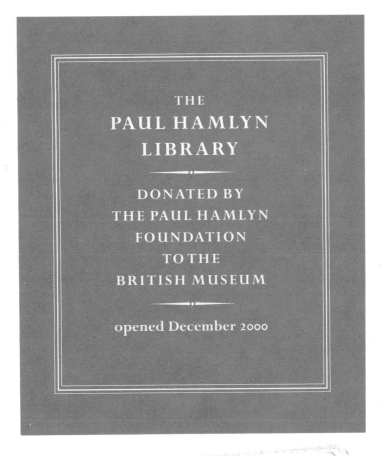

BYZANTINE EMPRESSES

BYZANTINE EMPRESSES

Women and Power in Byzantium, AD 527–1204

Lynda Garland

London and New York

First published 1999
by Routledge
11 New Fetter Lane, London EC4P 4EE

Simultaneously published in the USA and Canada
by Routledge
29 West 35th Street, New York, NY 10001

© 1999 Lynda Garland

The right of Lynda Garland to be identified as the
Author of this Work has been asserted by her in accordance with
the Copyright, Designs and Patents Act 1988

Typeset in Garamond by RefineCatch Limited, Bungay, Suffolk
Printed and bound in Great Britain by
TJ International Ltd, Padstow, Cornwall

British Library Cataloguing in Publication Data
A catalogue record for this book is available from the British Library

Library of Congress Cataloging in Publication Data
Garland, Lynda
Byzantine empresses : women and power in Byzantium, AD 527–1204 /
Lynda Garland.
Includes bibliographical references and index.
1. Empresses—Byzantine Empire—Biography.   2. Byzantine Empire—
History—527–1081.   3. Byzantine Empire—History—1081–1453.
4. Leadership in women—Byzantine Empire—History.   I. Title.
DF572.8.E5G37   1999
949.5′0099—dc21   98–23383

ISBN 0–415–14688–7

For Matthew,
Daniel Isaiah,
and Sophia

ἡ μόνη τῶν πασῶν ἐλευθέρα, ἡ τοῦ ξύμπαντος γένους δεσπότις

CONTENTS

ILLUSTRATIONS

Front cover.   Piriska (Irene), wife of John II Komnenos, from the panel in the south gallery of St Sophia depicting her with her husband and eldest son Alexios: detail (photo: Dumbarton Oaks, Washington DC)

Plates

Tables

PREFACE

This work presents a series of biographical portraits of the most significant
Byzantine women who ruled or shared the throne between 527 and 1204. Its
primary aim is to present and analyse the available historical data in order to
outline what these empresses did, what the sources thought they did, and
what they wanted to do. In this I am not breaking entirely new ground:
many of the empresses of this period were introduced to a wide readership
through the magnificent essays of Charles Diehl in his two-volume work
Figures byzantines. More recently Donald Nicol has constructed definitive
biographies of ten women of the Palaiologue era in his *Byzantine Lady*.
Ninety years of scholarship have, however, passed since Diehl was writing,
and while the present work does not hope to compete with him in read-
ability, it does attempt to present the reader with the documentation that he
omitted as well as the interpretations of modern scholars. To those who have
helped me in this task I would like to express my gratitude: in particular to
the staff at Dumbarton Oaks, where this work received its final touches, for
their assistance; to Richard Stoneman for his patience; and to my husband, as
always, for his encouragement.

ABBREVIATIONS

AASS	*Acta Sanctorum Bollandiana*, Brussels, 1643–1779; Paris and Rome, 1866–87; Brussels, 1965–70, 68 vols.
AB	*Analecta Bollandiana.*
ACO	*Acta Conciliorum Oecumenicorum*, ed. E. Schwartz and J. Straub, Berlin, 1914–83.
AIPHOS	*Annuaire de l'Institut de Philologie et d'Histoire Orientales et Slaves.*
Akropolites	*Georgii Akropolitae Opera*, ed. A. Heisenberg, rev. P. Wirth, 2 vols, Stuttgart, 1978.
Alexiad	*Anne Comnène, Alexiade*, ed. and tr. B. Leib, 3 vols, Paris: Budé, 1937–45, repr. 1967; English translation by E.R.A. Sewter, *The Alexiad of Anna Comnena*, Harmondsworth, 1979.
Angold, *Aristocracy*	M. Angold, ed., *The Byzantine Aristocracy IX to XIII Centuries*, Oxford: British Archaeological Reports, 1984.
Anth. Gr.	*Anthologia Graeca*, ed. H. Beckby, 4 vols, 2nd edn, Munich, 1957–8.
Attal.	*Michaelis Attaliotae Historia*, ed. E. Bekker, Bonn: *CSHB*, 1853.
BF	*Byzantinische Forschungen.*
BHG[3]	Bibliotheca Hagiographica Graeca, ed. F. Halkin, 3rd edn, Subsidia Hagiographica 8a, Brussels, 1957.
BMGS	*Byzantine and Modern Greek Studies.*
Bryen.	Nikephoros Bryennios, *Histoire*, ed. P. Gautier, Brussels: *CFHB*, 1975.
BS	*Byzantinoslavica.*
BS/EB	*Byzantine Studies/Études Byzantines.*
Buildings	Procopius, *Buildings*, ed. J. Haury, rev. G. Wirth, *Opera*, vol. 4: *De Aedificiis*, Leipzig: Teubner, 1964; tr. H.B. Dewing, vol. 7, Cambridge, Mass.: Loeb, 1940.

BZ	*Byzantinische Zeitschrift.*
Cass. *Variae*	Cassiodorus, *Variae*, ed. Th. Mommsen, *MGH* AA 12, Berlin: Weidmann, 1894; English translation by S.J.B. Barnish, *The Variae of Magnus Aurelius Cassiodorus Senator*, Liverpool: Liverpool University Press, 1992.
CFHB	*Corpus Fontium Historiae Byzantinae.*
Chon.	*Niketas Choniates, Χρονικὴ διήγησις*, ed. J.-L. van Dieten, Berlin and New York: *CFHB*, 1975; English translation by H.J. Magoulias, *O City of Byzantium: Annals of Niketas Choniates*, Detroit: Wayne State University Press, 1984.
Chon., *Orationes*	Choniates, Niketas, *Orationes et Epistulae*, ed. J.-L. van Dieten, Berlin and New York: *CFHB*, 1972.
Chron. Pasch.	*Chronicle Paschale* [Easter Chronicle], ed. L. Dindorf, Bonn: *CSHB*, 1832; English translation by M. and M. Whitby, *Chronicon Paschale 284–628* AD, Liverpool: Liverpool University Press, 1989.
CJ	*Codex Justinianus*, ed. P. Krueger, 11th edn, Berlin, 1954.
CMH	*The Cambridge Medieval History.*
Codex Marc.	Codex Marcianus 524, ''Ο Μαρκιανὸς Κῶδιξ 524', ed. S. Lampros, *NE* 8 (1911) 3–59, 113–92.
Corippus, *Iust.*	*Flavius Cresconius Corippus in Laudem Iustini Augusti Minoris Libri IV*, ed. and tr. Averil Cameron, University of London: Athlone Press, 1976.
CQ	*Classical Quarterly.*
CSCO	*Corpus Scriptorum Christianorum Orientalium.*
CSHB	*Corpus Scriptorum Historiae Byzantinae.*
CTh.	*Codex Theodosianus*, ed. Th. Mommsen, 3rd edn, Berlin: Weidmann 1962; English translation by C. Pharr, *The Theodosian Code and Novels and the Sirmondian Constitutions*, Princeton: Princeton University Press, 1952.
DAI	*Constantine Porphyrogenitus: De Administrando Imperio*, ed. and tr. Gy. Moravcsik and R.J.H. Jenkins, Washington DC: Dumbarton Oaks, rev. edn 1967.
de cer.	Constantine Porphyrogennetos, *De Cerimoniis Aulae Byzantinae*, ed. J.J. Reiske, 2 vols, Bonn: *CSHB*, 1829; partial French translation by A. Vogt, *Constantin Porphyrogénète. Le livre des cérémonies*, 2 vols, Paris: Budé, 1935–40.
DOP	*Dumbarton Oaks Papers.*
EEBS	Ἐπετήρις ἑταιρείας βυζαντινῶν σπουδῶν.

EHR	*English Historical Review.*
EO	*Echos d'Orient.*
Eustathios	*Eustathios of Thessaloniki: The Capture of Thessaloniki*, tr. J.R. Melville Jones, Canberra: Byzantina Australiensia 8, 1988; ed. B.G. Niebuhr, *De Thessalonica Capta*, Bonn: *CSHB*, 1842.
Evagr.	Evagrios, *The Ecclesiastical History of Evagrius*, ed. J. Bidez and L. Parmentier, London: Methuen, 1898; French translation by A.J. Festugière, 'Évagre, Histoire ecclésiastique', *Byzantion* 45(2) (1975): 187–488.
FHG	*Fragmenta Historicorum Graecorum*, ed. C. Müller, vol. 4, Paris: Didot, 1851.
Genesios	*Iosephi Genesii Regum Libri Quattuor*, ed. A. Lesmueller-Werner and I. Thurn, Berlin: de Gruyter, 1978.
Geo. Mon.	Georgius Monachus, *Chronicon*, ed. C. de Boor, rev. P. Wirth, vol. 2, Stuttgart: Teubner, 1978.
Geo. Mon. Cont.	Georgius Monachus, *Vitae Recentiorum Imperatorum*, in Theophanes Continuatus, ed. I. Bekker, Bonn: *CSHB*, 1838, 761–924.
GOTR	*Greek Orthodox Theological Review.*
GRBS	*Greek, Roman and Byzantine Studies.*
Gregoras	Gregoras, Nikephoros, *Byzantina Historia*, ed. L. Schopen, 3 vols, Bonn: *CSHB*, 1829–55.
Greg. Tur., *HF*	Gregory of Tours, *Historia Francorum*, ed. W. Arndt and B. Krusch, *MGH* Scriptores rerum Merovingicarum 1, Hanover, 1951; English translation by O.M. Dalton, *History of the Franks*, vol. 2, Oxford: Clarendon Press, 1927, repr. 1971.
HTR	*Harvard Theological Review.*
HUS	*Harvard Ukrainian Studies.*
JHS	*Journal of Hellenic Studies.*
JÖB	*Jahrbuch der Österreichischen Byzantinistik.*
John Biclar.	John of Biclaro, *Chronicle*, ed. Th. Mommsen, *MGH* AA, 11, Berlin: Weidmann, 1894, 207–20; tr. K.B. Wolf, *Conquerors and Chroniclers of Early Medieval Spain*, Liverpool: Liverpool University Press, 1990.
John Eph., *HE*	John of Ephesus, *Iohannis Ephesini Historiae Ecclesiasticae Pars Tertia*, ed. and tr. E.W. Brooks, *CSCO* 106, Scr. Syr. 54–5, Louvain, 1935–6, repr. 1952; English translation by R. Payne Smith, *The Third Part of the Ecclesiastical History of John Bishop of Ephesus*, Oxford: Oxford University Press, 1860.

John Eph., *Lives*	John of Ephesus, *The Lives of the Eastern Saints*, PO 17 (1923): 1–307, 18 (1924): 513–698, 19 (1926): 153–285.
John Lyd.	John Lydus, *Ioannes Lydus, On Powers or the Magistracies of the Roman State*, ed. and tr. A.C. Bandy, Philadelphia: American Philosophical Society, 1983.
John of Nikiu	*The Chronicle of John, Coptic Bishop of Nikiu*, tr. R.H. Charles, London: Williams and Norgate, 1916.
JRS	*Journal of Roman Studies*.
JTS	*Journal of Theological Studies*.
Kant.	Kantakouzenos, John (VI), *Ioannis Cantacuzeni Eximperatoris Historiarum Libri IV*, ed. L. Schopen, 3 vols, Bonn: *CSHB*, 1828–32.
Kedr.	George Kedrenos, *Historiarum Compendium*, ed. I. Bekker, 2 vols, Bonn: *CSHB*, 1838–9.
Kekaumenos	*Cecaumeni Strategicon et Incerti Scriptoris de Officiis Regiis Libellus*, ed. B. Wassiliewsky and V. Jernstedt, St Petersburg, 1896; repr. Amsterdam: Hakkert, 1965.
Kinnamos	*Ioannis Cinnami Epitome Rerum ab Ioanne et Manuele Comnenis Gestarum*, ed. A. Meineke, Bonn: *CSHB*, 1836; English translation by C.M. Brand, *Deeds of John and Manuel Comnenus by John Kinnamos*, New York: Columbia University Press, 1976.
Leo Diac.	Leo the Deacon, *Historiae*, ed. C.B. Hase, Bonn: *CSHB*, 1828.
Leo Gramm.	Leo Grammaticus, *Chronographia*, ed. I. Bekker, Bonn: *CSHB*, 1842.
Lib. Pont.	*Le Liber Pontificalis*, ed. L. Duchesne, 2 vols, 2nd edn, Paris, 1955–7; English translation by R. Davis, *The Book of Pontiffs (Liber Pontificalis): The Ancient Biographies of the First Ninety Roman Bishops to* AD *715*, Liverpool: Liverpool University Press, 1989; *idem, The Lives of the Eighth-Century Popes*, Liverpool: Liverpool University Press, 1992.
Liberatus, *Brev.*	Liberatus, *Breviarium Causae Nestorianorum et Eutychianorum*, ed. E. Schwartz, *ACO* 2.5, Berlin and Leipzig: de Gruyter, 1932, 98–141.
Malalas	John Malalas, *Chronographia*, ed. L. Dindorf, Bonn: *CSHB*, 1831; English translation by E. Jeffreys, M. Jeffreys and R. Scott, *John Malalas, The Chronicle*, Melbourne: Byzantina Australiensia, 1986.
Mansi	Mansi, G.D., ed., *Sacrorum Conciliorum Nova et Amplissima Collectio*, Florence, 1759–98, repr. Paris: Welter, 1901–27.

Men. Prot.	Menander Protector, fragments, in *The History of Menander the Guardsman*, ed. and tr. R.C. Blockley, Liverpool: Francis Cairns, 1985; also ed. C. Müller, in *FHG* 4.
MGH AA	*Monumenta Germaniae Historica*, Auctores Antiquissimi.
MGH SS	*Monumenta Germaniae Historica*, Scriptores.
Mich. Syr.	Michael the Syrian, tr. J.-B. Chabot, *Chronique de Michel le Syrien, Patriarche Jacobite d'Antioche 1166–1199*, 4 vols, Paris: Ernest Leroux, 1899–1924.
MM	F. Miklosich and J. Müller, eds, *Acta et Diplomata Graeca Medii Aevi Sacra et Profana*, 6 vols, Vienna: Gerold, 1860–90.
Monophysite Texts	*Monophysite Texts of the Sixth Century*, Syriac ed. and Latin tr. A. van Roey and P. Allen, Leuven: Peeters, 1994.
NE	Νέος Ἑλληνομνήμων.
Nicholas, *Ep.*	*Nicholas I Patriarch of Constantinople: Letters*, ed. and tr. R. Jenkins and L. Westerink, Washington DC: Dumbarton Oaks, 1973.
Nikephoros	*Nikephoros, Patriarch of Constantinople, Short History*, ed. and tr. C. Mango, Washington DC: *CFHB*, 1990.
Nov. J.	Justinian, *Novellae*, in *Corpus Juris Civilis*, vol. 3, ed. R. Schoell and W. Kroll, 6th edn, Berlin: Weidmann, 1954.
OCP	*Orientalia Christiana Periodica*.
ODB	*The Oxford Dictionary of Byzantium*, ed. A. Kazhdan, 3 vols, New York: Oxford University Press, 1991.
Patria	*Patria Constantinopoleos*, ed. Th. Preger, in *Scriptores Originum Constantinopolitanarum*, vol. 2, Leipzig: Teubner, 1907.
Paul Diac., *HL*	Paul the Deacon, *Historiae Langobardorum*, ed. L. Bethmann and G. Waitz, *MGH* Scriptores rerum Langobard. et Ital. saec. VI–IX, Hanover, 1878; English translation by W.D. Foulke, *History of the Lombards*, Philadelphia: University of Pennsylvania Press, 2nd edn, 1974.
PG	*Patrologiae Cursus Completus, Series Graeca*, ed. J.-P. Migne.
PL	*Patrologiae Cursus Completus, Series Latina*, ed. J.-P. Migne.
PLP	*Prosopographisches Lexikon der Palaiologenzeit*, ed. E. Trapp *et al.*, Vienna: Verlag des Österreichischen Akademie der Wissenschaften, 1976.

PLRE	The Prosopography of the Later Roman Empire, ed. J.R. Martindale et al., 3 vols, Cambridge: Cambridge University Press, 1970–92.
PO	Patrologia Orientalis.
PP	Past and Present.
Procopius	Procopius of Caesarea, Opera, ed. J. Haury, rev. G. Wirth, 4 vols, Leipzig: Teubner, 1962–4; ed. and tr. H.B. Dewing, 7 vols, Cambridge, Mass.: Loeb, 1914–40.
Psellos	Michel Psellos, Chonographia, ed. and tr. E. Renauld, 2 vols, Paris: Budé, 1926–8; English translation by E.R.A. Sewter, Michael Psellus: Fourteen Byzantine Rulers, Harmondsworth: Penguin, 1966.
Psellos, HS	Michaeli Pselli Historia Syntomos, ed. and tr. W.J. Aerts, Berlin and New York: CFHB, 1990.
Psellos, 'On Skleraina'	'Εἰς τὴν τελευτὴν τῆς Σκληραίνας', ed. M.D. Spadaro, In Mariam Sclerenam, Testo critico, introduzione e commentario, Catania: University of Catania Press, 1984.
Psellos, Scr. Min.	Michaelis Pselli Scripta Minora, ed. E. Kurtz and F. Drexl, 2 vols, Milan: Vita e Pensiero, 1936–41.
Ps-Symeon	Pseudo-Symeon, Chronographia, in Theophanes Continuatus, ed. I. Bekker, Bonn: CSHB, 1838, 601–760.
REB	Revue des Études Byzantines.
RH	Revue Historique.
Robert of Clari	La conquête de Constantinople, ed. P. Lauer, Paris, 1924; English translation by E.H. McNeal, The Conquest of Constantinople, New York: Columbia University Press, 1936.
RSBN	Rivista di Studi Bizantini e Neoellenici.
RSBS	Rivista di Studi Bizantini e Slavi.
Sathas, MB	K.N. Sathas, Μεσαιωνικὴ βιβλιοθήκη (Bibliotheca Graeca Medii Aevi), 7 vols, Venice and Paris: Gregoriades, 1872–94.
SH	Procopius, Secret History (Anecdota), ed. J. Haury, rev. G. Wirth, Opera, vol. 3: Historia Arcana, Leipzig: Teubner, 1963; tr. H.B. Dewing, vol. 6, Cambridge, Mass.: Loeb, 1940; and G.A. Williamson, Harmondsworth: Penguin, 1966.
Skyl.	Ioannis Scylitae Synopsis Historiarum, ed. I. Thurn, Berlin and New York: CFHB, 1973.
Skyl. Cont.	Skylitzes Continuatus, Ἡ συνέχεια τῆς χρονογραφίας τοῦ Ἰωάννου Σκυλίτζη, ed. E. Tsolakes, Thessalonika: Ἵδρυμα μελετῶν Χερσονήσου τοῦ Αἵμου, 1968.

Souda	*Suidae Lexicon*, ed. A. Adler, 5 vols, Leipzig: Teubner, 1928–38.
Stratos	A.N. Stratos, *Byzantium in the Seventh Century*, 6 vols, Amsterdam: Hakkert, 1968–75.
Syn. CP	*Synaxarium Ecclesiae Constantinopolitanae*, ed. H. Delehaye, *Propylaeum ad AASS Nov.*, Brussels, 1902.
Syn. Vetus	*The Synodicon Vetus*, ed. and tr. J. Duffy and J. Parker, Washington DC: Dumbarton Oaks, 1979.
Tabari	Tabari, *Annales*, ed. M.J. de Goeje *et al.*, 15 vols, Leiden: Brill, 1879–1901; tr. J.A. Williams, *The Early 'Abbasi Empire*, 2 vols, Cambridge: Cambridge University Press, 1988–9.
Theod. Stoud., *Ep.*	*Theodori Studitae Epistulae*, ed. G. Fatouros, 2 vols, Berlin and New York: *CFHB*, 1992.
Theophanes	Theophanes, *Chronographia*, ed. C. de Boor, 2 vols, Leipzig: *CSHB*, 1883; English translation by C. Mango and R. Scott, with the assistance of G. Greatrex, *The Chronicle of Theophanes Confessor: Byzantine and Near Eastern History AD 284–813*, Oxford: Clarendon Press, 1997.
Theoph. Cont.	Theophanes Continuatus, *Chronographia*, ed. I. Bekker, Bonn: *CSHB*, 1838.
Theoph. Sim.	Theophylact Simocatta, *History*, ed. C. de Boor, rev. P. Wirth, Stuttgart: Teubner, 1972; English translation by M. and M. Whitby, *The History of Theophylact Simocatta: An English Translation with Introduction and Notes*, Oxford: Clarendon Press, 1986.
Theophylact	*Théophylacte d'Achride*, vol. 1: *Discours, traités, poésies*, ed. P. Gautier, Thessalonika: *CFHB*, 1980; vol. 2: *Lettres*, Thessalonika: *CFHB*, 1986.
TM	*Travaux et Mémoires*.
TT	G.L.F. Tafel and G.M. Thomas, *Urkunden zur älteren Handels- und Staatsgeschichte der Republik Venedig*, 3 vols, Vienna: Hof- und Staatsdruckerei, 1856–7.
TTH	*Translated Texts for Historians*.
V. Euthymii	*Vita Euthymii Patriarchae Cp.*, ed. and tr. P. Karlin-Hayter, Brussels: Éditions de Byzantion, 1970.
V. Eutych.	Eustratios, *Vita Eutychii*, *PG* 86: 2273–390.
V. Ignatii	*Vita Ignatii*, *PG* 105: 487–574.
V. Irenes	'La vie de l'impératrice Sainte Irène', ed. F. Halkin, *AB* 106 (1988): 5–27.
V. Methodii	*Vita Methodii*, *PG* 100: 1244–61.
V. Philareti	'La vie de S. Philarète', ed. M.-H. Fourmy and M. Leroy, *Byzantion* 9 (1934): 113–67.

V. Sabas	*Vie de St Sabas: Kyrillos von Skythopolis*, ed. E. Schwartz, Leipzig: Hinrichs, 1939.
V. Symeoni Iun.	*La vie ancienne de Syméon Stylite le jeune*, ed. and tr. P. van den Ven, 2 vols, Brussels: Société des Bollandistes, 1962–70.
V. Taras.	'Ignatii Diaconi Vita Tarasii Archiepiscopi Constantinopolitani', ed. I.A. Heikel, *Acta Societatis Scientiarum Fennicae*, 17 (1891): 395–423.
V. Theodorae	'Βίος τῆς αὐτοκράτειρας Θεοδώρας (*BHG* 1731)', ed. A. Markopoulos, *Symmeikta* 5 (1983): 249–85.
V. Theophanous	'Zwie griechische Texte über die Hl. Theophano, die Gemahlin Kaisers Leo VI.', ed. E. Kurtz, *Zapiski Imp. Akad. Nauk*, 8th ser., *Hist.-Phil. Otdel*, 3.2, St Petersburg, 1898, 1–24.
Vict. Tonn.	Victor Tonnenensis, *Chronicle*, ed. Th. Mommsen, *MGH* AA 11, Berlin, 1894: 178–206.
Villehardouin	Geoffrey of Villehardouin, *La conquête de Constantinople*, 2 vols, ed. E. Faral, Paris: Budé, 1938–9; English translation by M.R.B. Shaw, *Joinville and Villehardouin: Chronicles of the Crusades,* Harmondsworth: Penguin, 1963, 29–160.
Wars	Procopius, *Wars*, ed. J. Haury, rev. G. Wirth, *Opera*, vols 1–2: *Bella*, Leipzig: Teubner, 1962–3; tr. H.B. Dewing, vols 1–5, Cambridge, Mass.: Loeb, 1914–40.
William of Tyre	William, Archbishop of Tyre, *Guillaume de Tyr: Chronique*, ed. R.B.C. Huygens, 2 vols, Corpus Christianorum: Continuatio Mediaevalis, 63, 63a, Turnhout: Brepols, 1986; also in *Recueil des historiens des croisades. Historiens occidentaux*, 1 (1 and 2), Paris: Imprimerie Royal, 1844; English translation by Emily Atwater Babcock and A.C. Krey, *A History of Deeds Done Beyond the Sea*, 2 vols, New York: Columbia University Press, 1943.
YCS	*Yale Classical Studies.*
Zach. Rhet.	J.F. Hamilton and E.W. Brooks, *Zacharias of Mitylene: The Syrian Chronicle Known as that of Zachariah of Mitylene*, London: Methuen, 1899.
Zepos, *JGR*	J. and P. Zepos (eds), *Ius Graecoromanum*, 8 vols, Athens: Phexe, 1931, repr. Aalen: Scientia, 1962.
Zon.	*Ioannes Zonaras. Epitome Historiarum*, ed. T. Büttner-Wobst, vol. 3, Bonn: *CSHB*, 1897.
ZRVI	*Zbornik Radova Vizantinoloshkog Instituta.*

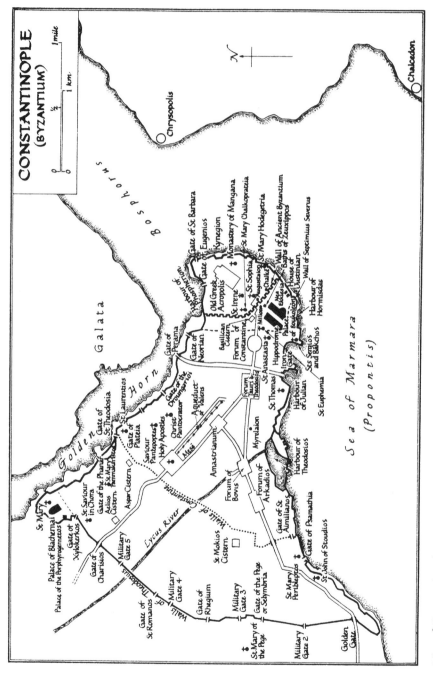

Map of Constantinople

INTRODUCTION

You were selected by divine decree for the security and exalta-
tion of the universe; you were joined to the purple by God's
will. Almighty God has blessed you and crowned you with his
own hand.

(de cer. 1.39)

These words formed part of the ceremony of the marriage of an emperor and
empress and reflect the ideology implicit in the act of imperial coronation. In
the Byzantine empire power was technically vested in the emperor. Nevertheless a number of empresses played an important part in government and
even took control of the empire in appropriate circumstances. Most commonly empresses came to power as regents for young sons, implying a fixed
period of caretaker government until the young emperor came of age, usually
at sixteen. But not all regents were ready to step aside – Irene finally had
her son Constantine VI blinded so that she could stay in power – and
Eudokia Makrembolitissa was appointed as regent for her son Michael, even
though he was technically of age. Co-ruling regents were officially acknowledged on coins, in acclamations and in dating formulas, although generally
(but not always) yielding precedence to the young emperor. Empresses could
also in exceptional circumstances rule in their own right, though it was
considered more normal that they should take the opportunity to choose a
husband and make him emperor. Irene and Theodora, the last Macedonian,
however, chose not to, while the sisters Zoe and Theodora ruled together as
autokratores for seven weeks until Zoe decided to marry again: the regime
could have lasted for longer had not the empresses been at loggerheads.
Empresses also possessed power as consorts, but in these circumstances they
were naturally bound by the wishes and temperaments of their husbands.
The principle of collegiality, however, ensured that in certain cases they were
seen almost as co-rulers. Indeed, Sophia, as niece of Theodora, seems to have
felt that her dynastic claim on the empire was as good as her husband's. Even
without official nomination as regent, the long absences of emperors on

1

campaign could still give empresses the chance to wield power and make executive decisions. This could also be formalised, as in the *chrysobull* of Alexios Komnenos appointing his mother Anna Dalassene regent, a position she retained for fifteen years or more. An empress interested in politics, like Theodora wife of Justinian, or Euphrosyne, was able to interview ministers, clerics and foreign ambassadors without reference to her husband, and correspond privately with world leaders. Euphrosyne, wife of Alexios III Angelos, held her own court, parallel to that of the emperor, and was noted for her role in government. This involvement was, however, totally at the will of the emperor and when Alexios wanted to get rid of her, he could send her instantaneously to a convent.

Empresses were known by a number of titles: Augusta, *basilis(sa)* and *despoina* being those most commonly encountered, while empresses ruling in their own right could adopt the masculine titles of *basileus* or *autokrator*: Irene used the title *basileus* in her *Novels*, while Zoe and Theodora during their joint rule were acclaimed *autokratores*. The title 'Augusta' was used to designate the principal empress, crowned by her husband and co-reigning with a *basileus autokrator*, and the principal duty of the senior empress was to hold the ceremonies pertaining to the wives of dignitaries at the court.

While the empress's constitutional importance was never defined, it was accepted that by her coronation, which was performed by her husband after the patriarch had prayed over the crown, an Augusta acquired something of imperial power, and empresses had their own imperial paraphernalia – they wore their own crowns, often with jewelled *pendilia*, the red imperial shoes, and had their own sceptres. That empresses were seen as possessed of the regal and almost numinous qualities of their husbands was of great significance when there was need for a regency, or the emperor died without nominating a successor. The status of Augusta itself was not automatically conferred by marriage and had to be formally granted by the emperor, either on his accession, or on their marriage, if he was already on the throne at the time, or after the birth of their first child.[1] In Late Antiquity, before 527, the title of Augusta had been awarded only rarely to the wives of emperors, though it becomes usual from the sixth century. Other women of the imperial family could be given the rank of empress, especially if there were no male heir. Constantine the Great had made his mother Helena empress at the same time as his wife Fausta *c.* 325, and Herakleios, Theophilos, Leo VI and Manuel I all granted the honour to their daughters. In Leo's case, as he was between wives at the time, this was specifically so there would be an Augusta to oversee imperial ceremonial. Constantine IX Monomachos even had his wife, the empress Zoe, confer the title *sebaste* (the Greek translation of Augusta) on his mistress Maria Skleraina, and she was officially called *despoina*. Alexios I Komnenos also gave his mother Anna Dalassene imperial rank, though she too was not crowned Augusta. With the sixth century it became increasingly common for the wives of emperors to be crowned, and except in the case of Alexios Komnenos and Irene Doukaina, the wives of the Komnenoi were automatically crowned at the time of their marriage or betrothal.

A number of redoubtable empresses preceded Theodora, wife of Justinian. Despite her dubious past, Helena mother of Constantine was celebrated for her pilgrimage to the Holy Land in 326, and for her piety and generous endowments to churches. The legend of her discovery of the True Cross led to her canonisation and she was to be the model of imperial sanctity for all future empresses. It also became customary for empresses to influence the transfer of power. Pulcheria, created Augusta at the age of fifteen by her brother Theodosios II, arguably imitated the piety and devotion of Helena, and was acclaimed as a 'second Helena' at the council of Chalcedon in 451 where she made a personal appearance. When her brother died in 450 it was Pulcheria as Augusta who made the choice of a new emperor, Marcian, and crowned him before the assembled army. She also married him, but in name only. Verina, widow of Leo I, crowned her brother Basiliskos, during his revolt against Zeno, her son-in-law, and when Zeno died in 491, his widow Ariadne was asked to nominate an orthodox successor by both senate and people; she picked the court official Anastasios.

On the death of an emperor, in default of a successor, the empress had the power to transfer the throne to a new incumbent. Zoe Porphyrogenneta, the heir to the throne in her own right, did so four times, to three husbands and an adopted son, in each case making the choice entirely on her own priorities. But imperial power was also seen as lodged in widowed empress consorts, who had no blood tie with the dynasty, but who were still considered as having the right of determining the imperial succession: it was usual but not necessary for the empress to marry this new candidate and thus legitimise his accession. When her husband, for example, lapsed into insanity, Sophia nominated an heir and successor. Even though she did not marry Tiberios – he was already married – her choice was sufficient to invest him with imperial prerogatives, and when Tiberios was on his death-bed the choice of a successor reverted again to Sophia. Had Irene wished to remarry after deposing her son Constantine VI she could have appointed her choice to the purple, and Michael III was warned by his advisers that his mother Theodora was possibly planning to marry to edge him out from power, one of the reasons for his removal of her to a convent. Emperors attempted to protect the succession by appointing co-emperors, juniors whose coronation ensured that they would succeed when appropriate. But the principle of dynastic succession was not well established in Byzantium – the eldest son need not necessarily inherit – and in times of transition this gave empresses great influence. Constantine Doukas, son of Michael VII and Maria of Alania, for example, remained co-emperor for some time under Alexios I Komnenos, even when Alexios had a son of his own; Manuel Komnenos was the youngest of John Komnenos's four sons, and came to the throne instead of his elder brother.

Similarly, both the emperors chosen by Sophia came from outside Justinian's family, even though there were family members who might quite suitably have been selected, including a son-in-law.

Empresses who were regents for minors often associated husbands with themselves in power – usually generals, as this was one area in which an empress regent could not be personally involved – in an attempt to help protect the rights of their young sons. Under such circumstances the young emperor technically remained the senior emperor, though decisions would be made by his stepfather until he came of age. For this reason Theophano married Nikephoros Phokas, while Zoe Karbounopsina was considered to be planning to marry the general Leo Phokas after her regime's debacle with the Bulgarians. Eudokia Makrembolitissa chose Romanos Diogenes as her second husband, and seems to have successfully protected the rights of her son Michael during Romanos's reign.

Empresses who did not remarry, or who, like Theodora, the last Macedonian, were single, ruled in the same way as emperors: they presided over the court, appointed officials, issued decrees, settled lawsuits, received ambassadors and heads of state, fulfilled the emperor's ceremonial role and made decisions on matters of financial and foreign policy. Their one disadvantage was that they could not personally lead an army: there were of course many emperors in the same position, but it had disastrous consequences in at least one case – Zoe Karbounopsina's regency foundered on inadequate military generalship.

During the reign of her husband the primary function of an Augusta was the orchestration of ceremonial at the imperial court, a highly stylised and intricate affair given the ceremonial nature of imperial life, which was based primarily around the Great Palace, a huge complex extending from the hippodrome to the sea walls, with its own gardens, sporting grounds, barracks, audience halls and private apartments; the Great Palace was the official residence of the emperor until 1204, though under Alexios Komnenos the imperial family usually occupied the Blachernai Palace in the north-west of the city, while there were other residential palaces in and outside of the capital. Empresses' public life remained largely separate from that of their husbands, especially prior to the eleventh century, and involved a parallel court revolving around ceremonies involving the wives of court officials. For this reason an empress at court was considered to be essential: Michael II was encouraged to marry by his magnates because an emperor needed a wife and their wives an empress.[2] The patriarch Nicholas permitted the third marriage of Leo VI because of the need for an empress in the palace: 'since there must be a Lady in the Palace to manage ceremonies affecting the wives of your nobles, there is condonation of the third marriage . . .'[3] While the empress primarily presided over her own ceremonial sphere, with her own duties and functions, she could be also present at court banquets, audiences and the reception of envoys, as well as taking part in processions and in services in St

Sophia and elsewhere in the city; one of her main duties was the reception of the wives of foreign rulers and heads of state. Nor were empresses restricted to the capital: both Martina and Irene Doukaina accompanied their husbands on campaign.

The empress was also in charge of the *gynaikonitis*, the women's quarters in the palace, where she had her own staff, primarily though not entirely composed of eunuchs, under the supervision of her own chamberlain; when empresses like Irene, Theodora wife of Theophilos, and Zoe Karbounopsina came to power they often relied on this staff of eunuchs as their chief ministers and even their generals. Theodora the Macedonian was unusual in not appointing a eunuch as her chief minister, perhaps because her age made such gender considerations unnecessary. The ladies of the court were the wives of patricians and other dignitaries: a few ladies, the *zostai*, were especially appointed and held rank in their own right. The *zoste patrikia* was at the head of these ladies (she was usually a relative of the empress), and dined with the imperial family. While it is difficult to gauge the size of the empress's retinue, Theodora wife of Justinian was accompanied by 4,000 attendants when she visited the spa at Pythion, though her escort included some of the emperor's officials and not merely her own. Seventy high-ranking ladies of the court met the young Agnes-Anna of France when she arrived for her betrothal to Alexios II, and at ceremonial functions the wives of dignitaries were divided into seven groups, whose title derived from that of their husbands (*magistrissai* were the wives of those with the rank *magistros*, for example). The number of courtiers in the tenth century has been estimated at some 1,000–2,000;[4] the empress would therefore have formed the focal point of ceremonies and functions for more than 1,000 women at court – 'the *sekreton* [court] of the women'.[5] While the *gynaikonitis* certainly did not involve harem-like seclusion, on a number of occasions it was the site of conspiracy and intrigue: the murders of Nikephoros II Phokas and Romanos III Argyros were plotted there by their wives, and Theodora, wife of Justinian, was said to have hidden the monophysite patriarch Anthimos in her quarters unsuspected for twelve years: the story is certainly apocryphal, though the anecdote is revealing in that it conveys the popular perception of the size and secrecy, and the quality of mystery and intrigue, seen as belonging to the *gynaikonitis*.

Marriage to an emperor generated great power for the woman's family: this can be seen most notably in the family of Theodora, wife of Theophilos, and in that of Euphrosyne, at whose accession the Kamateroi achieved practically a stranglehold on government. In the eighth and ninth centuries the birth and background of a future empress seems to have been of little importance: matches were chosen supposedly on the appearance of the bride, which explains some marriages which would otherwise seem unaccountable. Between 788 and 882 bride-shows were held five times to select a bride for the heir to the empire, and even if the decision were generally made by the emperor's mother or stepmother with a political agenda in view, there still was clearly a consideration that beauty was an essential prerequisite for an empress. In these bride-shows the background and family of the girls involved were not a primary consideration, and it was possible for a relative nonentity to be picked. It is possible that this was done to avoid pressure from aristocratic families who would have wanted a daughter chosen as empress. Theophano wife of Romanos II, though not selected in a bride-show, seems to have been chosen for the same reason. Aristocratic Byzantine women were very aware of their family background, as is shown increasingly in their nomenclature, which need not follow either that of their husband or their father. By the late twelfth century women, like men, openly displayed all their family connections, like Irene-Euphrosyne Komnene Doukaina Philanthropene Kantakouzene, an otherwise unknown nun who died c. 1202:[6] one of the two daughters of Anna Komnene used the names Irene Doukaina (after her grandmother) while the other called herself Maria Bryennaina Komnene (after her father and grandfather). Their seals show that Irene Doukaina and Euphrosyne Doukaina both retained their family name as empress. Imperial wives from abroad are rare prior to the twelfth century, though there were a number of marriage negotiations with the Franks for brides which failed to eventuate. Foreign princesses, such as Rotrud, daughter of Charlemagne who was betrothed to Constantine VI, were expected to learn Greek and be trained in Byzantine customs before arriving. Foreign brides were baptised in the orthodox faith, at which point they changed their names: that of Irene ('peace') is ubiquitous in the Komnenian dynasty, probably out of respect for Irene Doukaina.

Empresses, whether consorts or regents, could command very considerable wealth: a new empress distributed lavish amounts of gold to the patriarch, senate and clergy, and Maria Skleraina and Anna Dalassene, given the title of *despoina* by their lover and son respectively, possessed great financial resources and patronage. Their status was also signalled by the trappings of power and majesty – the heavy robes embroidered with gold and jewels, the precious gems, their omnipresent retinues, powers of patronage and spending money. The possession of their own imperial seals and the appearance of selected empresses on the coinage further reinforced their participation in *basileia*, imperial rule. The empress was also expected to demonstrate her piety and concern for her subjects in very practical ways – in the establishment of churches, monastic institutions and sometimes facilities for the poor and sick, as well as in more *ad hoc* donations to petitioners and courtiers. It was not unusual for empresses to take the veil on the death of their husbands, though in some cases they were forced into nunneries to prevent their reappropriation of power by marriage or other means.

While it is possible that Byzantine princesses were in some way trained for the diplomatic marriages they were expected to make abroad,[7] there was generally no education possible for a future empress, unless like some fiancées from abroad she was selected young. Imperial brides who married a co-emperor could also hope to benefit from 'on-the-job training' from the senior empress, until their turn came. However, for those women like Justinian's wife Theodora, whose background was on the stage, and others who were unexpectedly elevated to the purple, there was no transitional period in which they could learn the ropes of protocol and diplomacy. Eudokia, Anna Dalassene and Euphrosyne were aristocratic women, who had married between twelve and fifteen years of age and whose primary role since then had been managing their families and properties. Nevertheless, they were the empresses who make the greatest mark on government. Martina, Zoe Karbounopsina and Theophano had no precognition of the fact that they would be left in control of the empire, and no political training but what they had gained during their husbands' lifetimes, but the two former were certainly willing and competent to undertake the task.

Despite the fact that historical sources invariably express hostility, or at least surprise, at the concept of a woman in power, in the period between 527 and 1204 seven empresses ruled as regents for young sons, while others like Irene and Theodora the Macedonian ruled in their own right, and despite gender-based criticism did so extremely competently. Their contribution to Byzantine civilisation was immense, if only in terms of the maintenance of dynastic continuity, and while we encounter stereotypical criticisms based on the paradoxical combination of women and imperial power, in reality the validity of their rule was entirely recognised. And the least competent at government could be the most popular: when Zoe was exiled by her adopted son Michael V, the citizens took to the streets in her defence and their call for the restoration of 'the mistress of all the imperial family, the rightful heir to the empire' shows the loyalty and respect with which empresses could be viewed by their subjects.

Part I

FROM STAGE TO STATECRAFT

1

THEODORA, WIFE OF JUSTINIAN
(527–48)

Theodora, wife of the emperor Justinian, is one of the figures of Byzantine history of whom non-Byzantinists have sometimes heard. Indeed, the tales related by Procopius of her activities in the hippodrome, and outside of it, prior to her marriage, cast into insignificance stories of more modern royal scandals. More remarkable, however, than the fact that modern tastes for prurient gossip closely resemble those of earlier ages is the realisation that Procopius's narrative was not without foundation. Theodora, who was born *c.* 497, had been an actress, with all the connotations of sexual immorality and vulgar entertainment which the stage implied. A law had especially to be passed to enable her to marry a man of senatorial rank, let alone the nephew of Justin I and heir presumptive to the empire, and she had had an illegitimate daughter prior to her marriage. Yet Theodora rose triumphant against all possible obstacles: she became empress; advantageously married her family off with regard to their rank and wealth; possessed great sway in matters of state through her influence over her husband; and, like many a repentant prostitute, became a pillar of the faith, albeit of a heretic branch.

The contradictory nature of the sources makes it essential to revisit the story of Theodora's past given by Procopius in his *Anecdota* (or *Secret History*), despite its well-known features. Allegedly one of the three daughters of Akakios, a bear-keeper of the Green faction in Constantinople, at her father's death *c.* 500 Theodora and her family were left in poverty. Her mother remarried in the expectation that her new partner would take on her late husband's position. When their application for this was rejected, however, the girls were sent as suppliants into the hippodrome and enlisted the support of the Blues: from this point Theodora was a fanatic supporter of this faction.[1] As soon as she was old enough, Theodora followed her sister Komito both onto the stage and into the profession of courtesan, initially acting as a kind of male prostitute by indulging in anal intercourse with interested clients. Her performances both on and off stage were shameless, especially her speciality act with geese; her sexual appetites were such that at dinner parties she would have intercourse not only with all the guests but with the servants also. After accompanying Hekebolos, governor of Libya Pentapolis, as his concubine, and serving his unnatural appetites, she fell on misfortune when he threw her out and she had to work her way back to Constantinople through Alexandria and the cities of the Near East by prostitution, 'in every city following an occupation which a man had better not name'. During the period that she was on the stage, she performed numerous abortions on herself as well as conceiving a son named John, who was saved from infanticide by his father. In her early career, she was the friend of Antonina, whose background matched her own.[2] This friendship continued during their later lives. And this was only the beginning: Procopius goes on to discuss the empress's avarice, domination, autocracy and malice as empress.

After her return to Constantinople *c.* 522, Theodora met Justinian, some fifteen years her senior (he was born *c.* 482), who became infatuated with her; they were married at some point between 523 and 527, but a date in 523 or 524 is most likely; Justinian was crowned co-emperor on 1 April 527; and when Justin died, on 1 August 527 Theodora became empress, and remained so until she died on 28 June 548, whereupon she was buried with all due pomp in the Church of the Holy Apostles, Constantine the Great's foundation.

Given the 'rags to riches' nature of the story, clearly Procopius's account of the empress's past was not for public consumption. Contemporary works intended for a wider audience – Procopius's own *Wars*, his *Buildings*, Malalas's *Chronicle*[3] – leave untouched this aspect of the empress's career. Nevertheless, as Evans pertinently remarks, Procopius would not have written the *Secret History* unless he intended it to be read by someone,[4] and his contemporaries would have been able to verify (or otherwise) at least the bare bones of his account. The fact that the text did circulate in Byzantium is shown by the entry in the *Souda c.* 1000,[5] and though the date of the *Secret History*'s composition has been a matter of heated debate there is no reason to reject the reiterated statement of the *Secret History* itself, that it was composed thirty-two years after the commencement of Justinian's (i.e. his uncle Justin's) rule, hence in 550, at approximately the same time as the publication of the first seven books of the *Wars*.[6] As Theodora was but recently dead (in 548) the readership, and Procopius himself, would have possessed clear memories of her activities, and indeed the *Secret History* reads as if large sections of it were written or planned when she was still alive.[7] Scholars who have studied the work following its re-emergence in the Vatican archives in 1623 have apparently been more shocked by its contents than its original readers would have been, to whom the repentant sinner was a more acceptable construct than it is to the more modern-day reader,[8] and who were used to the rules and traditions of ancient invective.[9]

Theodora and her past

Despite the fact that Michael the Syrian, a twelfth-century monophysite chronicler, records in all seriousness that Theodora was the daughter of a priest and lived piously and chastely until her marriage with the emperor,[10] Procopius is not far from the mark. As the secretary and legal adviser to Belisarius from 527 until 540 and then a senator (whether or not he was the Procopius who also became prefect of the city is more doubtful) he was in a position to be able to chronicle her activities as well as those of her old friend Antonina, Belisarius's wife, whom he would have known intimately,[11] and who appears to have been his initial target in the *Secret History*, before he decided to broaden his attack to focus on the imperial pair. While the more extravagant details of the tales of Antonina's and Theodora's debaucheries would have been taken by the readership, as they were intended, as rhetorical flourishes in the invective tradition against wicked women,[12] the facts under-lying Procopius's account are confirmed by incontrovertible evidence else-where. The Syrian church historian and monophysite bishop John of Ephesos, a protégé and admirer of Theodora, who was made bishop of Ephesos at Theodora's instigation and was personally acquainted with affairs in the capital, describes her as 'from the brothel' (πορνεῖον).[13] This does not imply that she had been an actual prostitute, a *porne* based in a brothel and managed by a pimp (though the *Secret History* records that she became a *hetaira* or courtesan),[14] but actresses were considered available sexual partners and the profession of actress would certainly have involved both indecent exhibitions on stage and the provision of sexual services.[15] This casual remark of John of Ephesos informs us of two critically important facts: firstly that Theodora was an actress (*skenike*), living by her talents, both sexual and theatrical, in the sleazy entertainment business in the capital; and secondly, as John did not come to Constantinople until long after Theodora's rise to the purple, that her background was generally known when she was empress.

Interestingly none of Justinian's advisers was of noble origin (Narses, John the Cappadocian, Peter Barsymes and Tribonian), and Justinian's own back-ground was obscure enough, as he was of Thracian peasant family: Justinian was not class conscious and obviously capable of discerning merit apart from considerations of family and background. For, apart from the other obvious disadvantages to such a match, Theodora had an illegitimate daughter. While there is no mention of this daughter's name, it appears that she mar-ried into the family of the emperor Anastasios, and Theodora's daughters' three sons were prominent members of the court and establishment later in Justinian's reign: John had the rank of consul, Athanasios, a monk, was extremely wealthy and like John a leading monophysite, and Anastasios was betrothed to Joannina, Belisarius's daughter and the greatest heiress of the time.[16] Clearly Theodora's daughter was not Justinian's: not only is she always called the daughter of Theodora, she cannot have been born much later than 515 for her son to be married by 548. The *Secret History* also informs us that Theodora had an illegitimate son, John: there is no evidence to corroborate this, though there is no inherent reason to doubt it either.[17]

By the legislation of Augustus even the children of an actor or actress might not marry into the senatorial class.[18] While Theodora had been given patrician status after becoming Justinian's mistress, special legislation was still necessary to enable Justinian and Theodora to marry, and according to the *Secret History* the empress Euphemia, Justin's wife, though a barbarian by birth, illiterate and an ex-slave, prevented her husband from passing such a measure.[19] Indeed, ex-slaves were also forbidden to marry senators, and when her husband became a senator her own marriage would have been automatically annulled. It is likely that Justin, on becoming emperor, would have had to get round this by making her free born retroactively.[20] The law (*CJ* 5.4.23) framed to allow Justinian to marry Theodora is addressed to the praetorian prefect Demosthenes, in his first term of office, which had ended by 19 November 524. If Justin had to wait for Euphemia's death, this would date her death to 524 or before.[21] Presumably, therefore, the marriage of Justinian and Theodora can also be dated to 523 or 524.

The aim of Justin's law, doubtless framed by Justinian himself,[22] is stated to have been to help women who through the 'weakness of their sex' (*imbecillitate sexus*) have fallen into an unworthy lifestyle to return to an honest way of life; its exordium explicitly lays down, 'We [Justin] believe that we should, so far as is possible to our nature, imitate the benevolence of God and the great clemency to the human race of Him who deigns always to forgive the day-to-day sins of men, to receive our penitence and bring us to a better state. And if we delay doing the same for our subjects we shall deserve no pardon.'[23] The constitution permits actresses to renounce their errors and petition the emperor for an imperial grant of all marriage privileges: in other words they may contract legal marriage with men of any rank, just as if they had never led the immoral life of actress.[24] In addition an ex-actress who has been admitted to the patriciate may marry anyone, all previous blemishes (*macula*) attaching to her from the stage being wiped out, so that she has been so to speak 'handed back to her pristine, native condition'. Care was taken in framing the law to confirm the legitimacy of the children of such an actress who married after her rehabilitation: they are to be legitimate and a daughter from such a marriage does not count as the daughter of an actress, while daughters born to an actress before her mother's reinstatement are not ignored: they are entitled to an imperial conferment of unrestricted marriage capacity. This legislation thus ensured that any children of Theodora and Justinian would be legitimate, as well as removing any odium from Theodora's existing illegitimate daughter.

The paragraph which allows that a woman patrician, even if previously an actress, could marry anyone, ensured that Theodora did not need to apply to the emperor as a penitent actress. It also wiped out not only the blemish of the condition (of being an actress), but 'any other blemish whatsoever' which might impede a high union.[25] There was clearly the probability that Theodora might be accused of having been a prostitute, and it was out of the question that a prostitute could marry either a senator or even a free man: even Justinian's legislation never approaches the possibility.[26] This paragraph was clearly to obviate any later attack against Theodora in this regard which would endanger the legitimacy of any prospective children.[27] Procopius complains that this law opened the door for a number of marriages between senators and courtesans:[28] in fact it allowed senators to marry former actresses, but only those already raised to the patriciate had 'other blemishes' erased, and the number of patrician ex-actresses must have been minimal, to say the least. The law was clearly custom-made for Theodora.[29]

Theodora and women's issues

It has frequently been supposed that because of her past Theodora must have influenced Justinian's social legislation in its concern with improving the status of women. As a general rule, it should not be automatically assumed that Justinian's legislation to ameliorate the status of women was undertaken under the influence of Theodora, and it has to be seen in the context of his reforming legislation as a whole. Certainly Justin's edict *CJ* 5.4.23, often seen as concerned with women's rights, was not intended to improve the lot of actresses *per se* (or indeed, senators), in enabling them to marry men of senatorial rank, but to directly benefit Theodora and Justinian himself.[30] Nevertheless, there are indications that Theodora was involved in Justinian's reforms. In *Novel* 8.1 (AD 535), which banned the purchase of public offices by officials, Justinian himself mentions that he has taken counsel with 'the most pious consort given to Us by God', and the novel includes an oath to be taken by governors to her as well as to Justinian.

Justinian's legislation shows a 'determination to vindicate the status of women and their rights in marriage', and the 530s in particular saw a programme of law reform concerned in great measure with marriage and the family.[31] In a number of places he stresses the equality of the sexes: *Nov. J.* 5.2 (AD 535) states 'in the service of God there is no male or female, nor freeman nor slave',[32] while in divorce cases at least Justinian thought it wrong to have different penalties for men and women,[33] and he recognised a list of just causes for divorce.[34] In *CJ* 5.4.28 (AD 531 or 532) Justinian ruled that a marriage between a citizen and a freedwoman (an ex-slave, like his aunt by marriage Lupicina) was to remain intact even if the husband was made a senator. A similar reform to that of *CJ* 5.4.23, *Nov. J.* 117, published in 542, abolished the restrictions of *CTh.* 4.6.3 (Constantine, AD 336), and allowed senators to marry the daughters of female tavern-keepers or pimps (117.6).

Much of Justinian's legislation was concerned with protecting women and their rights. While the famous law on marriage enabled senators to marry ex-actresses, the stage features elsewhere in Justinian's legislation as something reprehensible: *Nov. J.* 51 (AD 537) allows women on the stage to renounce their profession and fines those who attempt to hold them to it by oaths or sureties,[35] while *CJ* 1.4.33 (AD 534) lays down that no woman, free or slave, can be forced onto the stage, and that a free woman who has been an actress has the right of marrying a man of any rank without the need to supplicate the emperor. His legislation on sexual offences (*CJ* 9.13, AD 528) covers the rape, abduction or seduction of all women, and in the case of *raptus* (abduction) prescribes execution even for the abduction of a woman slave, whereas previously there could be no charge of *stuprum* (unlawful sexual intercourse or rape) with a woman in the category of barmaid or below.[36] *Nov. J.* 134.9 (AD 559) rules that women are not to be imprisoned on charges of debt; sureties are to be found instead. If a woman has to be held on a major criminal charge she should be sent to a convent or guarded by reliable women for her own protection, in case she should suffer rape or other ill-treatment. Evagrios, generally antagonistic towards Justinian, noted the severity with which men charged with rape were treated.[37]

Justinian's legislation includes unexpectedly human touches: of particular importance is *CJ* 8.17(18).12 (AD 531) on the right of women to reclaim their dowry: '[the previous law] did not take into account the weakness of women, nor that the husband enjoys their body, substance, and entire life . . . who does not pity them for their services to their husbands, the danger of childbirth, and indeed the bringing into life of children . . . ?'[38] In another reforming law on legitimacy, *Nov. J.* 74.4 (AD 538), Justinian avows, 'for we know, though we are lovers of chastity, that nothing is more vehement than the fury of love', which as Daube noted must be a personal statement of Justinian rather than of one of his ministers.[39] In *Nov. J.* 22.3 (AD 535) the statement is made that it is mutual affection which creates a marriage, and that a dowry is strictly unnecessary, while *Nov. J.* 22.18 prohibits the repudiation of a woman who married without a dowry on that account. Before a husband could encumber an antenuptial donation with debt, the wife had to give her consent twice (*Nov. J.* 61.1.2, AD 537): this was because on the first occasion she might have been won over against her better judgement by her husband's blandishments and later change her mind.

A concern to control prostitution in the capital was shown by *Nov. J.* 14.1 (AD 535) which outlawed panders and procurers who exploited girls for prostitution and specifically stated that Justinian's aim was to clean up the city: 'It is Our wish that everyone should lead chaste lives, so far as is possible.' It legislates against girls being forced unwillingly into a life of unchastity. Apparently girls of ten or less were being compelled into becoming prostitutes after being enticed away from their parents by promises of clothes or food. Justinian also tried to stop such girls being led to believe that their contracts with or promises made to their pimps had the force of law. Prostitution was a fact of life in the capital and, as a number of emperors had previously attempted to legislate to control it,[40] we need not presume that Theodora was the motivating force. Nevertheless Theodora, who had first-hand experience of the evils which could face women of the lower classes, did take a personal interest in such issues, and this edict is closely reflected in the benefactions of the couple as recorded by historians.

Among their other charitable works, including foundations for the care of infants and the elderly and sick,[41] Theodora and Justinian put into effect practical measures designed to help unfortunates forced into prostitution. Procopius tells us in the *Buildings* that the imperial couple made a palace into a splendid monastery for former prostitutes who had been forced into working in brothels 'not of their own free will, but under the force of lust' because of their extreme poverty. This establishment was to be called 'Repentance'. To make the foundation of lasting benefit they endowed it with an ample income of money and added many remarkable buildings so that these women would never be compelled to depart from the practice of virtue.[42]

> For there had been a numerous body of procurers in the city from ancient times, conducting their traffic in licentiousness in brothels and selling others' youth in the public market-place and forcing virtuous persons into slavery. But the Emperor Justinian and the Empress Theodora, who always shared a common piety in all that they did, devised the following plan. They cleansed the state of the pollution of the brothels, banishing the very name of brothel-keepers, and they set free from a licentiousness fit only for slaves the women who were struggling with extreme poverty, providing them with independent maintenance, and setting virtue free.

The *Secret History*, in line with its normal practice of undercutting the motives of the imperial pair, tells us that more than 500 prostitutes were rounded up and that many of them went unwillingly, actually leaping from the parapet of the convent in order to escape the regime and being saved against their will;[43] elsewhere Procopius states that one of the main duties of the newly created office of *quaesitor* was rounding up pederasts and fallen women. According to Malalas, Theodora as early as 528 was involved in taking action against pimps and brothel-keepers who took poor girls as if under contract and made them into public prostitutes. She ordered that all such brothel-keepers should be arrested, and had them repaid the five *nomismata* (gold coins) they said that they had paid for the girls. From henceforth all brothel-keepers were to be outlawed, and she presented the girls with a set of clothes and dismissed them with one *nomisma* each.[44]

We may perhaps doubt that the pimps received their money back: under Justinian's legislation of 535 they would have been liable to corporal punishment and exile, though Theodora may well have made the girls an *ex gratia* payment to help them in their new lives. But the reference to the girls being 'as though under a contract' may be a reference to *Nov. J.* 14, which specifically legislated against those who entrapped girls into thinking that such arrangements were legitimate contracts. This may therefore be evidence that Theodora had some influence on this area of Justinian's legislation.

There is further corroborative evidence that Theodora was concerned with women's issues: Procopius tells us in the *Wars* that 'she was naturally inclined to assist women in misfortune'.[45] The case mentioned by Procopius referred to Praeiecta, the emperor's niece, who was in love with the Armenian Artabanes. Theodora stepped in to prevent a marriage, despite Justinian's concurrence, when Artabanes's existing wife came to court and begged for her help. Praeiecta was then married to John, a relation of the emperor Anastasios, in 548/9, and only Theodora's death cleared the way for Artabanes's divorce.[46] Another incident is recounted by Malalas, who tells us that in 528 Eulalios, a poverty-stricken *comes domesticorum* (commander of a unit of soldiers attached to the imperial household), bequeathed the charge of his daughters to the emperor, with insufficient assets to cover his dispositions for them. Justinian instructed the curator Makedonios to take up their inheritance and discharge all legacies and creditors, and 'as for his three daughters, I order that they be brought to the Augusta Theodora to be looked after in the imperial apartments'. He further ordered that they were to be given their dowries and property as bequeathed.[47]

Without assuming that Theodora necessarily played an influential role in Justinian's legislation on women's issues, she probably had an interest in removing some of the disadvantages from women of lower social status in the capital, and to this degree her past may well have had an impact on social conditions. But it would probably be a mistake to assume in view of her earlier career that Theodora was specifically championing the wrongs of prostitutes in her good works. Even Theodora would not have wished to have her subjects reminded too obviously of her past, though it may well have led historians to emphasise her charitable actions in this regard. Rather her work in this area was just one of the manifestations of the empress's beneficence and care for her people: it must be remembered that imperial women were traditionally expected to help the underprivileged, including prostitutes.[48] But she went down in tradition as a champion of the rights of prostitutes; John of Nikiu, the Coptic monophysite bishop of Nikiu in Egypt in the late seventh century, compares Theodora in her reforming capacity to Romulus, Numa, Caesar and Augustus: 'And subsequently came the empress Theodora . . . who put an end to the prostitution of women, and gave orders for their expulsion from every place.'[49] No doubt she brought greater knowledge to bear on the problems suffered by this class than the usual great lady in Byzantium, and it would be satisfactory to think that her measures were more successful than was customary.

The new empress

On her marriage to Justinian Theodora was suddenly transported to the highest rank in a strictly formalised and class-conscious society. Clearly she did not become empress without some social opposition. There were doubtless a number of formidable women at court whose views were antagonistic to the new regime of the Thracian upstart Justin and his nephew.[50] Justinian's marriage to Theodora, and her coronation as Augusta, would have been a further affront to these members of polite society, and the *Secret History* suggests that the marriage is sufficient evidence in itself for Justinian's moral turpitude.[51] One disapproving matron would have been Anicia Juliana (462–c. 528), the greatest heiress of her time; her mother was granddaughter of Theodosios II and daughter of Valentinian III; her father Olybrios had been emperor of the West; her husband Areobindos had been offered the throne of the East, when a revolt seemed likely to depose Anastasios in 512; her son Olybrios (consul in 491) had married Irene the niece of Anastasios himself, and Juliana had obviously intended her son for the throne. Noted for her other charitable foundations, between 524 and 527 Juliana built the Church of St Polyeuktos, which for some ten years was to be the most magnificent church in the city.[52] Juliana's consciousness of her imperial lineage and regrets for not having founded an immortal dynasty are evident in the verses of the epigram carved in large letters all round the nave of the church and outside the narthex.[53] Undoubtedly Juliana felt contempt for Justin and his heir, and even more, one assumes, for Theodora. As a champion of chalcedonianism, or orthodoxy,[54] Juliana's opinion of the monophysite Theodora would have been even more pointed. Doubtless her very presence in the city was a thorn in the flesh to the new imperial couple: Gregory of Tours tells us that when Justinian asked Juliana to make a contribution to imperial funds, she had all her wealth made into gold sheets which were used to decorate the roof of her church. She then invited Justinian to inspect her church and pointed out what she had done with the gold. When he sheepishly retracted his request, she took a valuable emerald ring from her finger and gave it to him, perhaps symbolising the transfer of imperial power.[55] In the poem which decorates her church (line 48) she is said to have surpassed Solomon: it has been suggested that when, after the building of St Sophia was completed in 537, Justinian exclaimed, 'Solomon I have vanquished thee!', it was Juliana and her church that he had in mind.[56]

Members of the upper classes who considered Justinian an upstart would have doubtless found Theodora an even more unsuitable empress than he was an emperor, and criticism of her elevation and behaviour is only to be expected. Yet, significantly, one of the few criticisms which the *Secret History* does not make against Theodora as empress is that of licentious behaviour and unfaithfulness to Justinian, unlike her friend Antonina who continued her affairs after her marriage with Belisarius. In fact the suggestion that

Theodora was suspected of an infatuation for Areobindos, a handsome young steward, resulted in his being flogged and disappearing immediately. Given Procopius's relish for descriptions of his targets' sexual misdemeanours he would certainly have reported any rumours of the empress's misconduct had they been current. What Procopius instead criticises is the way in which she extended and enhanced the submission implicit in imperial etiquette. The couple are said to have deliberately orientalised court ceremonial. Now, instead of senators genuflecting and patricians kissing the emperor's right breast, all had to prostrate themselves to Justinian. Theodora insisted on this tribute being paid to her too, on being called *despoina* (mistress), and even, it is said, on receiving ambassadors from Persia and other countries as if she were the mistress of the empire. The fact that no open protest was made, and that the highest officials of the empire were prepared to fall down before their new empress, doubtless intensified the hidden disapproval.[57]

Further criticisms, that she made serious matters a 'subject for laughter as if on the stage', are doubtless also an exaggeration. We can, however, envisage her using ridicule to put down the pretensions of those who might have looked down on her: she appears to have been no respecter of persons.[58] In the case that Procopius cites, a noble official of long standing asked Theodora to ensure that the debt owed to him by one of Theodora's servants be repaid. In response Theodora had her eunuchs chant in chorus 'you have a very big rupture' until the patrician gave up and retired from the audience. It is interesting that this scene is said to have taken place in the relative seclusion of the women's quarters, where Theodora had the luxury of enjoying a good joke in private: there is no hint that such vulgarity was introduced into imperial ceremonial, and indeed it appears that court etiquette took on new importance at this time and that Theodora deliberately used it to assert her new status. While the *Secret History* shows Justinian as being accessible to all, Theodora has all the magistrates awaiting her pleasure like slaves in a small stuffy anteroom, straining for hour after hour on tiptoe to be admitted, simply so that they could prostrate themselves and kiss her foot, and leave in silence. The court had in all things to give way to her convenience, even when she preferred to spend most of the year in the palace of Herion across the Bosporos.[59]

Theodora was quickly able to adapt to the realities of life at the head of an intricate and formal court. According to Malalas, when in 529 she visited the springs at Pythion (modern Yalova) with patricians and *cubicularii*, she was accompanied by a retinue of no less than 4,000 people, including the *comes largitionum*. After giving generously to the churches in the places she visited, she returned to Constantinople. Theophanes expands the entry, listing the high-ranking courtiers who escorted her.[60]

Under the year 527/8 Malalas lists Justinian's new constructions in Antioch – churches, a hospice, baths and cisterns. These were matched in munificence by Theodora, the new empress:

Likewise the most devout Theodora also provided much for the city. She built an extremely fine church of the archangel Michael; she also built what is known as the basilica of Anatolius, for which the columns were sent from Constantinople. The Augusta Theodora made and sent to Jerusalem a very costly cross, set with pearls.[61]

Early in her career Theodora is here showing her munificence in proper style. Procopius frequently links her name with that of Justinian in works of charity: in establishing two hospices for the destitute, including a *xenodocheion* or temporary lodging for visitors in the city; the building of the Convent of Repentance for prostitutes; repairing a highway in Bithynia; and in settlements after the reconquest of North Africa.[62] Theodora's marriage and status as empress gave her considerable financial independence, as a result of Justinian's generosity.[63]

There are no certain portrayals of her from the early period, but her portrait in the mosaic panel in the apse of San Vitale at Ravenna in Italy (Plate 1), completed after 547 when the Byzantines reoccupied the city, does not contradict Procopius's description of her appearance. Even the *Secret History* does not disguise the fact that she was worth looking at: 'she had a lovely face, and was otherwise attractive, but short, and while not completely pale, at least somewhat sallow; her glance was always keen and sharp.'[64] In San Vitale she is shown in full imperial regalia, her ornate jewels stressing her status. The deep embroidered border of her *chlamys* depicts the Magi bringing gifts to Christ, emphasising that like Justinian she too is bringing gifts to the church, in her case a communion chalice.[65] She would have been similarly depicted on the ceiling mosaic of the Chalke entrance to the imperial palace in Constantinople, which pictured Justinian's victories in Africa and Italy. The centre of the mosaic featured Theodora receiving with Justinian the homage of conquered monarchs:

> both seeming to rejoice and to celebrate victories over both the King of the Vandals and the King of the Goths, who approach them as prisoners of war to be led into bondage. Around them stands the Roman Senate, all in festal mood . . . they rejoice and smile as they bestow on the Emperor honours equal to those of God, because of the magnitude of his achievements.[66]

It would be safe to assume that Theodora relished her imperial honours and was concerned to ensure that her regality remained undiminished in the eyes of her subjects.

Plate 1 Theodora and her court, San Vitale, Ravenna (photo: Hirmer Verlag, Munich)

Theodora and the church

Whatever her background and education Theodora was able to make up for any such deficiencies. Like many an empress, one of her greatest spheres of activity was that of religious and charitable works, but with a difference; for Theodora was intensely interested in religious controversy and was an ardent monophysite. John of Nikiu relates that she had spent time in Alexandria and considered Timothy, patriarch of Alexandria (517–35), her spiritual father.[67] Despite this she was not bigoted: when the orthodox St Sabas visited the court in 531, she, like Justinian, prostrated herself before him in a typical gesture of veneration for desert ascetic saints and requested his prayers for a child.[68] Her support for monophysite bishops and monks was the main area in which her aims openly diverged from those of Justinian, one of whose primary concerns was to appear the champion of orthodoxy. Public opinion considered that the imperial couple deliberately fostered the appearance of disagreement in this regard to keep both sides happy,[69] but though the pair may have agreed to appear to 'divide and rule', there is little doubt that Theodora acted from conviction, albeit with Justinian's sanction. Before she was empress, perhaps in 523, John of Ephesos relates that Mare, the monophysite bishop of Amida, who had been banished to Petra, sent his deacon and notary Stephen to Constantinople to intercede for him. Stephen was directed by God to Theodora 'who came from the brothel', who asked her husband to present his case to the emperor Justin. Justinian spoke to the emperor and the appeal resulted in Mare's removal to Alexandria.[70]

That her monophysite leanings were well known is shown by the fact that it was on these grounds that St Sabas during his visit in 531 turned aside her request to pray to God that she might conceive. His failure to cooperate greatly grieved the empress. He had to refuse her request, he told his entourage, as 'no issue will come from her womb, in case it should imbibe the doctrines of Severos and cause more trouble in the church than Anastasios [the monophysite emperor]'.[71] Theodora's monophysitism presumably more than cancelled Justinian's orthodoxy in Sabas's view, and he was not prepared to risk another fervent monophysite emperor. John of Ephesos, who has nothing but praise for Theodora in her work on behalf of monophysite clerics and monastics and who was based at Constantinople in the 540s, calls her 'the Christ-loving Theodora, who was perhaps appointed queen by God to be a support for the persecuted against the cruelty of the times . . . supplying them with provisions and liberal allowances'.[72] Theodora's theological views and discussions of Christological issues at court were of interest to Severos of Antioch and are mentioned in his correspondence. Severos was patriarch of Antioch from 512 to 518, but exiled under Justin; he spent the subsequent years in hiding in Egypt, where he continued to be acknowledged as the uncontested leader of the moderate wing of the monophysites: Theodora is said by Zacharias of Mytilene to have been devoted to Severos.[73] Not only is she mentioned in Severos's correspondence in a letter to the palace chamberlain and deacon Misael in 537, but Severos felt that he could correct her on a point of theology, albeit an abstruse one. Clearly Theodora had been insulting the theology of the fourth-century church father Alexander, an orthodox bishop of Alexandria whose presbyter Arius instituted the Arian heresy:

> But I was much distressed that the serene queen presumes to say such grievous, not to say blasphemous things against the holy fathers in respect of doctrines which she does not understand, and mocks at the holy Alexander the archbishop . . . on the ground that even in the theology of the Trinity he termed person 'nature' and jeers at him as one of those who practise manual crafts, a coppersmith for instance or a carpenter of the name of Alexander, or as she says by way of accusation an advocate of the treasure-chambers . . . From what you now say, that the serene queen has not shrunk from saying such presumptuous things against the holy fathers, I certainly imagine that she has also spurned and despised, as vain trifling and superfluous futility, my little treatise on the question whether our Lord and God Jesus Christ should be said to be from two substances even as from two natures, which she thought good to accept when it was copied by you in large letters, or through fear of the king's laws which were put forth against my writings has not dared to accept it. I wrote to you at that time from Chios . . . but you wrote nothing at all to me upon these matters. He who writes an answer should reply to all the points contained in the letter.[74]

Theodora's fault here is in being unaware that the terms *physis* (nature) and *prosopon* (person), later distinguished, were not consistently used at the time of the Council of Nicaea. Misael is a frequent correspondent of Severos, who is here reporting Theodora's conversations to Severos, and while he does not specifically say so Severos obviously expects Misael to report the gist of this rather acerbic letter back to Theodora, to whom he has been sending reading material. Treatises were also specifically addressed to her by monophysite leaders. Theodosios of Alexandria, deposed from his patriarchate as a monophysite in 537, dedicated to her his *Tome against Themistios*, possibly in 538. This dealt with a refutation of the view of Themistios (a Severan monophysite) that Christ, because of his humanity, possessed human ignorance and not divine knowledge. Themistios and his followers were known as the Agnoetai, hence the issue is known as the Agnoetic debate.[75] A similar treatise was addressed to her by the more radical Constantine of Laodikeia, who had also been deposed from his see in 519 as a result of his monophysite beliefs. Both Theodosios and Constantine lived in Constantinople after their depositions, under the protection of Theodora. That Theodora could be appealed to by leading monophysite theologians in an internal debate on the ignorance of Christ shows that she was considered to take an intelligent interest in such controversies.

The period from 531 to 536 was one of détente between orthodox and monophysites and thus one in which Theodora's championship of the monophysites had full play. In 531 Justinian changed his tactics towards the monophysites, if not towards other heretical groups.[76] While Theodora's influence may have been at work here, it is more likely that his motivation was political because he wanted the East peaceful prior to his campaigns of reconquest in the West. Monophysite bishops and monks who had been exiled were allowed to return to their sees and monasteries and many came to Constantinople. The palace of Hormisdas, which adjoined the Great Palace, and which Justinian had built initially as his own residence in 518–19 and later connected to the palace proper,[77] became established as a monophysite monastery; in its heyday it came to provide shelter for some 500 clergy and monks under the protection of the empress, including for some time John of Ephesos, probably from 542.[78] Although there was already a church dedicated to Sts Peter and Paul in this palace, at some time prior to 536 the church of the Syrian saints Sergios and Bakchos was also built, as a centre of monophysite monastic worship. The great inscription on the entablature specifically honoured Theodora, praying that Sergios might 'in all things guard the rule of the sleepless sovereign and increase the power of the God-crowned Theodora whose mind is adorned with piety, whose constant toil lies in unsparing efforts to nourish the destitute',[79] a clear manifesto of her involvement with the community.

The early 530s was a time, therefore, when Theodora's and Justinian's ostensibly contradictory religious policies most closely cohered. In 533 Justinian decreed, with the pope's approval, that the Theopaschite doctrine ('that One of the Trinity suffered in the flesh') was orthodox.[80] This was an undeniable step on the road to monophysitism. In this climate, Theodora's influence may not have been needed to encourage Justinian to make Anthimos, bishop of Trebizond, patriarch in 535, but all the same it was a triumph for Theodora's cause. Anthimos was a pro-monophysite who initiated an open policy of discussion with leading monophysites.[81] During the debate over church union Theodora was able in 534/5 to persuade Justinian to invite Severos of Antioch, the leading monophysite of the day, from Alexandria to Constantinople.[82] She gave him accommodation in her palace (whether in the imperial palace or the palace of Hormisdas is not recorded) for over a year. This could have had momentous consequences, for during his stay Severos was able to convince the patriarch Anthimos of the correctness of monophysitism, at which Anthimos changed allegiance. He was, however, deposed by Pope Agapetus I in his visit to Constantinople early in 536, a blow for Theodora,[83] and a decision which Justinian, whose policy towards the monophysites was hardening, could not dispute because of his need to conciliate the western provinces where his campaigns were gaining momentum. Theodora also had Theodosios, a monophysite and a supporter of Severos of Antioch, made patriarch of Alexandria in February of the same year, 535, though Theodosios had to be installed by force against the wishes of a large proportion of the populace who held extremist monophysite views. Liberatus, archdeacon of Carthage, reports that Kalotychios, one of Theodora's *cubicularii*, happened to be in Alexandria when the patriarch Timothy died and it was Kalotychios who arranged for the consecration of Theodosios.[84] But Theodosios was soon banished from the city by Gaianos, a rival candidate: Gaianos like many of the Alexandrians was an Aphthartodocetist who believed in the incorruptibility of Christ's flesh, following the teachings of Julian of Halikarnassos. The 'History of the Patriarchs of the Coptic Church of Alexandria' records that Theodora reported this to Justinian, who 'wishing to please the princess, and to delight her heart, [he] gave her power to do by his authority in this matter whatever she desired'.[85] A general (the Persarmenian Narses) was sent with, according to Michael the Syrian, a detachment of 6,000 soldiers to confirm Theodosios in his see against this Julianist rival; 3,000 people were killed in the conflict. With the help of imperial troops and the support of Severos of Antioch Theodosios held on to his see for seventeen months of continuous street warfare. He was unable, however, to achieve a *modus vivendi* with the radical monophysites in the capital and in 536 left for Constantinople and never returned.[86]

On 6 August 536 an imperial edict banned Anthimos, Severos and their supporters from the capital and from all the great cities of the empire, and ordered the burning of all Severos's writings.[87] But this does not seem to have been systematically carried out and the palace of Hormisdas continued to flourish as a centre of monophysite resistance under Theodora's protection. Severos left the capital and died in Egypt in exile from his see in February 538. A letter of his to the eastern clergy is quoted in the *Chronicle* of Zacharias of Mytilene which speaks of his expulsion: 'As for the wickedness of these men, it is not sated with blood; the Christ-worshipping queen was a sufficient protection for me, and God, who through your prayers directed her to that which is good in His sight . . .'.[88] Theodosios too, now in Constantinople, was to be deposed by Justinian probably at the end of 537, for refusing to agree with Pope Agapetus's definition of orthodoxy. After being confined in the fortress of Derkos in Thrace with some 300 other monophysite clergy, he was soon brought back to the capital by Theodora's influence and housed in the palace of Hormisdas with his supporters, becoming after Severos's death the unchallenged leader of the monophysite church. Severos himself declined sending Theodosios any 'gift' after his deposition in Constantinople, 'seeing that he has the serene queen, who will provide him if he wish even with more than he needs'.[89] Severos had himself after all enjoyed Theodora's hospitality in the capital. Theodosios lived on to 566, and he and the community even after Theodora's death in 548 continued to be protected by Justinian for Theodora's sake, till 565 when John is writing, although they did not remain in the palace of Hormisdas.[90] Theodora is even credited by John of Ephesos in his *Lives of the Eastern Saints* with hiding the ex-patriarch Anthimos in her palace, where he remained secretly until her death twelve years later, unbeknownst to everyone except herself and two chamberlains: Anthimos must have been a special case, as other monophysite leaders openly remained in Constantinople. John's account here is somewhat suspect as he states that Anthimos abdicated after being patriarch for a number of years; it also differs radically from his later account in his *Ecclesiastical History*. He makes much of Justinian's wrath against Anthimos as a non-compliant patriarch, recording that as a consequence Theodora hid him in a chamber in her palace, and that Justinian and everyone else, except for Theodora and two chamberlains, thought that she had removed him from the city.[91]

The Hormisdas establishment was quite a complex one and the palace was adapted to monastic living: Theodora had cells made for the old and honoured among the inhabitants while halls were divided into cells and booths by means of planks, curtains and matting. Inmates included stylites and desert ascetics and solitaries who had been driven from their seclusion, and one large chamber was a monastery in its own right with an archimandrite, steward and servitors and its own regulations. Theodora herself was said to visit them regularly:

> The community of blessed men which was gathered together in the royal city by the believing queen at the time of the persecution, out of many peoples and various local tongues . . . was indeed composed of many blessed men who did not fall short of the number of five hundred . . . The believing queen also would regularly once in every two or three days come down to them to be blessed by them, being amazed at their community and their practices, and admiring their honored old age, and going round among them and making obeisance to them, and being regularly blessed by each one of them, while she provided the expenses required for them liberally in every thing; while the king also . . . marvelled at their congregation, and himself also was attached to many of them and trusted them, and was constantly received and blessed by them.[92]

The community consisted of monophysites from 'Syria and Armenia, Cappadocia and Cilicia, Isauria and Lycaonia, and Asia and Alexandria and Byzantium', and so many worshippers, including women and children, would gather for services that on one occasion the floor of one of the great halls gave way, though without causing any injury.[93] Theodora had similar institutions under her protection for monophysite nuns, and John records that some of these numbered more than 300 inhabitants.[94] There were other institutions too under her guardianship. When John of Hephaistu in Egypt came to Constantinople in the late 530s, Theodora received him with great joy, and she gave orders that spacious quarters also should be given him in the great mansion called Anthemiu, and an allowance also for him and his slave should be assigned to him there. And thenceforth the will and the zeal of the blessed man found expression; and from that time companies of men who were in distress, and had been for a long time beaten and buffeted and had none to relieve them, betook themselves to him . . .[95]

John soon left Constantinople to continue his missionary activities in Asia Minor and the Aegean.

After 536 Hormisdas continued as one of the main centres of clandestine monophysitism, which saw the consecration of bishops and aided the spread of monophysitism among the Ghassanid Arabs, Nubians and Syrians. In 541 the Ghassanid emir Harith directly approached Theodora to ask for 'orthodox' (i.e. monophysite) bishops for his tribe.[96] Accordingly, 'since the believing queen was desirous of furthering everything that would assist the opponents of the synod of Chalcedon', Theodosios in 542 consecrated two monks as bishops to work in the regions of Syria and Arabia. Jacob Baradaios (Bar'adai, a Syrian) was made metropolitan of Edessa and Theodore metropolitan of Bostra, capital of the province of Arabia.[97] Jacob Baradaios became the underground leader of the monophysites of Syria, and as a result of his achievements the Syrian monophysite church was known as the Jacobite church; while we should perhaps allow for a degree of pardonable exaggeration in his account, he tells us that by his death in 578 he had consecrated twenty-seven metropolitan bishops and some 100,000 clergy.[98]

Another area proselytised under Theodora's direction was Nubia, where the imperial couple sent alternative missionaries, and supposedly due to Theodora's generalship the monophysites prevailed. The idea of converting the Nobatai, a Nubian tribe, initially came from an elderly monk called Julian c. 541 in the entourage of Theodosios in Constantinople. Justinian, on being informed, thought the plan a good idea but that the mission should be orthodox. Theodora, it is said, thereupon wrote to the *dux* of the southern Egyptian province of the Thebaid, informing him that both she and the emperor intended to send a mission to the Nobatai, and that her emissary the blessed Julian would be in charge of her ambassadors. He should therefore give Julian every assistance to ensure that her mission arrived first or he would lose his head. The *dux* accepted her instructions, and Julian succeeded in converting Silko, king of the Nobatai, and a number of nobility and people, who became fervent monophysites and considered the emperor's mission when it arrived as nothing short of heretical.[99] While it seems laughable that the emperor and empress should each dispatch rival missions, it is of course possible that this too was part of their strategy of parallel diplomacy in religious matters. Justinian may have felt that the gesture of sending an orthodox mission was necessary to maintain imperial prestige, rather than expecting any success in converting the tribe to chalcedonianism, when their nearest neighbours were fervent monophysites: the same rationale may have accounted for his permitting the Ghassanids to be converted by monophysite clergy.[100]

John of Ephesos himself, though a monophysite, was sent by Justinian in 542 on a mission to convert the remaining pagans of Asia Minor. John tells us that in the four provinces of Asia, Caria, Phrygia and Lydia 80,000 inhabitants were baptised, and ninety-eight new churches and twelve monasteries built and seven other churches transformed from synagogues.[101] Again, the numbers involved should not necessarily be taken at face value. However, it is clear that Theodora was at the centre of a complex nexus directly responsible for the spread of monophysitism as a dynamic faith, which was to endure in the eastern provinces as an alternative church.

Theodora had great influence on church affairs, and it was in great measure due to her influence that the monophysite church endured and indeed came to flourish in the eastern provinces. John of Ephesos, as one of the monophysite leaders of the time, is naturally concerned to present the empress as a champion of monophysitism, and we should perhaps beware of taking his portrait too literally. Nevertheless, it appears that she sponsored several missions of proselytism, all successfully, and encouraged Justinian to send others, such as that of John of Ephesos in Asia Minor. Justinian's policies towards the monophysites continued to vacillate throughout his reign, and he seems personally to have honoured a number of their leaders. During the episode of the Three Chapters in the 540s, for example, he was prepared to upset the West in order to conciliate the eastern provinces. At the end of his life, in an attempt to bring his subjects to church unity, he issued an edict attempting to impose aphthartodocetism – a form of radical monophysitism which taught that the body of Christ was incorruptible – and he certainly respected individuals within the monophysite movement.[102] Theodora's monophysite activities were not always in opposition to Justinian's, and he must have tacitly permitted her involvement in the consecration of two patriarchs and the proselytisation of large areas of Asia Minor, Syria, Nubia and Arabia.

Theodora and power

Theodora's interference in religious issues mostly took place through unofficial channels, even if her actions were undertaken with the cognisance of Justinian. The extent to which she was concerned in other matters of imperial policy, such as Justinian's grandiose plans for reconquest of the West, is less clear. Justinian's aims were those of a conservative: as well as uniting the church he wanted to restore the empire, reform government, secure the eastern frontiers and leave behind him the monuments of an extensive and unparalleled building programme. In these aims it appears that he was supported by his powerful co-regent. Procopius's *Secret History* cannot be taken as unsupported evidence for their joint rule, but one of his reiterated complaints is their collegiality: 'neither did anything apart from the other to the end of their joint lives.'[103] Theodora is seen to be the dominant partner (where Justinian does not listen to her persuasions, she can entice him by suggesting a profit motive),[104] and Procopius considers that Justinian's love for Theodora must have been brought about by sorcery: in fact they are both demons incarnate intent on destroying the world.[105] Theodora's influence is corroborated elsewhere: even in the *Wars*, she is described as being greatly loved by Justinian, and John the Cappadocian is said to have slandered her to the emperor, 'neither blushing before her high station nor feeling shame because of the extraordinary love which the emperor felt for her'. Procopius in his published works frequently notes Theodora acting in cooperation with Justinian and gives an impression of mutual cooperation;[106] John the Lydian describes her as co-sharer of the empire.[107]

In the exaggerations of the *Secret History*, Theodora advances the careers of her favourites. She regularly attends meetings of the *consistorium* (the senate and emperor's advisers) and takes sides on issues. If Justinian entrusts any business to anyone without first consulting her, that man comes to a most unfortunate end. Theodora feels herself entitled to control every branch of public affairs, fills both church and state offices, and decides the composition of juries.[108] When she works behind the scenes, she has an army of spies in the city to keep her informed of events and conversations even in private houses; she can punish generals or create new ones; and is shown as pursuing and torturing her enemies, and incarcerating enemies in her private cellars under the palace. Procopius's accusations reveal that the empress had a very real presence in public affairs. The extent to which she misused her power may have been exaggerated but of the fact that she possessed power there is no doubt.[109]

Plate 2 A sixth-century gold marriage ring, with frontal bust portraits of the couple on either side of a monumental cross (Dumbarton Oaks Byzantine Collection: Washington DC)

The *Secret History*'s account is in at least one case documented by other sources, for example the case of a notary called Priskos. Priskos, according to the *Secret History*, had amassed a huge fortune by shady means. On the ground that he had treated her with scorn, Theodora denounced him to Justinian. This producing no result (we should note that Justinian does not always comply immediately with her requests even in the *Secret History*), Theodora had him put on board a ship and sent off to an unknown destination; he was then forcibly ordained. The emperor made no attempt to discover his whereabouts, but simply pocketed his money.[110] The official version of events is given by Malalas, under the year 529, who tells us that Priskos, 'ex-consul and former imperial secretary, incurred anger. His property was confiscated and he was made a deacon and sent to Kyzikos.'[111] Here it is apparent how Procopius's belittling technique has worked: Priskos, 'utterly villainous and as blustering as any Paphlagonian' (the reference here is to Kleon the politician attacked by Aristophanes), and who was probably a senior colleague of whom Procopius or his readership was glad to see the last, was actually an ex-consul. Moreover, the text of Malalas preserved in Constantine Porphyrogenitos's *de insidiis* records that he was in fact *comes excubitorum* (count of the excubitors and a very prestigious position) and exiled 'for having insulted and slandered the empress Theodora', while Theophanes adds that he was exiled by order of the emperor and ordained deacon.[112] The end result in each case is that his property is confiscated, but Procopius's picture of a private army and prison system and the empress's terrorist-like activities is revealed to be something more official and infinitely more effective. It is clear that slander of the empress was gravely punished by official means, no doubt to the chagrin of those who wished to criticise her and who were jealous of her influence with the emperor.[113]

The attack on Theodora in the *Secret History* for her punishment of the general Bouzes, who was accused of treasonable talk with Belisarius during Justinian's illness in the plague of 542, is similarly slanted. The two generals had apparently declared that if the emperor were to die they would not accept anyone appointed in their absence, and Theodora is said to have taken this as criticism of herself – as indeed it was. Theodora is said to have invited Bouzes to the women's quarters and thrown him into the labyrinthine cellars under the palace, only releasing him nearly two and a half years later.[114] While this episode is not corroborated by other sources, it is perhaps reasonable to suspect that Theodora was responding effectively to what she saw as treasonable practices: after all, it was to be considered quite acceptable for her successor Sophia to appoint two emperors.

Theodora's most famous role involved her actions reported in Procopius's *Wars*, when, during the Nika revolt in 532, with the throne at risk, she encouraged Justinian to stand up to the factional rioters rather than run away. Justinian had tried to curb the factions, the only means of expression of popular discontent at the burgeoning administration and taxation. This was unsuccessful and in January 532 minor riots and murders ensued; after the hanging of two of the seven rioters was bungled, and Justinian refused to pardon them, the factions determined to rescue them, burying their differences and adopting the watchword *Nika* (victory). As the government stood firm on their demands, the mob broke into the prison, set it on fire and burnt the city, calling for the dismissal of John the Cappadocian (the praetorian prefect), Tribonian, Justinian's legislator, and the city prefect Eudaimon. Justinian's removal of these officials came too late to placate the factions and on January 18 they compelled Hypatios, Anastasios's nephew, to accept the throne. Significantly Hypatios was also the choice of a large proportion of the senatorial class. An escape fleet was prepared and packed with the imperial treasure but Theodora intervened, according to Procopius, with a stirring speech, and saved the day:

> I consider that flight, even if it leads to safety, is especially wrong at this juncture. For just as it is impossible for a man who has come to the light not to die as well, it is intolerable for one who has been an emperor to be a fugitive. May I never be without this purple, and may I not live on that day when those who meet me do not address me as mistress (*despoina*). If you now want to save yourself, Emperor, there is no problem. For we have a lot of money, and the sea and the boats are here. But consider the possibility that after you have been saved you might not happily exchange that safety for death. A certain ancient saying appeals to me that royalty is a good funeral shroud.[115]

In actual terms the situation was saved by pragmatic means: while the mob was packed in the hippodrome acclaiming Hypatios, and insulting both Justinian and Theodora according to the *Chronicon Paschale*,[116] the generals Belisarius and Mundus (the Danube commander) went into the hippodrome at roughly opposite sides and turned their soldiers on the populace. Some 30,000 or more were slaughtered.[117] Hypatios and his brother were executed, despite their innocence of treason, and eighteen leading aristocratic conspirators were exiled and their property seized.

It has to be seriously doubted that Theodora actually delivered the speech as written by Procopius, though the sentiments, those of a woman who was determined to hang on to her imperial status at all costs, may have been hers. Cameron notes that the speech is a rhetorical set-piece, and an illustration of the theme of the resolute female, not actually a discussion of the matter in hand.[118] Procopius may here be making an ironical criticism of Justinian's government (equating it with the tyranny of Dionysios of Syracuse),[119] and at the same time making a further criticism of the regime by showing Theodora improperly taking on a masculine role, one that would more appropriately have been demonstrated by Justinian. On another level, we should however deduce that, even if Theodora did not deliver the speech as written, it was considered as something that she might well have said, and reflects her decisiveness and outspokenness in her relationship with Justinian.

Another episode in the *Wars* in which Theodora is depicted in Procopius's official works acting independently of Justinian follows on directly from his account of the Nika revolt, a juxtaposition which cannot be accidental. John the Cappadocian was Justinian's chief financial adviser at the time of the Nika revolt, and had been praetorian prefect since 530 or early 531. He was one of the emperor's hand-picked and trusted ministers, for Justinian had great need of money; the frontier wars with Persia were expensive and there were other wars in view. John was of low birth, avaricious, unscrupulous and libertine, as well as good at his job, and Procopius's picture of the Cappadocian, like that of John Lydus, is uniformly unflattering,[120] though he notes his financial expertise.[121] Dislike of his policies was one of the causes of the Nika riot in 532,[122] but he was so indispensable to Justinian that his successor Phokas was removed and he was reinstated by October.[123] Indeed, he was so close to Justinian that he could speak his mind: Procopius tells us that he alone could speak out forcefully against Justinian's projects of reconquest. This may have been one of the areas in which his advice to Justinian differed from that of Theodora and which may have caused her dislike: not only did he not flatter her, but he openly opposed her and kept slandering her to Justinian, despite her rank and Justinian's love for her.[124]

Theodora was determined to destroy the Cappadocian. John had been extremely ill-advised in trying to make a wedge between Justinian and Theodora, and she may also have realised the damage which the Cappadocian's unpopularity was doing to Justinian's regime. Another possibility is that she may have been jealous of the Cappadocian's power and influence with the emperor, which was great, and may even have seen him as a threat to the throne. It was in fact by his ambition and treachery that she finally entrapped him, but the fact that it took her eleven years shows his usefulness to Justinian and the reality of the relationship between the imperial couple: that Justinian would listen to her advice, providing there was no overridding reason not to do so.

Since Justinian would not remove the Cappadocian from office, Theodora decided to have him killed, but was unable to do so because he was so highly thought of by the emperor. Yet John was absolutely terrified of the possibility: every night he expected the imperial guard to slay him and 'kept peeping out of the room and looking about the entrances and remained sleepless, although he had attached to himself many thousands of spearmen and guards, a thing which had been granted to no prefect before that time'.[125] Theodora is here shown as concerned with the ill deeds committed by John (though her chosen manner of righting them – assassination – is somewhat drastic); John Lydus also describes her as being not only understanding towards those wronged but vigilant too in their concerns, and unable 'any longer to overlook the fact that the state was being ruined'. According to Lydus, Theodora even warned Justinian that his subjects would be ruined by John's evil deeds and that the empire was close to destruction.[126]

After suffering John for some eleven years, in May 541 with Antonina's help Theodora entrapped John's daughter Euphemia into getting John to commit himself to a conspiracy to gain the throne. Even though John was warned by the emperor of the danger involved, a secret meeting of John with Antonina outside the city at Belisarius's palace at Rufinianai was overheard by Narses and the commander of the palace guard positioned there for the purpose.[127] Procopius considers that even now had John gone directly to Justinian he would have been pardoned, but he fled to sanctuary, was disgraced, and exiled to a suburb of Kyzikos where he was ordained; a large part of his property was confiscated but returned by Justinian, so he could live in luxury even in exile. But further ill-luck continued to pursue John. When a party of senators was sent to investigate the murder of Eusebios, a bishop of Kyzikos, John, who had been at loggerheads with him, was accused of involvement, scourged and exiled once again to Antinoos in Egypt.[128] Theodora, according to the *Secret History,* then attempted to get proof of his involvement in Eusebios's murder by suborning two members of the Greens from Kyzikos who had supposedly been implicated. These young men were tortured to get a confession, the right hands of both being cut off when this was unsuccessful. Malalas confirms that they were implicated in the murder of Eusebios and that they were tried in public and their hands cut off.[129] Only after Theodora's death was John recalled, apparently in the same year, and he died in the capital still nominally a deacon.[130] The account of the *Secret History* typically shows Theodora as a vindictive monster but need not be taken at face value.[131] Far more important is the fact that in the *Wars*, the published history, Theodora and Antonina can be shown as conspiring in such a way against the finance minister by an author who clearly had inside knowledge of events and personalities. The episode is evidence that Justinian and Theodora differed in their views of John over a period of some years, and that not only did Theodora consider murder as a solution to the problem, but the praetorian prefect was well aware that he was in danger from the empress. While Theodora is here working through unofficial channels this made the position of her opponents no more secure. The Cappadocian's successor Barsymes had all John's skills in extracting money for Justinian's measures, but not his unpleasant personal qualities, and according to the *Secret History* was a nominee and favourite of Theodora.[132]

A further intrigue in which Theodora was said in the *Secret History* to have been involved was in the murder of Amalasuintha, the Gothic queen who started to intrigue with the Byzantines when her son Athalaric was dying in 534.[133] Justinian sent Peter of Thessalonika to pursue with her the matter of direct Byzantine control of the Ostrogothic regions of Italy. Amalasuintha, however, who had acted as regent since 526, decided not to come to

Constantinople and instead to retain power in her own right; as among the Goths kingship could not be held by a woman she married her cousin Theodahad after her son died. Theodahad had her imprisoned and she was soon murdered, in her bath, after the arrival of Peter, probably in April 535.[134] Amalasuintha was a woman of beauty and culture and according to the *Secret History* Theodora planned Amalasuintha's murder, as she feared her as a potential rival for Justinian's favours if she came to Constantinople. She assigned this task to Peter, who on his arrival persuaded Theodahad (whom Procopius here calls Theudatus) to undertake it.[135] This was a direct cause of Byzantine armed intervention in Italy and certainly Justinian welcomed the opportunity for such involvement as the action in Africa had reached a triumphal conclusion and Belisarius and his army were ready for further campaigns. Procopius's account is not entirely implausible,[136] and Theodora certainly appears to have been intriguing in some way with Theodahad, who was in hopes of a title, estates, and Justinian's friendship at Constantinople.[137]

Two letters in Cassiodorus's *Variae* are addressed to Theodora, one from Theodahad and one from his wife Gudeliva, both dated to spring 535. These are but two of the five letters addressed to Theodora by Ostrogothic sovereigns and their wives in the 530s.[138] Even if Theodahad's letter is not concerned with the murder of Amalasuintha, this document is one addressed to the empress, from the Gothic ruler, thanking her for her letters and verbal message, which had requested that she should have prior knowledge of any request being sent to the emperor, and trusting that he has responded to her delicate hint in a mutually satisfactory way:

> I have received your piety's letters with the gratitude always due to things we long for, and have gained, with most reverent joy, your verbal message, more exalted than any gift. I promise myself everything from so serene a soul, since, in such kindly discourse, I have received whatever I could hope for. For you exhort me to bring first to your attention anything I decide to ask from the triumphal prince, your husband . . . Hence it is that, advised by your reverence, I ordained that both the most blessed Pope [probably Agapitus] and the most noble Senate should reply without any delay to what you saw fit to request from them; thus, your glory will lose no reverence because a spirit of delay opposed it; but rather, speed of action will increase your favour that we pray for. For, in the case of that person too, about whom a delicate hint has reached me, know that I have ordered what I trust will agree with your intention. For it is my desire that you should command me no less in my realm than in your empire, through the medium of your influence . . .[139]

In an accompanying letter to Theodora, Theodahad's wife Gudeliva gives us a similarly enigmatic hint of some underground intrigue: 'For, although there should be no discord between the Roman realms, nonetheless, an affair has arisen of a kind which should make me still dearer to your justice.'[140] It has been conjectured that this too may refer to the murder of Amalasuintha. That Theodora's motive for such intervention in Amalasuintha's death was jealousy is absurd. We can only guess at other reasons for possible intrigue on her part, although the fact that Justinian may have been looking for a pretext for war could have induced the couple to encourage Theodahad to actions which would bring this about,[141] and Theodora may here have been acting as a conduit for unofficial hints from the imperial couple relating to Amalasuintha's death.

Theodora's religious concerns also caused her to interfere in western politics and it is possible that she played an important part in Justinian's treatment both of Pope Silverius (536–7),[142] and his successor Vigilius (537–55), whom she pressured Justinian to remove. Pope Agapetus, who had deposed Anthimos, the monophysite patriarch, in 536, was replaced on his death in Constantinople by the Gothic ruler Theodahad's nominee Silverius. That Theodora had hoped for her own candidate and tried to make a deal to establish Vigilius as pope after Agapetus is stated in western sources: Vigilius, a Roman deacon, had journeyed to Constantinople with Agapetus, where he seems to have concluded an agreement with Theodora promising to soften western opposition towards monophysitism. Since Silverius was already installed, Theodora decided to depose him, for this purpose employing her old friend Antonina, currently in Italy with her husband Belisarius who had taken Rome at the end of 536. Antonina succeeded in making Silverius appear a pro-Gothic traitor.[143] While the *Liber Pontificalis* (*Book of Pontiffs*) has Justinian initiate the request for Anthimos's re-installation as patriarch, it is interesting that Silverius replies directly to the empress:

> The emperor after discussing the matter with the deacon Vigilius sent a letter to pope Silverius in Rome with the request and demand: 'Do not hesitate to come and visit us, or be sure to restore Anthimus to his office.' . . . The most blessed Silverius wrote back to the empress: 'Lady empress, to restore a heretic who has been condemned in his wickedness is something I can never bring myself to do'. Then the empress was infuriated and sent orders by the deacon Vigilius to the patrician Belisarius: 'Look for some pretexts to deal with pope Silverius and depose him from the bishopric, or be sure to send him quickly over to us. Look, you have present with you the archdeacon Vigilius our dearly beloved *apocrisiarius*, who has given us his word he will restore the patriarch Anthimus.'[144]

Silverius was exiled by Belisarius,[145] and replaced by Vigilius who became pope in March 537. He, however, failed to fulfil his promises to Theodora, writing to her that despite his earlier agreement, he could not restore a heretic to the patriarchate.[146] Not only did he not work towards unity with the monophysites, he was not even prepared to condemn Justinian's edict issued between 543 and 545 known as the Three Chapters, which appealed to monophysite sympathies by anathematising the three Nestorian theologians Theodoret of Cyrrhus, Ibas of Edessa and Theodore of Mopsuestia, all long dead. Because of his failure to comply in this regard, Vigilius was forcibly taken to Constantinople where he arrived in January 547. He and Patriarch Menas soon excommunicated each other, but, according to Theophanes, one of Theodora's last official actions was to reconcile them on 29 June 547 after Vigilius had signed a condemnation of the Three Chapters.[147] Vigilius's position continued to waver, and he failed to attend the Second Council of Constantinople in May 553 which briefly imposed church unity. Finally in 554 he anathematised the Three Chapters and died soon afterwards.

Theodora's family

A further area in which Theodora demonstrated great managerial skill, as might be expected, was in her aggrandisement of her own family. She took steps in this direction immediately upon her accession, when in 528 her elder sister Komito was grandly married to Sittas (or Tzitas), in the palace of Antiochos near the hippodrome in Constantinople. Sittas, perhaps an Armenian, was made *magister militum per Armeniam* (commander-in-chief for Armenia).[148] Antonina, Theodora's old friend, was also married, to Belisarius, a great general of considerable wealth, who was from henceforth to receive Theodora's support.[149]

Theodora's illegitimate daughter made a good marriage into the wealthy family of the emperor Anastasios. A similarly grand marriage was arranged for one of Theodora's grandsons, also called Anastasios, to Belisarius's daughter Joannina. This was against Antonina's will according to Procopius, who records that it was only by prevailing on Anastasios to seduce Joannina (a very great heiress) while her parents were absent in Italy that Theodora was able to bring about the union.[150] Theodora had another grandson Athanasios, a monk who was a prime mover among the tritheists, a monophysite splinter group which arose in the 550s. Athanasios, who was apparently extremely wealthy, presumably from his father's side,[151] and who was known personally by John of Ephesos, was a candidate for the patriarchal see of Alexandria and eventually founded his own sect, the Athanasiani.[152] John of Ephesos mentions a third grandson named John, who was ambassador and consul and perhaps a patrician.[153] He married into another rich monophysite family, for his wife and mother-in-law Georgia and Antipatra are described by John as high-born and wealthy, of consular rank and patrician respectively.[154] A further kinsman of Theodora called George was curator of the palace of

Marina.[155] Theodora not only manoeuvred her grandchildren into the highest places in Byzantine society, she did the same for Sophia, her niece and the only other relative of Theodora's mentioned in the sources. Sophia was luckiest of all: she was married to Justin, the son of Justinian's sister Vigilantia, and was eventually to be Theodora's own successor. Sophia, like John and Athanasios, was a monophysite, and between them, Theodora's family – despite their lowly background and dubious origins – must have formed a distinctive group in the higher echelons of society in the capital.[156]

The succession to the throne was obviously a thorny issue. Theodora and Justinian had no children, a situation which obviously grieved Theodora greatly in the early 530s according to the life of St Sabas. There were numerous family members who were possibilities for imperial honours, but no successor was ever specifically appointed by Justinian. Theodora had disliked Germanos, Justinian's cousin, and his family, whom she saw as rivals, for Germanos was not only a highly successful general, but as another nephew of Justin he had as much claim to be emperor as Justinian: according to the *Secret History* Theodora would not even let anyone marry into his family.[157] It was only after Theodora's death in 548 that he emerged as favourite in the succession stakes, but he died in 550. Ironically, even though Theodora as it happened had no hand in events, it was the side of the family that she favoured which actually succeeded – not Germanos's sons, but Justin, the nephew whom Theodora had married to her own niece Sophia.

Death and aftermath

When Justinian died on 14 November 565, at the very advanced age of approximately eighty-three, his nephew was entrenched in the capital with the support of the aristocracy. In what appear to have been well-planned as well as well-orchestrated scenes, Justin II and Sophia assumed the mantle of power, and Justinian was conveyed to the Church of the Holy Apostles, a Constantinian foundation which he had rebuilt, and where there was a separate shrine north of the church intended for himself and Theodora.[158] Theodora had predeceased Justinian by seventeen years. She is generally thought to have died of cancer, and it is possible that Procopius's account of her luxurious lifestyle and liking for long baths is evidence for her attempts to ameliorate the symptoms.[159] Despite being without an obvious heir Justinian did not remarry, and while certain policy changes are apparent after Theodora's death, such as the recall of Belisarius from Italy, Justinian's inherent vacillation can also be seen to become more evident following Theodora's death.[160] After his victory over the Huns in 559, more than ten years after her death, Justinian had had his triumphal procession detour to the Holy Apostles so that he could light candles at Theodora's tomb.[161] It is possible that she played an important role in the practical shaping of measures during her lifetime, as well as in the concerted policy of maximising popular support through appeal to various sectors of society.

It is of course the case that Theodora worked indirectly, through intrigue, as in the downfall of John the Cappadocian. As with the wife of any head of state, she had no official power of her own and her influence depended on Justinian's readiness to take her advice, as on occasions he refused to do. The fact that it took Theodora more than a decade to rid the administration of the Cappadocian shows that her sphere of action had its limits. But officialdom and power are not synonymous: the fact that Theodora worked through unofficial channels does not mean that she was not a powerful force to be reckoned with, and the objects of her displeasure would have had little satisfaction in consoling themselves with the reflection that they were simply being targeted unofficially. But in fact Procopius's account of her underhand intrigues is somewhat suspect. Offenders like Priskos were punished for their sins against Theodora through official channels – perhaps a more horrifying prospect – while the Cappadocian was not assassinated, whatever Theodora's wishes on the matter, but entrapped into openly compromising himself with the establishment. In effect, Theodora may not have achieved her ends quite as surreptitiously as the *Secret History* would have us believe but doubtless she was equally effective. Procopius would, after all, not have written the *Secret History* unless there was a hostile faction which disapproved of her powerful position in the state, and perhaps one of the most annoying factors was the influence she had over the emperor. Her promotion of monophysitism can surely be seen as semi-official: while Justinian may not always have been aware of her actions, it is clear that they were not entirely in opposition to his private agenda, however much they might seem to have been in contradiction to his official policies. The part she played in the deposition of a pope and a finance minister and the consecration of two patriarchs, as well as in more routine matters, speaks for the correctness of Procopius's assertion of the collegiality of the imperial couple and for the degree of her influence on policies and events during Justinian's reign.

2

SOPHIA (565–601+)

Justin II and Sophia succeeded Justinian on 14 November 565; Justin was the son of Justinian's sister Vigilantia, though not the only candidate for the throne. Even at the time of their accession Sophia emerges as a prominent consort, who features markedly in the works recording both the event and the imperial couple's subsequent actions. Regrettably their reputation has suffered from unfavourable accounts in the works of contemporary historians, which have coloured views of their reign. The sources for Sophia and Justin have tended to be less than fair to the imperial couple: in particular John of Ephesos, a friend of Sophia's protégé Tiberios who was to become the emperor Tiberios Constantine,[1] vilifies the couple for their persecution of monophysite groups as part of which he was personally imprisoned, while for Evagrios the outstanding characteristic of the reign was Justin's avarice and stringent financial measures,[2] policies which in hindsight were also very much the concern of Sophia.

John of Ephesos describes her as Theodora's niece, and Sophia's own statement about her demented husband, 'The kingdom came through me, and it has come back to me: and as for him, he is chastised, and has fallen into this trial on my account, because he did not value me sufficiently, and vexed me',[3] implies a close relationship to the former empress Theodora. It also shows her as marked by a love of domination and a belief that the imperial power was hers by right. She even adopted the official nomenclature Aelia Sophia, using the title (Aelia) given to the empresses of the Theodosian house and their successors, which had been dropped by Euphemia and Theodora. Indeed, according to Averil Cameron, Sophia 'emerges as a figure as powerful and in many ways more interesting than her aunt'.[4] In fact, Sophia not only played an influential part in government, but one that was publicly recognised: something that Theodora never achieved or, indeed, aspired to.[5] Sophia is one of the prime examples of the dynastic marriages which Theodora orchestrated to the advantage of her family. She may have been the daughter of Theodora's elder sister Komito and the general Sittas, a marriage which Justinian (by which we may assume Theodora) arranged on his accession.[6] As Sophia already had a married daughter, Arabia, when she came to the throne, Sophia herself was presumably born no later than 535 and must have been married and Arabia born by 550: Arabia was married to Badouarios, Justin's successor as *curopalates*.[7] Theophanes records that a son, Justus, had died prior to the couple's rise to power.[8] It is in fact very probable that Sophia's marriage to Justin was arranged by Theodora, in the same way and at the same time as she arranged the match between her grandson Anastasios and Joannina, in both cases for the aggrandisement of her family. In this case the marriage must have taken place before 548, which would place Sophia's birth closer to 530, not long after the marriage of Komito and Sittas. As Theodora's close relative it is inconceivable that Sophia did not learn about the realities of power from Justinian's court, both during her aunt's lifetime and afterwards as wife of the *curopalates*, in charge of the running of the imperial palace. Theodora may herself have groomed her for power and apparently planned for her to assume the purple as her successor.

'Vivax Sapientia'

Sophia played a pivotal role in Justin's accession to the throne, apparently helping to orchestrate events behind the scenes. Justinian had nominated no successor, and Justin, who had the advantage over his cousin, the other main candidate, of being on the spot in the capital as *curopalates*, relied on a senatorial coup to engineer his rise to the purple, being secretly acclaimed in the palace on 14 November 565 by the senate prior to proclamation by the army, people and factions.[9] During the actual ceremonies Sophia wisely remained in the background, but the acclamations of the people treat the couple as a pair, the 'two lights of the world', according to Corippus,[10] and certainly the sources depict her as the dominant partner immediately upon their accession, if not before. Corippus's eulogistic poem on Justin's coronation dedicated to the quaestor Anastasios, of which the first three books were probably written in 566 and the fourth in 567, features Sophia very markedly. Both Vigilantia, Justin's mother, and Sophia are called goddesses, *divae*, at the commencement of the poem, and replace the Muses as a source of inspiration, while Sophia is invoked as queen of all, who protects the world ('summa regens Sapientia protegis orbem'): it is significant that this appeal is made prior to one to the Theotokos to give the poet divine aid.[11] Sophia in Greek means 'wisdom' and accordingly Corippus frequently translates her name as 'Sapientia', the Latin equivalent. He invokes her again in book three of the poem as 'divine and propitious empress, holy and venerable name, immortal good, the Wisdom (Sapientia) of our tongue' and the poet dedicates the work to her and asks her to aid his task. This in fact implies that she is his patroness and that he is fulfilling her wishes in writing the poem, while it appears that with Vigilantia she is his source for events which had taken place behind the scenes.[12] In Justin's accession speech in the palace, she is linked indelibly with him: 'this holy head Wisdom is made the consort, to rule with me together in honour the world entrusted to me, sitting in the same place', and Corippus puts into her mouth a moving prayer to the Virgin,[13] and pays her the forced compliment that the church of St Sophia was supposedly prophetically named for her by Justinian: he had either foreseen the future, or God had led him to dedicate the church to the 'pious auspices of the happy future'. This conceit of course takes no account of the fact that the church had been called St Sophia from the time of its foundation two centuries earlier. As well as speaking of power being given to the couple (rather than to Justin), Corippus also makes use of Sophia's relationship with Theodora, pointing out that Theodora was ruling when the church of St Sophia was built.[14] In other words, Sophia too had a dynastic claim on the throne.

It is Sophia who oversees the funeral arrangements for Justinian, organising the gifts for her 'father's' funeral, and ensuring that the mourners file past in a closely packed line, and the term 'vivax Sapientia', energetic Sophia, is used by Corippus in the context of the funeral pall which Sophia had had woven for Justinian with gold and precious gems, decorated with triumphal scenes from his reign.[15] The description may be applied more widely to her activities at Justin's accession and coronation. Just as Justinian's shroud must have been planned and put into commission well in advance, so must Sophia have prepared for the eventuality of his death in other ways. Corippus certainly thought her worth conciliating and flattering in 566.

Doubtless there had been jockeying for support as Justinian's reign was seen to be coming to its close, on the part of both the imperial candidates and others interested in ecclesiastical or senatorial honours. Two prominent churchmen, the patriarch of the time John of Sirimis (otherwise known as John Scholastikos) and the ex-patriarch Eutychios who had been exiled by Justinian in 565, claimed to have predicted Justin's accession. In both cases Justin is said to have been informed of their predictions before the event.[16] Justin's main rival for imperial honours was his homonymous cousin, son of Justinian's cousin Germanos, who was a general of note and currently engaged in campaigns against the Avars. Evagrios tells us that this Justin was at first welcomed in Constantinople in accordance with a prior agreement between the two cousins, but his bodyguard was then dismissed and he was expeditiously removed to Alexandria and murdered. Sophia certainly had a hand in both the planning of the deed and the subsequent celebrations: the Spanish chronicler John of Biclar, who was in Constantinople at the time, specifically ascribes the responsibility to the empress, and both she and Justin are said by Evagrios to have indulged their boiling spite by sending for the head and kicking it.[17] With the only real rival for the throne removed, Sophia had ensured that the transfer of power went smoothly. Her decisiveness may perhaps be similarly seen in the action taken against a conspiracy by leading senators Aitherios and Addaios in 566, which was scotched and the two leaders beheaded on 3 October on the grounds that they had attempted to poison Justin.[18]

Economic policies

At the commencement of the reign, indeed in an opening gesture to win popular support, Justin repaid debts and cancelled taxation arrears, further-more repaying loans which Justinian had demanded from the wealthy,[19] thus lobbying for support from all classes of society. His restoration of the consul-ship and consequent lavish largesse in the capital was similarly intended to buy support. Sophia was deeply involved in these financial measures and both now and later betrays such an interest in Justin's economic policies and concern for treasury reserves that they appear to be her own.[20] Justin himself claimed that he had inherited a financial crisis; this need not be taken too seriously.[21] Nevertheless Justinian's demands on wealthy bankers appear to have sparked off a bankers' conspiracy in 562/3, and it is these financiers whom Corippus portrays as beseeching Justin on his accession to have pity on them and their hardships. The conspiracy by Aitherios and Addaios in 566 may also have been connected with dissatisfaction on the part of leading financiers, for Aitherios had been involved in the earlier conspiracy.[22] Clearly they were not a class whom Justin and Sophia wished to offend, and Justin opened up his private treasuries and repaid the loans made to Justinian.[23]

Theophanes's account is somewhat confused, but he sees Sophia as the prime mover in this episode, stating that it was she who summoned the bankers and money-lenders and ordered that the financial records of contracts and receipts be produced. After reading the receipts, she handed them over to the creditors and repaid the amounts owed, for which she was greatly praised by the whole city.[24] Sophia's concern to maintain treasury reserves and avoid spending on anything but the most vital issues, for which she was later to scold Tiberios as both Caesar and emperor, can be seen in Justin's decision on his accession to cease paying subsidies to the Avars. This was shortly to have disastrous repercussions for the empire when Tiberios was to be defeated by them in 570 and 574, after which the empire returned to the policy of subsidies. While Corippus puts Justin's dismissal of the Avar embassy in 565 in ideological terms, that the imperial pride was unable to stoop to bribe barbarians, it is clear that the motive was primarily financial.[25] Furthermore, Justin saw no need for continuing the indemnity payment for the fifty-year peace with Persia. This financial policy was seen as resulting from avarice,[26] though Justin and Sophia clearly saw the need to replenish Justinian's exhausted treasury.

On his accession in 565 Justin had restored the consulship (which had lapsed since 541) and used this as an opportunity to make vast donations of largesse to the populace and gifts to the senatorial class in order to secure public support.[27] Perhaps this gave the wrong impression – that Justin and Sophia were amassing money to spend for their own purposes – and Justin took a second, though more low-profile, consulship in 568. His extensive programme of buildings and statuary in the city was also a visible means of expenditure, so clearly there was money to spend when the imperial couple felt it necessary. This may have added to the picture of avarice and conspicuous consumption which caused their unpopularity, which would have been further aggravated by his imposition of a customs duty on wine. In addition recipients of the bread dole at Constantinople had to pay four *solidi* for the privilege.[28] However, Justin's fiscal policy does not seem to have been extortionate despite the accumulation of large reserves in the treasury.

The most pious Augusta[29]

Sophia's influence on Justin can be seen prior to their accession in a very revealing episode. This is in her open adoption of chalcedonianism, orthodoxy, in the 560s. To this can also be linked Justin's specific statements of his orthodoxy on his accession as well as his work towards church unity in the early years of his reign. In the account of John of Ephesos both Justin and Sophia had shown an inclination to monophysitism, like other members of Theodora's family. Indeed he portrays Sophia as an open champion of the faith until the 560s, and describes how it was publicly known that a monophysite presbyter named Andrew used to administer the communion to her and all her household, while Justin was thought to take the monophysite communion more covertly.[30] Not only was her commitment to monophysitism more public than that of Justin, the couple's conversion to orthodoxy was said to have stemmed from Sophia's perception that their adherence to monophysitism might cost Justin the throne, after Theodore bishop of Caesarea warned her that Justinian was unwilling to see power pass into the hands of one who was not a committed chalcedonian.[31] As it was, her conversion took place only three years before she became empress, and Justinian was still not prepared even then to nominate an heir.

While it is true that all parties tried to claim imperial support for their religious stance, and thus any claims that the imperial couple had monophysite sympathies must be taken with some caution,[32] John is a remarkably informed source on the issue. He was one of the leaders of the monophysite party and was actually imprisoned in Constantinople during the monophysite persecution, as well as having been a friend of Tiberios, Justin's successor. In addition he would have had unrivalled contacts with the monophysite members of the imperial family, and the fact that his information may have come from this source may account for his mildness towards the imperial couple with regard to their apostasy: clearly after their accession the couple remained on comfortable terms with at least one member of Theodora's family, the wealthy monk Athanasios, who actually made the couple his main heirs.[33] It is perhaps surprising that Sophia's apostasy does not call forth more vilification from John than it does in his account. And it is also surprising that after such a background Sophia could become personally involved in the intensive persecution of monophysite believers. But

John's account can hardly be total fiction. At first Sophia's conversion may have been primarily a matter of expediency; it is noteworthy that, in his eulogy of Justin, Corippus includes a prayer to Mary spoken by Sophia which stresses the divine nature of Christ,[34] such indeed as would cause no discomfort to one who had monophysite leanings but who wished to appear unquestionably orthodox.

What is clear is that in the early years of their reign the couple show a deep desire for church unity while maintaining moderation in their dealings with controversial religious issues in their attempt to impose harmony. At the same time there is no doubt that Justin was concerned to display his own unexceptionable orthodoxy, perhaps because it was known that the couple had had dealings with monophysites. Even had they not, the connection with Theodora and the activities of other members of Theodora's family such as her grandson Athanasios would have called their religious allegiance into question. Accordingly, shortly after his accession, Justin issued an edict ordering that the Creed of Constantinople be recited in all churches. His patriarch John Scholastikos, whom he retained from the previous reign, and his quaestor Anastasios (the dedicatee of Corippus's poem),[35] were militantly orthodox. Corippus's poem proclaims Justin's adherence to chalcedonianism, with an excursus on the creed sitting strangely in the fourth book, while the gift of a fragment of the True Cross to the convent of Radegund at Poitiers in 568 made a similar statement to a western audience. Sophia's and Justin's gift to Rome of the 'Vatican Cross' bearing their portraits may also date from this period. Significantly Evagrios and Theophanes have no doubts whatsoever about Justin's orthodoxy, and such is Evagrios's opinion of Justin's mode of life that he would certainly have mentioned any criticisms in this regard had any been current. He in fact gives rare praise to Justin for his first edict against monophysitism, and Theophanes calls him thoroughly orthodox.[36]

There was doubtless difficulty in maintaining a balance and keeping all sides happy. Michael the Syrian shows Justin as entertaining Theodora's protégé, the ex-patriarch Theodosios, with all honour and promising to restore him to Alexandria, while at Theodosios's death in June 566 the homily at his funeral was delivered by the monk Athanasios, the tritheist grandson of Theodora and a fervent anti-chalcedonian, who used the occasion to anathematise the Council of Chalcedon.[37] While Michael's account may again be exaggerated in favour of monophysitism, a certain freedom of speech would certainly have been overlooked by rulers who were aiming to keep up good relations with both sides and were prepared to bend over backwards to achieve church union. The apparent thrust of their policies appears to have been that they were making sure that their orthodoxy was beyond question. If additional proof is required that the imperial couple were not strict adherents of monophysitism even prior to their accession, Justin was a devotee of the orthodox stylite saint Symeon the Younger, with whom he kept up a correspondence.[38] Symeon had foretold Justin's accession, and had cured his daughter of possession by a demon (presumably Arabia because no other is mentioned). Justin had asked that the girl be sent to him, but the saint replied by letter that she would be cured. And when Justin himself fell ill, the patriarch wrote for the saint's help, though in the event his advice was ignored by Sophia.[39]

Until 571 Justin and Sophia seem to have had as their main aim the restoration of unity in the church, to that end working towards a compromise with the monophysites. Indeed one of their main priorities was that of reconciling schismatic monophysite groups with each other. Upon his accession Justin sent out the monk Photeinos, elsewhere called Photios (Belisarios's stepson), to pacify the churches of Egypt and Alexandria where monophysite groups were at loggerheads, though Photeinos's bellicosity rendered his mission unsuccessful.[40] In the second half of 566 Justin convoked a series of conferences with various monophysite leaders and chalcedonians in the capital to help resolve their differences. Discussions were chaired by the patriarch John Scholastikos, an obvious choice in some respects but not one that boded well for any resolution of the differences within the church. A synod of prominent chalcedonians and monophysites was then assembled in an attempt to reach some *modus vivendi* on church unity, but after meeting for a year no compromise position was reached. Justin then arranged for a conference with the monophysites, including James Bar'adai the creator of the 'Jacobite' church, to be held first at Kallinikos on the Persian border, and then Dara, but, despite great concessions on the part of the chalcedonians, extremist monks rioted and caused Justin's edict to be rejected.[41]

Several years later, after further attempts at conciliation of the monophysites had failed, Justin proclaimed another edict, probably in 571/2, which, though relatively moderate, was more hard-line than that proposed at Dara.[42] The monophysite leaders in the capital, persuaded that they had been put in the false position of appearing responsible for the schism, were induced to submit to union and take orthodox communion on the understanding that the emperor would then anathematise the Council of Chalcedon. When this failed to take place, the monophysites felt that they had been deliberately put in the wrong and then deceived, and intensified their resistance to church union.[43] Justin's and Sophia's patience was exhausted and they were forced to change their policy with regard to monophysitism after their personal involvement in the attempt to restore religious unity in the empire had thus been met with repeated failure.[44] Intensive persecution of recalcitrant monks and clergy was initiated, for which John of Ephesos puts the main blame onto the patriarch: churches were shut, and priests and bishops imprisoned, while there were 'painful imprisonments, and heavy chains, and tortures, and the scourge and exile, and the like, in every land and city and village of the realm'; monophysite monastics were forced to take orthodox communion, including the nuns placed in convents in

Constantinople by Theodora.[45] The patriarch is presented as taking the primary role in forcing monophysite clergy to comply and may in this have influenced the imperial couple, though Justin was still receiving certain monophysite leaders cordially, even during the persecution.[46] In the 570s Justin and Sophia are seen as personally visiting monophysite monasteries in which John had performed divine service, and offering gifts in attempts to persuade monks to make their submission:

> The following day [after the patriarch's visit] the king visited the monasteries in person; and the next day the queen in like manner, offering each of them gifts, and restoring such monks as either had, or were ready to make their submissions. But such as resisted were exiled, or sent into close confinement, or made over without mercy to the praetorian guards to torture . . .[47]

John of Ephesos was one of the leaders of the monophysite bishops who were, as he tells us, imprisoned in the patriarchal palace and then in the penitentiary. He gives in some detail his sufferings from gout, solitary confinement and the ever-present vermin (flies, gnats, lice, fleas and bugs, the final straw being mice nesting under his pillow).[48] After over a year of such sufferings he was finally freed by the Caesar Tiberios. Members of Sophia's own family were even targeted in the persecution, including Georgia and Antipatra, the wife and mother-in-law of John, Theodora's grandson. John's name was also struck from the consular diptychs.[49] Whatever the motives of Justin and Sophia, their actions went further than was necessary to display their stance as champions of orthodoxy, and they must be held partially responsible for intensifying the split between monophysites and orthodox, even if this was not a major factor in the eastern provinces' fall to Arab rule in the seventh century.[50]

Justin and Sophia: the public face

Sophia was no shrinking violet. Even from the early days of Justin's reign the indissolubility of the couple was publicly presented to their subjects and others through a highly visible building programme and display of official statuary in the city. Their collegiality – the fact that it was a joint reign of two equal partners – was marked not only by epigrams of the reign describing dedications by the imperial couple and officials which speak of the couple as a pair,[51] but by their building activities. Justin had of course crowned her Augusta,[52] and the very nomenclature of Justin's constructions speaks of Sophia's paramount influence, for Justin rebuilt the harbour of Julian and named it after her (the Sophia), and called two new palaces after his wife, the Sophiai near the harbour of Julian, built before their accession, and the Sophianai across the Bosporos, probably built shortly afterwards.[53]

Theophanes also claims that Justin restored the public bath of the Tauros and named it Sophianai after Sophia.[54] The resulting confusion in the minds of scholars can only be equalled by surprise at the apparent lack of imagination employed and at Justin's overwhelming desire to flatter Sophia.

Further palaces included that of Deuteron in the north-west of the city with its extensive gardens and pleasure-grounds, involving the demolition of a number of existing houses, and one on the island of Prinkipo. It is notice-able that money was available for projects which enhanced the aura of imperial splendour in which the couple moved.[55] Statuary erected in the city demonstrated the united front presented by the pair: two bronze statues of Justin and Sophia are mentioned by John of Ephesos,[56] and a group of statues on pillars was set up by the chamberlain Narses at the harbour of Sophia comprising Justin, Sophia, their daughter Arabia and Justin's mother Vigilantia (or Narses himself in a different version). This was paralleled by a group of Sophia, Arabia and Helena, Sophia's niece, on the Milion in the centre of the city.[57]

The couple's works of philanthropy included a leper-house, orphanage, repair work on the great aqueduct of Valens and the construction of numer-ous churches,[58] while many more in the capital received renovation work or donations of relics, notably St Sophia and the Holy Apostles and the two great churches dedicated to the Virgin, for Sophia and Justin were equally devoted to the worship of Mary. This work displaying imperial splendour in the city was reflected in the palace itself by the new throne-room known as the Chrysotriklinos, or golden chamber, from now on one of the main set-tings for imperial ceremonial, and it has been argued that Justin's reign may have contributed to the possible scope and complexity of imperial ceremony during this period.[59] In the appreciation of the value of ceremonial Sophia obviously resembled her aunt.

The collegiality of the couple is similarly shown in their use of diplomatic gifts. The presentation of a relic of the Holy Cross to St Radegund in Gaul, probably in 568, provoked the composition of two hymns and a poem by Venantius Fortunatus in which Justin is called the new Constantine and Sophia the new Helena, and which makes clear (1. 57) that the request for the relic was granted on Sophia's initiative.[60] The Vatican Cross, also containing a fragment of the True Cross, bears the portraits of both rulers on its arms with a medallion of the Lamb of God in the middle, and was sent to Rome in their joint names.[61] While these diplomatic gifts had a political as well as a religious significance, they at the same time fulfilled a further, if secondary, purpose in affirming Sophia's role in government alongside Justin. Venantius's poem is significant in its emphasis on the role played by Sophia, and she dominates the second half of the poem; doubtless the envoys sent by Radegund to Constantinople in 568 with her request reported back on the realities of power in the capital and the expediency of giving the empress due consideration. Nevertheless, the poem is remarkable for presenting a portrait of Sophia which she herself would have appreciated (ll.71–2, 91–4):

> May the highest glory be to You, Creator and Redeemer of the world, because noble Sophia holds august rank . . . May you remain blessed as spouse of the Emperor Justin, Sophia, girt with the sacred patrician order. Ruling the kingdom of Romulus, may you grant its rights to the senate, and may the equestrian order revere you as mistress.

If Venantius had seen a copy of Corippus's poem brought back by Radegund's envoys, he would have had a chance to copy not only its trinitarian sentiments,[62] but its conciliatory stance towards Sophia.

Sophia and government

Whether Sophia was involved in other changes of policy from those pursued under Justinian apart from the financial, notably the disastrous resumption of hostilities with Persia, is a matter for debate. Evagrios criticises Justin's military neglect and the state of the Byzantine armed forces, and since the renewal of conflict with Persia was due to the desire to discontinue indemnity payments Sophia certainly had a hand in the decision.[63] There was also a tradition of conflict between Sophia and the general Narses: they are said by the late eighth-century historian Paul the Deacon to have exchanged insults on Narses's dismissal from his post in Italy. Complaints were made of Narses's oppressive rule by those jealous of his acquisition of great wealth and it was intimated that his behaviour might trigger treachery to the empire: the Romans would go over to the Goths. In response, Justin sent the prefect Longinus to replace the eunuch, whose anxiety, however, related more to the reaction of Sophia, whom he so greatly feared that he did not dare return to Constantinople. Clearly Sophia was not afraid to tackle Narses, veteran of many campaigns and now some ninety years of age, and she may have taken a jaundiced view of the immense wealth he had amassed in the province. Among other things, she is said to have sent him the message that she would give him the job of portioning out the weaving to the girls in the *gynaikonitis*, as a task more suited to a eunuch.[64] Paul links Narses's deposition with the incursions of the Lombards and has him retiring to Naples and urging them to invade Italy. That their invasion was due to his invitation is unlikely, but his command in Italy had been successful, and it is clear that his recall by Justin and Sophia in 568 helped to remove any obstacles to the Lombards' successful advance.[65]

With Narses recalled from Italy, and the Lombards moving in, and the Avar menace to the north, to recommence conflict with Persia was ill-advised to say the least.[66] A new instalment of tribute was due to Persia in 572, but

Justin refused to pay up and a pretext for war was presented by alleged Persian persecution of Armenian Christians. Hostilities began in summer 572 with an attack on Persian Nisibis, which failed; the Persians then proceeded to devastate Syria and besiege Dara, the greatest of the Byzantine fortifications in Mesopotamia, which fell in November 573.[67] This was a disaster for the empire and was directly related to Justin's lapse into dementia. His mental state had been precarious for some time: in October 572 he had his son-in-law Badouarios ejected from a *silentium* by the *cubicularii*, and ordered them to beat him with their fists. But even in this state it appears that Sophia still had some influence over him. When she upbraided him he immediately went after Badouarios and apologised ('I wronged you . . . it was through the work of the devil that this has happened') and invited him to dinner.[68] After he lapsed into total incapacity, his attempts to throw himself from the windows were thwarted by Sophia having carpenters fix bars on the side of the palace on which he lived, but there was no way of preventing him from biting his attendants (the rumour was current in the city that he had eaten two of them) except by frightening him with a bogeyman, at which he would hide under his bed. He was most successfully entertained by being pulled along on a mobile throne and by organ-music which was kept playing day and night near his chamber; even so, on one occasion the patriarch who had come for an audience was stunned by a blow on the head.[69]

As Justin became completely mentally incapacitated it was natural that Sophia should be turned to for advice on how to proceed with government. This would have been the situation in any case (the empress Ariadne in 491 had been asked to appoint an emperor on her husband's death), and Sophia had obviously been a formidable figure during her husband's reign up to this point. Her prominence is shown by her appearance with Justin on his bronze coinage, with both enthroned in full imperial dress, from the very first year of Justin's reign (Plate 3). Even in the early issues Sophia like Justin holds a sceptre, while the couple are shown as nimbate, and on coins minted at Carthage her name is added to that of Justin.[70] She is also named with him in the headings to decrees preserved on papyri.[71] Other empresses had

Plate 3 A *follis* of Justin II; the obverse shows Justin and Sophia enthroned. Minted at Kyzikos in 567/8 (Whittemore Collection: Harvard University)

appeared on the gold coinage – notably Helena, Fausta, Pulcheria and Licinia Eudoxia – but Sophia was the first empress to appear on day-to-day Byzantine coins and to be depicted together with the emperor, stressing their collegial status. Her status was thus undoubted and publicly stressed, and her position must have been unrivalled as Justin became increasingly ill.

When Justin's mental state deteriorated to a point where he could no longer publicly function as emperor, Sophia did not give in without a fight. Before a co-emperor could be appointed, she attempted to have him cured and called in a Jewish doctor and 'sorcerer', Timotheos, contrary to the patriarch's advice. The patriarch consulted the stylite saint Symeon the Younger in an attempt to have Justin cured through his intercession. The saint replied that Justin would be cured provided no methods of healing were employed which were contrary to the will of God. But Sophia persisted in consulting Timotheos, despite dire warnings from the patriarch when the saint observed what was being done in a vision and thereupon wrote a protest to the patriarch. The imperial couple, however, took no notice of the threats of divine chastisement and continued to consult the sorcerer who went further by introducing a female ventriloquist to the emperor.[72] When this treatment failed to work, an alternative solution had to be adopted: the government had nominally to be in the control of a man, and Sophia was responsible for selecting the candidate.

Despite the fact that there were members of the family who would have been appropriate choices, including Justinian's nephew Marcian, Justin's distant cousin Justinian (son of Germanos) and Arabia's husband Badouarios, she turned to Tiberios, the count of the excubitors, whom Justin, in one of his fits of lucidity,[73] made first his adopted son and heir with the title of Caesar, on 7 December 574 under the name Tiberios Constantine, and then in 578 joint Augustus. Tiberios had been made count of the excubitors not long before Justin's accession, and in that position had aided the transfer of power.[74] The choice was clearly Sophia's, and John of Ephesos reports that the senate took counsel with her on this matter.[75] Prior to the appointment, Sophia's diplomatic skills are shown by her request to Chosroes not to make war on a defenceless female with a sick husband, as a result of which she was able to buy first a one-year and then a three-year truce with Persia, with the exception of Armenia.[76] Her choice of Zacharias, one of the *archiatri sacri palatii* (the corps of palace doctors), as *de facto* leader of both embassies may have been due to her personal contact with him at court, though Justin had previously used Zacharias as a negotiator with monophysite bishops.[77] She also dealt personally with Jacob, the envoy sent to her by Chosroes after the negotiation of the one-year truce in February or March 574.[78]

It appears that Sophia not only had every hope of being able to influence Tiberios on matters of imperial policy, but that she also did not discount the possibility of marrying him on her husband's death. According to Theophanes there were rumours that even during Justin's lifetime she had taken Tiberios as her lover,[79] but these surely reflect gossip after the event. It is, however, obvious that despite the fact that Tiberios was her own nominee, Sophia was clearly concerned to secure her own position. Before he was appointed, Sophia required an agreement, confirmed by solemn oaths, that in the case of Justin's death Tiberios should pay every honour to her as empress and do her no evil.[80]

Even with Tiberios appointed as Caesar, Sophia had every intention of continuing in control. In fact, she behaved towards him as if towards a junior colleague. Her interest in treasury concerns certainly did not lapse with his appointment and she found it necessary to scold him for the lavishness with which he distributed largesse: in fact, she was so displeased by his expenditure that she finally took the keys of the treasury away from him and set aside a fixed sum of money for his disposal.[81] Tiberios found the treasury full, which speaks well for Justin's and Sophia's financial policies and accounts for their unpopularity.[82] Even after Justin's death, when Tiberios was sole emperor, she still felt herself able to rebuke him for his casual attitude to money: 'All that we by great industry and care have gathered and stored up, you are scattering to the winds as with a fan,' she is reported to have said after Tiberios had spent no less than 7,200 pounds of gold, besides giving away silver and robes of silk and other items.[83] Gregory of Tours records that Sophia had had to comment sharply to Tiberios on a number of occasions that he had reduced the state to poverty and that what it had taken her many years to accumulate he was squandering in no time at all.[84] Here she speaks in the singular and takes personal responsibility for the treasury. What is also remarkable is not just this relationship between dowager and ruling emperor, but the fact that such egocentric speeches by a female of the ruling family are recorded in historical sources.

The rivals

From Sophia's point of view the choice of Tiberios had its drawbacks, quite apart from his extravagance, for she was not prepared to share her rank or status with a competitor, and Tiberios was married. Ino, the new Caesar's wife, was middle-aged for she had previously been married, and Tiberios had been betrothed to her daughter. On this daughter's death, Tiberios had married Ino instead, and they had since had three children.[85] Sophia tried to ignore Ino and successfully prevented her from entering the palace for the whole of the four years that Tiberios was Caesar, even refusing Justin's appeals in his lucid moments that Tiberios might be allowed to have his wife with him. John of Ephesos records her as replying to Justin's request,

> 'Fool, do you wish me to make myself as great a simpleton as yourself? you! who have invested your slave with the insignia of sovereignty!' And then she vowed with oaths, 'I, as long as I live, will

never give my kingdom and my crown to another, nor shall another enter here as long as I am alive.'[86]

Sophia's perception of herself as empress was such that she was not willing to share her rank with anyone else, even a Caesar's wife: Justin may have taken a successor in Tiberios, but she was not prepared to accept one in Ino. And in this context should be seen her view of Justin's madness as retribution for his neglect of herself, and of the kingship as having come to him through her and now having returned to her control.[87] John records that she was thought to have spoken wickedly, but he is here commenting rather on her attitude towards the afflicted Justin and her sinful persecution of monophysites, rather than on her conception of herself as the embodiment of power.

For four years, therefore, Tiberios's wife Ino and two daughters, Charito and Constantina,[88] lived in the neighbouring palace of Hormisdas and he had to visit them at night. Sophia even went to the lengths of refusing to permit the noble ladies of the court to pay Ino their respects as the Caesar's wife. Ino remained in a state of constant terror, according to John, considering her life in danger, and as long as she stayed in the palace no one ventured to visit her. Considering the situation untenable, and obviously being in some fear for her life, Ino left Constantinople for Daphnudon and Tiberios had to commute backwards and forwards to see her when she fell ill there.[89]

Nevertheless, despite her view that the kingdom belonged to her by right, Sophia clearly felt that her position was insecure and that it would be strengthened by marriage to the reigning emperor. According to Theophanes Sophia had not even known that Tiberios was married until Ino arrived in Constantinople and was acclaimed, and was hoping to marry Tiberios and remain empress,[90] but Sophia indubitably knew of Ino's existence. She was, however, in hopes that Tiberios could be persuaded to cast off his wife and marry her instead. Proposals were therefore made to Tiberios on Justin's death in October 578, 'both through another person [presumably an emissary from Sophia herself?] and through the patriarch',[91] that he should divorce Ino and marry Sophia or her daughter Arabia, now a widow;[92] these Tiberios refused, despite the fact that they were presumably presented as a royal command. The fact that the patriarch Eutychios (who had been reinstalled after John Scholastikos's death) was an emissary is particularly striking in view of Tiberios's existing marriage, and the fact that Eutychios earlier in his career had been prepared to oppose Justinian. Being happily married to Ino, Tiberios instead invited Sophia to consider herself his mother, permitted her to remain in the palace (Sophia in any case had no intention of moving) and treated her with honour, though John comments that Sophia did not appreciate it.[93]

Since Tiberios would not marry her, Sophia had to give in gracefully, for she could hardly refuse Tiberios's request that Ino, the new empress, be sent for. Ino, however, clearly had doubts about the empress's good-will. She avoided the official escort, consisting of the commander of the praetorian guard accompanied by a large number of men of senatorial rank and a great retinue, which was sent to meet her, and left at midnight to slip into Constantinople with only her children and one boatman. On her arrival, in what appears to have been arranged between Tiberios and Ino as a pre-emptive strike to foil any plans of Sophia, Ino was met by the senate and patriarch in the palace and invested immediately with the royal insignia, after which she was saluted by the factions in the hippodrome by the imperial name of Anastasia.[94]

'Bitter malice and wicked violence'

As Tiberios had already been crowned prior to Justin's death,[95] there was no problem about his automatically succeeding to the throne. On the occasion of Tiberios's coronation on 26 September 578, nine days before Justin's death, Theophanes records Justin as exhorting Tiberios to honour 'your mother who was previously your queen. You know that first you were her slave, but now you are her son.' Theophanes seems deliberately to have shifted Justin's speech at Tiberios's appointment as Caesar in 574 to this point to add to the poignancy of the occasion, but is otherwise closely following his source, the seventh-century historian Theophylact Simocatta: Tiberios had been adopted by Justin and had promised to honour his 'mother'.[96] While Tiberios as emperor was prepared to honour his part of the bargain, the widowed Sophia was less willing to accept the change in their relationship. In the account of Gregory of Tours, Sophia was implicated in a plot against Tiberios in favour of Justin's distant cousin Justinian, obviously wishing to create a new emperor who might be more pliable to her wishes. She was not concerned in an initial plot, on Tiberios's accession, but she was involved in a further conspiracy, which she appears to have initiated. When Tiberios, who was out of the city, got wind of it, he hurried back and seized Sophia, deprived her of all her property, and left her only a small allowance. The fact that he removed her servitors and appointed others faithful to himself shows that he feared further machinations on her part. She appears to have been the prime mover behind the plot for, while Justinian was at first reprimanded, Tiberios later took him into high favour, and planned intermarriage between their two families.[97]

John of Ephesos confirms her involvement in the conspiracy:

> The queen Sophia, after the death of king Justin, set on foot plots without number against king Tiberios ... in bitter malice and wicked violence, being indignant at seeing him and his wife resident in the palace, and invested with the royal authority; and herself now in her lifetime deprived of her kingdom, in which she had conducted herself neither justly nor in the fear of God.[98]

He sees her misfortunes as punishment for her persecution of the mono-physites and failure to see that Justin's illness resulted from the same cause. According to John she was deprived of her property but continued to live in the palace, even after the plots had been discovered. Tiberios had also found that she had been removing several hundred pounds' worth of gold from the palace to her own house as well as other royal property: John will not commit himself to the precise amount, but states that it was said to be very large. Once again, Tiberios invited her to consider herself as his mother, and she stayed in the palace, but 'was bitter, and vexed, and out of temper, and full of grief and lamentation at her present state, to think that she was humiliated, and reduced in rank, and deserted by all men, and in her lifetime had become like one dead'.[99] This sounds almost like a verbatim report. The offer to consider herself as his mother must have been peculiarly bitter on two counts: not only had Sophia wished to marry him, but as his 'mother' her status was only that of a dowager empress consort, while Sophia wished to have the power of acting as an empress regnant. It must have been additionally galling to Sophia that her rival Ino, now renamed Anastasia, appeared with Tiberios on the coinage as early as 578/9, enthroned, sceptred and nimbate beside Tiberios, in the manner which Sophia herself had inaugurated (Plate 4).[100]

But Sophia was now unable to do more than prove recalcitrant over minor issues such as accommodation. John makes clear elsewhere that, whatever Tiberios's wishes, Sophia had refused to move or to let him reside with her,[101] and Tiberios had to rebuild part of the palace as accommodation for himself and his family. As Caesar under Justin inadequate apartments had been assigned for his use in one of the wings, and when Sophia showed no sign of changing her residence after Justin's death, Tiberios remodelled the whole of the northern side of the palace, as he did not wish to oppose or annoy Sophia. In order to do so he had to sacrifice a beautiful garden and extensive edifices already there; his magnificent new buildings included 'a noble bath, and spacious stabling for his horses, and other necessary offices'. And apparently she remained in the imperial palace, her wishes treated with respect, though John records a disagreement over which of them should finish the huge pillar begun by Justin in the baths of Zeuxippos: finally Tiberios had it pulled down and used the blocks in his own building extensions.[102]

Plate 4 A half-*follis* of Tiberios; the obverse shows Tiberios and Anastasia (Ino) nimbate and enthroned. Minted at Thessalonika in 579 (Dumbarton Oaks Byzantine Collection: Washington DC)

Theophanes recounts under the year 579/80 that Sophia moved to the palace of Sophiai, stating that it was built by Tiberios in Sophia's honour; according to this account she was not in disgrace, as he granted her *cubicularii* for her own service, commanded that she be honoured as his mother, and built her a bath and every other amenity. Theophanes has here misdated the construction of the Sophiai palace, which was built by Justin. His account may otherwise be correct in that Tiberios may have finally managed to remove Sophia from the imperial palace, though John implies otherwise; in any case she continued in every way to be treated as Augusta, and if she did remove to the Sophiai palace during Tiberios's reign this may well have been on her own initiative.[103]

Despite the fact that Sophia no longer took part in government, her influence was not yet over. As Tiberios approached death in August 582, supposedly from eating early mulberries which had gone bad, she as the senior empress was still seen as the repository of imperial power and accordingly she was sent for to give her advice on a successor.[104] She recommended Maurice, a successful general, who perhaps significantly was unmarried. Gregory says specifically that Sophia planned to marry him herself (she need not after all have been much more than fifty), but Tiberios outmanoeuvred Sophia on this occasion, and Maurice was married to Tiberios's daughter, Constantina.[105] Whatever Sophia thought of this alliance, she apparently remained on better terms with Constantina than with Ino, who died in 594 and was buried beside Tiberios.[106] Late in Maurice's reign, on 26 March 601, Sophia is shown as joining Constantina in making an Easter present of a *stemma*, or crown, to Maurice. Apparently Maurice hung the crown up above the altar in St Sophia 'by a triple chain of gold and precious stones', deeply offending both: 'the Augustas were greatly grieved when they learned this and the Augusta Constantina celebrated Easter in conflict with the emperor.'[107] This is the last that is heard of Sophia and it may be that she, like Constantina, fell victim to Phokas's regime, after his coup d'état and murder of Maurice in 602.

For some thirteen years, Sophia had been associated in power with an emperor whom she had easily been able to dominate. Without doubt she oversaw much of Justin's financial policy, which so successfully amassed wealth in the depleted treasury and without any undue degree of extortion, though it gained the imperial couple unpopularity. Their decision to cut back on the payment of subsidies, which was to be a direct cause of the renewal of the Avar incursions and of a war with Persia which was to drag on for decades, shows a similar concern for imperial finances and in retrospect has given the impression of serious mismanagement. Sophia's most marked characteristic was her love of power, which she equated with imperial status and which she was unwilling to share even with the wife of her husband's successor whom she had herself chosen. The same motivation may have inspired her adoption of chalcedonianism: once aware that her beliefs might be an obstacle to achieving the throne she was able to jettison them, and steer instead a course for church union under the banner of the championship of orthodoxy. As image was of such importance to her, it was natural that her presence and the collegiality of her rule with Justin should have been trumpeted throughout the city by the patronage of poets and artists, just as Justin's private building programme clearly pronounced under whose aegis it had taken place.

When compared to her aunt, it is clear that she possessed more real power than Theodora and wielded it more openly, but at the same time she had the misfortune of outliving her husband, from whom her status was technically derived. That she considered herself to be the repository of her husband's power, and that she mourned the loss of it, is clear from John of Ephesos's account. While her contemporaries reported that Sophia had a matrimonial aim in view in her selection of Justin's successors, there is no hint that she was being led away by her feelings; her overriding consideration was that she should retain her status as empress consort, which she viewed as giving her the right to share in the realities of imperial power, as she had seen Theodora do with Justinian. And in passing over members of her immediate family, and other more malleable yes-men as marriage partners, to choose first Tiberios and then Maurice as emperors, she showed excellent judgement and a perception of the military needs of the empire in the late sixth century, which may well have owed much to the training, or at least the example, of her aunt Theodora.

Part II

REGENTS AND REGICIDES

3

MARTINA (?615/16–41)

In 610 Herakleios, exarch of Carthage, sent a fleet under his son, also called
Herakleios, against the tyrant Phokas, who had murdered Maurice and been
put into power by a mutiny of the army, and whose misgovernment had lost
him support in all areas except that of the Blue faction. Herakleios was
acclaimed emperor on his arrival and Phokas executed.[1] Herakleios's fiancée,
Fabia or Eudokia, was already in the city, and according to Theophanes they
were married on the very day of Herakleios's coronation, 5 October 610, two
days later. Herakleios's reign was to be a mixture of triumphal success and
catastrophic defeat for the empire. His early years were marked by expeditions attempting to control the great military successes of the Persians.
Following Justin II's death in 578, Tiberios and Maurice had prosecuted the
Persian war, which Justin's policy of refusing to pay the usual tribute had
recommenced, and Maurice had brought the war to at least a temporarily
successful outcome. However, Persian power now revived, with a major
offensive resulting in the capture of Damascus and Tarsos in 613, and
Jerusalem and the True Cross in 614. In 615 the Persian army reached the
Bosporos, while Egypt came under attack in 619. From 622 to 628
Herakleios was to be preoccupied in campaigns with the Persians, ultimately
with great success, winning back Armenia, Roman Mesopotamia, Syria,
Palestine and Egypt. Unfortunately, in one of the more ironical of history's
blows, these territories were to be irretrievably lost to the Arabs from 633
onwards.[2] Furthermore, the empire which remained continued to be rent by
ecclesiastical dissension. In an attempt to resolve the schism between orthodox and monophysites which split the empire, Herakleios had proposed the
monothelete solution: that Christ had two natures but one will (*thelema*).[3]
With the patriarch Sergios's help, this was promulgated through the '*Ekthesis*
(statement) of the Orthodox faith', published probably in late 638 and
posted by Sergios in the narthex of St Sophia. In a vain attempt to head off
ecclesiastical debate, the *ekthesis* forbade discussion both of Christ's will and
of the single or dual natures of Christ.[4] Monotheletism was to be unsuccessful in uniting the church: the chalcedonians, like the West, reacted strongly
against this edict, while it failed to convert a single monophysite.

Uncle and niece

Herakleios had two children by Eudokia, Epiphaneia in 611 who was crowned Augusta with the name Eudokia at the age of one year, and the young Herakleios Constantine born in May 612, who was crowned early in 613.[5] The empress Eudokia herself died of epilepsy in August 612. Such was her popularity (or the respect paid to empresses generally) that a servant girl who inadvertently spat out of an upper window on to the empress's corpse as the procession passed through the city was summarily apprehended and burnt to death by the populace.[6] Herakleios's reign was to be complicated by his second marriage to his niece Martina and the hostility that this engendered.[7] Martina, who was crowned Augusta on their marriage, was the daughter of Herakleios's sister Maria by her first marriage to a certain Martinos. Considerably younger than her husband, she had a great influence on Herakleios. Theophanes places the marriage shortly after the death of Eudokia,[8] and it may have taken place in 613 or 614 though Nikephoros does not record it until after the Avar surprise attack of 623.[9] The marriage must have occurred, however, before 615/16 if Martina is the female figure who appears on the copper coinage with Herakleios and her stepson Herakleios Constantine from year six of the reign, and her appearance on the coinage at this point may be evidence for the recent date of her marriage. The fact that on one coin in the Dumbarton Oaks collection her figure seems to have been deliberately obliterated by a user who disapproved of her morals or political involvement implies that the empress on the coinage is Martina, rather than Epiphaneia-Eudokia, Herakleios's eldest daughter.[10] She has a crown adorned with pyramids and long *pendilia*, and her position on the left of the coin shows her as taking rank after her stepson. Martina's dynastic pretensions are shown by her appearance on these coins (Plate 5), and that she was apparently featured on them was no doubt a tribute to her personality and to the confidence placed in her by her husband, as in Sophia by Justin II.[11]

The patriarch Sergios considered the union of Herakleios and Martina incestuous and illegal, as indeed it was, but in the end he concurred and

Plate 5 A *follis* of Herakleios, showing Herakleios (centre), Martina (on l.) and Herakleios Constantine (on r.), minted at Nikomedia in 626/7. All three figures are practically interchangeable and wear plain crowns with crosses (Dumbarton Oaks Byzantine Collection: Washington DC)

actually performed the marriage ceremony himself, and Herakleios proclaimed her Augusta.[12] The populace strongly disapproved: the couple were greeted with insults even by the Greens, Herakleios's favoured faction, when they appeared in the hippodrome.[13] Even members of their own family considered the marriage unacceptable: Herakleios's brother Theodore earned his wrath during the Arab invasion of Palestine in 633 for continually criticising Herakleios because of his relationship with Martina and for saying 'his sin is continually before him', an insult which comprehended both Martina's incestuous marriage and her unconventional habit of travelling with Herakleios and the army.[14] Of their ten or so children at least two were handicapped, which was seen as punishment for the illegality of the marriage: Fabios, the eldest, had a paralysed neck and the second, Theodosios, was a deaf-mute, which was a disqualification for imperial office.[15] Martina accompanied Herakleios on all his campaigns even when pregnant: Herakleios II (known to later historians as Heraklonas), perhaps the fourth child of this remarkably productive couple, was born in Lazika in 626 while Herakleios was on campaign against the Persians.[16] No less than four of their children (two sons and two daughters), all of whom may have been born on campaign, were to die between 624 and 628, while Herakleios and Martina were in Persia.[17]

The last years of Herakleios

Martina was extremely unpopular in the capital, not only because of the incestuous nature of her relationship with Herakleios, but because of the pressure she put on him to secure the succession, or part of it, for her sons, despite the fact that her stepson Herakleios Constantine had been co-emperor since 613. In fairness to Martina, it should be noted that Maurice's will, drawn up when he was ill in 597, provided that the empire should be split between his sons, especially the two eldest.[18] Herakleios Constantine, in contrast, was well liked by the populace, who were afraid that he would lose his chance of the throne and be ousted by Herakleios, Martina's eldest surviving son eligible for the succession, usually known by the diminutive Heraklonas. Heraklonas, born in 626, was pronounced Caesar in 632 by his half-brother Herakleios Constantine during his consulship, a sign that Heraklonas would be next in line for the throne; that the act may have been unpopular is shown by the fact that it was Herakleios Constantine, the people's favourite, who was made to perform it.[19] Moreover, Martina's long absence from the capital in the 620s cannot have helped her to develop a more sympathetic public image in the city. Significantly she was eliminated from the coinage in 629, and thus she was obviously not associated in the popular mind with the triumphal victory over the Persian empire in 628 or the recovery of the True Cross;[20] nor does she reappear in 641, when her son came to the throne.

It may have been as a result of popular perceptions of Martina's manoeuvres on behalf of her children that a conspiracy was hatched prior to the death of Herakleios in late 637, a time when the Arab conquests of Syria and Palestine had quenched the euphoria of the late 620s and helped Herakleios to age considerably. The plotters included Herakleios's illegitimate son Atalarichos and his nephew Theodore: the noses and hands of all conspirators were cut off, one of Theodore's legs was also amputated, and they were exiled to Prinkipo.[21] Herakleios managed to overcome his pathological fear of water sufficiently to return from the palace of Hiereia to Constantinople at this point: for several months he had dispatched his sons to attend public functions and games in the capital in his place. In order to get across to the capital he had a bridge over the Bosporos especially made of ships, hedged with branches so that he could not even see the sea. Martina may have been involved in persuading him to return, for one result was that Heraklonas (officially Herakleios II) was crowned emperor in July 638, and his brother David made Caesar: Herakleios also had his daughters Augustina and Martina pronounced Augustae, probably in the following year.[22] There was perhaps need to settle the question of the succession, because even at that point Herakleios Constantine may have been suffering from severe ill-health, while the elder of Constantine's two sons, another Herakleios (later Constans II), was then only seven years old.

Martina: 'mother and empress'

Conflict between Herakleios Constantine and Martina was exacerbated during the late 630s, and Herakleios obviously foresaw that there would be problems following his death. After all, it can hardly have been easy for Constantine to work closely with a stepmother who was also his first cousin, even if she were some years older than he. When Herakleios's death was obviously approaching in 641, he made a will whereby his sons Constantine and Heraklonas (Constantine III and Herakleios II) were to be emperors of equal rank. His wife Martina was to be honoured by them as 'mother and empress'.[23] This implied not only that Heraklonas would have rights equal to those of his brother, but that Martina would have some direct influence on matters of government, even though Constantine at twenty-eight and with two sons of his own (Herakleios and Theodosios) was obviously fully competent to rule the empire.

The decision to leave the empire to both sons was presumably not due entirely to pressure from Martina; Constantine suffered from ill-health, and was in fact only to reign for some three months. Leaving the empire to both sons would secure the succession in the event of Constantine's death, as well as pacifying Martina, while she had clearly been put forward as regent in the eventuality of her son being left as sole ruler while a minor. It should be noted that succession in Byzantium was not hereditary: while the eldest son of an emperor would normally expect to rule, technically the emperor was elected by the senate and approved by the army and the people.[24] Herakleios was within his rights in nominating two of his sons as co-rulers, even if this were to mean by-passing his eldest son's young children. The situation was complicated by the terminal illness suffered by his eldest son: presumably Herakleios was intimating that, should Constantine die, he wanted his throne to pass to his second son rather than to his grandsons. In this he may have been considering not so much Martina's wishes but the relative age of the youngsters, for when Constantine died the empire was left in the hands of a fifteen-year-old (Heraklonas, who would reach his majority in a few months) rather than in those of Constantine's son Herakleios, a boy of ten. And the throne was not altogether a welcome legacy: at Herakleios's death the empire had lost Syria and Palestine, while the Arabs were making short work of Egypt; religious disturbances and ecclesiastical disputes over mono-theletism were endemic; and there was strife within the capital based on the factions of the two emperors and popular hatred of Martina. The government was also in desperate financial straits: Constantine actually had his father's tomb opened to remove the crown made of 70 pounds of gold which was buried with him.[25] Under the circumstances it was a compliment to Martina to assume that she could cope with the situation.

Herakleios died on 11 February 641 of dropsy.[26] After his three-day lying-in-state and burial in the Church of the Holy Apostles, his will was made public by Martina personally. She summoned the patriarch Pyrrhos, the senate and other dignitaries and called an assembly of the people in the hippodrome to show them the testament of Herakleios and the provisions for herself and Herakleios's sons. She demanded first place in the empire (in other words to assume authority herself), and clearly expected to be able to take over the business of government, despite the fact that her stepson had been co-emperor since 613 and was of more than an age to rule for himself. However there was opposition. Some of the crowd made their feelings quite plain:

> You have the honour due to the mother of the emperors, but they that of our emperors and lords ... Nor can you, O Lady, receive barbarians and other foreign emissaries who come to the palace or converse with them. May God forbid that the Roman State should come to such a pass![27]

This refusal to let her participate in government was a direct slap in the face for Martina, and Nikephoros's narrative may have been phrased with the regime of the empress Irene in mind.[28] The crowd paid particular respect to Constantine, rather than to Heraklonas, on the grounds that he was the senior emperor and had been co-ruler with Herakleios for most of his life. Martina then is said to have withdrawn to her palace. Normally she would have resided in the imperial palace: perhaps Nikephoros here is signifying that she withdrew to another residence, although this is unlikely. What is clear is that she was deeply unhappy with the turn of events.

Martina and Herakleios Constantine

Matters worsened between Constantine and his stepmother Martina, with the two factions openly hostile to each other. Constantine is said to have made the patriarch Pyrrhos disgorge monies which Herakleios had given into his care for Martina should she be driven out of the palace by her stepson. Presumably Constantine felt the financial state of the empire serious enough to warrant this appropriation, though Martina must have taken it as an act of personal hostility. Constantine was chronically ill; nevertheless, Philagrios the imperial treasurer was afraid that he might be harmed by Heraklonas and Martina and advised Constantine to write to the army that he was dying and that they should protect his children and their rights. Constantine thereupon sent the vast sum of 2,016,000 *solidi* to the army in the hands of Valentinos, an adjutant of Philagrios, to persuade the soldiers to oppose Martina and her children after his death and thus secure the succession for his sons. The money was perhaps distributed at the rate of five *solidi* per soldier and must have nearly exhausted the empire's cash reserves – in itself an act of aggression towards Martina and his co-ruler.[29] Constantine only ruled for 103 days according to Nikephoros and then died, perhaps on 24 May 641:[30] he was vomiting blood and probably suffered from tuberculosis.[31] Nikephoros does not accuse Martina of having poisoned him (though he does mention the treasurer Philagrios's fears on the subject), but this accusation was later officially propagated by Constantine's son Herakleios (who ruled as Constans II) and is found in all the chroniclers, often with the patriarch Pyrrhos mentioned as her accomplice. Theophanes, for example, tells us: 'When Herakleios had died and his son Constantine became emperor, Pyrrhos along with Martina killed him by poison.'[32] It is unclear why Pyrrhos would have been thought to cooperate with Martina in the murder of the emperor, unless because he felt that Constantine was not properly attached to the beliefs of monotheletism: Pyrrhos, appointed by Herakleios on Sergios's death in 638, was, like Martina, a fervent monothelete.[33]

The reign of Heraklonas: Martina's regency

Heraklonas, aged fifteen years, then automatically succeeded and was proclaimed emperor and shared the administration with Martina,[34] who as regent was naturally the *de facto* ruler. John of Nikiu records that the entire clergy was opposed to the new regime, declaring, 'It is not fitting that one derived from a reprobate seed should sit on the imperial throne: rather it is the sons of Constantine, who was the son of Eudokia, that should bear sway over the empire'.[35] Nikephoros says Heraklonas then dedicated to God the crown his brother had removed from their father's tomb, an act of filial *pietas* designed to put his half-brother in a bad light. All possible resources were mobilised: each soldier was given a donative of three *nomismata* in an attempt to mitigate the hostility of the army.[36] Measures were then taken against supporters of Constantine. Philagrios was tonsured and exiled, while many of his friends were scourged. This caused further waves of unpopularity in the capital, for John of Nikiu records that this gave rise to great dissension because Philagrios was greatly beloved. It also appears that the monothelete ecclesiastical policy was revived: Constantine appears to have been at least a moderate on the issue of monotheletism, but Martina was an enthusiastic supporter. She may have recalled George, eparch of Carthage, because he had circulated a report that an order she had sent him to free monothelete monks was not authentic.[37] As regent for Heraklonas Martina may also have been the one who decided to recall Cyrus the monothelete bishop of Alexandria from exile and send him back to Egypt. Cyrus like many of his predecessors had secular as well as ecclesiastical jurisdiction and had instructions to come to terms with the Arabs and to reorganise the administration there as a whole. Cyrus arrived in September and John of Nikiu informs us of the terms agreed for surrendering Egypt; the treaty was signed in November 641.[38]

Martina was unpopular with the factions, the senate, the army, the clergy and the people generally. Valentinos (Arsakidos), Philagrios's adjutant, who had been appointed commander-in-chief of the East by Constantine, then roused the soldiery against Martina and her children.[39] Following Constantine's instructions he distributed the money that had been sent by Philagrios and prevailed on the troops throughout the provinces to act against Martina and her sons and ignore Martina's orders. He also sent an agent to the army on Rhodes 'requesting that the expeditionary force intended for Egypt unite with him to march against Constantinople'.[40] He advanced to Chalcedon where he remained, supposedly in order to assist the interests of Constantine's children. Martina and Heraklonas, however, summoned the army from Thrace to the capital and held the city securely. Heraklonas guaranteed the safety of Constantine's son Herakleios, publicly swearing on the True Cross before the patriarch Pyrrhos in St Sophia that Constantine's two sons would not be harmed. He also counterattacked by asserting that Valentinos was not so much concerned with them as with securing the throne for himself. Heraklonas even took the young Herakleios over with him to Chalcedon where he addressed the army, according to John of Nikiu, and promised to adopt his nephew and make him co-emperor, as well as recall Philagrios from exile. Valentinos refused to move even on these terms, but the populace seem to have supported Heraklonas on his return.[41]

In September 641 (the harvest season) the army's ravaging of the vineyards on the Asiatic side of the Bosporos caused the people to urge that the young

Herakleios, Constantine's son who was now ten, be crowned to relieve the situation. Pyrrhos argued that the rebellion was intended to put Valentinos on the throne, but when the mob insisted the matter was laid before the emperor, Heraklonas took his nephew to St Sophia and invited Pyrrhos to crown him. The crowd, however, insisted that Heraklonas do it himself as was customary, and the young boy was crowned with the crown of his grandfather Herakleios and was then renamed Constantine by the populace.[42] The choice of his father's name significantly reinforced the populace's identification with that branch of the family. His coronation, however, did not quiet the underlying dissatisfaction of the people with Martina and her sons, and riots continued in the city. On the evening of the same day the mob, with 'Jews and other unbelievers', broke into the sanctuary of St Sophia and attempted to assault Pyrrhos, unpopular because of his support of Martina; not finding him, they profaned the altar and then carried the keys of the church through the city on a pole. Pyrrhos resigned his office on the following day (29 September 641) according to Nikephoros. Other sources record that he was deposed following a further rebellion by the army, which simultaneously dethroned Heraklonas, though these two events should be disassociated since Martina and Heraklonas appointed Paul, *oikonomos* of St Sophia, patriarch on 1 October, prior to their own dethronement.[43] Pyrrhos obviously left of his own volition, feeling that Constantinople was no longer a healthy place to be, especially as the clergy was solidly against Martina and her regime. He therefore decided on a trip to Carthage. He may in fact not even have resigned, but simply abandoned the capital: Nikephoros reports him as saying, as he removed his *pallium* (mantle) and left it on the altar, 'Without renouncing the priesthood I abjure a disobedient people!'[44]

The crowning of Herakleios Constantine (later Constans II) did not persuade Valentinos and his followers to leave Chalcedon and they were still causing damage. Heraklonas and Martina therefore came to an agreement with him and appointed him *comes excubitorum*, promising he would not be called to account for the money received from Constantine. In addition his soldiers would be rewarded with gold. In exchange, Martina's younger son David, who was the same age as Herakleios Constantine, was crowned as third co-emperor and renamed Tiberios.[45] Valentinos appears now to have made an attempt to declare himself emperor but the people of Constantinople rose against him and he renounced his plans: clearly he did not have the support of the populace. John of Nikiu also tells us that he was made commander-in-chief of the army and his daughter, Fausta, married to Constans, no doubt to buy his loyalty.[46] Valentinos then returned to duty.

Deposition

At some point shortly after this a revolt in the capital took place against Heraklonas and Martina. The senate seems to have played an important role

Plate 6 Marriage rings were typically exchanged during the marriage ceremony. This superb seventh-century octagonal gold marriage ring depicts on the bezel Christ and the Virgin crowning the couple, and on the facets scenes from the Palestinian Christological cycle. Inscribed on the hoops is the opening passage of John 14.27: 'Peace I leave with you, my peace I give unto you' (Dumbarton Oaks Byzantine Collection: Washington DC)

in events but the rebellion may also have been sparked off by further trouble with the army. John of Nikiu's account is not entirely reliable, but he tells us that the hatred between the two emperors (by which he presumably means their factions) continued to grow and that Satan sowed dissension between Heraklonas and the army, which must have continued to consider itself a champion of the rights of Constantine's children. The troops in Cappadocia, presumably unhappy with the settlement between Heraklonas and Constans, committed atrocities, producing a letter supposedly sent by Martina and Pyrrhos to David the 'Matarguem' (perhaps a *logothete*) to make 'a vigorous war, and to take Martina to be his wife, and to put down the sons of Constantine'. This letter, though possibly a forgery, was used as a catalyst for further trouble, and John tells us that as a consequence all the soldiers and people in the capital rose up and a large force marched to the capital, captured the palace and had Martina and her three sons – Heraklonas, David and Marinos – 'escorted forth with insolence' and deprived of their imperial status.[47]

According to Theophanes, Heraklonas and his mother were in power for six months; if this date is correct, the rebellion against them occurred in November 641. In the absence of any source material covering late 641 (there is a twenty-seven-year lacuna in Nikephoros's text at this point) it seems probable that following riots in the city instigated by the Blue faction the senate deposed Heraklonas and ordered his seizure and that of the rest of the family.[48] This was an unprecedented step. Theophanes records that the senate rejected Heraklonas together with his mother Martina and Valentinos (obviously now seen as one of the regime's supporters), and ordered that Heraklonas's nose and Martina's tongue be slit and that they be exiled. John of Nikiu adds that Martina and her sons Heraklonas, David and Marinos were escorted from the palace with insolence, that their noses were cut off and they were exiled to Rhodes: furthermore the youngest of Martina's sons was castrated.[49] The mutilation of Heraklonas was in order to assure that he did not return to the throne; that of Martina was presumably inspired by more personal opprobrium, and was perhaps an explicit comment on the vocal nature of her involvement in public affairs. The hatred felt for her by the people, clergy and army had certainly played an important part in contributing to the deposition of her son and the ending of their joint regime.

The young emperor, Constantine's son and Herakleios's grandson, was now known as Constans (a diminutive of Constantine) and reigned as Constans II (641–68). Constans did not assume real power until about 650 and Heraklonas's downfall was obviously orchestrated by those who assumed power of behalf of this rival branch of Herakleios's family. In his speech to the senate on his accession, Constans thanked the senators for their part in overthrowing his uncle, and indeed assigns the responsibility to them for deposing his uncle and expelling Martina. The speech as given by Theophanes also condemns Martina as responsible for the death of Constantine and justifies the deposition of Heraklonas on the ground of his illegitimate birth:

> My father Constantine, who begot me, reigned for a considerable time in the lifetime of his father . . . and, after his death, for a very short time; for the envy of his stepmother Martina both cut off his fair hopes and deprived him of life, and this on account of Heraklonas, her illicit offspring by Herakleios. Your godly decision rightly cast her out from the imperial dignity along with her child lest the Roman Empire appeared to be ruled in an unlawful manner.[50]

The assigning of responsibility to the senate may be something of a polite fiction: it was as well to assure the senate that everything that had happened was with their concurrence. It should perhaps occur to us to consider who might have written Constans's speech for him. A figure, who must have played a particularly vital part firstly in events leading up to Heraklonas's and Martina's exile, and then as regent after her son's accession, was Gregoria, Constans's mother and daughter of Herakleios's cousin Niketas.[51] Gregoria was thus not only the widow of Herakleios Constantine, but a member of the Herakleian dynasty in her own right.[52] Significantly the marriage of Gregoria and Constantine, at some point before 630,[53] had also been an incestuous one in the eyes of the orthodox church, since they were second cousins. Endogamous marriages may have been a family tradition stemming from the family's origins in Edessa;[54] a less charitable explanation might be that one of the motives for the match was to ensure that Herakleios and Martina were not the only imperial couple seen to be in an 'incestuous' union. Gregoria's activities are not featured in our sources, but it would be unrealistic to suppose that she took no part in the dynastic conflict stemming from Herakleios's death and the disposal of the empire, or that she remained uninvolved in the hostility which arose firstly between her husband and his stepmother, and then between her son and his uncle. Gregoria, though doubtless several years younger than Martina, stood in exactly the same relation to her as she did to her husband Constantine – Gregoria was second cousin to both – and must have been an important figure in the faction championing the rights of her son Constans against what was popularly seen as the involvement of Martina.

Martina's ambition for her family had inspired implacable resentment among the people of Constantinople, who were incensed by her marriage to her uncle and understandably blamed her for the union. But at the same time this ambition has perhaps been overstated. Doubtless, her unpopularity was such that she was better away from the capital with Herakleios on his campaigns, but this was in fact unfortunate: had she been present in the city during some of its vicissitudes in the 620s, notably the Avar siege in 626, this might have helped the populace to identify with her. In addition, the precarious financial state of the empire appears to have precluded her from taking part in the charitable foundations with which empresses endeared themselves to their subjects. But that she had dynastic ambitions is clear: on her husband's death she had hoped to take over the reins of government, and that she had imperial plans for her children is shown by her manoeuvring on their behalf and even by their nomenclature: why else would she name one of her sons Herakleios, giving him exactly the same name as his half-brother, if not to make the point that he was of equal rank and imperial status? But her sins have been exaggerated: Herakleios himself clearly expected her to take control of the administration after his death, and much of her involvement in politics on her family's behalf may have stemmed from the perception that her stepson was unlikely to survive long as emperor – a perception that was doubtless kept from the populace as much as was practicable. Blame for the conflict between Constantine and Martina cannot be laid entirely at her door, and there is no doubt that she did not poison her stepson. Her prolongation of the monothelete heresy was no more than a continuation of her husband's policies which were aimed at uniting the empire under one church. Nor was her treatment of Philagrios entirely without justification: he had after all exposed to Constantine the fact that Pyrrhos was custodian of monies left for Martina by Herakleios, which were then promptly taken away by her stepson, and had orchestrated the payment of the army explicitly to oppose Heraklonas and Martina, activities which under any circumstances can be classed as undermining Herakleios's settlement, if not as outright treason: she had after all been left by Herakleios as 'mother and empress'.

Martina left behind her the reputation of an ambitious schemer, who poisoned the rightful emperor for personal gain. This is almost entirely unjustified, and she was cast as one of the scapegoats to whom was assigned the responsibility for the loss to the Arabs of Syria, Palestine and Egypt: Herakleios's incestuous marriage and monothelete beliefs had inevitably turned God's favour from the empire, and the Arab victories were seen as evidence of divine displeasure.[55] The dynasty continued in a similarly violent manner: Constans's murder of his brother Theodosios, in order to secure the succession for his three sons, shows history repeating itself within the family. Finally Constans was to depart for the West – a decision which was not popular with the Constantinopolitans – and he was murdered in his bath by a chamberlain in September 668.[56] Martina's career coloured the reputation of empress regents, and of female members of the imperial family in general, for many years to come. It is some time before women again appear on Byzantine coinage, and many empresses in later years, perhaps like Gregoria, may have learnt from Martina's experiences that power can be just as effectively wielded without overt political prominence.

4

IRENE (769–802)

Irene was born in Athens, presumably between 750 and 755.[1] In 768 the
'Isaurian' emperor Constantine V Kopronymos (the 'dung-named' because he
was said to have defecated while being baptised as a baby), who, because of
his iconoclast policies, went down through Byzantine history as a monster of
depravity and wickedness, wanted a bride for his eldest son Leo IV. Historians offer no explanation of why Irene was chosen, and in view of Irene's
iconophile predilections it would seem that her religious views were ignored
in the selection process: an orphan, she was a member of the Sarantapechos
(Sarandapechys) family which must have been of political significance in central Greece. She was to place some of her family in positions of prominence:
a cousin later married the Bulgar khan Telerik and another relative married
the future emperor Staurakios.[2] Her uncle Constantine Sarantapechos
was a patrician and possibly *strategos* (commander of the theme) of the
Helladics, and his son Theophylact, a *spatharios*, is mentioned in connection
with the suppression of a revolt centring around Constantine V's sons in
799.[3] The fact that little is known of her family has led scholars to suggest
that Irene might have been the first instance of an imperial bride chosen
through a 'bride-show', a means apparently used for choosing a bride for
heirs to the throne from the late eighth century until the early tenth:[4] the
Life of St Philaretos, written *c.* 821–2, gives the details of the procedure
employed by which envoys were sent out through the empire to select girls
who met the strict standards of beauty laid down for potential empresses.
The girls were then presented to the bridegroom and he, or in fact his
mother, made the choice. There is no evidence to support the hypothesis that
this strange custom was introduced to Byzantium by Constantine V's first
wife Irene, a Khazar princess,[5] or that Irene took part in a bride-show, other
than the fact that there seems to have been no obvious reason for her choice as
an imperial bride.

Irene arrived in Constantinople on 1 November 769, escorted from
Hiereia by many *dromones* and *chelandia* (warships and galleys) decorated
with silken cloths, and met by the prominent men of the city and their
wives; she was betrothed in one of the palace chapels, that of Our Lady of the

Pharos, on 3 November and crowned empress on 17 December. This was followed by a marriage ceremony in the chapel of St Stephen in the Daphne Palace adjoining the Great Palace. On 14 January 771 she gave birth to Constantine, named for his grandfather, and on her father-in-law's death in August 775 her husband Leo IV succeeded to the throne.[6] Her father-in-law Constantine V receives a bad press in our main source: 'polluted as he was with much Christian blood, with the invocation of demons to whom he sacrificed, with the persecution of the holy churches and of the true and immaculate faith, furthermore with the slaying of monks and the profanation of monasteries: in all manner of evil he had reached a pinnacle no less than Diocletian and the ancient tyrants.'[7] Whatever Constantine's motives in pursuing Leo III's policy of iconoclasm – and a dislike of monastic power groups and monasticism as an institution may have been one – towards the end of his reign at least he tacitly tolerated monastic benefactions among his own family: according to the *Synaxarion* notice for Anthousa of Mantineon, his third wife Eudokia made generous donations to Anthousa's monastery, where she went during a difficult pregnancy. Theophanes tells us that Constantine's first wife, Irene, was also known for her piety (i.e. her iconophilism), and Constantine's daughter Anthousa was also an iconophile and became a nun.[8] Constantine's attitude towards relics and the worship of the Virgin Mary has no doubt been overstated in our sources – certainly the council which he convened in 754 at Hiereia only denied the propriety of venerating saints through material depictions[9] – and it appears that discreet iconophilism in imperial women was tacitly expected or at least tolerated.

Irene and Leo IV

At Easter 776 Leo crowned his five-year-old son emperor, at the same time imposing an oath on the army, senate and people that they would accept no other emperor but Constantine and his descendants. This sparked off a conspiracy by Leo's five younger half-brothers, focused round the Caesar Nikephoros, to whom Leo showed leniency: Nikephoros was to be the centre of opposition to Irene's regime on a number of occasions. In his religious policy Leo began by appointing bishops from among monks and removing the disabilities imposed on monasteries by his father: in this he seems to have been following a policy of promoting iconoclast monasteries subordinate to the ecclesiastical hierarchy. In 780, when patriarch Niketas died, Leo appointed Paul of Cyprus, who seems to have had iconophile sympathies, though he was made to swear oaths to uphold iconoclasm. Nevertheless, during Lent Leo seems to have renewed the persecution of iconophiles which Constantine V had instituted in the 760s. A number of prominent courtiers were arrested, scourged, tonsured and imprisoned; Theophanes the *cubicularius* and *parakoimomenos* died under the treatment.[10] Kedrenos, a later source, records that Irene was involved and that Leo had found two icons in her possession:

> In the mid-week of Lent he [Leo IV] found under [literally 'in'] the pillow of his wife Irene two icons. Having beheld them and made an investigation, he discovered that the *papias* of the palace and some others of the *primicerii* had brought them. He subjected them to many tortures and punishments. As for his wife Irene, he rebuked her severely and set her at naught, saying, 'Was this what you swore to my father the Emperor upon the fearsome and pure mysteries of our faith?' She affirmed that she had not seen them [the icons]. He spurned her and had no more marital relations with her.[11]

This tale is too consciously similar to that also told of the iconophile empress Theodora to be accepted as it stands. Nevertheless, Irene may have been trying to fill the palace with iconophile supporters, hence this crackdown, which shows Leo as a committed iconoclast trying to clean up his palace. Leo's death on 8 September 780 gave Irene the chance to pursue her own policies as regent for her ten-year-old son Constantine, and she took the opportunity to signal a change of direction. The rumour was current that Leo had died of a fever contracted after wearing the jewelled crown from the Great Church, dedicated by Herakleios or Maurice: whether Irene deliberately had this story circulated or not, it implies an attempt to smear her husband's memory, which her triumphant return of the crown in full imperial procession on Christmas Day 780 would have emphasised.[12]

The transfer of power did not go smoothly and her brother-in-law Nikephoros once more became the centre of revolt: it seems to have been instigated in October, only six weeks after Leo's death, by dignitaries who considered Nikephoros a better choice than Constantine with Irene as regent. Among others Bardas, former *strategos* of the Armeniacs, Gregory, the *logothete* of the *dromos*, and Constantine the count of the excubitors were arrested and scourged, tonsured and banished. Loyal supporters of the regime were appointed in their places. Irene had Nikephoros and his four brothers ordained and they were forced to administer communion publicly on Christmas Day in St Sophia,[13] a punishment which was prompt, effective and compassionate. It was on this occasion that Irene publicly returned the crown which her husband had removed, which she had had further adorned with pearls. Contemporaries might have recalled at this point the regency of Martina, the last female ruler, who had survived less than a year: it must have seemed very possible that Irene would be heading the same way. The conspiracy may have been sparked off by the dislike of a minor as emperor, or because Irene was suspected of iconophile leanings; the involvement of the *strategos* of the Armeniacs should not be taken as necessarily suggesting the latter.[14] Irene's proposal that Anthousa, her sister-in-law, should join her in the regency, if it can be accepted, may have been intended to conciliate the supporters of her husband's family: as it was, Anthousa refused the honour, and remained in the palace dedicating herself to good works.[15]

Irene as regent

Irene accordingly remained regent for the young emperor.[16] This was quite acceptable, but it does seem as if Irene was assuming more than the customary power of a regent from the start: her first coins had portraits of herself and her son on the obverse and commemorative images of Leo III, Constantine V and Leo IV on the reverse in the usual fashion. Significantly on these, she not Constantine holds the orb, and she is referred to as Constantine's co-ruler: in addition Constantine's name is placed on the reverse, the less important side of the coin.[17] She may have felt that her position was insecure, as indeed it was, and in order to strengthen it in 781 Irene decided on a matrimonial alliance between Constantine and Rotrud (Erythro), daughter of Charlemagne. This was not an entirely new departure: Pippin III, Charlemagne's father, had betrothed his daughter Gisela to Leo IV.[18] Presumably Irene's decision, a reversal of Constantine V's policy with regard to the Franks, was influenced by the fact that Charles's support would help Byzantium secure her territory in Sicily and Southern Italy. The proposal was a great honour for no western princess had as yet married into the imperial family. The *sakellarios* Konstaes and the *primikerios* Mamalos were sent to orchestrate the agreement and left the eunuch Elissaios, a notary, to 'teach Erythro Greek letters and language and educate her in the customs of the Roman empire'.[19] Another plot emerged early in the next year. Elpidios, whom Irene had sent out as *strategos* of Sicily in February 781, was reported two months later to be a member of the Caesars' party. When the Sicilians refused to surrender him, Irene had his wife and sons scourged, tonsured and imprisoned in the *praetorium*.[20] In the next year she sent a fleet under the patrician Theodore, a eunuch, against Elpidios; when Theodore's men were victorious, Elpidios fled to Africa where he defected to the Arabs, who received him as Roman emperor.[21] Michael the Syrian records that Elpidios defected because he had been found in a compromising situation with Irene: the tale is hardly to be accepted, attractive as it appears.[22]

In 781 the *sakellarios* John, a eunuch, was put by Irene in charge of supervising all the Asiatic *themata*. An Arab attack on the eastern frontier was defeated by Michael Lachanodrakon (Constantine V's general), though this success was neutralised by the defection of Tatzatios (Tatzates), *strategos* of the Bucellarii, who defected to the Arabs out of hatred towards the eunuch Staurakios, the patrician and new *logothete* of the *dromos*, who 'at that time was at the head of everything and administered all matters';[23] Staurakios must have replaced the conspirator Gregory in the position of *logothete*, and he was to maintain his position of influence until nearly the end of Irene's reign.

Tatzates's defection aborted the Byzantines' encirclement of Harun al-Rashid, the son of the Arab caliph, and a huge Arab army. Unlike Irene, Staurakios could lead an army, and it was Staurakios who, with the *magistros* Peter and the *domestikos* Antony, went to negotiate with the Arabs when, on Tatzates's suggestion, Harun asked for peace negotiations. Due to their failure to take adequate precautions and arrange for hostages, they were seized, Tatzates and his Bucellarion troops defected and Anatolia was left wide open to Arab attack. Irene therefore had to agree to pay a huge annual tribute of 70,000 or 90,000 dinars to the Arabs for a three-year truce, give them 10,000 silk garments and provide them with guides, provisions and access to markets during their withdrawal.[24] While Tatzates may well have been hostile to Staurakios, dislike of the eunuch's power seems an implausible reason for the experienced general, with a brilliant twenty-two year military career behind him, to defect: the Armenian historian Ghevond states that Tatzates turned traitor because he lost favour at the imperial court. On the face of it, if Irene were demoting Tatzates as part of her policy of removing Constantine V's generals from high command, this would have been a far more likely explanation for his actions, and one that does not reflect well on Irene's government.[25]

Irene's use of eunuchs to lead important expeditions may well have caused hostility among the armed forces. Doubtless she did not want to rely too heavily on the entrenched army leaders – the army, in particular the eastern army, was strongly pro-Isaurian and in general, though not invariably, iconoclast. Staurakios was also sent against the Slavs in northern Greece in the next year, where he recouped his military prestige, advancing to Thessalonika and making the Slavs of northern Greece pay tribute to the empire, and bringing back booty and captives; he even launched a raid on the Slavs in the Peloponnese. For this he celebrated a triumph during the hippodrome games in January 784. In May Irene, Constantine and a numerous force ceremonially visited Thrace 'taking along organs and musical instruments'. Beroia was rebuilt and renamed Irenoupolis ('city of Irene' or 'city of peace'), and she advanced as far as Philippopolis as well as decreeing the rebuilding of the Black Sea port of Anchialos. This appears to have been part of the successful strengthening of the Bulgarian frontier and resettlement of territory reclaimed from the Slavs. She also founded a new theme, called 'Macedonia'.[26]

With this success on the Bulgar front and the matrimonial alliance with the iconophile West secured, Irene could now begin to move on religious issues. Her devotion to icons has not been doubted, though it may have been over-emphasised, and she was to be responsible for the building of a number of churches and founding the Convent of the Mother of God on the island of Prinkipo.[27] While regent for Constantine, she was cured of a haemorrhage by the waters of Pege ('the spring'), outside of the walls of Constantinople, and as a result she presented rich gifts to the Church of the Virgin there – rich veils and curtains, a crown decorated with pearls and liturgical vessels – and set up mosaic portraits of herself and her son making their offerings to commemorate her cure.[28]

Theophanes implies that Irene's religious policy was becoming apparent by mid-781: 'From that time on the pious began to speak freely. God's word spread about, those who sought salvation were able to renounce the world without hindrance, God's praises rose up to heaven, the monasteries recovered, and all good things were manifested.' This change was marked by the discovery of a coffin by the Long Walls of Thrace, on which was prophetically engraved 'Christ will be born of the Virgin Mary and I believe in Him. O sun, you will see me again in the reign of Constantine and Irene'.[29] Clearly the regime was not above the fabrication of well-publicised iconophile propaganda where possible. From 780 a revival in monasticism is apparent as members of noble families take the monastic habit; Theodore the Stoudite and Theophanes Confessor himself became monks at this period. An opportunity for further measures arrived with the resignation of the patriarch Paul, who in 784 fell ill and retired to a monastery, apparently repenting of having served the cause of iconoclasm, but unwilling to take any steps himself in favour of restoring icon-worship. He is said to have made the statement: 'Would that I had not sat at all on the throne of priesthood while God's Church was suffering oppression, separated as she was from the other catholic thrones and subject to anathema!'[30] Irene summoned patricians and selected senators to hear Paul's advice that an ecumenical council should be convened to put an end to iconoclasm: the *Life of Tarasios* also has him designate Tarasios as his successor, though the choice of a public servant rather than a cleric must have been Irene's.[31] Theophanes speaks of Paul in eulogistic terms: venerable, charitable and worthy of all respect, and states that the public and government both had great confidence in him. If Paul could be publicly presented as repenting of his iconoclastic policies in the church this greatly strengthened the hands of the iconophiles, and from this point the question of the holy icons 'began to be openly discussed and disputed by everyone'.[32]

The Seventh Ecumenical Council, 787

Tarasios became patriarch on Christmas Day 784: he had had a high-flying secular career, and become *asekretis* or imperial secretary.[33] His selection sent a clear message of the change of ecclesiastical policy: while still a layman, Tarasios had founded a private monastery on his own estate at Stenon outside of Constantinople.[34] Irene convened a meeting of the people (senators, clergy and citizens) in the Magnaura palace, where he was unanimously acclaimed despite his own doubts on the subject, though there seems to have been some dissent on the subject of a council. His ordination was put in hand, though after being ordained deacon and priest he was not consecrated until

Christmas Day, a vacancy of nearly three months. Clearly Irene did not intend to rush matters or provoke opposition from iconoclast sympathisers. In August 785 Tarasios wrote an anti-iconoclast profession of faith to Pope Hadrian, while Irene asked the pope to dispatch emissaries for the ecumenical council: Tarasios also sent word to the patriarchates of Alexandria and Antioch. Hadrian's reply protested against a layman being elected to the patriarchate and demanded energetic action against the iconoclasts, giving his support for a council and sending Peter, the *oikonomos* of St Peter's, and Peter, abbot of St Sabas, as his representatives. In the following year bishops were summoned from throughout the empire in the name of the emperors Constantine and Irene. The council sat in the Church of the Holy Apostles on 1 August 786, with Irene and Constantine watching from the gallery. The chances of success were problematic if it came to open debate – the majority of the bishops would have been appointees of Constantine V and Leo IV. The iconoclast bishops gathering in the city in fact indulged in plots against the holding of a council and whispering campaigns against Tarasios, and proceedings were interrupted when according to Theophanes the *scholarii* and excubitors (the two divisions of the imperial guard) at their officers' instigation gathered in front of the church and threatened to kill the archbishop and other delegates. The empress's attempt to control them through using the men of her household was unsuccessful, and at the iconoclast bishops' shout of 'We have won!' the council was dissolved.[35]

Irene took prompt steps to retrieve the situation. She had gradually been able to remove from their posts many of the military commanders appointed under Constantine V and Leo IV, and the army was essentially loyal to her rule. Nevertheless that does not mean that it was in favour of the restoration of icons. Seeing the *tagmata* in particular, the elite unit in the city recruited by Constantine V, as a stumbling block to her reforms,[36] she used Staurakios to help her rid the city of iconoclast troops. On the pretence that she was undertaking an expedition to counter an Arab invasion in the East, Staurakios was sent out to meet the Asiatic *themata* serving in Thrace and ask for their assistance, and the imperial equipment was dispatched to Malagina, the assembly point in the Opsikion theme for eastern expeditions. In their place Irene ordered thematic regiments from Thrace and Bithynia to hold the city; as a large proportion of these were Slavs they would not have held strong iconoclast views. The rebellious troops were surrounded at Malagina and ordered to disband; after surrendering they were exiled from the city with their families and posted to the provinces. No doubt the disbanding of this elite force weakened the defences of the empire, but Irene thought the move a necessary one. Theophanes specifically tells us that Irene then formed her own army with men who were obedient to her, in other words she recruited into the *tagmata* soldiers loyal to herself. It may also have been at this time that she created the personal guard called the 'Watch'.[37]

In May 787 she summoned another council, this time to sit at Nicaea. The choice of venue is an interesting one – a site away from the dangers of popular riots and one which was bound to recall the first great ecumenical council at Nicaea at which Constantine the Great condemned Arianism.[38] The Seventh Ecumenical Council attended by 365 bishops, met in September to reject iconoclasm and anathematise the three iconoclast patriarchs and their supporters. Tarasios, who firmly controlled proceedings, allowed repentant iconoclasts to participate despite the protests of more extremist monks such as Platon of Sakkoudion. Iconoclasm was unequivocally condemned as a heresy and it was a document signed by all delegates, including previously recalcitrant bishops, that was brought to the Magnaura palace in Constantinople on 23 October to be presented to Irene and Constantine at a final session of the council at which Irene presided; Irene signed the document first, contrary to her usual practice, and was acclaimed with Constantine as the New Constantine and the New Helena.[39] The definition (*horos*) of the council justified the veneration of icons in the following terms:

> We define with all accuracy and care that the venerable and holy icons be set up like the form of the venerable and life-giving Cross, inasmuch as matter consisting of colours and pebbles and other matter is appropriate in the holy church of God . . . as well as the image of our Lord and God and Saviour Jesus Christ, of our undefiled Lady the Holy Mother of God, of the angels worthy of honour, and of all the holy and pious men. For the more frequently they are seen by means of pictorial representation the more those who behold them are aroused to remember and desire the prototypes and to give them greeting and worship of honour – but not the true worship of our faith which befits only the divine nature – but to offer them both incense and candles, in the same way as to the form of the venerable and life-giving Cross and to the holy gospel books and to the other sacred objects, as was the custom even of the Ancients.[40]

Mother and son: Irene and Constantine VI

Orthodoxy was now restored, though it would be naive to suppose that all opposition was at an end. The young emperor Constantine was seventeen years of age and technically capable of assuming control of government. But Irene showed no sign of retiring in his favour. In the following year, 788, she formally broke off the marriage contract with Charlemagne's daughter Rotrud. Charlemagne appears to have been unwilling to part with Rotrud (like many of his daughters) and prior to the Council of Nicaea he had refused to send his daughter to Constantinople, postponing the match indefinitely. Irene made the most of the situation. Instead of Rotrud a suitable bride was found for Constantine by means of a bride-show, the winning candidate being Maria of Amnia, whom the *protospatharios* Theophanes had escorted from Paphlagonia.[41] This is the first recorded case of a bride-show (the next being in 807/8, when Irene's relative Theophano was married to Staurakios, son of Nikephoros I), and Irene, who presumably instituted the custom, may well have used it as propaganda for her regime.[42] Irene dispatched a panel of judges, equipped with a set of ideal standards, to travel throughout the empire and select candidates from appropriate families: the girls' height, the size of their feet and probably their waists were measured by the commissioners. Irene of course ensured that Constantine was not allowed freedom of choice, even among these carefully picked possibilities, and Maria was the granddaughter of Philaretos, a magnate from the Armeniac theme, who had impoverished himself and owed his position to Irene. The *Life of Irene* makes it clear that it was Irene herself who picked the bride, and the *Life of St Philaretos* speaks of the thirteen girls as being presented to Irene, Constantine and Staurakios. Constantine, now of age to be making decisions for himself, was unhappy at the cancellation of his betrothal to Rotrud, being 'unwilling and very distressed' at the change of plan. This did not augur well for his wedding in November to Maria.[43]

With the alliance with Charlemagne broken off, hostilities were joined in Italy and the Byzantine forces under the command of the palace eunuch John, now the military *logothete*, were defeated: still worse, Irene had suffered setbacks at the hands of the Arabs and Bulgars.[44] From this point relations between Constantine and Irene worsened:

> The Devil, grudging the emperors' piety, inspired certain evil men to set the mother against her son and the son against his mother. They persuaded her that they had been informed through prophecies to the effect that: 'It is ordained by God that your son should not obtain the Empire, for it is yours, given to you by God.' Deceived, like the woman she was, and being also ambitious, she was satisfied that things were indeed so, and did not perceive that those men had offered the above pretext because they wanted to administer the affairs of State.[45]

This indictment by Theophanes of Irene's counsellors, notably Staurakios himself who had everything in his power while Constantine was essentially ignored, highlights the unconstitutional realities of the situation. Constantine therefore conspired with the men of his entourage ('who were few'), the *magistros* Peter, and two patricians to arrest Staurakios and banish him to Sicily, after which Constantine himself would assume Staurakios's position in ruling with his mother, surely not an unreasonable desire in view of the fact that Constantine was now seventeen and legally of age to rule. Perhaps significantly, one of Constantine's supporters, Peter the *magistros*, had been an appointee of Constantine V and one of his henchmen in the iconoclast persecution of 766/7. The emperor's plans were thwarted by an earthquake which caused the empress and emperor to go out to the palace at St Mamas for safety, and gave Staurakios the opportunity for a counter-plot: he stirred up Irene against Constantine and she had his men, including his tutor the *protospatharios* John, arrested, flogged and tonsured, and exiled. The *magistros* Peter and patrician Theodore Kamoulianos were put under house arrest, and the patrician Damianos was scourged, tonsured and banished to the fort of Apollonias. She also struck Constantine, 'addressed many reproaches to him', and confined him for several days, clearly trying to reinforce his subordinate and junior role in their relationship. The army was now asked to swear that as long as she was alive they would not suffer Constantine to rule and to place her name before Constantine's in the acclamations. Theophanes's comment that no one dared to object implies that there were many who would have liked to register their disapproval.[46]

The lack of military triumphs in Irene's regency may well have given rise to hopes that Constantine VI would emulate his grandfather and lead the armies to victory: both his grandfather and father had taken the initiative against the Arabs and achieved some successes. Constantine V had temporarily taken possession of Germanikeia, Melitene and Erzurum (Theodosioupolis), while under Leo IV Byzantine armies had undertaken extensive destructive raids in 776 and 778 and made a successful assault on Adata.[47] When the men administering the oath arrived at the theme of the Armeniacs in September 790, they not only refused to swear, but insisted on keeping Constantine's name before that of Irene in the acclamations. Alexios Mousele (or Mousoulem), commander of the Watch, was sent to deal with them, but they appointed him their commander after imprisoning their own *strategos*, Nikephoros, and acclaimed Constantine as sole emperor. The men of the other themes imprisoned their *strategoi*, Irene's appointees, and followed the Armeniacs' example in acclaiming Constantine. In October 790 all the regiments, more than half of the entire army, assembled at Atroa in Bithynia and demanded that Constantine, who was now nineteen, be sent to them. Irene was afraid of the army and let him go. The troops rejected Irene's authority and he was confirmed as emperor.[48]

Clearly Constantine had had his tutor John (Pikridios) recalled, for he sent John and the iconoclast Michael Lachanodrakon,[49] his grandfather's loyal general, to make the Armeniacs – his hard-core supporters – swear that they would not accept Irene as emperor ('εἰς βασιλέα'). Constantine also confirmed Mousele as their *strategos*. The choice of Lachanodrakon sent a message to the army that the emperor was identifying with the military priorities of his grandfather. Resentment against Irene's eunuchs had built up in both Constantine and the army. On his return to Constantinople in December 790 he had Staurakios flogged and tonsured and exiled him to the theme of the Armeniacs for their satisfaction; the eunuch Aetios the *protospatharios*, a confidant of Irene's, and all the other eunuchs were also exiled. She was confined in the palace of Eleutherios, which she had built overlooking the harbour of

Eleutherios and where she had hidden a large sum of money. However, she was not deposed and he continued to strike coins with her name and portrait, though she no longer held a *globus cruciger*, and the inscription was rearranged so that Constantine's name occurred on the obverse.[50]

Constantine's efforts as sole ruler were not impressive; in one small engagement with the Bulgars both armies fled; an expedition against the Arabs achieved nothing. But this was only a beginning, and he had shown his willingness to proceed against the empire's two greatest threats. The reason why he decided to bring Irene back into the limelight must therefore remain conjectural. On 15 January 792, after entreaties from her and many others in authority, he recalled her as his co-ruler and restored her title of empress and she was acclaimed, as before, after him. For the next five years the bust of Irene appears on the obverse of the *solidi* with the title 'Irene Augusta', and Constantine is shown on the reverse with the title of *basileus*, but as a beardless youth. It is clear that she once again took an active part in government and Staurakios too seems to have been recalled from exile. Only the theme of the Armeniacs refused to acclaim Irene (quite understandably) and rebelled, demanding Mousele, their ex-commander, back. Alexios Mousele was currently in Constantinople under a guarantee of safety; this request, plus the rumour that he would become emperor, caused Constantine to have him flogged, tonsured and confined in the *praetorium*.[51]

The severe defeat which Constantine suffered against the Bulgars in July 792 was badly timed – many officials, including Michael Lachanodrakon, were lost as well as the whole baggage train with the imperial equipment. When the *tagmata* reassembled in Constantinople they decided to bring Constantine's uncle Nikephoros out of retirement and make him emperor. As a result Constantine had Nikephoros blinded and his other four uncles had their tongues cut out: blinding was the chief form of punishment for political enemies and prevented the victim from assuming the throne. He also had Alexios Mousele blinded, persuaded by his mother and Staurakios that otherwise he would be made emperor.[52] Mousele may of course have been a focus for popular unrest and the threat may have been a real one. All possible contenders for power were now disposed of. Constantine may have been naive and malleable, but Irene's actions here show her at her worst: her deliberate manipulation of her son's fears in an attempt to lose Constantine the support of the army through the cruelty of his actions was underhand; in addition she must have had the satisfaction of taking her revenge on Mousele who had been instrumental in deposing her from power in 790. Staurakios too had achieved his revenge for being exiled to the Armeniac theme. Both had managed to put the emperor into an invidious position: Constantine had now been seen by the army to unfairly target Mousele, who had been his main supporter in 790.

Constantine had sent his supporter Theodore Kamoulianos, who had been involved in the abortive plot to remove Staurakios, to replace Mousele as *strategos*. On hearing of Mousele's blinding, the Armeniacs imprisoned their new *strategos*: they had been the one theme totally loyal to the interests of their emperor and Constantine had now lost their support. An expedition made against them by the *protospatharios* Artaser and Chrysocheres, *strategos* of the Bucellarii, in November 792 was defeated after many losses on both sides and both of Constantine's commanders were blinded. With the theme in revolt, Constantine took the field himself at the head of all the other *themata*. In May 793 the Armeniacs were defeated, due to the defection of the Armenian troops fighting with them. The Armeniacs had been a dissident element for over two years. Their leaders were put to death, the rest subjected to fines and confiscations, and a thousand men, those based at the theme's headquarters, were brought into the city in chains with their faces tattooed with the words 'Armeniac plotter', and were then banished to Sicily and other islands.[53] If this episode sent a message to the army generally, it was that services to Constantine were soon forgotten.

The Moechian ('adulterous') controversy

Irene and Constantine seem to have maintained some kind of détente, essentially keeping separate courts, but Irene continued to work against the interests of her son, the emperor. The *Historia Syntomos*, attributed to Michael Psellos, speaks of their joint reign like a battleground: 'They went for each other, hit and hit back in turn, and now Irene exercised absolute power, now Constantine took possession of the palace alone, again the mother, again the son, until their conflict resulted in a disaster for both.'[54] Constantine had formed a dislike for his unfortunate wife, perhaps initially because she had been chosen for him. Theophanes lays the worsening of their relationship to Irene's account: 'The emperor, who had conceived an aversion towards his wife Maria through the machinations of his mother (for she was yearning for power and wanted him to be universally condemned), forced her to become a nun and, after obtaining her consent, had her tonsured in January of the third indication [795].'[55] The *Life of Tarasios* says that Constantine fabricated the story of a plot by Maria to poison him, but could not gain credence for it; it was also said that he threatened to restore iconoclasm unless his divorce and remarriage were allowed.[56] Constantine had taken as his mistress Theodote, a *cubicularia* of his mother and cousin of Theodore the Stoudite,[57] and hence needed to divorce Maria to remarry. Maria seems to have gone willingly, and their two little daughters (of whom one, Euphrosyne, was later to be the wife of Michael II the Amorian) went with her to the convent on the island of Prinkipo, founded by Irene. Irene and Tarasios consented to the empress's becoming a nun, though Irene may have had an ulterior motive in view. Following a minor success against the Arabs in May, his first real victory against a foreign enemy, in August Constantine crowned Theodote as Augusta (a title Maria had not been granted) and betrothed himself to her, marrying her in September at the palace of St Mamas, his favourite residence: the wedding festivities lasted for forty days.[58]

Constantine was clearly hoping to avoid controversy with the church but, as Irene had foreseen, there was strong disapproval of this second marriage, which was against canon law, and the legality of his remarriage was hotly debated. Tarasios would not perform the ceremony himself but on the principle of 'economy' (*oikonomia*) had compromised by allowing his catechist to tonsure the empress Maria as a nun and Joseph, abbot of the Kathara monastery, to marry the emperor and Theodote. Platon, abbot of the monastery of Sakkoudion and uncle of Theodore the Stoudite, regardless of the fact that Theodote was his niece (or perhaps because of it),[59] led the opposition and broke communion with the patriarch, declaring him excommunicated for compromising with this 'adulterous' emperor; Constantine at first tried to conciliate them but early in 797 was driven to have Platon imprisoned, and the other monks including Theodore and his brother flogged and exiled to Thessalonika.[60] The controversy, known as the 'Moechian' or adulterous controversy, was doubtless worsened by the fact that Irene was openly on the side of the monastic establishment, against her son and the patriarch, 'because they opposed him [Constantine] and put him to shame'.[61] In an attempt to conciliate the monastic establishment and regain popularity generally, Constantine, with Irene and Tarasios, held in July of 796 a celebration to mark the return to the capital of the relics of the fourth-century saint Euphemia, believed to have been thrown into the sea by Constantine V, but which had been miraculously recovered by a passing ship, taken to Lemnos and were now restored. Theophanes, or his source George Synkellos, was himself present on this occasion at which Constantine's two young daughters Irene and Euphrosyne distributed parts of the saint's body to notables.[62] Tactfully no one seems to have commented on the discrepancy between the original undecayed body of the saint and the dry bones now on show. Euphemia's church, or *martyrion*, was also restored from its state as an 'arms-store and dung-heap' and reconsecrated.[63] Constantine V's antipathy towards relics, as evidenced in this story, may also have been part of the propaganda of Irene's reign.[64]

Death of an emperor

While Constantine and Irene were with the court at the hot springs at Prousa (Brusa) in October 796 for an extended stay, the news arrived that Theodote had given birth to a son, presumably prematurely; the baby, who was called Leo, died in the following May. Irene took the opportunity of her son's absence to plot against him:

> His mother addressed the commanders of the *tagmata* and beguiled
> them by means of gifts and promises with a view to deposing her son

and becoming sole ruler herself; some of them she coaxed personally, others through the men of her household, and she drew everyone to her side and was waiting to find the proper moment.[65]

The birth of a grandson and heir to the throne seems an unusual time for Irene to choose to make her move: presumably she felt that it weakened her position, as well as that of the eunuch officials who advised her. One of her moves may have been to stress the illegitimacy of the new heir, which might later give rise to conflict and controversy. Constantine was obviously unaware of the plots against him and was still allowing Irene and her ministers to make the decisions: when he mounted a campaign against the Arabs in March 797, he was accompanied by Staurakios and other friends of his mother. They were naturally afraid of the psychological value of a victory to Constantine at this juncture and the effect this would have on his prestige with army and populace. Scouts were bribed to report that the Arabs had left, and to his chagrin the emperor returned empty-handed.

His position was already under serious threat. Following the death of his son Leo on 1 May, Constantine crossed home to St Mamas after a racing contest: his mother's supporters followed him 'so as to catch him', presumably planning his arrest and blinding. Learning of this Constantine embarked on his *chelandion* intending to take refuge in the theme of the Anatolics. His wife also fled the city, and he was accompanied, 'without his knowledge, by his mother's friends': this speaks of treachery from within the emperor's own retinue. Irene had the bureaucracy and *tagmata* on her side. She assembled the officers loyal to her in her palace of Eleutherios and then entered the imperial palace. The news that an army was gathering around Constantine almost caused her to decide to retire and send a delegation of bishops requesting a promise of safety, but this would not have protected her supporters. Instead she wrote to her adherents in the emperor's retinue who had accompanied Constantine to Pylai in Bithynia. These had fears on their own account of their deeds coming to his notice, and Irene now threatened to tell Constantine of their plans unless he were handed over to her. As a result they seized him, put him on board the imperial *chelandion* and bringing him to the city confined him in the Porphyra, the purple palace where he was born, on 15 August 797, blinding him there 'in a cruel and grievous manner with a view to making him die at the behest of his mother and her advisers'.[66] Irene cannot escape responsibility for this: she had manipulated events and personalities to this conclusion. She was clearly aware of the decision to blind him and appears to have made it herself. Whatever the degree of Constantine's unpopularity, the deed was generally abhorred: Theophanes tells us that the sun was darkened for seventeen days and 'everyone acknowledged' that this was because the emperor had been blinded. Whether Constantine actually died from this treatment is a matter that has been much debated, and if he did it was certainly hushed up.[67] Irene was now in sole control.

Irene 'basileus'

Irene's constitutional position was now an anomalous one, though in general, it was accepted. There were, however, four sons of Constantine V unblinded. But she does not seem to have considered the possibility of choosing to marry and thus reign with or through her husband. In fact she struck gold coins with her portrait on both sides to emphasise that she was sole ruler (Plate 7) and in at least one of her *Novels* used the title emperor ('Irene the pious emperor'), not empress,[68] though she used the title *basilissa* or Augusta on her coins, as well as on her seals. She thus became the first Byzantine empress to mint coins as sole ruler with the title *Eirene basilissa*. While her love of power has perhaps been overstated, she was clearly not averse to displaying her imperial status to her subjects: on the gold coins of her sole reign she is depicted in a robe embroidered like the consular dress of the emperors, holding a cruciform sceptre and *globus cruciger*.[69] Irene's blinding of her son may have encouraged Charlemagne to assume the title of emperor of the Romans: he was crowned by Pope Leo on 25 December 800, the pope arguing that the imperial throne was technically vacant as it was occupied by a woman.[70]

Nearer home the brothers of Leo IV were once again the centre of a plot in October 797: they were persuaded to take refuge in St Sophia, the idea being that once there the populace would spontaneously proclaim one of them emperor. No uprising took place and the eunuch Aetios managed to extract them and banish them to Athens. A further plot in March 799 planned to bring them out of confinement and make one of them emperor, and the four as yet unblinded all lost their eyes. This plot was prompted by the 'Helladics', and Irene's uncle Constantine Sarantapechos – possibly *strategos* of the theme of Hellas (Greece) – may have informed her of the plot.[71]

As sole ruler one of Irene's first actions was to release Platon and Theodore; she was to establish them as abbots of the monastery of Stoudios in Constantinople.[72] Furthermore Tarasios defrocked Joseph of Kathara who had

Plate 7 A *solidus* of Irene, with her portrait on both sides, carrying a *globus cruciger* and sceptre, minted at Constantinople in 797–802 (Dumbarton Oaks Byzantine Collection: Washington DC)

performed the 'adulterous' marriage. Both actions explicitly damned Constantine VI's remarriage and persecution of his monastic opponents. But Irene's rule was not to be trouble-free. Her son's death had changed the dynamics of power at court and her administration was now marked by the rivalry between the eunuchs Staurakios and Aetios, both of whom were aiming at securing the empire for their relatives after Irene's death. In 797/8 their hostility now came to the surface in public. Irene's procession on 1 April 799, Easter Monday, from the Church of the Holy Apostles, in her chariot drawn by four white horses led by patricians (namely Bardanes, *strategos* of the Thrakesians, Sisinnios, *strategos* of Thrace, Niketas, domestic of the *Scholae*, and Constantine Boilas), during which she scattered gold coins to the people, should perhaps in this context be seen not as triumphal but as deliberate propaganda in an attempt to bolster her public image and maintain popularity.[73]

When Irene fell critically ill in May 799 the rivalry at court intensified: Aetios won the support of Niketas Triphyllios, domestic of the *Scholae*, and they informed the empress that Staurakios was aiming for the position of emperor. Irene held a state council at the palace of Hiereia but did little more than rebuke and threaten Staurakios, who apologised and prepared to protect his back in future. In February 800, as part of his revenge against Aetios and Niketas, he prepared the way for a rebellion by bribing the imperial guard and their officers with money and gifts: he seems to have lacked the support of higher-ranking officers. Although no eunuch had ever been emperor, he seems to have cherished imperial ambitions in his own right. Aware of the situation, presumably by the instrumentality of Aetios, Irene called another state council in the Great Palace and forbade any contact with him, which according to Theophanes introduced a degree of order in the situation: governmental stability now depended precariously on the opposition of the equally powerful factions of Aetios (now *strategos* of the Anatolics) aligned with Niketas, and of Staurakios. The situation was resolved when Staurakios fell fatally ill, coughing blood; even so he refused to forgo his dreams of kingship. He had been persuaded by doctors, monks and magicians that he would live to be emperor, and on those grounds started a revolt against Aetios among Aetios's troops in Cappadocia. He died in June and did not live to hear how it fared, but the rebels were arrested and exiled.[74] Government was obviously breaking down: not only the army but also the administration must have been disturbed at a state of affairs where eunuchs were openly squabbling over the throne and jockeying for support and power at the court.

Discontent and revolution

It was in this climate that Charlemagne was crowned emperor in December, which must seriously have damaged Irene's prestige even further. Following this, Theophanes informs us that after considering a naval expedition against Sicily Charlemagne then changed his mind and decided to marry Irene. Aetios was now essentially in charge of government and armed forces. In 801/2 Aetios tried to make his brother Leo emperor: he appointed him *mono-strategos* of Thrace and Macedonia, while he himself controlled the Asiatic themes (the Anatolic and Opsikion): Aetios himself had led his themes and won a victory over the Arabs in 800, but in the next year was defeated. These four themes were strategically close to Constantinople and had more than a third of the empire's troops.[75] Confident of his position he felt free to insult other officials: 'Being filled with pride, he humiliated dignitaries in positions of authority and took no account of them.' One of these officials was clearly Nikephoros, Irene's finance minister (*logothete* of the *genikon* or treasury). The disgruntled courtiers decided to revolt, and their plans were confirmed by the arrival of the ambassadors from Charlemagne and Pope Leo, asking Irene to marry him and unite the two halves of the empire. This was a proposal which could only fill a Byzantine bureaucrat with dread, but Irene appears to have been happy to consent and was only prevented from agreeing by the influence of Aetios, 'who ruled by her side and was usurping power on behalf of his brother'. While the ambassadors from Charlemagne were still in the city (and it is difficult to doubt that the timing was deliberately chosen to impress them with the finality of events), at dawn on 31 October 802 Nikephoros assumed power. He was backed by a number of high-ranking conspirators, including Niketas Triphyllios the domestic of the *Scholae*, the quaestor, and a relative of Irene, Leo Sarantapechos. Irene was currently at her palace of Eleutherios. They tricked the guards at the Chalke Gate into believing that Aetios was forcing the empress to proclaim his brother Leo as emperor and that she had therefore sent for Nikephoros to proclaim him emperor instead to forestall Aetios's plan; the guards themselves willingly joined in the ceremony. The palace of Eleutherios was surrounded and at daybreak the empress was sent for and confined in the Great Palace. Nikephoros was then crowned in St Sophia by Tarasios. Theophanes's view of Nikephoros is less than impartial and he stresses the unpopularity of Nikephoros's accession with the populace. His account, however, gives the impression that Irene's removal was supported by the nobility and her own friends:

Men who lived a pious and reasonable life wondered at God's judgement, namely how He had permitted a woman who had suf-fered like a martyr on behalf of the true faith to be ousted by a swineherd and that her closest friends should have joined him out of cupidity, I mean Leo of Sinope (who was patrician and *sakellarios*), and the accursed Triphyllii, and the above-mentioned patricians who had been enriched by her many liberalities, who had often dined at her table, and had assured her through flattery and under terrible oaths that they considered her goodwill more essential than anything else in the world.[76]

Doubtless Irene was still popularly revered for her part in restoring the icons, but it is also clear that she was being deserted by her former supporters at court: Nikephoros himself may have been the *strategos* of the Armeniacs deposed in 790 for backing Irene; Niketas Triphyllios was still domestic of the *Scholae*; Leo Sarantapechos was her own relative.[77] The rebellion seems to have been triggered off by fears that the greatly disliked eunuch Aetios would move to put his brother on the throne before Irene could accept the Franks' marriage proposal.[78] On the following day she was visited by Nikephoros who made his apologies for assuming the throne (it had been against his will, naturally) and wore black buskins rather than the imperial purple as more suited to his modest tastes. Assuring her of her safety, and that she would be treated as a mistress by a servant, he condemned the vice of avarice and urged her not to conceal any of the imperial treasures: there must have been rumours current that Irene had stashed a lot away. Theophanes puts into Irene's mouth an ennobled speech about the fluctuations of fortune, and has her state that she had been aware of Nikephoros's imperial ambitions but was too noble to act on them. Nikephoros promised to allow her to keep her palace of Eleutherios as long as she did not hide any of the imperial treasures, and she swore to that effect on a fragment of the True Cross 'down to the last penny'. However he exiled her to the convent on the island of Prinkipo which she had herself built, and later in November had her removed to Lesbos and ordered her to be severely guarded; perhaps in the interim she had rallied some support. Michael the Syrian records that Irene and Aetios had attempted to have Nikephoros assassinated by some monks: Irene was then exiled to Athens but Aetios was spared in consideration of past services. While the destination is implausible it is not impossible that Irene was involved in some plot against her successor.[79] A rebellion against Nikephoros in July 802, in which Bardanes Tourkos, *strategos* of the Anatolics, was proclaimed emperor by his men, may have been in support of Irene, though Theophanes does not say so;[80] Bardanes as domestic of the *Scholae* had been one of Irene's main supporters in bringing her to power and had been one of the four patricians who led her horses in her triumphal procession in 799. The revolt was not welcomed by the inhabitants of the capital and Bardanes withdrew to a monastery. Nevertheless, Nikephoros's decision to marry his son and heir Staurakios to Irene's niece Theophano (even though 'she was betrothed to another man and had slept with him many times'[81]) was doubtless to strengthen the dynastic claims of their family: Theophano was supposedly selected in a bride-show but, as always, the primary concern in the selection was not the appearance of the candidate but her political suitability. Irene died on 9 August 803, after which her body was transferred to her monastery at Prinkipo.[82]

Irene: a successful ruler?

As ruler Irene was severely handicapped by being unable to lead an army, the more so because she seems to have preferred to bypass experienced commanders who might have been tainted with iconoclast beliefs in favour of her own trusted eunuchs.[83] While these could on occasion win respectable victories and command themes, this can hardly have been popular with the army or conducive to its smooth running. She also weakened the empire militarily by removing capable iconoclastic *strategoi* appointed by Constantine V, like Michael Lachanodrakon, and putting her own appointees in command: this may however have been exaggerated, as in 789/90 the *magistros* Peter (her father-in-law's man) was still in office despite the part he played in the persecution of iconophiles. Irene's relations with the *themata*, notably the Armeniacs, was precarious throughout: the soldiers who had served so loyally under the outstanding general Constantine V were unwilling to be commanded by a woman who was instrumental in keeping Constantine's grandson from power and whose administration was unable to reproduce the great victories of the 740s and 750s. But Irene, faced with the Arab caliph Harun al-Rashid (789–809), knew her limitations, and those of her officials. As sole ruler she immediately attempted to sue for peace with the Arabs, who were devastating Cappadocia and Galatia: this was unsuccessful. In 798 the Arabs even advanced as far as Malagina and succeeded in capturing the herd of imperial war horses. This humiliating episode was followed by other raiding parties, including an expedition in 798/9 which inflicted a severe defeat on the soldiers of the Opsikion theme and captured their camp equipment. Harun then consented to a four-year truce for which Irene had to pay an annual tribute.[84] After Irene assumed sole power military activity was kept to a minimum. Nevertheless, Byzantium suffered no major loss of territory and she was successful in containing the Arab forces. In the long term she had been more successful in Bulgaria: the four new Byzantine strongholds there were reasonably effective in protecting the Bulgar frontier and by the end of her reign the Byzantines were no longer paying tribute to the Bulgars.

Her financial policy was not unsuccessful. Even despite the huge tribute paid to the Arabs and her tax concessions, at the end of her reign she still had large cash reserves to hand over to Nikephoros. In fact she seems to have had an appreciation of money and its importance and is said to have concealed treasure in her own palace. It was doubtless this she used to win over the *tagmata* and officials against her son. But she may have been thought to have been profligate with the empire's reserves: in 801 Irene remitted civic taxes for the capital and cancelled the customs dues, *kommerkia*, of Abydos and Hieron, which controlled maritime traffic reaching the capital.[85] These measures, and 'many other liberalities', led to great thanks on the part of the people and have generally been assumed to have been made, like her donation of gold coins in 799, for the sake of maintaining popularity,[86] though there is evidence that she was also concerned with philanthropic measures. Theodore the Stoudite in a letter addressed to Irene in the most flattering language gives fuller details of these reductions and the relief that these caused in lowering prices – he speaks of dues not only on sea-borne traffic, but on roads and narrow passes, and exactions on fishermen, hunters and a long list of artisans and petty traders being removed: much of this may however be the rhetoric of flattery. He also refers to her abolition of payments demanded apparently from soldiers' widows in lieu of their deceased husbands' military service. It appears as though she had exempted philanthropic institutions, the orphanages, hostels, homes for the aged, churches and imperial monasteries from the hearth taxes (*kapnika*); these were restored by Nikephoros.[87]

The return to icon-worship

Irene's greatest triumph, which led to her canonization, was not simply in restoring icon-worship, but in doing so peacefully and without controversy. No bishop dissented at the Council of Nicaea, when only a year earlier iconoclast bishops had triumphantly claimed victory when the council in Constantinople was disbanded. In this she relied heavily on Tarasios, who accepted the iconoclast bishops back into the fold without rancour. As a choice of patriarch for the occasion he was an inspired one, and Irene seems to have had the knack of selecting her ministers for their innate skills: it was her misfortune that she felt it incumbent on herself, for whatever reason, to rely where possible on eunuchs, even for military expeditions. She seems too to have had a flair for time and place – the holding of the council at Nicaea showed a nice awareness of the propaganda value involved, while the orchestration of the 'discovery' of the coffin near the Long Walls and the return of the 'relics' of St Euphemia bear the mark of a master diplomat, albeit one not too concerned about the veracity of the reporting of events.

Was Irene's task in restoring icons a difficult one? Probably not, though Irene seems to have moved relatively slowly in order not to upset any hardline iconoclasts. The fact that she replaced the Christ icon on the Chalke Gate of the imperial palace, the removal of which signalled the beginning of iconoclasm in 726 (in the ensuing riot women were said to have been prominent), and endowed some iconophile church decoration seems to imply that iconoclast sensibilities were not too easily ruffled, although the Chalke icon was not replaced until 797 or later. According to the *Scriptor Incertus* the restored icon had an inscription placed over its head which read, '[The image] which Leo the emperor had formerly cast down, Irene has re-erected here',[88] and the lack of a reference to Constantine VI makes it certain that the restoration of the image was not made until after 797, the delay perhaps being in deference to the iconoclast party. Under her rule there is evidence of the return of monastic investment of money in art, and a number of churches can be attributed to her reign, such as St Sophia at Thessalonika and Bizye in Thrace, and several monastery churches in Bithynia: St Sophia in Thessalonika can be dated by the monograms of Constantine and Irene.[89] The *Patria* tells us that she was said, with Constantine VI, to have built a church to St Anastasios, as well as restoring the Church of the Theotokos at Pege; she also established a small monastery of St Euphrosyne known as 'ta Libadia', and built churches to St Luke and St Eustathios.[90] As part of this artistic revival a number of major works were also undertaken, such as statues of Constantine VI and Irene themselves:[91] Constantine erected a bronze statue of his mother in the hippodrome,[92] and their mosaic portraits were dedicated at Pege. Irene was also an active philanthropist: she established several homes for the aged, hospices for the poor, *xenodocheia* (hostels for travellers without accommodation and the sick) and a cemetery for the poor.[93]

The worst accusation that can be made against Irene, of course, concerns her deposition of her son. Constantine's own actions cannot be used to justify her. Constantine VI may not have been the world's most dynamic ruler, but he had hardly, after all, had a chance. When he died at twenty-six he was still dominated by his mother and her ministers. The worst that can be said of him is that he seems to have lacked the capacity to carry things through – on three occasions he failed to give battle: against the Bulgars in 791 and 796, and against the Arabs in 797, when his mother's supporters informed him that they had withdrawn. With experience and the advice of skilled commanders his military expertise would no doubt have improved or he would have learnt to rely on those good at the job. The main accusation that can be made against him is one of immaturity, no doubt deliberately fostered by his mother and her advisers. His decision to have the 1,000 ringleaders of the Armeniac revolt in 793 tattooed on the face with the words 'Armeniac plotter' is probably not to be seen as childish: it is after all paralleled by the method used by the grave and humourless Theophilos to deal with the 'graptoi', when Theophilos had an entire poem (metrical irregularities and all) branded on the faces of two recalcitrant iconophile monks. The sending of a parcel of horse excrement to the Bulgarian khan in 796 by Constantine is less excusable and suggests a certain lack of diplomatic finesse in one who had technically been ruler since 780.[94]

There is no evidence to show that Irene was inspired by anything other than a wish to secure her own position in her blinding of Constantine. It is true that he was associating with army commanders and officials who had served under his grandfather and father, but that is only to be expected: they were after all his only power base. Had Constantine been planning to reintroduce iconoclasm Theophanes would certainly have told us and used it to justify Irene's actions. Constantine was involved with his mother in the Council of Nicaea and the restoration of icon veneration and in the retrieval of the relics of Euphemia, as well as in their building programme: there is nothing to suggest that he was a closet iconoclast. Theophanes's negative verdict on Irene as a ruler is echoed by her *vita*, written in the mid-ninth century, which contains a number of critical comments derived from Theophanes on her ambition for political power, the fact that she was easily deceived (being a woman) and her brutal treatment of her son and his associates.[95] Her niece Theophano, who married Staurakios, son of Nikephoros I, also cherished imperial ambitions, according to Theophanes. When her husband was dying of his mortal wound incurred in Nikephoros's catastrophic defeat against the Bulgars, it was Theophano's desire to obtain the empire like Irene that caused the proclamation of Staurakios's brother-in-law Michael I emperor.[96]

Part of Irene's problem may have been that she never felt secure in power. Her regency began with a revolt on the part of her brothers-in-law, and she knew she could not count on the *tagmata* and some of the *strategoi*. Her main allies were her eunuch officials, whom she relied on even to direct military operations, and they proved to be treacherous and corrupt. She does not deserve the depth of criticism given her by one modern scholar: 'She was, by any standards, medieval or modern, a bad woman; and, what was worse, an incapable and irresponsible prince.'[97] The fact that she was an able politician is shown by the fact that she survived the threat of her five brothers-in-law, given her lack of support in the army and bureaucracy – an impressive feat indeed and one for which she deserves full credit.

5

THEODORA, RESTORER OF ORTHODOXY (830–67+)

Despite Irene's success in restoring the icons, iconoclasm resurfaced as imperial policy between 815 and 842, and was finally terminated by another empress-regent, Theodora wife of Theophilos, in 843. Theodora had much in common with Irene: both were iconophiles married to iconoclasts, with whom they were reputed to have been in conflict over the issue of personal icon worship; both convened important church councils; both empresses relied on eunuchs to help them rule; both were left as regents for young sons, each of whom turned out to be immature and in want of guidance, even after reaching maturity, as well as being susceptible to the charms of young women; and in both cases their sons resented this influence of their mothers and attempted to depose them from power. And both empresses could be single-minded and ruthless in their pursuit of power: while there is no suggestion that Theodora wished to emulate Irene and depose her son or was doing anything other than maintaining the government for him until he was ready to rule, she was however privy to a plot to assassinate her brother Bardas, after he had removed her from power.

A proportion of the army, especially the *tagmata*, as well as some churchmen, appear to have remained iconoclast at heart. The disasters suffered by Nikephoros I and his son Staurakios against the Bulgars in 811 (after which the khan Krum used Nikephoros's skull lined with silver as a toasting-cup) revived a wave of nostalgia among army officers, exacerbated by the dislike of the monastic party that had heavily influenced Nikephoros's son-in-law Michael I.[1] The soldiers of the *tagmata* broke into the tomb of their hero Constantine V and called on him to lead them again: they had previously installed a mechanism in the mausoleum in the Holy Apostles which caused it to open suddenly as if by a divine miracle.[2] Leo, *strategos* of the Anatolics, was proclaimed emperor in 813 and Michael I, Nikephoros's son-in-law, abdicated. Leo V returned to a policy of iconoclasm, but was murdered in 820 at Christmas Mass and was succeeded by his comrade Michael II. Though an iconoclast himself Michael married Euphrosyne, daughter of Constantine VI and Maria of Amnia and a committed iconophile. Michael's son Theophilos was, however, brought up as a fervent iconoclast by his tutor

John the Grammarian, and under Theophilos iconophiles, especially foreign monks, were actively persecuted in the capital.

Women seem to have been particularly attached to the veneration of icons, not merely because they were less likely to be able to read the Scriptures, but because of the nature of their employments at home.[3] The veneration of the Theotokos intensified in the empire in the late sixth and early seventh century, and she was adopted as the especial protectress of Constantinople.[4] This expansion of the cult of the Virgin was at least in part the result of women's devotion to the Mother of God, to whom Irene was to dedicate her convent on the island of Prinkipo. The letters of Theodore the Stoudite document a number of iconophile women during the second iconoclast phase which commenced in 815, who remained loyal to the veneration of icons, when their husbands or fellow monks apostatised; one of his correspondents was Mary of Amnia.[5] Iconophilism is especially evident among royal women: Theodosia, widow of Leo V, converted to orthodoxy, and for this was exiled by Michael II,[6] and Irene, Mary of Amnia, Euphrosyne, Theodora and (surprisingly) Irene, the first wife of Constantine V, are just some examples of imperial women who were said to have been devoted to icon worship. The first half of the ninth century is also a period when female hymnographers briefly flourished – Kassia, Theodosia and Thekla.[7]

Theodora, like Irene, was so highly regarded by later generations that she was canonised by the church for restoring orthodoxy. Born in Ebissa in Paphlagonia, she was probably of Armenian origin and the daughter of an army officer called Marinos and Theoktiste Phlorina.[8] On 5 June 830 she married Theophilos, after a bride-show held in the palace.[9] They had two sons: Constantine, born probably in 834, who was unfortunately drowned in a palace cistern at the age of two, and Michael III; and five daughters: Thekla, Anna, Anastasia, Maria and Pulcheria (Plate 8). Like many imperial women, Theodora was portrayed as a devout iconophile, despite the views of Theophilos: as well as privately venerating icons, she is said to have had Lazaros the icon painter released from prison, and to have encouraged Euphrosyne, Theophilos's stepmother, to teach her step-granddaughters to venerate icons on their visits to her convent.[10]

Theodora and Theophilos

Theophilos, who was born in 812/13 and crowned co-emperor in 821, came to the throne in 829. In the first months of his reign his stepmother Euphrosyne was also his co-ruler, and it was she who arranged his marriage six months after his father's death, when Theophilos was seventeen. In 830 Euphrosyne sent out to every theme to collect beautiful and well-born candidates, who arrived in May 830. In choosing to hold a bride-show for the young emperor, Euphrosyne was continuing the tradition by which her father Constantine VI and her mother Maria of Amnia had been married. The

Plate 8 The daughters of Theophilos and Theodora – Thekla, Anastasia, Anna, Pulcheria and Maria – are taught to venerate an icon of Christ by their grandmother Theoktiste. (Taken from A. Grabar and M. Manoussacas, *L'illustration du manuscrit de Skylitzès de la bibliothèque nationale de Madrid*, Venice: Instituto ellenico di studi byzantini et post-byzantini)

show was held in Theophilos's new Hall (*Triclinon*) of the Pearl, a palace complex he had just completed, and according to Symeon the Logothete Theophilos chose Theodora more by accident than from a considered judgement:

> Having sent out into all the themes, [Euphrosyne] summoned beautiful girls so that her son Theophilos might marry. Escorting them into the Palace, to the Triclinum called the Pearl, she gave Theophilos a golden apple, and said, 'Give this to whichever one you like'. Among the girls of noble birth was an extremely beautiful girl named Kassia. Seeing her and admiring her greatly for her beauty, Theophilos said, 'Yet / Through a woman evils came to man'. She, though modestly, replied, 'But / Through a woman better things began'. He, wounded in his heart by her reply, passed her by and gave the apple to Theodora, a Paphlagonian girl.[11]

If Kassia who here was so quick at capping Theophilos's verse was the hymn-writer who founded a convent in Constantinople and was a correspondent of Theodore the Stoudite, then iconophilism was certainly not an obstacle for participating in the show. As with previous bride-shows, the whole thing was probably stage-managed, in this case by Euphrosyne, who may only have selected iconophiles, like Kassia and Theodora, for the show, and possibly herself was responsible for the choice of Theodora as the bride-elect.[12]

Theodora was crowned in the Church of St Stephen in Daphne on 5 June 830 and the couple then married in St Sophia. Euphrosyne retired to a convent called the Gastria, which she founded in Constantinople, and left the imperial stage to the newly-weds.[13] As empress, Theodora was immediately possessed of the wealth with which to emphasise her new status: following her coronation she presented the patriarch and clergy with fifteen pounds of gold each and the senate with fifty.[14]

Iconoclasm under Theophilos

Theophilos's measures in favour of iconoclasm seem to have been inspired by what he considered an iconophile plot in 831: a pamphlet that was circulated predicting his death. The suspected perpetrators, who had connections with Theodora's family, were imprisoned and Euthymios, a former bishop of Sardis, died under his treatment, becoming an iconophile martyr.[15] In June 833 Theophilos issued an edict ordering the arrest of iconophile clergy and monks not in communion with the official hierarchy; anyone who sheltered them would have their property confiscated. A number of monks were imprisoned and beaten, some dying under the treatment. This can hardly have been welcomed by Theodora, if she were a devout iconophile.

Nevertheless, their family life started propitiously. Even though their first three children were daughters Theophilos had them crowned Augustae and in the late 830s struck an issue of ceremonial gold *solidi* with the portraits of himself, Theodora and Thekla on the obverse, and Anna and Anastasia on the reverse (Plate 9).[16] It was probably in 834 that Constantine was born and he too was crowned: coins were minted showing Theophilos on the obverse and Constantine on the reverse.

In 838 when the patriarch Anthony died, it was natural for Theophilos to appoint his old tutor the iconoclast John the Grammarian in his place. The regime then became more overtly iconclast and Theophilos issued a second edict, ordering that all icons be destroyed or plastered over. This resulted in the beating and imprisonment of the monk Lazaros, a famous icon painter. At the same time there are hints that things may not have been going well with the imperial couple, especially after the Arab capture of Amorion in 838 – an unparalleled defeat which shattered Theophilos and seriously undermined his health. In consequence the emperor devoted himself increasingly to building projects, scholarship and divination, and also seems in 839 to have begun an affair with one of Theodora's attendants. When Theodora, not unnaturally, took this badly and showed it, Theophilos begged her pardon, swore it was his only offence, and built a new palace for their daughters, the Karianos.[17] It was shortly after this that Theodora's predilection for icons was forced on Theophilos's notice: Theodora often sent her daughters to Euphrosyne's monastery, where they were taught to venerate icons (Plate 8). The older girls were wise enough to keep quiet about it, but in early or mid-839 the youngest daughter Pulcheria, then about two, 'a mere baby in both age and sense', told her father about the beautiful dolls kept in a box and held up to their heads and faces to kiss. Theophilos went into a rage and forbade his daughters to be taken to their stepmother again; he may also have forced Euphrosyne to leave the Gastria.[18]

The story is also told that Theodora kept icons in her bedroom in Theophilos's lifetime: the emperor's jester named Denderis was said to have burst into Theodora's bedchamber one day where he found her reverently lifting icons to her eyes. Theodora explained that they were dolls whom she loved dearly, but going to the emperor, who was at dinner, Denderis told

Plate 9 A *solidus* of Theophilos celebrating the coronation of his three eldest daughters as Augustae: the obverse shows Theophilos with Thekla (l.) and Theodora (r.), the reverse Anna and Anastasia. Minted at Constantinople in the late 830s (Dumbarton Oaks Byzantine Collection: Washington DC)

him of the 'pretty dolls' he had seen 'nurse' (i.e. Theodora) taking out from a cushion. Theophilos understood the allusion and sought out Theodora to shout at her. Theodora, however, explained that she and her maids were looking in a mirror and Denderis had mistaken their reflections. Denderis when later asked by Theophilos if he had seen 'nurse' kissing any more dolls, put one hand to his lips and the other to his behind and asked him not to mention them again.[19] The incident is so related as to reflect badly on both Theophilos and Theodora and should not perhaps be taken at face value, though Symeon the Logothete confirms that Theodora secretly venerated icons while her husband was alive.[20] However, relations between the couple may have been strained, and it was after this incident that Theophilos inflicted his savage punishment on the brothers Theodore and Theophanes, iconophile monks from the Holy Land who had come to Constantinople; he had twelve iambic verses stating that they had come to propagate heresy tattooed on their faces, and exiled them to Apamea, and they were thence known as the *graptoi* ('written on'). Theophanes was a well-known hymnographer and to add insult to injury Theophilos's poem contained deliberate metrical errors.[21] Theophilos also heard that Lazaros had been painting icons in prison, and had his hands branded with red-hot plates. Theodora, however, it is said, was able to persuade him to allow Lazaros to recover at the monastery of St John the Baptist at Phoberos.[22] But the sources with regard to Theodora's closet iconophilism must be read with caution: it is unlikely that Theophilos would have tolerated any heretical practices at the centre of the court, and while both Theodora and her minister Theoktistos are presented in hagiographical works as fervent iconophiles this is little more that the inevitable rewriting of history consequent upon the final iconophile triumph.

Theodora as regent: the 'triumph of orthodoxy'

Shortly after this Theophilos contracted dysentery. Before he died, on 20 January 842 probably at the age of only twenty-nine, he summoned a group of leading officials and citizens to the Magnaura and asked for their aid in helping Theodora and Michael, their two-year-old son. Clearly he intended Theodora to succeed as regent but the eunuch Theoktistos, the *logothete tou dromou*, and Theodora's uncle Manuel, the *protomagistros*, were appointed as guardians to assist her, according to the sources, though there is some doubt as to whether Manuel was in fact still alive at this point; Theodora's brother Bardas may also have been included.[23] With Irene's reign in mind Theophilos might have felt it important to associate experienced administrators and generals with Theodora in power. There is no suggestion that Theodora's religious beliefs affected Theophilos's decision. Certainly she had had some experience in financial transactions, over which she had apparently fallen out with Theophilos: when he spotted a fine merchant vessel sailing into the harbour of Boukoleon, he asked about its owner. On learning that it belonged to Theodora, he immediately ordered the ship and all its cargo to be burnt, exclaiming: 'What! has my wife made me, an emperor, into a merchant?'[24]

Michael, who was born on 9 January 840, was only two years old,[25] and Theodora ruled in his name until 856 relying mainly on Theoktistos, her co-regent and chief minister, rather than on her male relatives. Theoktistos had been an iconoclast under Theophilos, but now was fully in agreement with Theodora as to the advisability of a return to icon-worship. Like Theodora he was later canonised by the orthodox church, and the council which appointed Methodios patriarch and restored the sacred icons was held in his residence.[26] Another moving spirit may have been Methodios himself, who had lived in the palace for many years, and who may well have acted secretly as a spiritual adviser to Theodora.[27] While all three have been presented as venerators of icons, one of the reasons behind the restoration may have been the belief in ruling circles that iconoclasm no longer brought the empire God's favour.[28]

Theodora did not act precipitously: it was not until March 843 that she moved to restore icon veneration, and the whole episode seems to have been kept very low key, presumably in order not to offend unrepentant iconoclasts.[29] Theodora's attitude towards these iconoclasts was deliberately conciliatory and she attached as a condition to the restoration of the icons that her husband Theophilos would not be anathematised as a heretic. The story is told that Theodora, while in a state of contrition, had a vision on Friday of the first week of Lent (9 March 843) in which she saw Theophilos naked and being dragged off to torture. She followed the procession and when they reached the Chalke Gate of the palace she saw an awesome man sitting on a throne in front of the image of Christ. When she fell at his feet, the man proclaimed that her husband was forgiven because of her tears and faith.[30] A further apocryphal tale in the *Vita Theodorae* concerns the miracle by which Methodios wrote the names of all the iconoclast emperors in a book which was then deposited on the altar of St Sophia: when Methodios returned Theophilos's name was found to have been miraculously erased.[31]

The ecclesiastical council which restored orthodoxy was held in Theoktistos's house early in March 843, the main protagonists being Theodora, Theoktistos and her two brothers, as well as a further relative Sergios Niketiates: it was very much a small family affair.[32] John the Grammarian was deposed by the council and Methodios elected patriarch in his place.[33] The whole affair seems to have passed peaceably, except that when John came to be expelled from the patriarch's residence, he refused to leave, demonstrating wounds inflicted on his stomach by the excubitors: the tradition then arose that he had inflicted them on himself.[34] Theophilos himself was not anathematised, and according to the Continuator of Theophanes Theodora herself addressed the assembly, pleading that he had repented of his errors, and threatening to withdraw her support unless he were excluded from the anathema against practising iconoclasts. This may not have been so much out of marital affection as from the realisation that anathematisation of Theophilos would antagonise his numerous followers.[35] Monks and bishops exiled by Theophilos were recalled, and the 'triumph of orthodoxy' was celebrated in St Sophia following a great procession on the first Sunday in Lent (11 March 843). Monastic foundations again became fashionable: it was presumably during her regency that Theodora turned an estate called Armamentareas into a monastery of St Panteleimon and endowed it with landed property.[36] There was doubtless some hostility to the restoration felt in certain circles: Genesios recounts that a young woman was suborned to accuse Methodios of having seduced her. Methodios however visibly proved to the gathering the impossibility of this accusation and the lady confessed that she had been bribed.[37] John the Grammarian, who was forcibly retired to a monastery on the Bosporos, was also said to have ordered a servant to poke out the eyes of an icon in the church there, and for this received 200 lashes by order of the empress, who at first wanted to put out his eyes also.[38] But on the whole, while iconoclast churchmen are documented as late as 870,[39] there seems to have been little if any concerted opposition, due mainly to the prudent policies of Theodora and Theoktistos.

In the first year of the regency the gold *solidi* of the reign show the figure of Theodora on the obverse, with Michael and Thekla, her eldest daughter, on the reverse (Plate 10): significantly the other regents are not depicted, while Theodora is the only one given a title in the inscription ('Theodora *despoina*'). Similarly, an imperial seal of the early regency gives Michael, Theodora and Thekla the title of 'Emperors of the *Romaioi*'. Perhaps as early as the end of 843 Christ's image reappears on the gold coinage, with Theodora and Michael on the reverse (Plate 11).[40] The restoration of icons in places of public worship took longer: the first important mosaic, that of the Virgin in the apse of St Sophia, was inaugurated by the patriarch Photios on 29 March 867.[41] This delay may have been due either to a lack of competent artists, or to the strength of the iconoclast opposition, and it appears that it was not until the 860s that sacred decorations were displayed outside of the palace: the earliest examples of sacred art occur in the palace chapels and the Chrysotriklinos of the Great Palace.[42] However, at some point before 847, Theodora did replace the image of Christ over the Chalke, or Brazen Gate;

Plate 10 A *solidus* of Michael III from the first year of Theodora's regency, with Theodora on the obverse, and Michael (l.) and his eldest sister Thekla (r.) on the reverse. Minted at Constantinople 842–3(?) (Whittemore Collection: Harvard University)

Plate 11 A solidus of Michael III, with a beardless Michael in the place of precedence
(1.) and Theodora shown larger (r.). Minted at Constantinople in 843(?)–56
(Dumbarton Oaks Byzantine Collection: Washington DC)

this new image was a mosaic, with Christ depicted full-length, and it was
supposedly made by the monk Lazaros, who had suffered under Theophilos.[43]
A twenty-nine-line epigram by the patriarch Methodios (who died in June
847) seems to have been inscribed beside the restored icon:[44]

> Seeing Thy stainless image, O Christ, and Thy cross figured in
> relief, I worship and reverence Thy true flesh. For, being the Word of
> the Father, timeless by nature, Thou wast born, mortal by nature and
> in time, to a mother. Hence in circumscribing and portraying thee
> in images, I do not circumscribe Thy immaterial nature – for that
> is above representation and vicissitude – but in representing Thy
> vulnerable flesh, O Word, I pronounce Thee uncircumscribable as
> God . . . Refuting their [the iconoclast emperors'] lawless error, the
> empress Theodora, guardian of the faith, with her scions arrayed in
> purple and gold, emulating the pious among emperors, and shown to
> be the most pious of them all, has re-erected it with righteous intent
> at this gate of the palace, to her own glory, praise and fame, to the
> dignity of the entire Church, to the full prosperity of the human race,
> to the fall of malevolent enemies and barbarians.[45]

This triumphal praise of Theodora's judgement and piety might be said to
have set the scene for a successful regency. It is difficult in hindsight to
determine who was primarily responsible for the smooth running of the
empire from 842 to 855, the period of the regency of Theodora and
Theoktistos, the *de facto* prime minister,[46] but one or both should be considered remarkably successful in government. As Theoktistos had not only
had long and loyal service under Theophilos, but had been instrumental in
bringing Michael II to the throne, he obviously contributed a great deal to
the regency and its policies, which should not, however, be taken to imply
that Theodora was a cipher. What is clear, is that the two of them deliberately excluded Theodora's brothers from power, despite their unimpeach-
able military qualifications and experience. Under Theophilos, Theodora's
family had been placed in positions of importance, married off well, and

treated with respect:[47] the title of *zoste patrikia*, the highest court rank for women, which was marked with a particular girdle (*zoste*), was created by Theophilos for Theodora's mother Theoktiste.[48] Nevertheless, Bardas and Petronas and their sons were now relegated to a passive role in the government of the empire. One of her sisters, Kalomaria, a widow, lived in the palace with her sister, but dressed in cheap clothing and spent her time paying monthly visits to the prisons and distributing alms.[49]

As might have been expected, the members of the Stoudite monastery were not prepared to accept the leniency shown to former iconoclasts by the patriarch Methodios: indeed, in the interests of church harmony, Methodios was finally forced to excommunicate them,[50] and the election of Ignatios, a strict monk, on Methodios's death in June 847, may have been intended to conciliate the Stoudite faction. The treatment of heretic Paulicians was less lenient, however, and they were savagely persecuted and their property confiscated by the state.[51] In military matters Theoktistos, who took the field personally, achieved considerable success against the Arabs, and actually restored Byzantine rule in Crete for a short time in 843–4, while Cyprus was reoccupied and an expedition against Arab Egypt was undertaken in 853, in which Damietta was burnt.[52] The Slavic tribes in the Peloponnese were also reduced and forced to pay tribute.[53] Financially, the empire had profited from the regency: Theodora in 856 is said to have been able to show the senate 190,000 lb of gold and 300,000 lb of silver (13,680,000 *nomismata*) in the treasury.[54]

The regency is terminated

The regency of Theoktistos and Theodora was abruptly ended in November 855, when Theoktistos was murdered by Bardas with the backing of the young ruler Michael III.[55] Both were unhappy at Theoktistos's role in government, but for different reasons. In 855 Theodora and Theoktistos, concerned at Michael's liaison with Eudokia Ingerina, a noble lady at court possibly of Scandinavian background, 'on account of her impudence or shamelessness',[56] had married him to Eudokia Dekapolitissa.[57] The marriage was again arranged through the preliminaries of a bride-show, though Eudokia Dekapolitissa was certainly of noble birth and belonged to court circles.[58] As with previous bride-shows, the potential groom had little say in the selection. The decision was orchestrated by Theodora and Theoktistos: Eudokia Ingerina was actually allowed to take part, but Michael was not allowed to choose her.[59] The fact that she was the emperor's mistress was obviously not a qualification. Michael, now sixteen and of an age to rule for himself, appears to have ignored his new wife and continued his liaison with Eudokia Ingerina. Unhappy with having his judgement overridden, he brought Bardas secretly to court on the advice of the *parakoimomenos* Damianos. Bardas persuaded him that his mother intended to marry or marry off one of her daughters and in that way depose Michael and blind him (the memory of Irene's take-over must have been a powerful factor here), and that in any case he would have no say in power while Theodora and Theoktistos continued to work together.[60] Kalomaria (i.e. 'Good Maria'), Theodora's sister, and Theophanes, chief of the wardrobe, also joined the conspiracy.[61] The accounts of the actual assassination are contradictory in many of their details,[62] but it appears that Bardas may not have intended to murder Theoktistos, merely to humiliate and exile him. At the critical moment, however, it was Michael who called on the guards to kill the cowering *logothete*. Theodora was not without courage for, according to Genesios, she learnt of what was happening and rushed out to save Theoktistos, but was frightened away by one of the conspirators, and Theoktistos was dragged out from the chair under which he had taken shelter and stabbed in the stomach. Michael was then proclaimed sole ruler.[63]

The actual control of affairs of state, however, devolved not on Michael, but on his uncle Bardas. Theodora herself was bitterly resentful at Theoktistos's murder, and remained unrelenting towards his assassins, despite Michael's attempts to conciliate her; the Continuator of Theophanes describes her as berating her brother and son and filling the palace with her wails and lamentations.[64] Theodora's daughters were sent to a convent, and Theodora was formally deposed as Augusta on 15 March 856, but remained in the palace until August or September 857, plagued by her son who attempted to drive her into retirement. She then joined her daughters in the monastery of Gastria and was tonsured with them (the patriarch Ignatios refused to perform the ceremony on the grounds that they were unwilling to become nuns). Their possessions were taken away and they were compelled to live like private citizens.[65] The catalyst for her expulsion from the palace may have been her involvement in a plot to murder her brother Bardas, which was master-minded by the imperial *protostrator*. The plot was discovered and the conspirators beheaded in the hippodrome.[66]

Bardas was designated *epi tou kanikleiou* in Theoktistos's place, *magistros* and then domestic of the *Scholae*. In 859 he was given the important post of *curopalates*, and then in 862 Caesar; his two sons were also given important military posts. The decade of Bardas's administration (856–66) was one of great cultural renaissance, including the conversion of Bulgaria, while campaigns in Asia Minor led by the emperor himself and his uncles achieved some successes, especially after the defeat by Petronas of an Arab army in September 863.[67] But this run of success was broken when Michael started associating with Basil, a groom from Macedonia said to be of Armenian origin, whose start in life had been given him by a wealthy lady Danielis, who met Basil in Greece, and who enriched him supposedly because of a prophecy that he would gain the throne.[68] Basil, whose strength was immense, first attracted Michael's notice by his skill at handling horses,[69] and Michael unhesitatingly sacrificed his uncle and the interests of the empire for Basil's company: according to Genesios Michael honoured Basil with many offices and he is praised for his agility in the hunt, ball-playing, wrestling and jumping, discus-throwing, weight-lifting and running.[70] Theodora is said to have warned Michael of the potential danger from Basil, but he took no notice: the sources date Basil's meeting with Michael prior to Theodora's forced retirement in 857.[71] Basil was made patrician and *parakoimomenos* in 865, and when the army was assembling in the Thrakesion theme for an expedition against the Arabs on 21 April 866 Michael stood by while Basil assassinated Bardas.[72] Basil was made co-emperor in May 866. The next year Basil was to kill Michael himself, who was not yet twenty-eight years old.

Before this, however, an unusually sophisticated matrimonial arrangement was entered into by Basil, Michael and Michael's mistress, when Eudokia was pregnant in 866 with Leo, later to be Leo VI, who was born in September 866. It appears that Eudokia had remained Michael's mistress during the past decade, though it is possible that Michael married her to a son of the Caesar Bardas *c.* 856 to legitimise her social status, and when this son died, she may have taken up with Bardas.[73] Bardas may have deposed patriarch Ignatios for condemning his relationship with his daughter-in-law as incestuous, though it is more probable that Ignatios's refusal to tonsure the empress and her daughters was responsible.[74] Basil was made to divorce his wife Maria, by whom he had two children, and marry Eudokia Ingerina, on condition that he treated her with respect. At the same time he was given Michael's sister Thekla, the ex-nun, as his mistress, who would now have been about thirty-five years old,[75] and made co-emperor. The whole point of the charade seems to have been to ensure that Michael's son by the pregnant Eudokia would be 'born in the purple', albeit to the wrong father. In fact, the liaison between Michael and Eudokia seems to have continued up till Michael's death: Symeon the *logothete* implies that Eudokia's next son Stephen was also Michael's.[76] Basil had reason to believe he might lose Michael's favour: at a race meeting at the palace of St Mamas after Leo's birth in September 866 a patrician Basiliskianos, who had just flattered the emperor, was invited to put on the imperial shoes, an incident which concerned both Basil and Eudokia the new empress that Basil might be losing favour. Basil may have started to conspire against Michael, from concerns at how long his imperial status was likely to last, and in 867 Michael was warned by a monk of a plot by Basil while he was out hunting.[77]

Michael was murdered later that month, on 24 September 867, after Basil and Eudokia had been to dinner in the Palace of St Mamas. The bolt of Michael's bedroom door was tampered with by Basil so the door could not be locked, and he was encouraged to get very drunk by Eudokia.[78] While he was sleeping off his wine Basil and eight friends dispatched him.[79] Eudokia, seven months pregnant with Stephen, was then escorted to the imperial palace 'with great honour':[80] the implication that she had been involved in the conspiracy is very strong. The other Eudokia, Michael's actual widow, was returned to her parents. Theodora had been restored to liberty, if not to any active part in government, by this point, and was on speaking terms with her son: on the day of his murder she sent Michael a dinner invitation, and Michael told some of his entourage to hunt something suitable to send her. Our last glimpse of Theodora is when she was found by Paul the *cubicularius*, who had been sent to arrange Michael's burial, weeping with her daughters over the body of Michael, which was wrapped in the blanket belonging to the right-hand horse that he drove.[81]

What Theodora, an Augusta again at least in name, thought of the empress who succeeded her can be guessed with some certainty: it cannot have been favourable. Theodora died sometime after the accession of Basil I and was buried in the Gastria monastery.[82] As empress, Eudokia Ingerina went on to have one other son and, it seems, three daughters, who were made nuns by their father Basil. Her wild life was not yet over, for in about 878 she had an affair with a certain Xylinites, who was punished by Basil by being made a monk. He was later promoted to *oikonomos* of St Sophia by Leo VI.[83] In 879 Basil's eldest son by his first marriage, Constantine, died, and Eudokia was to see her son Leo, Theodora's grandson, as next in line for the succession.

Theodora's misfortune as regent was, like Irene, that of having a son who had interests other than simply running the empire. We should of course beware of taking the later Macedonian assessment of Michael's character at face value: he was not as black as he has been painted by historians of the Macedonian dynasty, who, Genesios and the Continuator of Theophanes in particular, were later concerned to blacken his name in order to justify Basil's usurpation and murder of Michael.[84] Symeon the *logothete* in contrast gives us the counter-view to Macedonian propaganda. Though he has gone down in history as 'Michael the Drunkard', the soubriquet is not entirely justified.[85] Later historians recorded that his favourite jester Gryllos ('Pig') dressed up as the patriarch, while the emperor and eleven of his other companions robed themselves as ecclesiastical officials and roamed the city singing lewd songs (on one occasion reportedly meeting the patriarch Ignatios himself).[86] He is recorded as having given a fortune to his jockey Cheilas and as having been profligate in presents to the children of his jockeys, giving as much as 100 pounds of gold as christening presents.[87] He is said to have become an intolerable tyrant, and issued orders for the execution of innocent men in his fits of drunkenness.[88] But not all these stories can be accepted, at least as they stand. Michael's taste for wine, women, song, buffoonery and indecent stories,[89] and horse-racing,[90] vilified in the Macedonian sources, is confirmed by Symeon the *logothete*, who speaks of his devotion to hunting and horse-racing and 'other depravities', and of his stables adorned with marble and serviced with running water.[91] But his reputation has suffered unduly: he was a popular ruler, and led his army in person, though he was overshadowed by other greater administrators, first Theoktistos (when Michael was not in any case of an age to rule) and then Bardas. Photios could certainly praise Michael in glowing terms as a military victor, referring to his successes over the Arabs in September and October 863 and his humbling of Bulgaria without fighting in 864, while he rebuilt the cities of Nicaea and Ankara, and reconstructed the Church of Our Lady of the Pharos in the palace.[92] Indeed, certain tales of his more idiosyncratic behaviour, as reported to us, read favourably in modern eyes – notably the tale of his dining without notice with an ordinary woman in the city and laying the table himself, though they have been deliberately recast by the Macedonian historians to put him in a bad light.[93] And his comment on the Photian–Ignatian schism, if it can be attributed correctly to him, shows some wit, and a proper appreciation of Bardas's motives in deposing Ignatios: 'Theophilos [Gryllos's proper name] is my Patriarch, Photios is the Patriarch of the Caesar, Ignatios of the Christians.'[94] As an emperor in his early twenties one might expect him to have had extra-curricular interests, especially when encouraged to do so by parties such as Bardas and Basil, who for their various reasons wanted him entertained and kept away from government.

Theodora has similarly suffered from the desire of the Macedonian historians to blacken both the reign of Michael III and the regency which preceded it. She is shown as lying to her husband about the icons kept in her bedroom, and teaching her daughters to deceive their father about what happened during their visits to their step-grandmother's monastery; she is said to have ranted and raved hysterically after Theoktistos's murder and gone into a fit of sulks, refusing to be appeased by her son; she even connives in an assassination attempt on her brother Bardas, presumably in order to regain her ascendancy over her son and control of the administration, though it could have been simply out of revenge for Bardas's murder of Theoktistos. Even the anecdote of her highly successful mercantile ventures, which today would win praise for her initiative and business enterprise if nothing else, is told in such a way as to impugn her imperial status. Doubtless in some of these cases the incident has been deliberately retold in order to discredit the empress, in the same way as happened with the biography of her son Michael.[95] Nevertheless, even allowing for the bias of the sources, the picture emerges of a woman of character, who was able to exclude her brother from power without difficulty, who was not afraid to speak her mind when necessary, and who was fully capable of governing the empire.[96]

6

THE WIVES OF LEO VI (886–919)

The tetragamy issue, the question of the fourth marriage of Leo VI and Zoe Karbounopsina, was 'perhaps the most significant event of early tenth-century Byzantine political and ecclesiastical life'.[1] The question was not one of the legality of a fourth marriage, which all ecclesiastical parties considered to be totally unacceptable, but of the degree to which the needs of the empire and the will of the emperor could be accommodated by the church when necessary. The issue resulted in the church in schism, and with an empress once more regent for a minor. In this case the regency was held by an empress, the legality of whose marriage was in doubt, and who had come to power by a palace coup and overthrown the patriarch as head of the regency council. To make her position even more difficult, her son's legitimacy and right to the title of heir and emperor had been the subject of heated and to some degree unresolved controversy.

Leo VI, whose scholarly tastes were such that he became known as 'the Wise', ruled from 886 to 912. He was the son of Eudokia Ingerina, and technically the second son of Basil the Macedonian, but as he was born only four months after the wedding and Eudokia was known to have been the mistress of Michael III his paternity may rightly be doubted.[2] By his first wife Basil had had a son, Constantine, his favourite and heir to the throne, but he died in 879, and Basil was succeeded by Leo, whose paternity is therefore of importance. It would certainly demonstrate the irony of history if the founder of the brilliant 'Macedonian' house was not in fact Basil I but Michael III 'the Drunkard', the Amorian. One of Leo's first official acts was to collect the remains of Michael III and bury them with due imperial honour in the Church of the Holy Apostles,[3] which implies that at the very least he identified with Michael and is strong grounds for presuming that he thought Michael was in fact his father.

Leo is best known for his four marriages – a sign not of his licentious tendencies (though he does seem to have had a weakness for attractive women) but of his intense desire for an heir. This was of critical importance for the dynasty, since his detested brother Alexander was also childless.[4]

St Theophano

Leo's first wife, Theophano Martinakiou, does not seem to have been an ideal choice. Like Eudokia Ingerina herself she was one of the Martinakes (Martinakioi) family, the daughter of the *patrikios* Constantine Martinakios.[5] According to her *Life*, at the age of six her father found her a tutor so she could learn Holy Scripture: she soon knew the Psalms and hymns by heart and devoted herself to reading the Bible and prayer.[6] Theophano was chosen by means of a bride-show arranged by Eudokia Ingerina, her new mother-in-law, probably in the second half of 882, when Leo was nearly sixteen and Theophano fifteen.[7] As with previous bride-shows, the decision was not made by the groom-elect but by his mother. In this obviously apocryphal version of events, Eudokia is said to have selected three of the candidates and told the others to return home, presenting them with gifts and money:

> Then she took only those three with her to the Palace and made a trial of them in the bath. When she saw that the beauty of the saint greatly surpassed the others', she clothed her in imperial garments and, taking her by the right hand, went before Basil, the emperor and her consort. Casting her at his feet, she pronounced her a worthy bride for his son. And the Emperor [Leo], himself also amazed by the unexceptional beauty of the girl, took from the fold of his robe his little ring fashioned from jasper and put it on the young lady's hand.[8]

We have two versions of the marriage: Leo's statements as reported in the *Vita Euthymii* (*Life of Euthymios*) and the 'official' version of the *Vita Theophanous* (*Life of Theophano*), by an anonymous contemporary, which presents the marriage as ideal. In the *Life of Euthymios* Leo is reported as saying that 'all the Senate knows that it was not at my wish that I married her, but in fear of my father and in utter distress'.[9] His reluctance may have been caused by the fact that he perhaps already had a mistress, Zoe, daughter of Stylianos Zaoutzes the captain of the palace guard; if not, she was certainly his mistress soon afterwards, and when Theophano reported this to her father-in-law Basil he threw Leo on the ground and beat him up (Basil's past as a wrestler doubtless made this a memorable experience), while Zoe was forced to marry.[10] We can only conjecture why Eudokia chose such an unsuitable bride for her son. Eudokia may well have thrown in her lot with Basil and the Macedonians, as was only sensible under the circumstances, especially if she had joined in the assassination conspiracy against Michael. This may have resulted in her feeling antagonistic towards her son Leo, particularly as there was conflict between him and his father. Leo's funeral oration for Basil speaks of his mother in glowing terms as beautiful, aristocratic and destined by fate for the throne, but like his eulogistic portrait of his father Basil I this should not be taken literally.[11]

There was tension between father and 'son' and in 883 Leo was found to be plotting against Basil and spent three years in prison.[12] He narrowly escaped being blinded. Then on 21 August 886 Basil fell victim to a hunting accident, which left him with fatal wounds.[13] This has frequently been assumed to have been the cover for a conspiracy, masterminded by Stylianos Zaoutzes, but the fact that the *Vita Euthymii* states that Basil lived on for nine days and took no reprisals seems a serious objection to this.[14] On the other hand the Arab source Tabari specifically states that Basil was killed by his sons.[15] The practical arrangements behind the conspiracy, if indeed there were one, were probably in the hands of Zaoutzes, father of Leo's mistress Zoe, and the government now fell essentially into the hands of Zaoutzes.[16] Leo also deposed Photios as patriarch and installed his brother Stephen[17] – the idea being that patriarch and emperor would henceforth work hand in hand. The monk Euthymios, a personal friend of both Leo and Theophano, had sympathised with Leo during the reign of Basil, and after Basil's death Leo made him *hegoumenos* of a monastery, a member of the senate and *synkellos* as well as his spiritual director. There was mutual animosity between Zaoutzes and Euthymios. Zaoutzes is presented as the embodiment of evil in the *Vita* of Euthymios, while Euthymios was disliked by Zaoutzes for his influence over the emperor.[18]

Leo and Theophano had a daughter, named Eudokia after her grandmother, born soon after their marriage and before Leo's imprisonment,[19] and when she died after a few years Theophano, unhappy in her relationship with Leo, wanted a divorce. The *Vita Euthymii* implies that both Euthymios and Theophano expected that his marriage to Zoe would result from such a divorce.[20] Euthymios therefore persuaded Theophano of the sinfulness of such proceedings, and there was no official separation, but Theophano from then on lived an austere and devout life, until she died on 10 November 895 or 896 at the age of approximately thirty,[21] though presumably she continued to perform the essential imperial duties of her position. She was proclaimed a saint shortly after her death, following miracles at her tomb, and Leo built a church in her honour and a sanctuary for her relics.[22]

Zoe Zaoutzaina: 'miserable daughter of Babylon'

Stylianos Zaoutzes (or Zaoutzas in Skylitzes) was a Macedonian of Armenian descent.[23] Stylianos held the post of hetaireiarch under Basil I and according to the *Life of Theophano* persuaded Basil to release Leo VI from prison; at this point his daughter Zoe Zaoutzaina was already Leo's mistress, so he had a vested interest in Leo's well-being.[24] He was present at Basil's fatal accident in 886, which he may have orchestrated, and at Basil's death-bed.[25] Basil left him as guardian for his son and Leo swiftly promoted him: before Christmas 886 he became *magistros* and *logothete tou dromou*.[26] In 894 he received the title of *basileopator* (not because he was the father of the emperor's mistress, a relationship which though not secret could not be officially recognised, but because he was Leo's 'spiritual father').[27] He formulated much of government policy during Leo's early reign, including the legislation, and most of Leo's Novels were addressed to him. His subordinates' mishandling of Bulgarian trade helped cause the Bulgarian war in 894, and Leo seems to have been becoming restive under his management, prior to his marriage to Zoe.[28] Antony Kauleas, the patriarch who succeeded Stephen on his death, was his partisan. Zaoutzes lived to see his daughter as empress, for he died in mid-899 and was buried in the monastery of Antony Kauleas.[29]

Zoe Zaoutzaina thus had influential connections at court and Skylitzes gives the detail that she was of outstanding beauty, probably from the belief that imperial mistresses had to be unusually attractive.[30] The relationship had certainly commenced long before Basil's and Theophano's deaths: in 900 the couple's daughter Anna was old enough to marry. The *Vita Euthymii* could well be correct when it recounts Theophano's informing on her husband to her father-in-law, and the *Life* paints a clear picture of her jealousy early in their marriage, though according to other sources she apparently became resigned to Zoe's relationship with her husband and the fact that she was publicly overshadowed by Zoe, consoling herself instead with prayer and devotional practices.[31]

Zoe seems to have accompanied Leo in a semi-official capacity in Theophano's absence: the chronicle of Symeon the *logothete* speaks of both Zaoutzes and Zoe travelling with the emperor to the monastery of Damianou, while Theophano was at Blakhernai praying, and it was Zoe who informed the emperor of an assassination attempt made there by her brother Tzantes and other relatives, when they masterminded a plot against Leo's life.[32] She heard a noise while she was sleeping with the emperor and looked out the window to see what was happening, reporting to Leo that there seemed to be a conspiracy against him. Leo leapt on board ship and escaped to Pege and took prompt action against the conspirators, being for some time on bad terms with Zaoutzes.[33]

Shortly after the death of Theophano, Zoe's husband Theodore Gouzouniates died.[34] Rather than simplifying matters, this actually complicated things for the couple because Zoe was said to have murdered both the empress and her husband.[35] Despite the scandal involved, Leo and Zoe, who already had an illegitimate daughter Anna, decided to marry and the wedding eventually took place in 898. Zaoutzes, presumably from a desire to see his daughter an empress, urged that the marriage take place as soon as possible, but there was opposition from Euthymios, Leo's spiritual adviser, not because this was a second marriage but because Zoe's 'evil conduct was notorious' and if they married this would prove the rumours of their past conduct to be true.[36] Euthymios was sent off to the monastery of St Diomedes and the marriage was celebrated, despite objections from Antony Kauleas the patriarch. The ceremony was performed by a palace priest named

Sinapes, who was later deposed, and Zoe was crowned empress.[37] Zoe, however, died in less than two years, towards the end of 899 or in early 900, of 'a frightful illness and loss of her wits';[38] they had been married only twenty months. Inside her coffin she had 'the miserable daughter of Babylon' inscribed.[39] Leo built a church to St Zoe in her honour in May 900, and had his daughter Anna crowned Augusta so imperial ceremonies for which an empress was necessary could continue to be performed as usual.[40] Anna, however, was soon sent to the West to marry Louis III of Provence; her marriage was being negotiated when Leo's third marriage to Eudokia was under discussion in the first half of 900. She bore Louis a son Charles Constantine, who survived to the 960s as Count of Vienne, and she was the first of the 'new female ambassadors for Byzantium', princesses sent abroad as diplomats for the empire;[41] though illegitimate, Anna's status had been regularised by her parents' subsequent marriage, and the part she played both as 'temporary' empress in Byzantium and abroad should not be underrated.

The third marriage

In the eastern church second marriages were only reluctantly tolerated, and third marriages were even more severely discouraged: in the imperial house only the 'heretic' iconoclast emperor Constantine V had been married for a third time. Basil the Great in his canons did not allow the name of marriage at all to a third marriage, calling it *polygamia* or 'moderated fornication', and he imposed a penalty of four years before the sacrament, the eucharist, could be received.[42] Prior to Leo VI, and probably under Irene, civil law had forbidden third marriages and stated that the children of them were illegitimate.[43] In 899 or earlier Leo had himself issued a law (*Novel* 90) condemning third marriages and insisting on the canonical penalty, though allowing such marriages to be legal, while ironically in *Novel* 91 he outlawed concubinage.

Since multiple marriages were traditionally regarded with hostility by the orthodox church, Leo after Zoe's death was in an invidious position. In the *Procheiros Nomos*, between 870 and 879, Leo had joined with his father Basil in absolutely forbidding fourth marriages.[44] Even Leo's second marriage to Zoe had caused disciplinary problems within the church, and the priest who celebrated it had been deposed. Nevertheless, the patriarch, Antony Kauleas, issued a dispensation permitting Leo to marry for a third time without the normal canonical penalties, on the Byzantine grounds of 'economy' (*oikonomia*). Even the patriarch Nicholas Mystikos, who came to be Leo's main opponent on the issue of the fourth marriage, later granted that this third marriage was allowable because of the need of an empress for imperial ceremonial,[45] though this in itself suggests that there was opposition at the time. So, a few months after Zoe's death Leo married and crowned as empress the 'very beautiful' Eudokia Baiane.[46] This marriage perhaps took place in early August 900; there are no grounds for assuming that Eudokia was selected in the last of the bride-shows. Eudokia, unfortunately, died on Easter Day 12 April 901, while giving birth to a boy, who was christened Basil after his grandfather, but who also died shortly afterwards.[47] Euthymios advised the emperor that he was the author of his own misfortunes and that Eudokia's funeral should be as quiet as possible – advice which Leo ignored.[48]

The tetragamy issue

Leo had been unlucky: the pious Theophano had been imposed on him and died childless. Zoe Zaoutzaina had died less than two years into their marriage and left him with only a daughter. In spite of the canonical prohibitions and opposition on the part of some of the clergy, Leo had managed to obtain a dispensation and marry Eudokia Baiane in 900. She died in childbirth the next year. So at the age of thirty-five Leo had had three wives and still had no male heir. To make things worse, his only surviving brother Alexander, whom Leo detested and whom with some truth he suspected of plotting against him, was also childless, and their three sisters were nuns. The problem of the *tetragamia* (the fourth marriage) was a very real dynastic one for the future of the Macedonian house.

After the death of Eudokia, Leo began a liaison with a noble lady at court, also named Zoe, who is usually known as Zoe Karbounopsina ('Zoe of the coal-black eyes'). She was of good family, though we do not know her parentage: her uncle Himerios, who was *protoasekretis*, came to power with her and was appointed to the command of the imperial navy in 904 when an Arab fleet menaced Constantinople. After a further success in 905 he was then created *logothete* and in 910 led an expedition against Syria and successfully sacked Laodiceia. Her family was also distantly related to Theophanes the chronicler, and to Photeinos, *strategos* of the Anatolikon theme.[49]

Had they remained without an heir, Leo would doubtless have been satisfied with Zoe's being recognised as his *maitresse en titre*, his official mistress, and not attempted to embroil the church in controversy over another imperial marriage, like that of the 'adulterous' marriage of Constantine VI. Zoe's first child appears to have been a daughter.[50] We cannot be certain when the liaison commenced, but Zoe was certainly living in the palace as Leo's mistress in the summer of 903; when Leo was attacked in the church of St Mokios in May 903 by a dissident named Stylianos, the *parakoimomenos* Samonas was not with him because he was escorting Zoe to the palace.[51] On 3 September 905 Zoe gave birth to the long-awaited son, Constantine (VII); Zoe had become pregnant after wrapping a cord round her waist that had been measured around an icon of the Virgin at the church at Pege.[52] The fact that the birth took place according to custom in the Porphyra, the purple chamber of the palace, showed from the start that the couple intended to claim that their son was a 'porphyrogennetos' – a true imperial heir born to a reigning emperor. But the problem was how to legalise his position. The patriarch Nicholas Mystikos knew all about the situation: as Leo reminded him at this juncture, he had after all blessed Zoe's pregnancy and prayed for a male heir.[53] He too was now in a difficult position. Even though Nicholas had been an imperial private secretary (*mystikos*),[54] and was presumably appointed by Leo in March 901 as a patriarch on whose support he could count, granting a dispensation for a fourth marriage out of hand was out of the question.

Nicholas was so far successful in calming the opposition, that he orchestrated an agreement with the extremists by which Zoe was to be expelled from the palace, and in return the boy be christened in St Sophia on 6 January 906.[55] Only two of the opposition spokesmen, Arethas of Caesarea and Epiphanios of Laodiceia, remained intransigent.[56] In the event they were proved to be right, for, whatever the agreement that had been made, it was not adhered to. Both Leo and Zoe clearly realised that Constantine's legitimacy and consequently his right to the throne depended on the regularisation of their position. Therefore, three days after the baptism Leo restored Zoe to the palace with full honours, and before mid-year their marriage was celebrated by Thomas, a palace priest, and she was proclaimed empress of the Romans.[57] Nicholas wrote to Pope Anastasius in 912 that:

> The third day after the baptism was not past when the mother was introduced into the palace with an escort of imperial guards, just like an emperor's wife . . . for now not in word only but in very deed the plan concerning the wife prevailed, and the imperial marriage ceremony was – as we thought – celebrated; the very crown was set on the woman's head . . . This was what happened; and the whole City, not just the archpriestly and priestly body, was in uproar, as though the whole faith had been subverted.[58]

Thomas was of course later deposed, but apparently by Euthymios not Nicholas.[59] Leo must have considered that he had the private consent of Nicholas, but they both seem to have underestimated public indignation, marshalled particularly by Arethas of Caesarea. The canonical penalties were clear: according to the canons of Basil the Great Leo had to be banned from participation in all church services for four years, and the emperor was therefore forbidden to enter the church by Nicholas.[60] This ban lasted until February 907.

Nicholas continued to work towards finding ground for granting a partial dispensation; it was doubtless his idea to appeal to Pope Sergius in Rome for a ruling, and on three occasions in 906 he actually offered to admit Leo to the church, but withdrew these offers on each occasion, fearing a split in the church and hoping to gain the support of as many metropolitans as possible in favour of *oikonomia* beforehand.[61] He wanted Leo and Zoe to be separated until a council could be convened, at which the ruling of the papacy would certainly be in Leo's favour, multiple marriages being perfectly acceptable in the West. But Leo flatly refused to be separated from Zoe for a single day, and would do nothing to compromise her status as wife and empress. The other patriarchs were eventually to give their permission for a dispensation, as did the pope, and Nicholas seems to have had an agreement from the leading metropolitans that they would act in concord or inform him of any move they made.[62] Nevertheless there were remnants of implacable resentment within the church at Constantinople, chaired by Arethas. By Niketas Paphlagon, for example, Nicholas was called the 'rapist of the bride of Christ' (i.e. the church) because of his leniency. Arethas himself wrote to Leo: 'Why can you not now dismiss with thanks the woman who has given you the child you desired, as we dismiss a ship when her cargo is discharged or throw away the husk which has brought the fruit to maturity?'[63] The same view was voiced in retrospect by Nicholas in his letter to Pope Anastasius, in which he appears to put much of the blame on Zoe herself:

> The tyranny of his desire prevailed, and the fourth wife allured to herself the in all ways good, but, in this, evilly persuaded Emperor. The excuse seemed to be the son that [had] been born to him; though it would have been easy to adopt the child, since, as is only human, he wanted a son, and dismiss the mother, with whom from the first his connection had been illicit, together with whatever provision he cared to bestow on her.[64]

What is remarkable here is not the cavalier dismissal of the personal relationships involved, but the failure to understand the concern of Leo and Zoe that their child's status had to be above reproach, which involved the acceptance of their marriage. On Christmas Day 906 Leo was formally denied entrance at the central door of St Sophia by Nicholas. He returned twelve days later for Epiphany in 907 and was again refused: opposition clearly continued among sections of the church and Nicholas was afraid of causing a schism. Having failed to force the Constantinopolitan church hierarchy to admit him before public intervention by the Roman legates took place, on 1 February Leo had nothing to lose and exiled Nicholas and all the metropolitans.[65] He presumably had in mind the master-stroke of appointing as patriarch Euthymios, a devout monk and his own spiritual director, and thus undercutting opposition. Euthymios was already recognised as head of the ecclesiastics who were in favour of the dispensation.[66] Nicholas was forced to resign – he was actually arrested during dinner with the emperor[67] – and exiled to his own monastery of Galakrenai near Constantinople.

Although not given to ecclesiastical administration (he preferred to remain away from the capital, if possible, and seems to have given minimal time to the duties of *synkellos*),[68] Euthymios accepted the patriarchate to stop Leo legislating in favour of third and fourth marriages.[69] Later in February a council was held in the presence of the papal legates, which granted the partial dispensation to the emperor. Some of the metropolitans changed to the emperor's side, but a schism took place between the followers of Nicholas, now turned into an ardent opponent of the fourth marriage, and the new regime.[70] Euthymios agreed to crown Constantine co-emperor (on 15 May 908),[71] but deposed Thomas, the priest who performed the marriage, and he appears to have forced Leo in 907 to issue a law forbidding fourth marriages, and stipulating that they should be forcibly dissolved. Leo was received into communion, but through the last five years of his life he was only admitted as a penitent in St Sophia and not allowed into the sanctuary.[72]

Although Euthymios had accepted the patriarchate and was prepared to grant Leo's dispensation, he was not prepared to accept that the fourth marriage was legal in principle. He flatly refused the request of Zoe's relatives that he should proclaim her Augusta in St Sophia ('God forbid that ever that should be!'),[73] and even though Zoe herself wrote to him twice with the same request he replied that her name would never appear in the sacred diptychs:

> His first answer affirmed it was impossible. The second time he made no excuse. Thereupon, seized with rage, through one of the eunuchs who served her, she sent word to him: 'Are you unaware, father, what you were before, and to what honour you have acceded, through me? Then why do you not proclaim me in church, but that you disdain and disparage and make small account of me, who am joined to a prince and emperor, and have a son likewise crowned and born in the purple? Know assuredly that if I had not been cause of the whole matter, never had you ascended the patriarchal throne. Therefore be pleased to proclaim me, as the Senate has done.'[74]

Zoe's concern to see her status recognised comes through clearly here, as does her belief that it was through her that Euthymios became patriarch. When she asked that Thomas, the priest who had performed their marriage, be reinstated, this request too was rejected, and Euthymios replied that Thomas had been completely removed from the list of serving clergy.[75] In his view, she was only allowed to be married to Leo VI as an exercise of *oikonomia*.

Alexander: the 'man of thirteen months'

Leo died on 11 May 912 when Constantine was only six years old; Leo had been ill since March, perhaps from typhoid fever.[76] He appointed his brother Alexander as Constantine's guardian, although earlier he had not allowed him a share in government and had suspected him of plotting against him. Doubtless Zoe's standing was such that she could not serve as sole regent: perhaps Leo also felt that giving Alexander the official position might in some way make him more protective towards the young heir. One of

Alexander's first actions was to recall Nicholas from exile:[77] Nicholas's later claim that Leo had restored Nicholas before he died is relatively unconvincing in view of the unanimity of the other sources.[78] Zoe was expelled from the palace by her brother-in-law,[79] and with her went her friends, including the *parakoimomenos* Constantine and her uncle Himerios, who was put into prison. This Constantine was an especial favourite of Zoe: in fact, even though Constantine was a eunuch, Samonas the *parakoimomenos* who had brought him to Zoe's notice was so jealous of the affection felt for him by Zoe and Leo that he slandered the relationship between Zoe and Constantine as being too intimate. Leo therefore had him tonsured, though he later restored him to favour.[80]

Nicholas began to settle old scores: Euthymios and Nicholas's old friends, who had at first failed to support his attempts at compromise and then sanctioned the very marriage themselves, were deposed and anathematised, with Alexander's blessing.[81] Euthymios was called before a meeting of the *silentium* and treated with contempt: his beard was plucked out by the roots, two of his teeth were knocked out and he was punched, kicked, spat on and trampled before being carried off into exile.[82] Nicholas removed the pope's name from the diptychs and Constantinople and Rome were not in communion for the next eleven years. The ordination of Euthymian bishops and clergy was declared invalid and their successors were appointed. But many refused to go, and in the end, after riots and bloodshed, only four archbishops were actually dismissed.[83]

Alexander, addressed by his brother on his death-bed as the 'man of thirteen months',[84] which was taken in retrospect as a prophecy of ill-omen, was given to amusements and debauchery, and to magical practices in the hippodrome in the hope of improving his health.[85] He now dismissed his wife and mother-in-law from the palace to make way for his mistress: Nicholas showed the flexibility of his principles by himself marrying Alexander to his lady-love.[86] It must have been an anxious time for Zoe; our sources inform us that Constantine was not a strong boy and that Alexander frequently considered having him blinded or castrated, but was persuaded against this by those whom Leo had assisted.[87] Alexander's death in June 913, perhaps of cancer, must have been a relief for Zoe, even when it left Nicholas as *de facto* head of government.[88]

Zoe and Nicholas

The next six years were marked by a fierce struggle for power between Nicholas and Zoe, followed by an uneasy *entente cordiale* after Zoe emerged the victor. Alexander left a council of seven regents to govern for his young nephew, headed by Nicholas, and which included Gabrilopoulos and Basilitzes, two of Alexander's Slavic favourites. The empress was pointedly excluded.[89] Her presence on the council would not, in any case, have been palatable to Nicholas. Nicholas's position was in itself unenviable: he was responsible for protecting the interests of a monarch who, according to his viewpoint, was illegitimate and had been crowned by an illegal patriarch.

Zoe challenged Nicholas's position as regent; she was the empress and, as the mother of the young emperor, by all custom and tradition she had first claim to the regency. At Alexander's death she returned to pay him a death-bed visit, only to be expelled again to a convent by Nicholas, who also deprived her of all imperial prerogatives and made the senate and bishops sign that from henceforth they would not accept her as empress; four months later he had her tonsured as Sister Anna. When she complained of ill-health, however, he did kindly allow her to eat meat on fast-days.[90] Nicholas may initially have supported or even instigated the revolt of Constantine Doukas, Domestic of the *Scholae*, in June 913, which was only foiled by the prompt action of John Eladas,[91] one of the regency council. Constantine Doukas was killed, almost in the moment of victory, and Nicholas then brutally suppressed the remnants of the conspiracy. His purge of blinding, scourging and impaling caused general shock-waves in the capital, especially as his initial involvement in the plot was suspected and cast doubts on his loyalty to the regime.[92] Then in August the forces of Symeon of Bulgaria swept up to the land walls. Symeon demanded the crown and that the emperor should marry one of his daughters. Nicholas agreed to the marriage of the young emperor with Symeon's daughter Helena at some future date and crowned Symeon 'emperor of the Bulgarians' in a ceremony improvised with his own head-dress.[93] This marriage of course did not take place: it was against all precedent.[94] While this rapport achieved with Symeon was no doubt the result of great diplomatic finesse, the subtlety was not appreciated in Constantinople and the rapprochement with the Bulgarians again lost Nicholas popularity. Finally, because the young emperor was calling for his mother, implying that there were personalities in the palace favourable to her interests and identifying them with those of the seven-year-old emperor, Zoe managed to stage a successful coup in February 914: the sources at this point comment on her persistence and the tenacity with which she grasped at power.[95]

In her recovery of power she was assisted by John Eladas, a member of the regency council, whose invitation to Zoe to return shows that Nicholas had lost control of the council. She was to retain power as empress-regent for the next five years, and ruled with the support of the *parakoimomenos* Constantine, whom she restored to his position, and the general Leo Phokas, his brother-in-law.[96] Eladas died shortly after her return to power, and her executive was formed from Constantine the *parakoimomenos* as head of the government, his relatives the brothers Constantine and Anastasios Gongylios, who were also eunuchs, and a fourth eunuch Constantine Malelias, the *protoasekretis*, head of the imperial chancellery.[97] Symeon of Bulgaria contemptuously considered her government to be dominated by eunuchs, and in writing to him in 921 Nicholas concurs that the troubles of Zoe's regime were their doing.[98]

Nicholas's creatures were removed, notably the Slavic co-regents Basilitzes and Gabrilopoulos, on the advice of Eladas.[99] Nicholas was now deprived of political power, though he was not deposed from the patriarchate. Zoe offered it again to Euthymios, but he refused to return on the grounds that he found retirement more congenial.[100] Zoe, without a nominee with whom to replace Nicholas, instead plotted to turn him into a cipher. This was achieved without subtlety. The *Vita Euthymii* tells us that she sent fifty men 'with instructions to enter the archbishop's chamber with their swords drawn, running all about hither and thither, and with their fearful aspect and arms to terrify him'. Nicholas at once fled to St Sophia, by his own passage-way, the *Life* here caustically commenting that he had not seen the inside of the church for eight months.[101] After hiding there for twenty-two days claiming sanctuary, following unsuccessful requests to the empress for his release from asylum, Zoe finally agreed that he could resume his duties as patriarch on the following conditions: he had to stay out of politics and not come to the palace unless invited, to mention Zoe's name in church prayers, and to proclaim her Augusta.[102] Nicholas, despite all his political experience, was effectively neutralised.

While Zoe and her eunuchs held the reins of government, she still used Nicholas's skills and experience in diplomatic dispatches.[103] But Nicholas's position had changed: his letters make clear to his friends that at this juncture he no longer had the patronage with which to help them,[104] and his support of Zoe's government is at times obviously unwilling: in 915 and 916, during the build-up to the Bulgarian campaign, his correspondence shows a frenzied concern that church lands should not be appropriated to assist the state's finances, or money levied from the church to help with military expenses, as well as with the draft status of clergy.[105] Nicholas's own views of the change in his fortune are expressed in a letter to Ignatios, metropolitan of Cyzicus, probably written in 914, where he speaks of:

> this huge black cloud of distresses upon me and all the community. In face of it I have given up in despair, and endure a living death, and am weary of the sunlight, and would rather be numbered among those who are in their graves than among those who live under the sun.[106]

The Bulgarian campaign

Zoe's regency was initially a success, and its achievements have in great measure to be ascribed to Zoe herself, even though she relied heavily on Constantine the *parakoimomenos*. Her status is emphasised on the coinage of her regency where she takes the title emperor with her son, and they are called 'βασιλεῖς 'Ρωμαίων', 'Emperors of the *Romaioi*', though Constantine

Plate 12 A *follis* of Zoe's regency, with Constantine VII (l.) and Zoe Karbounopsina (r.), minted at Constantinople in 914–19. Zoe wears a *chlamys* and crown with *pendilia* and cross flanked by two pinnacles (Dumbarton Oaks Byzantine Collection: Washington DC)

VII is always shown in the position of precedence (Plate 12).[107] Zoe came to terms with Symeon of Bulgaria, as a result of which Adrianople was handed back to the Byzantines in 914;[108] Ashot, king of Armenia, was put back on his throne in 915 by a Byzantine army; and in Italy the military governor of Longobardia, who had been appointed by Nicholas, won a glorious victory at the head of an allied force over the Arabs near Capua, which greatly enhanced Byzantine prestige in the area.[109] Nevertheless, with Nicholas no longer in power, and the betrothal with Symeon's daughter not ratified, Symeon renewed his pressure on the empire and caused great destruction in Thrace, Macedonia and mainland Greece. Peace was therefore made with the Arabs, and Zoe decided to throw everything into the scales for an all-out confrontation with the Bulgars[110] – for this the levy of money, so disliked by Nicholas, was exacted from the churches, probably in 916, and all possible sources of manpower explored. In fact in a letter to Constantine the *parakoimomenos* in 915/16 Nicholas informs him that even though the treasury has suffered by the war, it would be better to sell the emperor's purple cloak than that the church should lose the revenues given them of old by pious emperors: such a theft would anger God. His views were clearly meant to be passed on to Zoe, but were ignored, and Nicholas lacked the power to orchestrate any effective or concerted opposition to these measures.[111]

The government made an agreement with the Pechenegs, that they should attack the Bulgars from the rear; Nicholas also strongly protested about the pagan sacrifice of cattle, dogs and sheep, which accompanied the conclusion of this treaty with the Pechenegs.[112] The Byzantine force was ready in August 917, the army commanded by Leo Phokas and the navy by Romanos Lekapenos. The aim was to strike into north-eastern Bulgaria, and possibly capture Preslav, but the strategy failed due to mismanagement. The Pechenegs in fact went home because of disagreements between Lekapenos and John Bogas, the military governor of Cherson. Symeon saw his opportunity, and at the river Achelous near Anchialos on 20 August 917 the whole Roman army was massacred. Leo the Deacon, writing at the end of the century, records that piles of bones lying on the ground there could still be seen in his own time.[113]

Romanos Lekapenos the admiral had already played an important part in the defeat. Now, instead of staying to rescue fugitives, he sailed for home. Symeon followed up his victory by a further attack on the capital and Leo Phokas took a force out of the city to meet him. It was taken by surprise at Katasyrtai near Constantinople late in 917 or early in 918 and the majority of the soldiers were killed: with this further defeat the last hopes of survival for Zoe's government disappeared. In addition the Arabs of both West and East immediately recommenced operations against Byzantine territory.[114] Nicholas in his capacity as patriarch wrote to Symeon pleading for moderation in his moment of victory, and even putting some of the blame on himself.[115]

Conspiracy and intrigue

The struggle for the crown now entered a new phase, and the personal influence of Zoe, never very popular, was at an end. Nevertheless, she held on to power for more than a year after the defeats at the hands of the Bulgarians. The players in this new contest for the throne were Zoe and Nicholas, Leo Phokas and Romanos Lekapenos. Zoe held an enquiry into Romanos's conduct in the campaign and he would have been sentenced to be blinded had not Constantine Gongylios and Stephen the *magistros*, two of the ministers closest to Zoe, influenced the decision to the contrary.[116] This condemnation was of course justified, but it confirmed Romanos as an opponent of the regime on the grounds of personal survival. As she had throughout her period of government, Zoe continued to rely on Phokas. It appears that his wife, who may have been the sister of her trusted minister Constantine, had died, and Zoe was thought to be planning to marry him to secure her hold on the throne: we have an elegant letter from Nicholas to Constantine, consoling him on his sister's death, dated to between 914 and 918, and it is generally assumed that this sister was Leo Phokas's wife.[117] That they planned to remarry was the sort of accusation generally made against empresses whose regime was not secure, and we need not assume it to have been true: the fact that Phokas had been married twice already might also have been an obstacle.[118] What was important was that the accusation was generally believed, even in the highest court circles.[119]

Public opinion was solidly against the rise of Phokas to the purple through marriage to the empress, and the catalyst in the circumstances was the young Constantine VII's well-meaning but politically inept tutor Theodore, who seems to have been highly suspicious of Phokas and of his brother-in-law Constantine the *parakoimomenos*. Theodore worked on his pupil's fears and persuaded him, without consulting his mother, to write to Romanos Lekapenos asking his protection against the usurpation of Phokas.

This gave Romanos the perfect excuse to intervene in the interests of Constantine VII. When Zoe discovered that the letter had been sent, the *parakoimomenos* was dispatched to tell Romanos to pay off his soldiers and disband the fleet, but instead of complying Romanos kidnapped him. At this juncture Zoe took council with her patriarch and ministers, and when she sent envoys to Romanos to complain of his behaviour, they were showered with stones by the populace. Zoe's remonstrances to her son and court, in the 'solar' (*heliakon*) of the palace, when she asked what had been going on behind her back, were countered by Theodore's reply that the rebellion had taken place to stop Phokas destroying the 'Romans' and the *parakoimomenos* the palace.[120]

Power had slipped from Zoe: her greatest mistake was that of keeping Phokas in command of the army. She also miscalculated in listening to Constantine Gongylios and Stephen the *magistros* and pardoning Romanos, after he had been condemned for high treason. Romanos was to take over the government, but Zoe was deprived of power two days before this, on 23 March 919, by Nicholas. Nicholas attempted to remove Zoe from the palace, and sent John Toubakes to expel her, but she remained there due to the pleading of her son; her embraces, tears and lamentations overwhelmed Constantine into crying that he could not bear to part with her, and his wishes overrode the orders of Nicholas. Leo Phokas, however, was deposed as Domestic of the *Scholae*.[121]

Nicholas had no intention of handing over power to Romanos Lekapenos, but when he refused to agree to a request of Romanos along these lines, he was outmanoeuvred when Constantine's tutor Theodore (presumably still suffering from paranoia about Leo Phokas) once again took a hand in proceedings and invited Romanos to sail round to the harbour of Boukoleon, the harbour of the Great Palace. On 25 March 919 Romanos staged his successful coup, sailing into Boukoleon and occupying the palace. The marriage of his daughter Helena to Constantine VII was arranged and took place on 4 May 919, when Constantine was only thirteen.[122] For his own part Romanos was appointed to the highest administrative offices, and given the title *basileopator* (father of the emperor). It is hard to believe that Zoe was not involved in the rebellion which took place shortly afterwards, ostensibly on behalf of the young emperor, which involved not only Leo Phokas, but Constantine the *parakoimomenos*, the Gongylios brothers, and Constantine Malelias, her entire executive team; nevertheless, though the revolt was crushed, Zoe suffered no repercussions.[123] Romanos became Caesar in September and was crowned co-emperor by his son-in-law in December. With this for some time the young emperor's interests went into eclipse: he was only to gain control of government in 945.

The schism is ended

Nicholas and Romanos, perhaps surprisingly, became allies, and Nicholas continued as patriarch. The question of the fourth marriage, and the schism in the church, was finally settled in July 920, when a council was summoned in Constantinople, in which the followers of both Nicholas and Euthymios participated. On 9 July the famous *Tomus Unionis* (Tome of Union) was published. The church decreed that third marriages were permissible, though there were limitations: a man over forty, for example, who already had children, was not allowed to marry for a third time. Fourth marriages were declared to be out of the question. This however was not made retrospective, and Constantine's 'legitimacy' was therefore protected. The tome did not in fact mention either Leo VI or Zoe, but dealt in generalities.[124] Jenkins has noted that every year from then on Constantine would hear read out on the first Sunday in Lent this edict implying that 'his father had been a lecher, his mother a concubine and he himself a bastard'.[125] In fact, the dynastic issues involved must have been clear to everyone; what was also clear was that Constantine's legitimacy had been protected, but only precariously.

One month later, in August 920, Zoe was deposed as Augusta and sent to the monastery of St Euthymia in Petrion, again under the name of Sister Anna. She was accused of having attempted to poison Romanos with food prepared by a *notarios* named Theokletos. This was probably not true.[126] Not that Zoe was not capable of drastic measures, but the time for such actions had passed by: they would have had little effect now Romanos and his family were entrenched in power. At this point she disappears from history.

Zoe's abilities and her government in general have been overshadowed by the issue of the fourth marriage as a whole, a perception which automatically relegates her to the status of fourth wife and subsidiary to the problem of the relationship of church and state. But this does her less than justice. In many ways Zoe achieved far more than Irene and Theodora, wife of Theophilos. From the time she was proclaimed Augusta, she had to live with the perception that she was regarded by a large, vocal and influential part of the population as an empress purely under sufferance – even the supporters of her son's imperial status, like the patriarch Euthymios, considered that her marriage had been permitted by dispensation simply to ensure the empire of an heir. Two patriarchs refused to grant her full imperial status. Her brother-in-law relegated her to a convent and even failed to nominate her as one of the regents for her son. She was again removed to a convent and tonsured by the patriarch and the head of her son's regency council. While her son had been crowned emperor in 908, Zoe must have been continually aware that any slight on her position as empress tacitly implied that his status too could be in doubt: if she were not an empress, then he, by definition, could not be legitimate.

Under the circumstances Zoe's tenacity of purpose, and still more her strength of personality, has to be admitted. It was not simply noteworthy that she could make a come-back as regent in February 914 when Nicholas's regime was becoming unpopular, and take over the government: what was really remarkable was that in so doing she could neutralise Nicholas – the patriarch and one of her most virulent opponents – as a threat, and further retain him as patriarch and compel him to work with her for more than five years. The fifty armed men who impelled him to seek sanctuary in St Sophia for over three weeks must have made an impression on him, but even the trauma of this harrowing experience must have been reinforced by the personality and abilities of the empress for the relationship to have lasted for so long. Nicholas was considered no novice to treachery: for Zoe to compel cooperation from such a man, who chose to remain in the influential position of patriarch, is no small testimony to her diplomatic and executive skills. Arethas, too, initially one of the more virulent opponents of her marriage, referred to her with respect in his funeral oration for Euthymios in 917, blaming Alexander for expelling her from the palace.[127] Her regime actually foundered on the realities of the inadequate command of the armed forces, but it should be noted that Symeon of Bulgaria was no mean enemy and was to wreak havoc on the empire up until his death in 927. Furthermore Zoe's control of government and potential opposition is shown by her continuation in power for more than eighteen months after the catastrophic defeat at the Achelous, and her diplomatic abilities and the loyalty of her executive by the fact that it was not until more than a year after his coup that Romanos was able to remove her from the palace.

While Constantine was still a minor, she had at least guarded the empire for him until he was of marriageable age and had preserved the succession of the Macedonian dynasty, even though this was to be punctuated briefly by the intervention of his in-laws the Lekapenoi. Moreover under her the empire had regained its prestige. Her achievement has to be viewed in the light of the fact that all this was achieved by an empress the legitimacy of whose marriage was generally questioned, whose past as the emperor's mistress was well known, and whose son was, strictly speaking, illegitimate. But her motives were clear: despite the fact that Constantine was not strong, it was her overriding purpose to see him survive and reach the throne. Even when the possibility of her marriage with Leo Phokas was canvassed, not one of her contemporaries questioned her motives in such a scheme. Had she been able to rely on more competent, and loyal, military leadership, and not have had to depend so heavily on eunuchs as her officials, she might well have seen Constantine reach his majority under her regency.

7

THEOPHANO (*c.* 955–76+)

With the later Macedonians we meet two empresses who had a great impact on government, not only through direct political involvement, but by their use of indirect, indeed underhand, means to remove their husbands from power. Theophano, wife of Romanos II, was directly involved in the assassination of her second husband Nikephoros II Phokas in 969, while her granddaughter Zoe Porphyrogenneta in 1034 helped to organise the murder of her first husband Romanos III Argyros to allow her to marry and crown her lover. In their successful dynastic plots, these empresses interfered very directly in the succession, showing the extent to which plots could be hatched in the *gynaikonitis* and their own capacity for intrigue and assassination in the selection and installation of a new ruler.

Theophano and Romanos II

Theophano was originally named Anastaso, but it was changed to the more suitable name of Theophano when she married Romanos II, the only son and heir of Constantine VII Porphyrogennetos, who had been born in 939 after five daughters.[1] Romanos had previously been married to Bertha-Eudokia, the illegitimate daughter of Hugo of Provence, king of Italy (927–47),[2] though the marriage, which took place in 944, was not consummated because of the age of the couple, and when Bertha died in 949 another alliance was then negotiated with Hedwig of Bavaria, niece of Otto the Great. A eunuch was sent to teach the girl Greek, but this alliance did not eventuate, and Hedwig married Burchard II of Swabia in 954. Romanos was in fact to make a totally different match, and in 955 or 956 married Theophano, a very beautiful girl who had been born in Constantinople supposedly of less than noble parentage. The contemporary sources Leo the Deacon and Skylitzes concur in noting the obscurity of her family, but we need not accept the account of the invariably hostile Skylitzes that her father was an innkeeper. Leo tells us that she was more beautiful than any other woman of her time, which might imply that she captivated the young heir who accordingly forced a *fait accompli* on his family. The reasons for

126

Theophano's selection therefore remain unresolved, though as in the bride-show tradition, appearance, rather than high birth, may have been an important factor in the choice of a potential empress.[3]

Theophano served her apprenticeship as junior Augusta under her mother-in-law Helena Lekapena. The most notable example of the involvement of empresses in imperial ceremonial in the reign of Constantine VII was on the occasion of the reception of Olga of Kiev in the Great Palace, probably in 958. On this unusual occasion, the visit of a female head of state, the empresses held a special reception for Olga and her delegation in the *triklinos* of Justinian II, at which Helena as empress sat on Theophilos's great throne, and her daughter-in-law on a golden chair at the side. They first received the seven groups of the wives of court dignitaries and then Olga and her entourage and attendants. As well as the formal banquets, Olga was also received in the empress's bedchamber for an audience with the emperor and empress and their children.[4]

Romanos came to the throne on 9 November 959 and on his accession retained Constantine's closest supporters, such as the general Nikephoros Phokas,[5] but entrusted the administration to the eunuch Joseph Bringas.[6] While Romanos has been generally portrayed as weak and pleasure-loving, his reign saw some outstanding military successes, such as the victory over the Arabs in Crete which was regained by Phokas in 961. Phokas also achieved great triumphs in Asia Minor, capturing Aleppo in December 962.[7] What part, if any, Theophano played during the short reign of her first husband is not known, and Skylitzes's assertion that Romanos and Theophano attempted to hasten their accession by poisoning Constantine VII, the attempt being unsuccessful only by chance, may be attributed to his general dislike of Theophano rather than to any basis in fact; his further suggestion that the emperor's death might have been due to a more successful second attempt is purely hypothetical.[8] However, Theophano did attempt to get Romanos to remove his mother from the palace, an exercise which was very poorly viewed by Helena, who had to resort to tears and the threat of a mother's curse to maintain her position. But Theophano did manage to have Romanos's five sisters dispatched to convents and tonsured, perhaps in the following year, though they were allowed to eat meat by special dispensation: clearly they went unwillingly.[9] Theophano had thus certainly supplanted the dowager empress, herself no stranger to intrigue, who was greatly grieved at the removal of her daughters and lived only a short time afterwards.

Theophano may have been concerned to rid the palace of in-laws whom she found uncongenial, but it is more likely that she was aiming at removing any source of influence on the rather immature Romanos. Helena, his mother, seems to have inherited the resourcefulness of her father Romanos Lekapenos: in December 944 her brothers Stephen and Constantine removed their father from power and sent him off to a monastery, and she certainly was instrumental in encouraging her husband to depose and exile her brothers, before they could depose him as well. On 27 January 945 they were arrested at dinner and sent to monasteries themselves.[10] Once Constantine VII was installed as sole emperor she seems to have worked alongside Basil the Nothos ('Illegitimate'), her half-brother, in managing at least some aspects of government. Skylitzes accuses the pair of appointing discreditable people to provincial governorships and the most important civil offices and of putting offices up for sale.[11] Theophano may also have seen Romanos's sisters as a threat: when Constantine VII fell ill, his daughter Agatha assisted him with chancellery work, not just as an amanuensis but because she understood the work and was well informed about official government matters.[12] Under the circumstances, Theophano may have felt more comfortable with them removed from the palace.

Theophano's regency

Theophano and Romanos had at least three children: the dates of the births of their two sons are debated but Basil was probably born in 958 and Constantine in 961, while Anna was born on 13 March 963, two days before her father's death; there also seems to have been an elder daughter Helena, who was old enough to be present for dessert during Olga's visit to the court.[13] Romanos had reigned for less than three and a half years and was only twenty-four when he died. He is reported as having died while hunting deer during Lent; but, according to Leo, most people suspected that he had been poisoned with hemlock (κώνειον), the poison originating from the women's quarters.[14] As he had made no provision for a regency, Theophano therefore came to the throne as regent for her sons Basil and Constantine on the authority of the senate and patriarch.[15] Joseph Bringas had administered the empire as *parakoimomenos* under Romanos II and was essentially left as head of the state. Nevertheless there was bad blood between Bringas and both the general Nikephoros Phokas and Basil the Nothos, and Theophano sided with the latter faction. This hostility was to ensure that the regency was a brief one, from 15 March to 15 August 963, and Nikephoros is recorded as having resolved on seizing the throne prior to his visit to the city in April 963 to celebrate his triumph for his victory in Crete.[16] With the support of the patriarch Polyeuktos he was confirmed in his appointment as commander-in-chief and bound by an oath not to conspire against the rule of the young emperors (an oath which he later found it convenient to forget).[17] Bringas, however, continued to plot against Phokas, attempting to deprive him of his position, and offering the throne to Marinos Argyros, commander-in-chief of the western armies. Accordingly, on the advice of his nephew Tzimiskes, Phokas decided to seize power.[18] Skylitzes gives an alternative explanation that Phokas was driven by love not only of the throne, but specifically of the empress Theophano, with whom he was in close communication. According to Skylitzes, Phokas had been having an affair with Theophano when he was in the capital and this was one of the reasons why Bringas was so ill-disposed towards him. The affair was widely spoken of and helped to exacerbate the unsettled state of affairs.[19] Judging from Nikephoros's character and tastes, this seems yet another attempt to marginalise Theophano as a wicked seductress, directly or indirectly responsible for the misdeeds of both Nikephoros and John Tzimiskes his successor.

Nikephoros Phokas was acclaimed emperor by his troops in Cappadocia on 2 July 963. He at first is said to have refused the honour, giving as an excuse the death of his wife and young son Bardas, but then was persuaded to accept and marched against the capital. Nikephoros clearly felt that he needed to secure his own position against the machinations of Bringas. The populace and patriarch supported Nikephoros, Basil the Nothos brought his 3,000 retainers onto the streets, and the opposition dissolved when Nikephoros reached the capital. He was crowned on 16 August of the same year.[20]

Leaving aside Skylitzes's report that Theophano and Nikephoros were lovers, Theophano's reason for siding with Phokas was clearly because she realised that the best chance of retaining the throne for her sons was to support Phokas, especially following his proclamation by the army. The *Historia Syntomos*, perhaps by Psellos, suggests that her second marriage may have been a consequence of her being confronted with an unstable political situation and states that, according to one of his sources, she had wished Tzimiskes, not Nikephoros, to become emperor, but Tzimiskes himself supported Nikephoros. She may, given a choice, have preferred not to remarry, and one source at least speaks of her being energetic enough to handle affairs by herself.[21] It does, however, appear that she had played a definite part in Phokas's bid for power, and according to Zonaras it was on her orders that Nikephoros came to Constantinople to celebrate his triumph in April 963.[22] The degree to which she participated in government during the months of the regency is unclear, though she is said by Skylitzes to have been involved in the poisoning of Stephen, son of Romanos Lekapenos, who had been crowned co-emperor by his father and was hence a possible contender for the throne. Stephen was in exile at Methymne on Lesbos and he died suddenly on Easter Sunday.[23] The removal of Stephen, if such it was, was an act of political consolidation of the regime, not one of personal vengeance, but the accuracy of the information must be questioned: Skylitzes associates all unexpected deaths with poison and attributes them to Theophano's agency, and it is probably as unhistorical as his statement of Theophano's and Nikephoros's affair.

Nikephoros Phokas may well have wanted to marry the beauteous empress, even if only to legitimise his own claim on the throne, but considering that he had long wanted to become a monk and was given to ascetical practices, an extra-marital liaison between them is out of the question. In fact following his accession he removed Theophano from the Great Palace to the palace of Petrion, but in the next month, on 20 September, he married her and became the protector of the rights of the two young emperors. As further evidence for his sexual continence, Leo the Deacon tells us that Nikephoros had abstained from sex and eating meat since the accidental death of his son Bardas, who had been killed by a spear while playing with a cousin: his monastic advisers now persuaded him, however, to marry and to start eating meat again. He therefore married Theophano, who was a veritable Helen of Troy in her appearance.[24] The rights of the young emperors were assured: Theophano had gained a new imperial husband, retained her status as empress, and ensured the continuation of the empire for Basil and Constantine, now aged five and three or two years respectively. Like Zoe Karbounopsina in 918/19, she had backed a general to take over the throne, but unlike Zoe she was successful.

Nikephoros II Phokas

A slight hiccup was caused by the report that Nikephoros was actually the godfather of one or both of Theophano's sons, which would make the marriage uncanonical and alarmed the devout and uncompromising patriarch Polyeuktos. Nikephoros refused to be separated from Theophano, and the situation was cleared up when it was explained, perhaps with an economical regard for the actual truth, that it was Nikephoros's father Bardas Phokas, not himself, who was their godfather.[25] Theophano was treated extremely generously by Nikephoros – she was showered with rich garments and profitable estates – and according to the Armenian source Matthew of Edessa the young emperors were treated with honour and lived in splendour in the palace.[26]

Phokas's reign was one of further military triumphs under Phokas himself and the new Domestic of the East, his nephew John Tzimiskes: Cyprus was regained for the empire, and Cilicia and Syria were reconquered; even Antioch was to fall in October 969. Theophano accompanied Nikephoros on campaign with her children in Cilicia in 964, and he left her in Drizion while he took a number of cities, including Adana.[27] The match, however, does not seem to have been an ideal one. Phokas, a widower, was fifty-one when they married and thus considerably older than Theophano; he was much given to ascetical practices, such as wearing a hair-shirt and sleeping on the floor, especially prior to the festivals of the church;[28] and his appearance, at least in the description given by Liutprand of Cremona (who had failed to negotiate an imperial match for the heir of the western empire), was not particularly inspiring:

> a monster of a man, in height a pygmy, with a fat head and little eyes like a mole. He is disfigured by a short, broad beard, thick and greying, while a short neck scarcely an inch long further diminishes his dignity. His thick, copious hair gives him a porcine look, and he

has the swarthy complexion of an Ethiopian. He is 'the sort of man you would not want to encounter in the middle of the night'.[29]

Perhaps more importantly for Theophano's opinion of her husband, Phokas during his reign lost popularity because of his fiscal policy, in which heavy taxation, inflation and increased military obligation were the prices paid for the programme of reconquest, and because of a disastrous campaign in Sicily between 964 and 967.[30] But the sources should be read with caution: Skylitzes's account of Nikephoros's reign, in particular, is deliberately slanted to put Nikephoros in the worst possible light,[31] and Nikephoros continued to be popular with the people, as the historical tradition and a cycle of songs and legends shows,[32] though aspects of his government were generally deplored by the church and aristocratic rivals. Nikephoros was made aware that his regime was unacceptable to some. After the capture of Antioch, he was warned by a monk of his approaching death; he therefore took entirely to sleeping on the floor instead of in a bed.[33] Nevertheless, according to Leo the Deacon, even at this point his relations with Theophano remained cordial, so he cannot have suspected her of any disloyalty. When she privately petitioned him on behalf of his nephew John Tzimiskes, who had been demoted from the position of Domestic of the *Scholae*, perhaps as early as 965, and was in disgrace,[34] and requested that he should be given another command and married to a wife of noble family (his previous wife Maria Skleraina having died), Nikephoros concurred. Leo comments on the fact that Nikephoros 'habitually granted Theophano more favours than were proper, under the impact of her beauty'.[35] Other sources state that relations between the couple had deteriorated, perhaps because the marriage was never consummated; Zonaras says that Nikephoros kept away from Theophano, because he had no desire for sexual relations; Skylitzes records that Theophano was the distancing partner, presumably disgusted by his puritanism.[36]

Intrigue in the *gynaikonitis*

Our sources agree that at some point Theophano and John Tzimiskes became lovers, and that in 969 they conspired to murder Nikephoros and place John on the throne.[37] Whatever Theophano's reason for having Nikephoros pardon John, John was recalled to Constantinople and told to visit the palace every day. But many of his visits were made clandestinely, through secret passages prepared by Theophano, so that they could confer secretly on how to remove Nikephoros from power. Leo the Deacon tells us that at intervals he would send her strong men, vigorous warriors, whom she kept in a secret room near her quarters, who would take part in the conspiracy. The couple agreed to use force, and in secret meetings at his home John planned the murder of Nikephoros with his fellow conspirators. When Nikephoros was warned in a note handed him by one of the priests of the court that his assassination was in view, and that he should have the women's quarters searched, a search was carried out by the chamberlain Michael. This, however, failed to explore the room containing the murderers, either out of respect for the empress, or through some neglect of duty.[38]

On the evening of 10 December Theophano, as normal, went to the emperor and told him that she was going to give some instructions about the princesses who had just arrived from Bulgaria as brides for the young emperors, but that she was coming back and that he should not close the bedchamber door for she would do that when she returned. Theophano then left, while the emperor made his customary lengthy devotions, apparently in a small chamber for meditation adjoining the Church of the Pharos, and then lay down on the floor.[39] But John's retainers had meanwhile emerged from hiding and were awaiting John's arrival on the terrace of the imperial quarters. When John sailed into the Boukoleon with his fellow conspirators (the general Michael Bourtzes, Leo Abalantes, Atzupotheodoros, Leo Pediasimos and Isaac Brachamios)[40] they were hauled up in heavy snow in a basket attached to ropes. They then entered the bedchamber and were terrified to find the bed empty; however, a eunuch from the staff of the women's quarters pointed out where the emperor was asleep on the floor, and they proceeded to dispatch him brutally. Nikephoros's head was shown to his bodyguards to prevent any violence against John who had seated himself on the throne and was acclaimed emperor.[41] John played a critical role in the actual murder, striking Nikephoros on the head with his sword, though the *coup de grâce* was delivered by one of the other conspirators, Leo Abalantes. The involvement of John and Theophano was, however, to be played up by later sources: Matthew of Edessa has Theophano actually handing John his sword and, like Michael the Syrian, John personally butchering Nikephoros.[42]

The aftermath of the conspiracy

Basil the Nothos, who appears to have fallen from his position of influence under Nikephoros, had played an important part in the conspiracy and in the acceptance of John as emperor, and was restored to the position of *para-koimomenos* as a reward. John's prompt actions prevented any resistance; he made it clear from the outset that the two sons of Romanos were to remain co-emperors, and the city was quiet.[43] But when he went to St Sophia to be crowned, the patriarch refused him entry and presented him with three ultimata: Theophano had to be banished from the palace, the murderer of Nikephoros had to be dealt with, and the measures taken against the church by Nikephoros had to be revoked, Nikephoros having forced through the passing of a decree that the bishops would not take any action in church affairs without his approval. Theophano was therefore immediately banished to the island of Prote or Prokonnesos, and Nikephoros's 'murderer' Leo Abalantes, or murderers according to Skylitzes and Zonaras who have John putting the blame on both Abalantes and Atzupotheodoros acting under the instructions of Theophano, were exiled. John was then absolved of his involvement and crowned on Christmas Day 969.[44]

Nikephoros was fifty-seven when he died, some twenty years older than the empress.[45] Moreover he rather tiresomely wanted everyone to be as virtuous and clean-living as himself and made himself offensive to those with different views. Tzimiskes, on the contrary, as well as being a noted and successful general like his uncle, was extremely handsome and athletic, despite being short, and not averse to a good time: he sometimes used to drink more than he should, was extraordinarily generous, and was given to the enjoyment of physical pleasures as well as addicted to luxury and elegance.[46] As a husband he was a better proposition than Nikephoros, who had long planned to become a monk, wore a hair-shirt, was given to lengthy devotions and used to sleep under the bear-skin of his uncle the hermit Michael Maleinos, whom he especially venerated.[47] He appears to have led an entirely celibate life, even during his marriage to Theophano, which historians consider as the major factor in her hatred for him, though he still seems to have been devoted to her.[48]

Only two of the sources even consider that Theophano's part in Nikephoros's death may have been politically motivated. Zonaras suggests that she may have been concerned for the future of her children in view of the fact that there were rumours that Nikephoros was planning to have Basil and Constantine castrated and put his brother, Leo the *curopalates*, on the throne. The *Historia Syntomos* similarly states that there was a rumour current that Nikephoros was planning to castrate her sons and leave the throne to his brother, and presents Leo as ambitious and the cause of the trouble between Nikephoros and John Tzimiskes. Theophano, tired of Nikephoros's continence and suspicious about the report, therefore decided to get rid of him. According to Bar Hebraeus too, Theophano had not wished to marry Nikephoros, and she heard that he was planning to make her sons eunuchs; hence she brought men in women's dress into the church of the palace to have him assassinated. Yahya of Antioch gives the most circumstantial account, involving a family quarrel between the imperial pair, stemming from Nikephoros's decision to leave his brother Leo, the *curopalates*, as regent while he was on campaign. Theophano thought that her sons might be at risk during Nikephoros's absence, but was unable to persuade her husband of the truth of this possibility despite repeated discussions which led to angry words between the couple. She therefore persuaded John, who became her lover, to kill the emperor.[49]

It is only fair to say that while Tzimiskes may well have seemed a more attractive proposition as a husband than Nikephoros, Theophano's part in the assassination has certainly been stressed overmuch in our sources. Certainly it was in the interests of the new regime to shift as much blame as possible onto the dowager empress, and the driving force behind the conspiracy must be assigned to a group of discontented aristocratic former supporters of Nikephoros, most notably the generals Tzimiskes himself and Michael Bourtzes. Theophano was a convenient scapegoat, and if rumours about her possible involvement in the deaths of previous family members were circulating at this time, this would have helped John and Basil the Nothos in their portrayal of her wicked treachery. Even the patriarch Polyeuktos, known for his intransigence on moral issues, had a vested interest in clearing the reputation of John Tzimiskes, though John was clearly guilty of first-degree homicide. The argument that his anointing at the coronation washed away the sin of the murder, in the same way as baptism cancels out previous sins, was pure sophistry.[50]

Theophano's exile

According to Skylitzes, Theophano did not accept her fate without a struggle and she actually managed to escape from Prokonnesos and fled to Constantinople, taking sanctuary in the great church, from where she was removed by Basil the Nothos. She was then sent to the newly created monastery of Damideia in the distant Armeniac theme. Her mother was also exiled. Theophano's removal from St Sophia was not peaceable and she is said to have 'insulted first the emperor and then Basil, calling him a Scythian and barbarian and hitting him on the jaw with her fists'.[51] Theophano was obviously upset at being ditched by her lover, who had used her as a stepping-stone to power and then abandoned her: as a member of a dynasty which began with Eudokia Ingerina who was clearly involved in the murder of Michael III but went on unchallenged to be empress of Basil I, and included Zoe Karbounopsina who had outmanoeuvred her opponents to come to power, Theophano might have expected her role in Nikephoros's murder to have been accepted or at least overlooked, but she was unlucky. John, too, had to rethink his plans. Her removal may not have been what John originally planned but he was happy to settle for it in return for ecclesiastical support. A marriage to Theophano would have legitimised John's claim on the throne. His forcible separation from her meant that he now had to seek some other alliance with the Macedonian house, and in November 970, on the advice of Basil the *parakoimomenos*, he married Theodora, daughter of Constantine VII Porphyrogennetos and aunt of the two young emperors, who was not distinguished for her beauty and grace, but who, Leo tells us, indisputably surpassed all other women in prudence and every kind of virtue. The marriage greatly pleased the citizenry, who saw it as protecting the rights of the dynasty.[52]

Theophano receives an overwhelmingly hostile press in the contemporary sources. Skylitzes calls her an adulteress,[53] and in Nikephoros's epitaph by John Geometres, archbishop of Melitene, apparently inscribed on Nikephoros's tomb in the Church of the Holy Apostles, the blame for his murder was laid squarely at her door, and he is apostrophised as 'conqueror of everything except his wife'.[54] The contrast between Nikephoros's far-flung conquests and the domestic manner of his death was a piquant one, and, in another poem by Geometres, Nikephoros states, 'I fell in the heart of the Palace, unable to flee the hand of a woman.'[55] In addition, a satirical song about Theophano's failure to marry John has been preserved in a late sixteenth-century Cretan manuscript, which records how she was exiled by her lover and made the subject of a satirical parade in the streets of Constantinople.[56] The ditty appears to reflect a procession in which Theophano, who has exchanged her coronation robe for a skin, was shown riding on a mule, and the patriarch Polyeuktos and Basil the Nothos, 'the matchmaker', are implied as being the main agents of her downfall.

After John's death in January 976 Theophano's son Basil soon brought her back to the palace, according to Skylitzes at the instigation of Basil the Nothos.[57] For Theophano to be restored to the palace by her sons and the *parakoimomenos* suggests that her reputation cannot have been too tarnished, in her sons' view at least. There she no doubt resumed her rightful position as empress, remaining the senior Augusta when her son Constantine married Helena Alypia, for Basil was never to marry.[58] A Georgian tradition made her again into a prominent figure, later directing negotiations with the Georgian prince David of Taiq following Bardas Skleros's revolt early in her son's reign, and she may have been partially responsible for supporting the foundation of the 'Iviron' monastery on Mt Athos reserved for monks of Georgian nationality: a manuscript preserved in Moscow points to her as a benefactor.[59]

Even though Theophano was certainly not guilty of all the crimes and conduct attributed to her by both medieval and modern authors, she was none the less an awesome lady. She almost certainly did not murder her father-in-law Constantine VII or her first husband, and the suggestion that as she was 'sexually promiscuous' Basil may have been her son by one of the Varangian guard is quite unsubstantiated.[60] Her involvement in the murder of her second husband, Phokas, on the other hand is well documented, and she clearly had it in mind to become empress for the third time by marrying her second husband's assassin, said by all to have been her lover. The hostility of the sources has made them reject any motive for her in this but the purely personal, but this should not be taken at face value. She may well have been motivated by the desire to protect the throne for her children in the face of a possible threat to their well-being. Theophano certainly shows the potential for intrigue possessed by a reigning empress. She is remarkable in having attempted twice to influence the transfer of power, in both cases hoping to ensure the protection of the rights to the throne of her young sons: in the case of Nikephoros Phokas her support was critical for his rise to power, while in that of John Tzimiskes she unfortunately chose a fellow conspirator who was only too willing to make her the scapegoat for his own actions.

8

ZOE PORPHYROGENNETA
(1028–50)

The Macedonian house had come to power in 867 through the assassination of Michael III, in which the new empress Eudokia Ingerina was implicated, while a hundred years later Theophano had been involved in the murder of her second husband. This was not the last display of murderous tendencies by an empress of the Macedonian house, however, for Theophano's grand-daughter Zoe was to succeed in having three husbands, each an emperor by right of marriage to her, and like her grandmother she was to have one of them removed for her convenience, in order to marry her young lover.[1] Zoe, however, succeeded in her aims, perhaps because Zoe and her sister Theodora, as brotherless daughters of Constantine VIII, were the legitimate successors and heirs of the dynasty. That was certainly how the populace saw it when Zoe's position was threatened, firstly by Michael V her adopted son and then by Maria Skleraina, the mistress of her third husband. In her murder of Romanos III, Zoe was activated by purely personal motives – overpowering infatuation for a younger man. She had no children for whom to plot, no plans for the government of the empire, only a totally egotistical concern to satisfy her own desires: the fact that Romanos was not an extremely success-ful emperor was not relevant to her plan to remove him, for Michael was not chosen for any potential imperial qualities. At least Theophano had picked on two generals for the purple, and was concerned that they protect her sons' position. Zoe was also said to have plotted against her second husband, Michael IV, and her adopted son Michael V, and to have attempted to have poisoned her husband's brother, John the Orphanotrophos, the *de facto* ruler of the empire. While these accusations need not be taken as necessarily true, they are a pointer to the deference and suspicion with which she was regarded by her contemporaries.

Zoe: the heir of empire

Theophano's son Basil II reigned for forty-nine years (976–1025), which were spent with great success in campaigns against the Bulgars and Arabs. He died in 1025 while preparing an expedition against Arab Sicily, leaving the throne to his brother Constantine, and by implication to Constantine's daughters, since neither of the brothers had made any other provision for the succession. The eldest daughter, Eudokia, had been disfigured by a childhood illness and gone into a convent.[2] The other two, Zoe and Theodora, remained in the women's quarters of the palace, clearly in a state of some mutual tension and animosity,[3] until their father Constantine VIII was on his death-bed in 1028, at which point Zoe was fifty or so years of age (she was born c. 978) and Theodora somewhat younger.[4] There had been a plan by which one of the princesses, probably Zoe, was dispatched to the West to marry Otto III, in the same way as Theophano, niece of John Tzimiskes, had been sent as the bride of Otto II in 972.[5] But the bridegroom had unfortunately died prior to the princess's arrival at Bari in February 1002,[6] and in any case this marriage would not have solved the problem of the empire's succession. The disastrous failure to make provision for the continuation of the dynasty must be attributed to Basil II's distrust of women in positions of influence and unwillingness to let in-laws interfere in the government of the empire.[7] But when Constantine's life of dissipation and enjoyment – horse-racing, gaming, hunting and the concoction of sauces[8] – was drawing to a close some-thing had to be done. The solution was somewhat drastic: after briefly review-ing possible candidates, and deciding initially on Constantine Dalassenos, Constantine changed his mind and picked on Romanos Argyros, the eparch, prefect of the city, whose suitability for the position had been generally canvassed: even if the emperor had been unwilling to plan for his eventual demise, the question of his successor had clearly been a matter of interested speculation.[9] Romanos had been quaestor and *oikonomos* of St Sophia and his background was impeccable: indeed, his sister Maria Argyropoulina had been chosen by Basil II to marry John the son of Peter II Orseolo, the doge of Venice, in 1005. Maria appears to have offended the opinion of local churchmen by her luxurious style of living, including her use of forks, for which she was seen to be justly punished when she and her family died of the plague in 1006.[10]

Perhaps in dynastic terms Romanos's age should have been considered a drawback (he was born c. 968),[11] but the only fact regarded as an obstacle to the union – that Romanos was already married – was swiftly dealt with. Romanos's wife Helena was told that if she did not retire immediately to a convent, her husband would lose his eyes. She retired, under the monastic name of Maria, and Romanos and Zoe were married and crowned in Novem-ber 1028, three days before Constantine breathed his last. Romanos must have valued Helena's self-sacrifice, for he gave her the title of *sebaste* (the Greek translation of Augusta) and made extravagant charitable donations on her death.[12] According to Skylitzes and Zonaras, Theodora was said to have been given the choice of marrying Romanos, but declined it. Her reasons were based either on the degree of kinship between them or on the fact that his wife was still living.[13]

Zoe and Romanos III

Zoe was very aware of her imperial status – Psellos comments on her arrogance, as well as on her quick temper and willingness to inflict blinding at the slightest provocation[14] – but her only recorded political activity in Romanos's reign seems to have been confined to forcing her sister to retire to the convent of Petrion. Theodora was apparently involved on two occasions in treasonable activities with Constantine Diogenes, and as Romanos was on campaign it was Zoe who scotched the conspiracy.[15] Otherwise her rank was displayed in spending as much money as possible, while Romanos attempted to show himself a great builder, general and administrator. He failed in all these, just as he had failed in the hope of founding a dynasty: the couple consulted medical experts, and Zoe even took to the use of magic amulets and other practices. When it was clear that no children were going to eventuate, he made the mistake of ignoring Zoe, not sleeping with her and instead keeping a mistress.[16] Worse, he barred her access to the treasury and made her live on a fixed allowance.[17] Being unable to squander money was a disaster for Zoe. Such insults were not to be borne by the princess of the Macedonian dynasty, who spotted in an imperial audience Michael, the handsome brother of John the Orphanotrophos, a high-ranking eunuch at the court whose title ('director of an orphanage') belies the importance of his position in the hierarchy. She was instantly struck by Michael's attractions. Being unable to control her passion, she wasted no time in inviting him to visit her and then making her intentions known to him.

The young man, Michael, despite initial objections on his part, was schooled by his brother in the arts of pleasing the empress and nature took its course. Zoe was wildly infatuated with him and the couple were discovered together in a number of compromising situations, even in bed, and Zoe was not only found sitting Michael on the throne, complete with sceptre, and embracing him, but boasted that she could make him emperor – or indeed that he was so already.[18] This was clearly what Michael had in mind.[19] The emperor Romanos's sister Pulcheria (wife of the blinded Basil Skleros), with a circle of like-minded friends, warned her brother that he might be in danger, and spoke to him of a plot against his life, but to no avail. Romanos chose to take no notice of the affair, preferring Zoe to be occupied with one liaison, rather than sleeping around more widely, as she appears to have done prior to this infatuation; at least the names of Constantine Katepanos and Constantine Monomachos were linked with hers in this context.[20] The affair with Michael was generally suspected and a matter for open discussion at the court and in the capital.[21] Romanos seems even to have encouraged the affair. If so, he miscalculated: on Good Friday, 11 April 1034, Zoe, who may have been trying to have him poisoned but got impatient for results, had him drowned while swimming in his bath by Michael's attendants. She came in, took one look at him while he was gasping his last, and disappeared to marry Michael and set him on the throne.[22]

Zoe and Michael IV

Power had returned briefly to Zoe's hands: as soon as Romanos was dead Zoe took control, behaving as if she had a divine right to the throne, though she was not concerned to seize power for herself but for her lover Michael, persisting in her desire to make him emperor instantly, and entirely ignoring the advice of all her officials and family retainers. Michael was therefore proclaimed emperor that evening and the patriarch Alexios the Stoudite, summoned by 'the emperor', was surprised on his arrival to find Michael dressed in cloth-of-gold sat on the throne beside Zoe awaiting him. The payment of 100 lb of gold, 50 lb to the patriarch personally and 50 lb to the clergy, removed any scruples he might have felt in marrying the couple, though widows were legally obliged to observe a year's mourning.[23] Pleased to fall in with the empress's wishes, the whole city joined in rejoicing at Michael's accession, Romanos was forgotten, and the populace blithely and light-heartedly acclaimed Michael as emperor, the day after Romanos's death.[24]

Michael IV Paphlagon ('the Paphlagonian') and Zoe settled down as the new imperial pair, and initially the relationship seems to have been a happy one, with Michael arranging amusements for her.[25] But soon things went sour: Michael may have been feeling guilt at his predecessor's murder which intensified the epilepsy from which he suffered.[26] At the instigation of his brother John (whose rapacity, like that of Michael's other brothers, was well developed) he also seems to have been afraid that he too might be thought dispensable like Romanos, and on the pretext of a plot by Zoe had her confined to the women's quarters. The captain of the guard had to give permission for any visitors, after careful scrutiny. Her eunuchs and the most trustworthy of her maid-servants were dismissed, baths and walks were curtailed and she was physically confined to her rooms. Michael himself stopped seeing her, and she had to put up with the threats and abuse of his brothers, which she did, let it be said, with gentleness and diplomacy. Psellos himself applauds Michael's fear of Zoe, and considers it justified, lest some 'accident' should happen to him too. Significantly, despite all these precautions, the emperor's family were still extremely afraid of her, viewing her like a lioness who had only temporarily laid aside her ferocity,[27] and clearly she was still considered a force to be reckoned with.

Whether or not Zoe had been involved in a plot against Michael, she seems to have accepted the situation philosophically, though not without one attempt to remedy the situation. Skylitzes reports in some circumstantial detail how in 1037 she attempted to have John the Orphanotrophos poisoned by a doctor who was giving him a purgative. One of her eunuchs,

Sgouritzes, successfully corrupted the doctor with large presents and promises of immense wealth in return for his cooperation, but the plot was discovered when one of the doctor's servants reported it to John. The doctor was exiled to his home at Antioch, the *protospatharios* Constantine, who had provided the poison, was exiled, and the empress was kept under closer supervision.[28] While Skylitzes is inclined to attribute all sudden deaths to poisoning, especially by a woman, in this case his account reads plausibly; John had schemed relentlessly for his own and his family's accession to power, in defiance of Zoe's rightful status as heir, and was responsible for her ill-treatment.

In default of a successor to Michael, whose epilepsy forecast a short reign, Zoe had been prepared to sanction in *c.* 1035 the choice of Michael's nephew, another Michael, known as Michael Kalaphates ('the Caulker'), as heir to the throne. This solution was suggested by John the Orphanotrophos, who now had the government of the empire in his own hands and who feared that his brother's death might leave him out in the cold as far as power was concerned, and whose treatment of Zoe had not made him popular with her or her supporters. On this occasion Psellos puts into John's mouth a speech to his brother which explicitly outlines Zoe's rights as heir to the empire, as well as stressing the way her generosity had won her subjects' hearts.[29] The young Michael was adopted by Zoe, who does not seem to have had much choice in the matter, and proclaimed Caesar, or official heir. John the Orphanotrophos now believed that, even should his brother die, the family fortunes were secured.[30] But Michael V, at least according to Psellos, possessed no consideration for benefactors and no gratitude, though he was skilled at dissimulation. Accordingly, though he succeeded Michael IV without conflict, he planned treachery towards his uncle John and the empress from the inception of his reign.[31] Michael IV prepared for his death by building a magnificent church and monastery of Sts Kosmas and Damian, as well as charitable foundations such as a *ptochotropeion* (hostel for beggars or the destitute) and a home for repentant prostitutes, who swarmed for admission.[32] As he was dying on 10 December 1041, Zoe, who had obviously been released from confinement and had clearly forgiven Michael his crimes against her, heard that he had been tonsured and was close to death in his monastery of Kosmas and Damian. Despite her appreciation of her regal status she crossed the city on foot, against all precedent, 'overcoming very natural disinclination', to see him: however, he refused her entry.[33]

The adopted son: Michael V

The legitimatist principle had worked successfully in Zoe's choice of a husband and an adopted son, and Michael V succeeded Michael Paphlagon without trouble. But Michael's accession only came about because of Zoe's consent: between 10 and 13 December 1041 Zoe was empress and in control, and only after consideration did she decide to carry out the plans of Michael IV and his family, even though Psellos speaks of John and his family manoeuvring her into agreeing to their plans:

> Heaping upon her all the flattering names suitable to such a moment, they assured her that their nephew would be emperor only in name, while she, apart from the title, would have, besides, the power that she inherited by right of descent. If she so desired, she would administer the State in person; if not, she would give her orders to him [Michael] and use him as a slave-emperor to do her bidding.[34]

Zoe was convinced by their flattery and deviousness, as well as by their solemn oaths, and agreed. Michael V was thus crowned three days after the death of Michael IV, with Zoe's full approval, which was vital to the new emperor's accession. Skylitzes makes it clear that the realm was seen to have devolved back upon herself and that she was free to make whatever decisions she chose concerning the succession, in the interim taking decisions with the help of the eunuchs who had served her father, and ensuring, before she agreed, that Michael would treat her correctly 'as sovereign lady, mistress, and mother'. She also used the opportunity, according to Skylitzes, to banish three of Michael's uncles: the Orphanotrophos was sent off to the monastery of Monobatai; Constantine, the domestic of the *Scholae*, was removed from his position and dispatched to his estates in the Opsikion theme; and George the *protovestiarios* sent to his estates in Paphlagonia. The first few days of Michael's reign were also marked by his constant repetition of the deferential expressions, 'the empress', 'my mistress', 'I am her servant', 'whatever decision she makes', as if he were simply a junior colleague, and Zoe was of course acclaimed before him.[35] There are no known coins of Michael V's reign, but patterns for *histamena* have been identified as belonging to his reign, which, significantly in this regard, depict not Michael but Zoe.[36]

Unhappily for Zoe herself, however, she was no luckier with her adopted son than with her husbands. Michael began to feel hatred for her and could not bear to hear her name mentioned in public proclamations before his own; he therefore refused to listen to her, did not allow her access to the council chamber and – worst of all – barred her from the treasury. Furthermore, she was kept under surveillance and her ladies-in-waiting were controlled by the emperor.[37] After only five months of rule Michael, who also removed the members of his family who had brought him to power, except his uncle Constantine, then planned to get rid of her entirely and, after consulting his councillors and then his astrologers, had her sent to a monastery on Prinkipo on the night of 18/19 April 1042, asserting that she was plotting against him and attempting to poison him.[38] On this sad occasion, Psellos puts into Zoe's mouth a speech while on board ship which is hardly historical, but which well expresses her image in popular eyes as the heir of the Macedonian house. Apostrophising the great ruler, her uncle Basil the Bulgarslayer, she is said to have lamented, with tears in her eyes, as the ship bore her away:

'It was you, my uncle and emperor, you who wrapped me in my swaddling clothes as soon as I was born, you who loved me, and honoured me too, more than my sisters, because, as I have often heard them say who saw you, I was like yourself. It was you who said, as you kissed me and held me in your arms, "Good luck, my darling, and may you live many years, to be the glory of our family and the most marvellous gift to our Empire!" It was you, also, who so carefully brought me up and trained me, you who saw in my hands a great future for this same Empire. But your hopes have been brought to nothing, for I have been dishonoured . . . I beg you, watch over me from Heaven and with all your strength protect your niece.'[39]

Whatever the realities of the situation, Psellos here intends us to believe that Basil had Zoe trained for her position as purple-born princess and possible heir of the empire, and his statement in her defence at this point, that she had no intention of meddling in state affairs – indeed could not when in exile with one lady-in-waiting – implies that under other circumstances she might well have intended to do so.[40]

Nevertheless, Michael saw her as a threat, she was tonsured and he informed the senate of the state of affairs, and of the occasions on which she had supposedly plotted against him, on one occasion being caught red-handed, but which he had previously concealed out of deference to the senate. Psellos roundly dismisses these statements as lies, which however won the senate's approval, though later events show that many of them had reservations. Nevertheless, a feeling of anxiety gradually permeated the city, with the empress's banishment being a topic of intense debate by the elite, the palace staff, the clergy, businessmen and especially the imperial guard, who doubtless felt Zoe's safety was their prerogative. The indignation grew, while the populace was the first to action, inspired not only by a concern for Zoe's safety but for her imperial status relative to that of Michael V.[41] According to Skylitzes, the catalyst was Michael's public proclamation of 19 April read by the eparch Anastasios in the forum of Constantine, stating that Zoe had been banished for treason and Alexios the patriarch deposed.[42]

Revolution

The populace erupted in defence of the empress. A voice from the crowd shouted 'We don't want the cross-trampling Kalaphates as our emperor, but our ancestress and heir and mother Zoe'. The crowd yelled 'Dig up the bones of the Kalaphates!' and broke into violent rioting. There followed three days of anarchy, in which women and children joined, Psellos describing how they took to the streets in defence of the empress:

'Where can she be,' they cried, 'she who alone is noble of heart and alone is beautiful? Where can she be, she who alone of all women is free, the mistress (δεσπότις) of all the imperial family, the rightful heir to the Empire, whose father was emperor, whose grandfather was monarch before him – yes, and great-grandfather too? How was it this low-born fellow dared to raise a hand against a woman of such lineage?'[43]

Psellos bears witness to the frenzy with which the mob, including young girls and children, attacked the mansions of the emperor's family and the palace.[44] Michael and his uncle Constantine the *nobilissimos* determined to recall the empress, who remained remarkably pacific, even failing to blame Michael for her misfortunes – perhaps because she feared retribution at his hands. In fact Michael and Zoe appear to have done a deal – Zoe would remain a nun, and acquiesce in his decisions, and on these terms they made a covenant to face the danger together.[45] Whether or not this was known to the people at large, when Michael showed Zoe to the people in the hippodrome still dressed in her nun's robes instead of her imperial regalia, the situation was only exacerbated, with some pretending not to recognise her.[46]

As the rebels were afraid that Zoe might be able to persuade her supporters to give up the struggle, a new plan was adopted. Zoe was ignored, as in any case she was in the Great Palace where they could not reach her, and the populace, inspired by the palace eunuchs, members of the senate and Constantine Kabasilas, one of Constantine VIII's retainers whom they appointed as their 'general', rushed to the monastery of Petrion and released Theodora. She at first refused to cooperate, but they dragged her from the sanctuary, clothed her magnificently, made her sit on a horse and with due honour led her to St Sophia, where homage was paid to her, not just by a fraction of the people, but by the whole elite as well. At some point after midnight on 20 April, everyone proclaimed her empress together with Zoe.[47] The report was that some 3,000 people died in the rioting of 19–21 April, though popular songs expressed the people's satisfaction at the turn of events.[48]

Theodora seems at this point to have taken charge of the situation. While in St Sophia she mustered her power-base, deposing Michael V and appointing her officials.[49] Despite the fact that Zoe seems to have been prepared to pardon Michael, Theodora was inexorable: Psellos was a member of the party as her supporters went to seize Michael and his uncle Constantine as they sheltered as suppliants in the Stoudios monastery. Theodora and her supporters clearly saw that Zoe was so jealous of her sister that she would rather see a stable-lad on the throne than share the throne with her herself. Hence, fearing that she would promote Michael to the throne a second time, they determined to obviate this possibility and have him blinded. An order from Theodora was received to remove the refugees from sanctuary, and Skylitzes records that while Zoe recoiled from giving the order to have them blinded, Theodora had no such qualms. It was on her orders to the new eparch Nikephoros Kampanarios that the punishment was inflicted.[50]

Theodora and Zoe

For the third time the empire had returned to Zoe, but this time with a difference. Power now rested not just with Zoe but with Theodora too, and their joint status needed to be defined. With one empress in the Great Palace and one in St Sophia, the senate was unable to make a decision. Zoe was the elder, while it was due to Theodora that the revolt had been brought to a conclusion and who had saved them from the 'tyranny' of Michael V. Interestingly, the problem was solved by Zoe, who took the initiative according to Psellos, greeting her sister with affection, and agreeing to share the empire with her:

> The question of the government was thus resolved by agreement between them. Next, Zoe brought her to live with herself, escorted by a procession of great magnificence, and made her joint-ruler of the Empire. As for Theodora, she lost none of her respect for her sister, nor did she encroach on her prerogatives. On the contrary, she allowed Zoe to take precedence and, although both were empresses, Theodora held rank inferior to the older woman.[51]

Zoe may have been making a virtue of necessity, because in Skylitzes's account Zoe was ordered by the populace to co-rule with Theodora, and she did so unwillingly, while Zonaras says that Zoe was excessively jealous of Theodora and the senate had to persuade her. It was, however, Zoe who spoke to the senate and to the people, asking their advice as to what should happen to the emperor, Michael V.[52] They were acclaimed as *autokratores* ('emperors'),[53] and there followed seven weeks of joint rule, from 21 April to 12 June, in which Zoe and Theodora issued coinage and ruled jointly.[54] Psellos complains that 'they tended to confuse the trifles of the women's quarters with pressing matters of state', which implies in view of Theodora's later reign that Zoe set the tone of this period of joint rule; certainly, as the junior empress, Theodora sat slightly behind Zoe during their court appearances.[55] But members of Michael's V's family were removed from their positions, and the sisters abolished the sale of offices, raised many to the senate, and offered the people generous donatives. The *nobilissimos* Constantine was brought back from exile and examined concerning the appropriation of taxes: he revealed that he had 5,300 lb of gold hidden in a cistern in his house, and was then returned to exile (Theodora's priorities may perhaps be seen in this interrogation, for she was noted for her parsimony). The eunuch Nikolaos was made domestic of the *Scholae* of the East, and Constantine Kabasilas *dux* of the West, while George Maniakes, an excellent choice of appointment, may have been given the rank of *magistros* and sent back as commander-in-chief to Italy.[56]

Psellos stresses that all was peaceable, with the civilian population and military working in harmony under them, and that outwardly their government cohered with that of previous emperors. They settled lawsuits, made judgements on administrative and taxation issues, held audiences with ambassadors and performed all other duties. Most of the talking was done by their officials, but when necessary they gave orders in a soft voice, and replied to queries either on their own judgement or by the advice of their officials. Nevertheless, Psellos believed neither of them temperamentally fit to govern: they knew nothing of administration nor were capable of sustained argument on political matters, though Theodora later showed herself well aware of the priorities and practices of government in her own reign.[57] The major change in government, notes Psellos, was a larger-than-life quality: the officials began to act as if they were on stage and had been promoted to better roles, while money was poured out lavishly. Zoe in particular opened up the treasury, and 'any trifles hidden away there were distributed by her with generous abandon'. She was the sort of woman who could exhaust a sea teeming with gold-dust in a single day, remarks Psellos. Still worse, army pay and expenditure was diverted to courtiers and sycophants.[58]

This extraordinary co-regnum was ended by Zoe. She was tired of sharing government with Theodora, and they disagreed over the division of power. A further criticism of Psellos refers to the sisters' desire for power *vis-à-vis* each other: 'The love of power, or the lack of power, the apparent freedom and the absence of supervision, and the desire for even greater power – these were the things that made the emperor's apartments into a *gynaikonitis*.'[59] The sisters seem to have been unable to distinguish between substance and image, a situation exacerbated by their strong feeling of rivalry and jealousy for their own status and prerogatives. If Zoe and Theodora also differed radically on matters of policy and expenditure that was a further factor in the unreality of the drama taking place. There was a strong feeling that the empire needed an emperor, while Zoe herself, unlike Theodora, was not temperamentally inclined towards government and may well have been tired of the details of administration. The situation was clearly becoming unstable and rumour and gossip were rife, with the supporters of the empresses canvassing their respective right to rule. Some thought that Theodora should be empress, on the ground that she had championed the people in the face of Michael V, and had never married; others thought that Zoe, because of her experience and imperial rank (having been crowned empress at her marriage to Romanos), was more suitable, not least because she was more attracted to power.[60] In the face of these spreading rumours, Zoe, now aged perhaps sixty-four, therefore staged a coup and seized all power for herself a second time.

For Zoe it was inconceivable that she should rule single-handed and the next move was to find a suitable husband. According to Psellos, 'she sought in marriage someone not from afar but from nearby, from her own court circle, thus keeping power for herself'. The choice of a possible emperor sparked wide-ranging debate, and numerous candidates of the Constantino-politan nobility were rejected for one reason or another.[61] Constantine Dalassenos, a front-runner for the position, was considered unsuitable despite being a most handsome man. Summoned to the palace on some other matter, he was presented to the empress as a possible candidate on his visit. Unfortunately he spoke with abruptness, displaying bold ideas on the subject of the empire, and showing himself incapable of compromise. He was there-fore ruled out, thus losing his chance of the throne by marrying Zoe for a second time. Another possibility, the handsome Constantine Katepanos, or Artoklines, whom Zoe was said to have had an affair with in Romanos's lifetime which was rumoured to have recently resumed, was also considered. He, however, died suddenly, some said poisoned by his wife who did not choose to lose him to the empress while she was still alive, perhaps a reflec-tion on the fate of Helena, the first wife of Romanos Argyros, who had departed for a convent and seen her husband marry Zoe. As a result, Zoe decided on the twice-married Constantine Monomachos as the winning candidate.[62]

Constantine IX Monomachos

Monomachos was no stranger to Zoe, for Zoe had been fond of his company during Romanos's reign, when they engaged in clandestine meetings to the disgust of most of the courtiers, and his second wife had been the daughter of Romanos III's sister Pulcheria. He had even been seen as a possible successor by Michael IV because of his intimacy with Zoe.[63] Zoe spoke on the subject to her bodyguard and personal staff, and, when they were unanimous in their agreement, she informed the senate of her plans, and Constantine was recalled from his exile on Mytilene, where he had been sent on suspicion of treasonable activities by John the Orphanotrophos.[64] This marriage, com-ments Psellos, marked the end of the authority and personal intervention of the empresses in state affairs.[65] Their failure to work cooperatively, and Zoe's desire to oust her sister, had brought about the end of their joint rule, which lasted less than two months. However, during this period they had fulfilled all imperial duties, including issuing their own coinage, on the reverse of which was depicted the busts of the empresses, wearing jewelled robes with deep collars and the traditional crowns with triangular plaques, holding between them a *labarum* (see Plate 17, p. 163).[66]

Constantine, another civil aristocrat without military experience like Zoe's first two husbands, was encumbered by a mistress, Maria Skleraina, who had spent seven years in exile with him on Lesbos, putting all her assets at his disposal.[67] Otherwise there were no impediments, apart from the fact that each was marrying for the third time, and for this reason the patriarch Alexios did not personally perform the ceremony, though he did crown Constantine. Instead a priest called Stypes married the couple; the marriage is depicted in the Madrid manuscript of Skylitzes (Plate 13), in which the patriarch is shown crowning Constantine: Zoe as empress is already wearing her crown.[68] Maria Skleraina was to be an important figure at court for the first years of Constantine's reign. She was the great-granddaughter of Bardas Skleros, who in the reign of Basil the Bulgarslayer, Zoe's uncle, had three times proclaimed himself emperor, and she appears to have been the widow of a *protospatharios*: she has been identified with the *protospatharissa* Maria, daughter of Skleros, who is recorded in the *Peira* of Eustathios as demanding repayment of 62 lb of gold from an impoverished patrician Panberios who was indebted to her, receiving instead the *charistikion* of the monastery of St Mamas.[69]

Constantine and Skleraina, the cousin of his second wife,[70] were devotedly attached to each other and were unable to endure separation. Only the fact that canon law prohibited third marriages, as well as their degree of relationship, meant that their liaison remained unregularised. Zoe was therefore faced with a situation which she may not have anticipated, though it is unlikely that such a long-standing relationship would have gone unnoticed. Skleraina was also possessed of political dreams. Not only was she interested in seeing Constantine on the throne, 'no less than himself' (says Psellos) 'she was sustained by hopes of power; nothing else mattered if only in the future she might share the throne with her husband. I say husband because at that time she was convinced that their marriage would be legally sanctioned, and all her desires fulfilled when Constantine, as emperor, overruled the laws [banning third marriages].'[71] When Constantine did reach the throne, but on the condition of attaining it through marriage to Zoe, she despaired altogether, even of losing her life, expecting that Zoe's jealousy would bring retribution on herself.

Constantine must have been sure of his position for he was quite prepared to lay his cards on the table and is said to have spoken openly to Zoe about Skleraina even at their first meeting. He was regardless of the possibility that Zoe might be jealous, as well as of all entreaty from disinterested parties. Like Romanos III he was possessed of an outspoken sister Pulcheria, one of the cleverest women of Psellos's generation, but his conduct was exactly contrary to her 'excellent advice', for at this very first meeting with Zoe he not only spoke to her of Skleraina, but mentioned her as his wife, rather than as a prospective mistress, as well as one who had suffered much at the hands of the imperial family. He therefore begged Zoe to recall her from exile and grant her reasonable privileges. To this quasi-bigamous proposal Zoe

Plate 13 The marriage of Zoe and Constantine IX Monomachos: coronation of Constantine. (Taken from A. Grabar and M. Manoussacas, *L'illustration du manuscrit de Skylitzès de la bibliothèque nationale de Madrid*, Venice: Insituto ellenico di studi byzantini et post-byzantini)

immediately consented, being according to Psellos too old to be sexually jealous, though it is more likely that she was expecting some such request and was prepared to be complaisant. To her surprise (and initial dismay), therefore, Skleraina received two letters, escorted by an imperial bodyguard, one from Constantine, written the day after his marriage and on the day of his actual coronation, and one from Zoe, promising a friendly reception and encouraging her to return to Constantinople. In other words Zoe not only knew of the liaison at the time of their marriage, she actively encouraged Skleraina to join Constantine, though she might not have anticipated the degree to which Skleraina was to become involved with the imperial family.[72]

The 'ménage à trois'

Skleraina at first, with an 'undistinguished' bodyguard, moved into an inconspicuous house at Kynegion, which Constantine treated as a private residence of his own so that he would have grounds for frequent visits. Around it he began important construction works, the complex of St George of Mangana south-east of the Great Palace, to justify his time, and entertained the members of Zoe's faction who accompanied him with a table loaded with delicacies outside the house (the menu being chosen by themselves). In this way he mitigated the indignation they felt at the way he was treating their empress, and they had a reason for actually finding excuses for Constantine's visits when they saw him debating pretexts for another one. In the end, Constantine stopped keeping his assignations a secret, and openly lived with Skleraina, treating her not as a mistress, but as his wife. Psellos comments that the liaison had a strange air of unreality about it: 'whether one saw what was going on with one's own eyes or merely heard of it from others, it was hard to believe' – clearly Constantinople must have been buzzing over the affair.[73] St George of Mangana ended as a vast foundation of buildings and gardens, with a palace, a monastery and church of St George, a home for the elderly, a home for the poor, a residence for foreigners and a hospital, as well as the school of law. This was combined into an independent financial institution as a bureau of public finance (*sekreton*). Among other things, it possessed a wheat mill, a bakery, real estate in the capital and extensive lands in the provinces. The concession of this *oikos* (foundation), in other words the surplus of the financial income, was assigned to Skleraina (Plate 14).[74] On her arrival Constantine had also sent her enormous sums of money as gifts, and Skleraina's financial resources are shown by her gift of 10 lb of gold to St Lazaros Galesiotes, with which the saint built a church to the Theotokos.[75]

Eventually Constantine summoned up the courage to suggest to Zoe that Skleraina move into the palace, and she was soon installed. Even though Zoe consented to her publicly living there as Constantine's mistress, Constantine

Plate 14 A seal of the *sekreton* of St George the Tropaiophoros (Mangana), *oikos* of
the *sebaste* Maria Skleraina, mistress of Constantine IX Monomachos, here
called the '*hyperperilambros* ("most brilliant") and *eutychestate* ("very
felicitous") *sebaste*', 1042–5 (Dumbarton Oaks Byzantine Collection:
Washington DC)

was concerned to protect her to the full, and an official document was drawn
up in which Zoe promised to treat Skleraina with due honour:

> A treaty of friendship was set out in a document and an imperial
> pavilion built for the ceremony of ratification. In front sat Zoe, Con-
> stantine, and Skleraina, while the Senate filed in to witness this
> extraordinary contract, blushing and for the most part talking in
> undertones. Despite their embarrassment, the senators still praised
> the agreement as if it were a document sent down from heaven. They
> called it a 'loving-cup' and lavished on it all the other flattering
> epithets that deceive and cajole frivolous and empty-headed persons.
> The contract being signed and the oaths administered, she who had
> hitherto been only a lover, was now introduced to the private apart-
> ments of the palace, no longer called 'mistress', but 'My Lady'
> (δεσπότις) and 'Empress' (βασιλίς) officially.[76]

What surprised everyone, including presumably Constantine, was that
Zoe evinced no emotion at this, but warmly embraced her new partner, and
Skleraina was accorded by the empresses the title of *sebaste* (the Greek translation of 'Augusta') at Constantine's instigation. From this point, Skleraina
took rank after Zoe and Theodora as a quasi-empress, being called *despoina*,
mistress, like them and taking her place behind them in official processions.[77] She even discussed the same problems with the emperor as did Zoe
(though on occasion he allowed himself to be influenced more readily by
Skleraina, the 'junior empress', τῇ δευτέρᾳ βασιλίδι). Their living-quarters
were settled in very civilised manner, with Zoe's, Theodora's and Skleraina's
apartments all adjoining Constantine's. Skleraina's were the more private,

and Zoe never visited her husband without first ascertaining whether he were alone.[78]

Skleraina's influence on Constantine cannot now be ascertained, but she certainly used her influence to promote the career of her brother Romanos Skleros: Skylitzes tells us that her relationship with Constantine accounted for the high rank of her brother.[79] Zoe and Theodora were flattered by presents made from the fund, presumably the *oikos* of St George of Mangana, which Constantine had especially given Skleraina from which to make presents to win the sympathies of courtiers of either sex and the two empresses in particular, who showed no resentment at her promotion and participation with them in imperial ceremonial.[80] It is even possible that Skleraina had borne a daughter to Constantine prior to his accession, which would have made her position at court more prestigious; this princess was to marry Vsevolod of Kiev at some point after 1046 and to give birth to Vladimir II Monomachos in 1053.[81] Skleraina appears to have been good company, and as she was prepared to flatter and pander to the tastes of the empresses she was not unwelcome. She was not extremely attractive (though she had a beautiful voice); on the other hand she was susceptible to flattery about her appearance which again implies the relationship to have been widely known, not least because Constantine diverted streams of wealth in her direction with lavish generosity. Due to the fact that she knew everyone was talking about her, she developed a very sensitive ear, ready to hear comments reflecting on her appearance and behaviour. Psellos speaks highly of her speech, in particular her beauty of expression, the sweetness of her diction and the grace in her manner of telling a story, though part of the point of this anecdote is doubtless to emphasise his own learning and ubiquity at court, for he is pleased to tell us that she had frequent conversations with him about Greek mythology.[82]

However, there were popular fears for the safety of the empresses. Constantine's well-known devotion to his mistress led to a spontaneous popular revolt on 9 March 1044, when a sudden cry went up as Constantine prepared to mount at the Chalke Gate for his ride to the shrine of the Holy Martyrs: 'We don't want Skleraina as empress, nor our mothers, the purple-born Zoe and Theodora, to be killed for her sake.' Only the prompt action of the elderly empresses gesturing from the palace saved Constantine from being lynched.[83] Psellos himself suggests that Skleraina's original ambitions may have justified such fears, but these were not realised and the *ménage* in the palace worked quite amicably. Perhaps she was satisfied with the status and recognition she had achieved as the emperor's concubine: had Constantine not already been married three times it might have been a different matter. Nor did she and Zoe have any real ground for conflict: Zoe was not sexually jealous, or concerned with her rival's position at court. She did not have any interest in Monomachos's imperial concerns, according to Psellos, but preferred to leave government in his hands and be relieved of all responsibility in this direction.[84] The fact that Constantine tended to rely more on Skleraina's advice, therefore, would not have been too inflammatory.[85] Nevertheless, the relationship caused concern outside the palace: Zoe and Theodora were after all the legitimate 'rulers' and were seen as linked with Monomachos in sharing the imperial dignity. John Mauropous, in a letter to Constantine asking him to spare the soldiers who took part in Tornikios's revolt in 1047, speaks of Constantine, Zoe and Theodora ('our most holy mistresses and empresses') as an indivisible triad.[86] When Constantine celebrated his triumph over the rebel general George Maniakes in 1043, Zoe and Theodora were sat either side of him, though it was not usual for empresses to be present at triumphal processions and ceremonies: their presence highlighted the fact that they were the source of Constantine's imperial authority.[87]

Monomachos was still making plans for Skleraina's future: 'It is possible that the emperor intended to found an empire for her in the future – at least there was much talk of it. How it was to be done I do not know, but he certainly cherished ambitions in that direction.'[88] After all, in the nature of things, Zoe could be expected to predecease Skleraina. But as it happened the liaison ended with Skleraina's untimely death *c.* 1045, after severe chest pains and asthma. She was buried in the Church of St George of Mangana, and Constantine was later buried not by Zoe but beside her.[89] Constantine was overwhelmed with grief at her death,[90] and part of the estate at Bessai which belonged to St George of Mangana was donated by Constantine to St Lazaros Galesiotes, in return for prayers for Skleraina (now deceased) and himself.[91]

Psellos declines to describe the emperor's grief in the *Chronographia*, though we have a lengthy composition in verse (446 lines) on Skleraina's demise written by Psellos, where, in the *persona* of Skleraina's mother, he dwells on the relationship between the 'empress' (*despoina*) and Constantine. The poem ends by advising the emperor to take comfort in the empresses Zoe and Theodora and makes no attempt to tone down the nature of the relationship.[92] In fact in the *Chronographia* he inserts his description of Zoe's occupations after the narrative of Skleraina's liaison with Constantine, implying that Zoe amused herself with such pursuits while Constantine was occupied with his mistress. He closes the description of Zoe's appearance and occupations with the comment, 'Let us return once more to the *despoina* and Constantine. Perhaps it may be the readers' wish that we rouse them from their slumbers and separate them.'[93]

Zoe as empress

Zoe did in fact have other interests, which Psellos describes at some length. The statement that she left the administration of the empire entirely in Constantine's hands implies that she could have interfered if she wished, and it is true that she by no means renounced her imperial status or the very real power at court that it brought. Her generosity and ability at emptying the treasury were remarkable, and she was much given to inflicting blinding on those who committed even the slightest error. Indeed Constantine had to countermand her orders in this regard, or many men would have been blinded for no reason. But Psellos stresses his personal knowledge of her absolute ignorance of public affairs, and the way her judgement was warped by the vulgar and tasteless extravagance prevalent in the palace; while implying that she was not without some intellectual advantages he makes it clear that her addiction to vulgar pursuits detracted from her regality.[94]

Instead of matters of imperial concern, Zoe occupied herself with more practical pursuits. Her rooms in the palace were constantly filled with boiling pots and pans, making ointments and perfumes, and she refused to spend time in the normal female pursuits of weaving and spinning. As contradictory as ever, she enjoyed ribald buffoonery, while at the same time being very pious, with a particular devotion to Christ Antiphonetes. Most of all, she was dedicated to spending money, and was the most generous of women: an especial key to her favour was praise of her family, especially the deeds of her uncle Basil II. The treasury emptied faster than revenues could come in. The right to empty the treasury was in Zoe's view an integral part of the perquisites of the heir to the empire: courtiers who wished to flatter her – and Psellos states that many did – would throw themselves on the floor at her approach, as if struck by lightning at the sight of her, and she would reward them magnificently with 'chains of gold' (on the other hand over-effusive thanks would see the recipient in chains of iron instead). At least in old age, Zoe was not especially vain, as she disdained cloth-of-gold, necklaces, diadems and the beautiful heavy robes, normal for her rank, preferring instead thin dresses. But that does not mean that she was not appreciative of the effect of her appearance and majesty on others, nor above being flattered on those grounds.[95]

She clearly was beautiful and a commanding figure, even in old age when Psellos knew her – in her heyday plump, though not very tall, with a perfect figure, large eyes and imposing eyebrows, golden hair and a beautifully white complexion. Clearly, even as an old woman she was imposing, with her smooth skin, though her hands were unsteady and her back bent.[96] The famous depiction of Zoe on the panel in the south gallery of St Sophia (Plates 15, 16), in which she offers a legal document to Christ, while Constantine offers a donation of money, is evidence for her appearance, and for her perception of it, in old age, showing her as fair-haired, with a plump, skilfully made-up face and wearing sumptuous court attire.[97] It also acts as a statement of Zoe's imperial status, as empress and legitimate heir of the empire.

On the grounds of Psellos's description of her passion for inventing and preparing perfumes and unguents Zoe has been generally assumed to have been greatly concerned with her appearance:

Plate 15 Zoe, from the panel in the south gallery of St Sophia depicting her with
Constantine IX Monomachos (photo: Dumbarton Oaks, Washington DC)

Her own private bedroom was no more impressive than the work-
shops in the market where the artisans and the blacksmiths toil, for
all round the room were burning braziers, a host of them. Each of her
servants had a particular task to perform: one was allotted the duty of
bottling the perfumes, another of mixing them, while a third had
some other task of the same kind. In winter, of course, these operations were demonstrably of some benefit, as the great heat from the
fires served to warm the cold air, but in the summer-time the others
found the temperature near the braziers almost unbearable. Zoe herself, however, surrounded by a whole bodyguard of these fires, was
apparently unaffected by the scorching heat. In fact, both she and her
sister seemed to be by nature perverse. They despised fresh air, fine
houses, meadows, gardens; the charm of all such things meant
nothing to them.[98]

154

Plate 16 Detail of Plate 15

155

But the nature of this information is contradictory: why, after all, if she had lost all desire to charm and all interest in her appearance – a fact mentioned again later[99] –·should she spend her time manufacturing cosmetics? Rather than assuming that this workshop was concerned with personal ointments which helped to keep Zoe free from wrinkles even at the age of seventy, it is possible instead that she was involved in marginal magical practices, with a religio-political rather than a cosmetic aim in mind.[100] Psellos continues his description of Zoe with an account of her fervent piety, especially with regard to a certain icon of Christ which she had commissioned, a copy of the icon of Christ Antiphonetes in the Church of the Virgin in the Chalkoprateia. This icon was so lifelike that it responded to questions put to it by changing colour, and foretold coming events.[101] Psellos reports that he often saw Zoe clasping it and talking to it as if it were alive, or lying on the ground in front of it beating her breasts, tearing at them with her hands: 'If she saw the image turn pale, she would go away crestfallen, but if it took on a fiery red colour, its halo lustrous with a beautiful radiant light, she would lose no time in telling the emperor and prophesying what the future was to bring forth.' Psellos continues by discussing the qualities of certain perfumes which drive away evil spirits, commenting that precious stones and certain herbs and magical ceremonies have the power of invoking deities, and stating that Zoe was not involved in pagan practices, but offering to God 'the things we regard as most precious and solemn'.[102] The logical conclusion is that these perfumes and ointments were offerings, and confirmation of this is provided later in the *Chronographia*, where Psellos tells us again that Zoe was not interested in the things that appeal to women – spinning and weaving – but on one thing alone: 'the offering of sacrifices to God. I am not referring so much to the sacrifice of praise, or of thanksgiving, or of penitence, but to the offering of spices and sweet herbs, the products of India and Egypt.'[103] So it appears that the manufacturing process in her apartments was for the purposes of offerings in the context of divine worship, very probably connected with the Antiphonetes icon and its 'magical' divinatory properties: a borderline activity no doubt in conventional religious terms, but one that was surely not without precedent among women of the imperial family.[104]

Zoe died in 1050, perhaps at the age of seventy-two, after catching a fever. Before her death she made a final statement of her own imperial standing by remitting debts and granting an amnesty to condemned criminals, and taking for the last time the chance to squander wealth from the treasury: Psellos comments that it poured forth gold like a river.[105] She was buried in the church that she founded in honour of Christ Antiphonetes,[106] and Constantine (who chose to be buried next to Skleraina) is shown as desolate, shedding tears at her tomb, and even wanting to pay her divine honours. Psellos is scathing about his interpretation of the growth of a mushroom on her tomb as a miracle showing that her soul was numbered amongst the angels, though other courtiers were less intellectually honest and supported Constantine's belief through fear, or through hope of gain from their flattery.[107]

Zoe had four times been the channel for the renewal of imperial power, legitimating emperors by marriage or adoption.[108] She had on occasion been at the mercy of those whom she had associated with herself in power, but has been generally underestimated as a political figure: 'Empress Zoe, though historically significant (along with her sister, Theodora) as the last in the line of the Macedonian dynasty, was politically a pathetic figure, more concerned with unguents, ointments and the marriage bed than with the affairs of state.'[109] This judgement is less than fair, both for Zoe and certainly for the politically adept Theodora. Episodes like the murder of Romanos, in which she played a decisive role, have been played down because of Zoe's status as imperial heir (whereas in the case of Theophano her involvement in Nikephoros's murder was considered heinous). Moreover, even the *maîtresse en titre* Skleraina had imperial ambitions, and it is inaccurate to say that Zoe's female contemporaries, as described by the chroniclers, remained figures of the *gynaikonitis*: they were not confined to quarters of their own, nor were they excluded from political comment. Imperial politics were inseparable from the person of the emperor and women of the imperial family had every chance to express an opinion on events, and many of them did.[110] Zoe and Theodora were in a unique position as the legitimate descendants of the dynasty, and that Zoe did not take any overt interest in government was entirely her own choice. Her sister Theodora, however, chose differently, and with some success, while the transfer of power to Michael Paphlagon, Michael Kalaphates and Constantine Monomachos had in each case depended completely on Zoe's own judgement and wishes.

Part III

EMPRESSES AS AUTOCRATS

9

THEODORA, THE LAST
MACEDONIAN (1042–56)

Zoe's death in 1050 was not the end of the Macedonian dynasty, for Theodora remained in the palace. Theodora had long been overshadowed by her sister: she was not as beautiful, though she was cheerful and a better talker, 'curt and glib of tongue',[1] and was less flamboyant and more placid (far more self-controlled, and almost dull, comments Psellos).[2] Her main interest appears to have been counting her money, and she was far more restrained in her generosity than Zoe, though Psellos comments that her resources were more limited.[3] Historians, like her contemporaries, have tended to ignore Theodora, but she was still a force to be reckoned with, as Constantine Monomachos found to his cost. Indeed, she was not just a satellite to Zoe, and in fact made one of the more successful rulers of the eleventh century.

Theodora as revolutionary

Initially on Zoe's marriage to Romanos III in 1028, Theodora had remained in the palace and shared in imperial honours, except that, not being empress, the privilege of acclamation was not extended to her, and her position was inferior to that of Zoe. Romanos granted her titles and imperial favours, but even her lower rank excited her sister's jealousy, and Zoe had her removed from the palace to a convent, according to Psellos after certain people had spread malicious rumours about her.[4] Theodora may well have been given the chance to marry Romanos – in which case she, and not Zoe, would have become empress – and turned it down; Zoe should clearly have taken precedence as the elder, but Constantine and his advisers must have been aware that Zoe was past child-bearing age and that in this case the younger sister might perhaps stand a slightly better chance of continuing the dynasty. Certainly at Romanos's accession she was placed under the guard of John the *protonotarios*, presumably to ensure a smooth transition of power, perhaps implying that there were suspicions as to her loyalty. Within a few months, in the first year of the reign of Romanos III, she was to be charged with involvement in the conspiracies of both Prousianos and Constantine Diogenes. Prousianos was suspected of plotting against Romanos, probably early in 1029, with the aid of Theodora and his mother Maria, the 'zoste patrikia', the highest rank for a court lady. Prousianos and his mother were dispatched to monasteries, and he was blinded. Shortly afterwards, before the end of October 1029, Constantine Diogenes, *dux* of Thessalonika and Romanos's nephew by marriage, was accused of a conspiracy. He was first made *strategos* of the Thrakesion theme, and then brought back to Constantinople and imprisoned; he was later blinded. His fellow conspirators were named as John the *protospatharios* and *synkellos*, Daphnomeles a patrician and general, and Theodora, who was then removed to the convent of Petrion.[5] Zoe had her suddenly tonsured in the following year on the grounds that this would prevent any further plots and scandals: nevertheless, she seems to have been further involved with Constantine Diogenes, who planned to escape to the Illyrikon theme in 1030 while Romanos was in Asia Minor preparing for his second invasion of Syria. Zoe was informed of the plot by Theophanes, metropolitan of Thessalonika, and had the conspirators Diogenes, the metropolitan of Dyrrachion and the bishop of Peritheorion seized, though the latter were later released by Romanos. Diogenes was brought to the palace of Blachernai for interrogation by the eunuch John, later the *orphanotrophos*, where he committed suicide.[6]

During the reigns of her in-laws Theodora was not simply an adjunct of the imperial house, she was a focus for conspirators and possibly an instigator of revolt in her own right. To what extent the disagreement between the two sisters may have brought about such a state of affairs cannot now be decided. But even in her convent, according to Psellos, Theodora was treated with courtesy and retained the semblance of majesty in Romanos's reign, though she was forgotten by Michael IV and his nephew.[7] Despite her initial unwillingness to become involved in the popular riot of 19 April against Michael V, she was quick to act and quite prepared to take responsibility. Once she had been taken from her convent and acclaimed in St Sophia, it was on her orders, in the face of Zoe's hesitation, that Michael V and Constantine the *nobilissimos* were removed from the monastery of Stoudios and blinded, and she may also have been responsible for inflicting summary punishment later on John the Orphanotrophos, who on 2 May 1043 was blinded in his monastery, it was said on Theodora's orders and against the wishes of Constantine IX Monomachos: John died on the thirteenth of the same month.[8] It was his machinations that had brought Michael IV to the throne, at a time when Theodora might have expected to take a hand in government, and she can hardly have approved of his attempts to keep the throne in his family.

After Theodora had reigned jointly with Zoe for seven weeks (Plate 17), she was ousted by Zoe's coup of June 1042, when Zoe took power for herself and then associated Constantine Monomachos with her as her husband. Theodora may well have been planning something for herself along the same lines (at least the instability of the regime was apparent to contemporaries),[9] but under Constantine Theodora remained in the palace and was treated

Plate 17 A *histamenon* with busts of Zoe (l.) and Theodora (r.) holding a *labarum* between them and wearing crowns with *pendilia* and alternating triangular plaques and pinnacles; the obverse shows the Virgin with a medallion of Christ. The legend reads 'Mother of God, help the empresses Zoe and Theodora'. Minted at Constantinople in 1042 (Dumbarton Oaks Byzantine Collection: Washington DC)

by him with respect, being associated in processions and official functions alongside her sister. The 'crown of Monomachos' depicts Theodora together with Zoe in full imperial regalia, and a miniature in a manuscript of the Homilies of St John Chrysostom (Codex Sinait. gr. 364) shows Constantine flanked by Zoe and Theodora (Plate 18): the trio are described as 'the shining trinity of earthly sovereigns'. Zoe is dressed in red and Theodora in blue, and Zoe is shown with dark hair in two plaits: unfortunately Theodora's face is considerably damaged. However, her regalia match Zoe's, the only distinction being that while both are described as Augustae and porphyrogennetae, Zoe is additionally given the epithet 'most pious'. Rays descend to the heads of Zoe and Theodora from the hands of the Christ above the trio, while rays from his feet reach Constantine through a crown.[10] Clearly, therefore, Theodora possessed all visible imperial prerogatives in Monomachos's reign. Together with Zoe she conferred the title *sebaste* on Skleraina, and she seems to have been content with the state of affairs. Skylitzes's statement that she was involved in the blinding of John the Orphanotrophos shows that contemporaries saw her as possessed of some influence, though, significantly, Theodora was seen as ill-disposed to Monomachos during her reign.[11]

Zoe and Theodora clearly liked entertainment, and one of Psellos's criticisms of Constantine IX was his acquiescence in their luxurious, laughter-loving habits. In fact he took care to provide them with every amusement.[12] It cannot be entirely fortuitous that the 'crown of Constantine Monomachos', now in Budapest, shows Zoe and Theodora flanked by dancing girls, for like Constantine they dearly loved entertainment, which was available at the court in many forms. Psellos considers Constantine quite unusual in preferring to be amused by nonsense-talk or stammering rather than by music, singing, dancing or mimes.[13] An example of the type of humour enjoyed by the empresses is described by Psellos and gives an unexpectedly uninhibited view of the imperial court. Romanos Boilas, a courtier and favourite of

Plate 18 Zoe, Constantine IX and Theodora (Codex Sinait. gr. 364, f. 3r). (Taken from J. Spatharakis (1976) *The Portrait in Byzantine Illustrated Manuscripts*. Published by Brill, Leiden, The Netherlands)

Constantine, used to entertain them in the women's quarters by jokes, banter and mime:

> Indulging in all kinds of silly talk, he maintained he had been born of the elder sister. Further than that, he swore most solemnly that the younger sister, too, had given birth to a child. His own birth, he said, had taken place thus – and then, as if recalling how he had been brought into the world, he gave a description of her labour, with shameless details. His most witty anecdotes, however, concerned Theodora's accouchement, the conversations she had during the pregnancy, and the manner of her delivery. These foolish women, captivated by the clown's stories, allowed him to come and go as he pleased by secret doors.[14]

After Zoe's death, however, Theodora came into conflict with Constantine, who was still devoted to pleasure and frivolity, and showed signs of wanting to marry his mistress, who was an 'Alan' or Georgian princess hostage at court. This would have been his fourth marriage, a thing not to be tolerated, and Theodora peremptorily put her foot down, both on these grounds and because she was not prepared to accept this insult. The girl, who had broken out into precious jewels, curiously shaped necklaces and bracelets, had been given the title *sebaste*, and acquired an imperial bodyguard and important revenues. She even performed the part of 'empress' at receptions for her father's envoys from Georgia, but the liaison had to remain unofficial.[15] On a further occasion, when Constantine's favourite, Romanos Boilas, made an attempt on the emperor's life *c.* 1051, according to Psellos because he was in love with this mistress of Constantine, Constantine wanted to pardon him, refusing to take the plot seriously. Boilas, however, who was a senator and commander of the imperial bodyguard, was exiled on the insistence of Theodora and Constantine's sister Euprepia, and both of them 'instead of being agreeable constantly criticised the emperor's stupidity'.[16] Boilas was recalled ten days later because the emperor could not do without him.

Theodora *despoina*

When Constantine died in January 1055 of a cold caught when bathing in his favourite pool, Theodora pre-empted discussion by taking the throne herself as the last of the Macedonian dynasty. At this point, though still at court, she seems to have been in relative retirement, and Constantine failed to consult her about possible successors, fixing on Nikephoros Proteuon, governor of Bulgaria, following the advice of his main counsellors the *logothete* John Leichoudes, the *protonotarios* Constantine, and Basil the *epi tou kanikleiou*. Nevertheless, her advisers, Niketas Xylinites, Theodore and Manuel, presumably members of her retinue, encouraged her to act decisively. When she learnt that the decision about Nikephoros Proteuon had been made, she at once left the emperor at Mangana and returned to the palace by warship. Using her purple-born status as a spring-board to sole rule, as well as the fact that her character was well known, she won over the support of the imperial bodyguard, and was acclaimed emperor ('*autokrator*'). Constantine was seriously worried at the news, but was unable to do anything about it; his illness took a turn for the worse and he died 'cursing his fate' on 11 January 1055. He was buried in his own foundation of St George of Mangana.[17]

Theodora thus, as Skylitzes remarks, took over her 'ancestral rule', and made an exceptionally good ruler until she died in August 1056, especially bearing in mind that our sources are prepared to criticise a regime with a woman in charge. Nikephoros Proteuon was held in Thessalonika and then sent to a monastery in the Thrakesion theme, while Theodora removed his supporters, confiscating their property and banishing them. Initially she promoted eunuchs to the most important offices, and rewarded her supporters: Theodore was made domestic of the eastern *Scholae* and sent off to cope with the Turks in place of Isaac Komnenos. Niketas was made *logothete tou dromou*, and Manuel *droungarios* of the Watch.[18]

Psellos notes with some surprise that instead of associating one of the leading noblemen in power with her, she preferred to reign on her own, explaining this by her observation of her sister's experiences with her husbands. She therefore ruled in her own right, with the help of her retinue and officials, quite openly taking on the role of a man.[19]

> She herself appointed her officials, dispensed justice from her throne with due solemnity, exercised her vote in the courts of law, issued decrees, sometimes in writing, sometimes by word of mouth. She gave orders, and her manner did not always show consideration for the feelings of her subjects, for she was sometimes more than a little abrupt.[20]

Her failure to issue the customary donatives to the people and army on her accession roused a certain resentment, though this was quelled by the explanation that she was simply resuming the throne, rather than being installed for the first time.[21] Here was a public display of her well-known parsimony, and it is interesting to note that she was not afraid to break with custom when she chose. More generally, rule by a woman was considered improper, and her appointment of clerics, deemed a masculine privilege, and the fact that the empire was ruled by a woman, roused the enmity of the patriarch Michael Keroularios, whom once she was firmly in power Theodora refused even to meet and perhaps planned to depose.[22] After at first relying on her eunuchs, she then deliberately went outside of the circle of her courtiers and appointed Leo Paraspondylas as her chief minister, with the titles *synkellos* and *protosynkellos*, whom Psellos treats with less than justice perhaps for personal reasons: Paraspondylas, like Theodora herself, was inclined to be curt, especially with people who failed to come to the point.[23] Psellos was certainly at court at the time and alleges that she recalled him from his self-imposed exile as a monk and that he was one of her advisers, having been consulted by her about confidential dispatches and private affairs even in the lifetime of Constantine IX.[24]

In an emergency her regime coped well: when early in her reign the rebel general Bryennios brought his army to Chrysopolis, her supporters seized and exiled him.[25] A long life was foretold for her, because she remained physically upright, and her mental powers were more than equal to long spells of work, and she took her duties seriously, studying problems beforehand on occasion, while on others she was capable of considering them and clearly expressing her opinion without previous deliberation.[26] Psellos judges her reign successful,[27] though criticising her for her naivety in believing that she would live for ever and failing to make provision for the succession.[28] A severe gastric disorder warned the court of the need for some decision, and on the advice of her councillors as she was dying she consented to the choice of the elderly and inept general Michael VI Bringas (or Stratiotikos), selected by her officials not so much for his capability as for the fact that he would protect their interests; he was crowned as her successor on 22 August 1056.[29] Her death on 31 August finally marked the end of the Macedonian dynasty.

Theodora is remarkable for having assumed government in her seventies, and for having succeeded so well, without any formal training. It appears, however, that she had long had her eye on the throne. While she may have chosen not to marry Romanos Argyros out of moral considerations, she was thought to have been implicated in two revolts early in his reign, which implied her dissatisfaction with her own position, and she was quick to take charge in the events of April 1042, make executive decisions and establish herself as empress. The fact that she had a well-organised body of supporters suggests that even in the convent she had not been idle. The co-regnum with her sister failed to work because of their suspicions of each other's ambitions, and clearly Zoe's method of proceeding was not to the more parsimonious Theodora's taste. But even in the reign of Monomachos she remained entrenched in the palace, and was ready and willing, as well as competent, to reassume the purple on his death. Theodora was aware only too clearly of her status as purple-born princess: she was one of only three emperors in this period to term themselves 'porphyrogennetos' on their coinage.[30] Finally acclaimed sole 'autokrator', she ruled as an emperor – the first woman since Irene to do so. More remarkably, except in the initial stages of her reign, she does not seem to have relied on her eunuchs, but on normal ministers of state. An object lesson of what can be achieved by tenacity of purpose, Theodora was a fitting end to the Macedonian dynasty.

10

EUDOKIA MAKREMBOLITISSA
(1059–78+)

With Eudokia Makrembolitissa, niece of the patriarch Michael Keroularios,[1] and second wife of Constantine X Doukas (1059–67), there emerges the first of a number of women of Byzantine birth, who, despite unexpectedly reaching the throne, wield power once there with confidence and finesse. In this Eudokia was to be followed by Alexios Komnenos's mother Anna Dalassene, and Euphrosyne Doukaina. Indeed, Eudokia was one of the more masterful of Byzantine empresses, and Psellos, who knew her well and liked to think of himself as one of her most intimate advisers, points out that her conduct resembled that of an emperor: her pronouncements had the imperial note of authority.[2] Eudokia, the daughter of John Makrembolites and Michael Keroularios's sister, was also a literary lady,[3] as well as the mother of seven children by Constantine Doukas, one of whom died in infancy.[4] Two of these, Constantios and Zoe, were porphyrogennetoi born after Constantine's accession, and she was to have two further sons by her second husband Romanos IV Diogenes.

Constantine X and Eudokia

Constantine and Eudokia came to the throne on the abdication of Isaac I Komnenos in 1059, who, two years after replacing the elderly Michael VI Stratiotikos on the throne, was himself persuaded to abdicate in favour of Constantine Doukas, president of the senate. Constantine had also been a potential candidate for the throne in 1057, but had bowed out in favour of Isaac who had superior support from the army. But Isaac's programme of reforms in the army and bureaucracy offended too many vested interests and in the autumn of 1059 Psellos, against the very clearly expressed wishes of the empress Aikaterina, daughter of John Vladislav of Bulgaria, was able to persuade Isaac that he was ill and should retire to a monastery.[5] This left the throne clear for Constantine, who may have first offered it to his brother John who turned it down.[6] Constantine had previously been married to a daughter of Constantine Dalassenos, but she died before he came to the throne (the family was unlucky, for her father had twice missed out on marrying the empress Zoe). After his first wife's death, to prevent any scandal Constantine Doukas married Eudokia Makrembolitissa. This was probably before 1050, since they had five children before their accession. It was a good match. The Makrembolites family had bureaucratic connections in the capital, and in the early 1050s the patriarch Michael Keroularios was at the height of his power:[7] he worsted Constantine IX over the issue of the schism with Rome in 1054, the empress Theodora was unable to depose him, and he was responsible for the abdication of Michael VI Stratiotikos and the transfer of power to Isaac I Komnenos in 1057.

When Constantine fell ill in October 1066, he entrusted the regency to his brother, the Caesar John Doukas, and the patriarch John Xiphilinos. On this occasion he recovered, but when his death approached in 1067 he decided on Eudokia as the regent for their children, of whom he was extremely fond: Psellos, who likes to picture himself as a close friend of the emperor, describes him as a family man, joining in his children's games, laughing at their baby-talk and romping with them.[8] Eudokia had already been given the title Augusta,[9] and it is not her choice as regent which is surprising but that on the earlier occasion Constantine had made other arrangements excluding her.

Psellos's picture of Eudokia has to be seen through the medium of his flattery of her son Michael VII, whose tutor he was and in whose reign he was writing.[10] In addition, Psellos, who was an old friend and 'spiritual brother' of the empress's father,[11] in one letter calls her his 'niece',[12] while he speaks of Constantine Keroularios, Eudokia's cousin, as his nephew.[13] In a flattering letter to the empress, written apparently during the reign of Romanos IV, Psellos also points out that he was her father's closest friend and that Eudokia had often called him her uncle.[14] Psellos also takes care to put his own conduct during the reign in the best possible light, which further distorts his portrait. Nevertheless, the picture emerges of a woman of intellect and foresight, and he introduces her as a lady of 'noble birth, great spirit, and exceptional beauty',[15] who, when she initially takes on the role of regent, behaves in a suitably modest and decorous manner: 'neither in the imperial processions nor in her own clothing was there any mark of extravagance', as he implies might have been expected of a normal, more fallible, empress.[16]

No excuse should have been needed for Constantine's decision to leave the regency to his wife, but, perhaps in view of events and her later remarriage, Psellos takes care to tell us that Constantine considered Eudokia as the wisest woman in the world, and that he felt that no one was more qualified to educate their sons and daughters.[17] Nevertheless, Constantine must have had suspicions of her intentions, if not of her qualifications for ruling. He clearly felt it necessary to exact a promise from her that she would not remarry and that she would do all in her power to guard the throne for their children. A similar guarantee was required from the senators that they would accept no other emperor but his sons. Eudokia's oath was made in writing in the presence of the patriarch, a church synod and the senate, shortly before Constantine died on 21 May 1067, and was witnessed by the patriarch, John Xiphilinos. It stated that she would not only be faithful to the memory of her husband (that she 'would not defile their marriage bed'), but protect her children's interests as heirs to the throne, guarding them from all obstacles that might endanger their reign. Furthermore, she had to swear that she would not bring her own cousins or relatives into government but leave it in the hands of Constantine's brother John Doukas. Should she break her oath and remarry, the patriarch, or his successors, would subject her to anathema.[18]

Clearly Constantine foresaw a potential threat to the dynasty. The cousins in question were presumably the two nephews of Keroularios, Nikephoros and Constantine, who were correspondents of Psellos and already in positions of importance in the hierarchy: Constantine appears to have been the *logothete tou genikou*.[19] While Constantine Doukas surely did not suspect her of putting her family's interests before those of her children, he obviously considered that she would be liable to make use of the skills of her cousins and promote them to positions in which they would be able to undermine the long-term interests of the dynasty. The oath was to ensure that the government would remain in the hands of Eudokia and her children, assisted by John Doukas, without the intervention of Eudokia's in-laws or outsiders, whom she might bring to the throne by marriage. In the event Constantine's forebodings were proved correct: Eudokia did remarry, and her remarriage (or at least the reaction of the members of the Doukas family to it) did endanger the dynasty. But it could be argued that the oath itself, and the consequent need for secrecy and intrigue, did little but complicate events and provide material for propaganda for the Doukas family to use against Eudokia and Romanos, her second husband.

Eudokia as 'supreme ruler'

The empire was thus entrusted to Eudokia and her two sons Michael and Constantios, both minors. The transfer of power went smoothly. Constantine may even have prepared the way for this regency, for Eudokia appears on Constantine's silver and copper coinage, while the children are not shown, even though Michael and Constantios were co-emperors; both the absence of his sons and the presence of Eudokia are unusual.[20] Moreover, she was given titles of importance on the coinage, signifying her role as *basilis*, and allowed a degree of collegiality with Constantine: on his silver coinage, the *miliaresion*, for example, she and Constantine are together called '*pistoi basileis Romaion*', 'faithful emperors of the *Romaioi*', while on one type of the copper coinage she apparently stands in the place of honour, on the spectator's left, though her hand is placed on the *labarum* below that of Constantine.[21] In the silver octagonal reliquary of St Demetrios in Moscow, a scene on the lower zone of rectangular panels shows a half-figure of Christ crowning or blessing an emperor and empress, identified as Constantine X and Eudokia. Eudokia's inscription reads, 'Eudokia in Christ the Lord, Great Empress (*megale basilis*) of the *Romaioi*', and she holds an orb. The title 'the great' usually implies the senior empress, though here it does not mean that she is equal to Constantine. It does, however, suggest that her status was not unlike that of a co-emperor or successor to the throne. Certainly she was a major figure in the dynasty prior to Constantine's death, and the fact that she was linked with him in the term 'emperors of the *Romaioi*', implies that she was an Augusta of more than usual importance.[22] Constantine may have thought that the dynasty would only survive through her, while still feeling the need to circumscribe her actions after his death.

The couple's eldest son was Michael VII. His age is not known, but in 1067 he was long past his youth[23] and must have been born before 1050. He was not, therefore, technically a minor, as emperors had been known to assume the throne at sixteen. Nevertheless, neither he nor the rest of the family made any objection to Constantine's proposal, and Eudokia became supreme ruler ('τῶν ὅλων ἐγκρατής'),[24] in charge of the whole administration, ruling in conjunction with Michael and Constantios, her first and third sons (the porphyrogennete Constantios, the third son, had been proclaimed emperor at his birth and hence ranked above Andronikos, his elder brother).[25] The experience of John Doukas was there to help her if she needed it, but she preferred not to entrust the administration to other hands. While she may have taken the position of emperor, '*basileus autokrator*',[26] it is more likely that her rule was technically that of a regent, while in practice all power was centred in her.

> When the Empress Eudokia, in accordance with the wishes of her husband, succeeded him as supreme ruler, she did not hand over the government to others . . . [but] she assumed control of the whole administration in person . . . She made herself conversant with all her duties, and wherever it was practicable she took part in all the pro-cesses of government, the choice of magistrates, civil affairs, revenues, and taxes. Her pronouncements had the note of authority which one associates with an emperor. Nor was this surprising, for she was in fact an exceedingly clever woman. On either side of her were the two sons, both of whom stood almost rooted to the spot, quite overcome with awe and reverence for their mother.[27]

Constantios, who was born after his father's accession, was still a child, but Michael at least was of an age to rule. Nevertheless he left the whole administration to his mother. Psellos sees this as to his credit, and praises him for keeping silent in his mother's presence when he could have spoken, and for not taking part in matters concerning the empire: other historians were less impressed by Michael's lack of aptitude for government.[28] Psellos was one of his tutors, and Psellos's works written for Michael include explanations, in verse, of legal concepts and church doctrine, a work on physics, some chapters on theology and a collection of riddles.[29] Eudokia while training Michael for kingship reinforced his junior status: personally training him for his career, and allowing him to appoint magistrates or act as a judge, while she reinforced her lessons with kisses and commended him for his contribution.[30] In this building up of his character and overt preparation for rule, she could be seen to be deliberately marginalising him, though it also appears, to put it charitably, that she was working with unpromising material.

Eudokia's status as ruler is reflected in her public iconography. On the gold coinage (*histamena*) of late 1067, we see Eudokia in the centre, with Michael at her right and Constantios at her left (Plate 19); in other words she is taking precedence over her children. On a *tetarteron* probably of the same date she is associated with Michael VII but takes the place of honour. The inscription reads 'Eudokia and Michael, emperors', and this is the first time that a regent takes precedence over her son: both Irene and Zoe Karbounopsina were named after their sons, not before. Similarly, in the dating clauses of South Italian charters Eudokia's name takes precedence over those of her children and she is often the only one to receive the imperial title.[31] It is possible that Psellos's statement as to the imperial audiences, in which she was flanked by her two sons, reflects the public iconography of the coinage.[32] Her status is further reinforced by seals, probably from the period of her regency, which give her the title 'Εὐδοκία εὐσεβεστάτη αὐγούστα (Eudokia, most pious Augusta)' and 'Εὐδοκία αὐγούστα', with no mention of Michael or Constantios; another, which can be dated to between May and December 1067, shows her standing between her two sons, with the inscription 'Eudokia, Michael and Constantios, emperors of the *Romaioi*'.[33] Clearly she was the *de facto* emperor, even if she were not proclaimed as such.[34]

Plate 19 A *histamenon* of Eudokia Makrembolitissa, with Michael (l.) and Constantios (r.), minted at Constantinople in 1067. Eudokia stands on a dais and carries a knobbed sceptre; her sons hold a *globus cruciger* and *akakia*. The obverse shows Christ on a square-backed throne (Dumbarton Oaks Byzantine Collection: Washington DC)

The second marriage

Eudokia was remarkable not so much for taking over the throne when her husband died, as for preferring not to give it up again to her son. In fact not only did she not hand over the rule to Michael, she chose to break her oath and remarry, selecting a general, Romanos Diogenes, for that purpose. This was to Psellos's consternation; he considered her action extremely unwise, despite her explanation to him that the empire needed a competent military man to take charge.[35] The fact that she might remarry had clearly been canvassed by contemporaries, despite her oath, and there were widespread rumours about who the lucky man might be.[36] As it was, Psellos was stunned by the choice, though he is careful like Zonaras to exonerate Eudokia of any self-indulgent and licentious motives in her decision.[37] He does, however, state that when Romanos was acquitted by Eudokia of conspiring with the Hungarians in the wake of Constantine X's death that this was an error of judgement on her part and she should have had him put to death.[38] Romanos was recalled to Constantinople and on 25 December 1067 named *magistros* and *stratelates* (commander-in-chief).[39] At this point there is evidence for some excellent undercover work by Eudokia in the attempt to win support for her marriage to Romanos. Some of the senate were apparently in favour of a remarriage, but the patriarch John Xiphilinos had to be won round. One of the stories to which the secrecy of the whole affair gave rise was that when her plan to remarry was blocked by the patriarch, one of her eunuchs was sent to inform him secretly that Eudokia was intending to marry his brother (or nephew). The patriarch therefore summoned the senators individually and got them to revoke their signatures, stating that in demanding such an oath Constantine X had been actuated by jealousy and not the public good. He therefore released the empress from her oath.[40] The tale as it stands is meant to redound to Eudokia's discredit and cannot be taken at face value, but she certainly managed to achieve her aim without patriarchal disapproval.

On the night of 31 December 1067 Romanos was introduced discreetly to the palace and presented by Eudokia and Psellos to Michael Doukas for his consent, Michael having been woken up for the purpose. Michael's lack of expression at the news and at his presentation to his new stepfather ('becoming at once his colleague on the throne and his friend') might be taken as displaying either his disapproval at events or his fear of his mother.[41] There had been whispered rumours and it had been impossible to keep the matter entirely a secret,[42] but this occasion seems to have been the first that Psellos himself heard about the affair: his statement that the empress only told him about it on the night of 31 December has an unmistakable air of pique. John Doukas was summoned to the palace and presented with a *fait accompli*.[43] John was more diplomatic than Michael: after a not unreasonable inquiry about his nephew's well-being, he was able to say a few words in commendation of Romanos and offer his congratulations to the happy pair. The next morning, New Year's Day 1068, Romanos married Eudokia and was crowned and acclaimed *autokrator* in St Sophia. Only the Varangian guard seem to have had objections and these were removed when Michael VII showed himself willing to accept the situation.[44]

Eudokia seems to have thought that Romanos would be subject to her influence. When she woke Michael to tell him that he was to meet his future stepfather, she informed him: 'Although he takes the place of your father, he will be a subject, not a ruler. I, your mother, have bound him in writing to observe this arrangement.'[45] Psellos here gives us evidence that some form of written agreement had taken place between Eudokia and Romanos, presumably to the effect that Romanos would protect the dynastic rights of Eudokia's sons. Eudokia's experiences in her second marriage, as depicted by Psellos, can in many ways be compared to those of Zoe. Having saved his life, she considered that by making him emperor she would be preserving her own power, and that he would never oppose her wishes. A reasonable conjecture, but according to the picture promulgated by the Doukas faction she was proved wrong. Only for a little while is he said to have acted like her loyal subject (in itself an interesting pointer to the agreement between them); soon he began to treat her with contempt, almost like a captive, and would willingly have driven her from the palace: 'the more she tried to dominate him, to treat him, who was really her master, like a lion in a cage, the more he fretted at her restraining influence, and glared at the hand that kept him in check. To begin with, he growled inwardly, but as time passed his disgust became obvious to everyone.'[46] Psellos is here overstating the case, trying to promote the picture of a rupture between Romanos and Eudokia, which he, when the empress was stirred to indignation at Romanos's insults and refusal to take advice in his military schemes, vainly attempted to heal. But his statement that he treated her like a prisoner has to be taken with some caution and is perhaps belied by Eudokia's later conduct.[47]

In fact, after coming to the throne Romanos did protect the rights of the dynasty:[48] he crowned Eudokia's second son Andronikos Doukas co-emperor, doubtless at Eudokia's request,[49] and even kept John Doukas in power.[50] His constitutional inferiority to Michael and his brothers is shown in his coins; on the gold *histamena* (the most valuable coins of the reign) Michael and his brothers occupy the obverse – the important side – while on the reverse Christ is shown blessing the marriage of Eudokia and Romanos, a depiction not seen since the fifth century, stressing that like Anastasios in 491 Romanos had come to power through marriage (Plate 20). Romanos's appearance on the reverse of his own coinage clearly shows that he ranks after Eudokia's sons and that he is not the senior emperor. There also exists in the Bibliothèque Nationale in Paris the pattern for a gold *tetarteron*, depicting Eudokia on the obverse with the title of *basilissa*, holding the *labarum* and a *globus*, and Romanos on the reverse with the title *despotes*, with the *akakia* (a cylindrical bar with knobbed ends) and a *globus*. Not only the respective

Plate 20 A *histamenon* of Romanos IV Diogenes. The obverse shows Michael VII with
Constantios (l.) and Andronikos (r.); on the reverse Christ crowns Romanos
(l.) and Eudokia (r.). Minted at Constantinople in 1068–71 (Dumbarton
Oaks Byzantine Collection: Washington DC)

titles, but the fact that she holds the sceptre gives a clear indication of her
precedence over Romanos. The coin may never have been minted because it
made this statement in too categorical a way,[51] and in fact only four empresses have the term *basilis*(*sa*) applied to them on coins: Irene, Zoe and
Theodora, and Eudokia.[52] We also have imperial seals of the period which
closely resemble the *histamena*: one is dated to early 1068, while others follow
Romanos's crowning of Andronikos. These link Romanos and Eudokia as co-
rulers with the title 'Romanos and Eudokia emperors of the *Romaioi*'. On the
later seals the obverse depicts Christ crowning Romanos and Eudokia, while
the reverse depicts Michael and his two brothers.[53] In the same way the
'Romanos ivory' in Paris, which depicts Romanos IV and Eudokia, describes
them as 'Romanos, emperor of the *Romaioi*' and 'Eudokia empress (*basilis*)
of the *Romaioi*'.[54] In the official iconography of the reign of Romanos and
Eudokia there is clear evidence that Romanos was protecting the interests of
the Doukas dynasty, and it expressly states that he ruled by right of his
marriage to Eudokia and was junior to her sons. And we must assume that
the official presentation of the couple on coins and seals expressed Eudokia's
own view of her position as empress and almost co-ruler, as the legitimating
factor of her husband's government (Plate 21).

Plate 21 A *tetarteron* of Romanos IV. The reverse shows Romanos (l.) and Eudokia (r.), holding between them a globe supporting a long cross. Minted at Constantinople in 1068–71 (Dumbarton Oaks Byzantine Collection: Washington DC)

The Doukas response

Eudokia's plans for the regime were hampered by her having two sons by Romanos, Nikephoros and Leo, in quick succession, whom Romanos crowned, thus associating them with himself, Michael, Andronikos and Constantios in power, weakening the position of Eudokia's sons.[55] Following unremitting hostility from the Doukas faction John Doukas was also in disgrace, and Eudokia's son Andronikos was said to have been with the army in 1068 more as a hostage than a general.[56] It was the treachery of John Doukas's son Andronikos at the battle of Mantzikert which led at least in part to the Byzantine defeat and Romanos's capture by the Turks on 19 August 1071.[57] This caused great consternation at Constantinople, and finally the government passed to Michael and Eudokia jointly. According to Psellos the decision at the conference called by Eudokia was unanimous that Romanos, alive or dead, should be ignored and the government be carried on by Eudokia and her sons, but opinion was divided as to whether the government should pass to Michael and his brothers, or whether Eudokia should be restored to sole authority and her sons excluded. According to Psellos, both he and the emperor Michael favoured the idea that Eudokia and Michael should be joint rulers, though he notes that there were some who were urging Eudokia to rule alone with an eye to governing the state for their own profit, to this end trying to force a quarrel between Michael and his mother.[58] Though now well into his early twenties, Michael supposedly continued to show great respect towards his mother, even, it is said, to the extent of being prepared to abdicate if she so desired. But in fact, there seems to have been a split between mother and son: Psellos speaks of trying to effect a settlement between them, which was obviated by the fact that even the thought of meeting his mother face to face made Michael blush.[59] John Doukas's arrival in Constantinople from Bithynia settled the question. He was received in the palace by Eudokia and her sons and given back an active part in government, while power was restored to Eudokia and Michael jointly.[60] Eudokia's competence and influence must be seen in the plan to associate her again in power with Michael, who was after all twenty-one or more: his lack of interest in government is hardly an excuse.

176

This new regime only lasted a month, from September to October 1071. The news that the Seljuq sultan Alp-Arslan had freed Romanos and that he was intent on regaining power put Eudokia into a position of some embarrassment: at this vital moment she lost her grip. A letter from Romanos to the empress informing her of what had happened caused wild confusion in the palace. Psellos himself advised that Romanos not be received back.[61] Letters were sent out to the provinces instructing them not to accept Romanos.[62] The Caesar John stepped in; considering Romanos's return as threatening both his nephews and himself, he proceeded to a coup. He was obviously concerned at the news that Romanos and Eudokia were in correspondence: clearly her policies might turn out to be in direct opposition to those of John. So, with the collaboration of his sons, he had the Varangians proclaim Michael emperor and Eudokia was deposed and sent off to her own convent of Piperoudion on the Bosporos, together with her two sons by Romanos, who lost their imperial honours.[63] Psellos is alone in attributing the coup to Michael himself, on the advice of the Caesar's sons, and describes Eudokia as losing her nerve on hearing the racket made by the guards acclaiming Michael – pulling her veil over her head and hiding in a secret crypt, the entrance to which Psellos stood by waiting on events (having pretty much lost his nerve himself).[64] When John decided to depose Eudokia and send her to her convent Michael opposed this, ineffectually. Propaganda directed against Eudokia, doubtless manipulated by the Caesar and his sons, led to a second decree that she should be tonsured.[65]

Anna Dalassene, sister-in-law of the ex-emperor Isaac I Komnenos, was also exiled. The Komnenoi had been promoted to positions of influence under Romanos, and Manuel Komnenos, nephew of Isaac I and eldest son of Anna Dalassene, had been made *curopalates* and given the command of the army in Asia Minor. His mother Anna was also supposed to be scheming with Romanos, and was banished to Prinkipo with some of her children.[66] Two campaigns were waged by the Caesar's sons against Romanos, who was viewed by the Doukas faction as a rebel, and he was captured in the spring of 1072; despite becoming a monk he was savagely blinded on 29 June, dying in a monastery which he had founded on the island of Prote on 4 August 1072:[67] sources agree that his blinding was entirely the doing of the Caesar and not of Michael VII, who was ignorant of the decision until it was irrevocable.[68]

Eudokia and Botaneiates

Eudokia's career was not, however, entirely over. In Michael's reign the eunuch Nikephoritzes, his favourite and chief adviser, managed to convince Michael that Eudokia and some other relatives were scheming against him, so she was still a force to be reckoned with even in her convent: this was apparently some time after the Caesar had retired to his estates in late 1073, but before the corn depot outside Raidestos was set up in the winter of

1076/7.[69] Then, after nine children and two husbands and several years in a convent, she nearly succeeded in marrying for a third time. When the general Nikephoros III Botaneiates deposed Michael VII in 1078, he not only recalled Eudokia to Constantinople, but was strongly attracted to the idea of marrying her: Botaneiates was an elderly widower, whose second wife Vevdene had just died. As another possibility he considered marrying Maria of Georgia or 'Alania', Eudokia's daughter-in-law, the wife of Michael VII Doukas. Michael had entered monastic life and was to become bishop of Ephesos. Eudokia had no objections at all to becoming the new empress, and Anna Komnene reports that it was whispered that Eudokia had written to Botaneiates even before his arrival in the capital to propose a match with herself or her daughter Zoe; Botaneiates was actually married, but his wife died shortly after his accession. She was outmanoeuvred, however, by the Caesar John Doukas, who was not prepared to see Eudokia again on the throne, and advised Botaneiates instead to marry Maria because of her lack of relatives in the capital, the implication presumably being that Eudokia's would be desirous of a place in government.[70] Eudokia, though very eager to marry him, also seems to have been influenced by a holy man Panaretos, who reminded her of 'many things' that put an end to her eagerness.[71] Botaneiates instead presented her with honours and a lavish income, including three *sekreta*, despite the fact that Alexios Komnenos had worked hard to persuade her son Constantios to proclaim himself emperor instead of Botaneiates.[72] We do not know the date of her death, except that it was probably after 1081, but her connections with the Komnenoi would have ensured that her retirement was spent in suitably regal conditions.[73]

Eudokia's perception of her own standing can be seen from a copy of the *Sacra Parallela*, excerpts from the Church Fathers, including St Basil, St Maximos, St Gregory Nazianzus, St John Chrysostom and St John Damascene, which was prepared for her. In the manuscript she is depicted with Constantine and two of their sons, Michael and Constantios; the Virgin is shown as crowning Constantine and Eudokia.[74] Eudokia is shown as taller in stature than the emperor, though her face is too damaged to trace the features. The dedication poem, which provides further evidence for Eudokia's perception of herself as sharing the empire with her husband, includes an acrostic on her name and is addressed to her:

> Christ, having come across conjugal love,
> has bestowed on you the glory of wielding the sceptre . . .
> For this reason you are now adorned with the crown of power
> in all the hymns and holy books,
> together with the children, resplendent in the crown,
> the light-bearing branches of the purple.
> You have heard, oh mistress and ruler of the world (κοσμοκράτορ),
> all these exist for you and through you.[75]

Eudokia had a remarkable and tempestuous career. Most striking is the fact not only that she was willing and able to take on the empire as sole ruler on more than one occasion, but that her contemporaries considered her competent to do so. That her own family were prepared to see her enthroned as supreme ruler, even when she had a son of an age to take power, speaks highly for her managerial abilities. Unlike Zoe she was actively encouraged not to marry, both by her first husband's family and also by her officials such as Psellos, to avoid any dynastic conflict of interest. And her own ambitions are shown by her intention of keeping her hand on the tiller even after remarrying, though this may have been due not simply to the desire to wield power but to the wish to protect her children's position. She did not hide her light under a bushel: the iconography of three reigns, of Constantine X, her own and Romanos IV, displays her status as *basilis Romaion*, and emphasises the collegiality of power as it was seen in the Doukas dynasty. Her decision to remarry was a calculated risk: as it was it misfired, both because of the hostility of the Doukas clan, and also because of the secrecy surrounding the circumstances of the marriage, which her first husband's oath made imperative. In a sense Constantine X had been right: Eudokia's remarriage and the birth of new sons to a second husband who then crowned his own heirs as additional co-emperors had put the dynasty into jeopardy.[76] But, as in the case of Constantine VII, it is quite possible that the legitimatist principle would have triumphed, even had Romanos stayed on the throne. In the event, the dynasty was vested in the person of Michael VII, and Eudokia's actions may have been decided by a dispassionate assessment of his abilities: even when he was installed as sole ruler the dynasty in any case ended with him.

11

THE EMPRESSES OF ALEXIOS I
KOMNENOS (1081–1118)

MARIA OF ALANIA

Any discussion of Komnenian empresses has to commence with a consideration of Maria of Georgia, or Maria 'the Alan' as she was generally known by contemporaries,[1] for it was Maria who was one of the two women responsible for bringing Alexios Komnenos to the throne. Originally called Martha, Maria was a daughter of the Georgian king Bagrat IV (1027–72), and married Michael VII Doukas probably before the death of his father Constantine Doukas. While the reasons behind the break with tradition can only be conjectured, Maria was only the second empress in the eleventh century to be chosen from outside the empire's borders: in fact, every wife selected for a Byzantine senior emperor or heir to the throne after Constantine V's first wife Irene came from a Byzantine family, though Byzantine princesses had been sent abroad; the other exception was Bertha, daughter of Hugh of Provence, who married Romanos II.[2] Maria would, however, have had at least some knowledge of what to expect at the Byzantine court for her father's previous wife was connected with the imperial family: Helena Argyropoulina was married to Bagrat by her uncle Romanos III Argyros in 1032. Helena, however, lived for only a year or so after her marriage, and it was Bagrat's second wife, Borena, who was to be the mother of George II, Maria and Martha. Martha may well have resided in Constantinople as a young girl, perhaps as a hostage at the court of Theodora, as her father had been, under Basil II.[3] Martha, now Maria, and Michael had one son, Constantine, who was born early in 1074, and who received the co-emperorship at an early age.[4] In August 1074 he was betrothed to Olympias, who was a daughter of the Norman Robert Guiscard, and who was brought to Constantinople to be educated by her new mother-in-law under the new name of Helena; the betrothal was ended when Michael VII abdicated.[5]

Psellos in his *Chronographia* eulogises Maria's beauty and modesty, and, according to Anna Komnene, Maria was so beautiful that like the Gorgon's head she was capable of rendering a bystander speechless or rooted to the spot; Plate 22 (Coisl. 79, f. 1), which shows her alongside Michael VII,

Plate 22 Maria of Alania and Michael VII Doukas, labelled as Nikephoros
Botaneiates (Coisl. 79, f. 1). (Taken from J. Spatharakis (1976) *The Portrait in
Byzantine Illustrated Manuscripts*. Published by Brill, Leiden, The
Netherlands)

depicts her in official guise, but still manages to convey something of her
attractions.[6] Like her mother-in-law Eudokia Makrembolitissa, Maria
appears on the coinage alongside her husband, which perhaps belies Psellos's
description of her as retiring (Plate 23). Psellos's account need not be taken
at face value, for he is concerned to flatter his pupil Michael VII and his
family, and Maria's readiness to marry the elderly general Nikephoros III

Plate 23 A *tetarteron* of Michael VII; the reverse shows half-length figures of Michael
and Maria of Alania holding a long cross between them. Maria has a
modified *loros* with collar-piece and crown with pinnacles and *pendilia*.
Minted at Constantinople in 1071–8 (Dumbarton Oaks Byzantine
Collection: Washington DC)

Botaneiates after her husband's abdication and Nikephoros's accession to the
throne is a sign rather of her willingness to risk alienating the patriarch and
clergy in her concern to protect the imperial inheritance of her young son
than of her bashful nature.

Nikephoros, Maria and Alexios

Botaneiates's second wife, Vevdene, died shortly after his accession,[7] and it
was the Caesar John Doukas who advised Botaneiates to marry Maria, wife of
Michael VII, in preference to Eudokia Makrembolitissa: Maria, now shelter-
ing in the convent of Petrion, was outstandingly beautiful and had no
troublesome relations.[8] The suggestion may actually have come from Maria
herself.[9] Botaneiates, who was considered a great catch, seems to have preferred to have married Eudokia given the choice, but in either case what he
was aiming at was 'placating the Byzantine sentiment for legitimacy' in
marrying the wife of one of his predecessors.[10] This factor must have been of
great weight, for his choice of Maria was not without its difficulties and the
marriage was openly called 'adulterous': it was also 'trigamous', though the
fact that this was his third and Maria's second marriage was of less concern to
the church establishment than the reality that Maria was not a widow.[11] The
Armenian source Matthew of Edessa goes so far as to state that Maria hated
her husband Michael because of his ascetic life and his refusal to have sexual
intercourse with her: she therefore had an affair with Botaneiates and encouraged him to seize the throne.[12] This account is somewhat embellished, but
the marriage of Botaneiates and Maria was considered as adultery and was
not well regarded by the church establishment; the priest who performed it
was deposed.[13]

If Maria's motivation was to preserve the rights of her young son, she
failed, for after Botaneiates's accession Constantine lost his rank and
prerogatives, and despite the fact that Maria worked hard at having him
recognised as his stepfather's heir Botaneiates finally decided on one of his
own relatives, Nikephoros Synadenos.[14] Nevertheless Maria appears on

Nikephoros's silver coinage and her own status was thus publicly emphasised.[15] In her efforts to have Constantine acknowledged as heir to the throne Maria was supported by the Komnenoi, and Anna Komnene reports that Maria was even driven to intrigue with the brothers Isaac and Alexios because of Botaneiates's refusal to recognise Constantine's rank.[16] The preliminaries of the coup demonstrate the power and influence of the empress, as well as the degree of independence she could enjoy. Alexios, with his brother Isaac, visited her regularly, and privately, to gain support for their coming coup against Botaneiates. Alexios's elder brother Isaac had married her cousin Irene, and now Maria adopted Alexios as her son. This was managed by Isaac, who advised the officials of the *gynaikonitis* to persuade Maria to this step.[17] In this way she formed a kinship tie between Alexios and Constantine, who were now adoptive brothers, and strengthened Alexios's bond of allegiance and subservience to herself, as both his empress and mother, as well as giving him the right of access to her with no possibility of slander. Clearly the fact of the adoption was widely known and incited jealousy towards the brothers. In return Isaac and Alexios formally swore that Constantine would not lose the throne through their doing.[18] Maria's ability to create her own network of supporters demonstrates the degree to which she was the legitimating factor in Botaneiates's reign,[19] as well as her lack of loyalty to the regime: she had married Botaneiates for certain personal reasons, and as these had not worked out she felt herself justified in masterminding a conspiracy against her husband and emperor. Anna states quite clearly that had Botaneiates decided to leave his throne to Constantine, Maria's son, he would not have been deposed. Moreover, Alexios and Isaac were anxious to keep Maria's goodwill, without which they would fall prey to their enemies at court.[20] She was also an unrivalled source of information as to potential threats towards the Komnenoi: in fact it appears to have been Maria who made sure that Alexios was informed of the 'plot' against them which precipitated their actual revolt.[21] Having thus thrown in her lot with the faction of Alexios Komnenos, Maria obviously expected a *quid pro quo* once his coup was successful, and when Botaneiates abdicated on 1 April 1081, dying soon afterwards, she looked for the agreements to be implemented.[22]

The accession of Alexios I Komnenos

Alexios came to the throne as a direct result of the efforts of his two 'mothers', through the network of the contacts of his biological mother Anna Dalassene who had put years of planning behind events, and the support of his adoptive mother, the current empress. Anna was happy in seeing her son on the throne: Maria, for her part, had gained the recognition of her son Constantine once again as emperor and heir to the throne, and she may also have hoped to strengthen her own and Constantine's position by marrying Alexios. This may also have been the view of Anna Dalassene, who perhaps preferred to see Alexios married to Maria than to Irene Doukaina, a marriage she had only countenanced with the greatest reluctance. While the reaction of the patriarch to the marriage of an adoptive mother and son could be forecast as being exceptionally hostile in the current climate,[23] Maria had challenged the establishment once on a similar issue, and the sources do seem to suggest that a marriage between Alexios and Maria was on the cards. When the new emperor moved into the palace at Boukoleon, while Maria was still resident in the Great Palace adjacent, he took all his relations including his brothers with him, but his fourteen-year-old wife, Irene Doukaina, whom he had married in 1078, stayed with her family in the 'lower palace'. Even more strikingly the Komnenoi tried to stop the fleet in the harbour of Boukoleon acclaiming 'Alexios and Irene'.[24] Moreover, while Alexios was crowned on 4 April 1081, Irene's coronation only took place a week after his public proclamation, following pressure from the patriarch Kosmas and George Palaiologos, Alexios's brother-in-law, who was married to Irene's sister Anna and had gained the sympathies of the fleet.[25] Irene's grandfather John Doukas also appears to have manipulated events to ensure Irene's coronation; she was as yet childless, and if she were removed to a convent the blow to the family prestige would have been immense. A further factor was that Anna Dalassene may have been plotting to remove the patriarch in favour of the monk Eustratios: if so, she was unable to remove him in time and was outmanoeuvred by John Doukas. The patriarch Kosmas refused to retire unless Irene was crowned and the coronation of Irene took place: with it went Maria's hopes of the crown for the third time. Zonaras's comment, that as a young man Alexios was much given to amours and that Irene was very jealous, may perhaps refer to an affair with Maria either before or after his accession, though on the face of it it reads as a general comment on his habits of immorality.[26] Certainly Maria, who was now perhaps in her mid-twenties, would have had more seductive glamour than Alexios's fourteen-year-old wife, whose role and status were additionally marginalised by her mother-in-law.

The 'alternative' empress

Alexios seems to have preserved Maria's interests throughout his reign – she was after all his adoptive mother – though inevitably the birth of Alexios's own son John in September 1087, after two daughters, was eventually to have an impact on the status of her son Constantine. The Doukas family now had two strings to their bow: Constantine was again officially regarded as co-emperor, while Irene, the Caesar John Doukas's granddaughter, was empress consort. It was on the advice of John Doukas that Maria, before she left for the Mangana palace 'with an escort worthy of her rank', induced Alexios to issue a *chrysobull* to confirm the special privileges granted to Constantine. In fact, so faithfully did Alexios keep his promises to Maria that Constantine as co-emperor even outranked Alexios's elder brother, the *sebastokrator* Isaac. For a few years, therefore, he acted as junior emperor and his signature appeared in state documents, while he accompanied the emperor on public occasions.[27] A few days after the birth of Alexios's eldest daughter Anna Komnene, on 2 December 1083, the young princess and Constantine were betrothed and their names were included in acclamations as the heirs-apparent; Anna recalls these days with regret.[28] In the manner customary among the Byzantine aristocracy, Anna was brought up with Constantine under the care of her future mother-in-law Maria.[29]

Maria was obviously a devoted mother, and, in imitation of the atmosphere of virtuous sobriety for which Alexios's court became noted under Anna Dalassene, Maria strove to present the picture of a pious, educated, virtuous mother and preceptor.[30] At some point it appears that she had voluntarily become a nun: Zonaras tells us that she was a nun at the time of Michael VII's death, *c.* 1090, for she went to visit Michael when he was dying and asked his pardon for marrying Nikephoros.[31] Taking the veil may have been part of her policy of toning down her past, though it was not uncommon for empresses who had nothing to repent, and it made no difference to her standing and political influence in the capital. But, as was only to be expected, the birth of a son to Irene in September 1087, who was himself to be crowned co-emperor in 1092, meant that Constantine lost his status as heir. He may, however, have remained engaged to Anna until his death in or after 1094; there was, after all, every reason to keep such imperial connections and ambitions in the family, though with the birth of each child to Irene Doukaina Constantine's chances of the throne looked more and more remote.[32] But he was still treated as an honoured member of the family: early in 1094 he entertained Alexios on his extensive estate at Pentegostis, near Serres, and Maria herself enjoyed large estates called Petritzos and Pernikos at Christopolis.[33] Though Maria's hopes of seeing her son an emperor were diminishing, she had her compensations. Indeed, she seems to have held her own 'alternative' court at the Mangana palace, where she removed after Alexios's accession with a full imperial retinue, and where her talents as scholar and literary patroness had full play: she had received the Mangana palace and monastery and the Hebdomon monastery by *chrysobull* from Botaneiates, and was well provided for financially. Her profile in the capital remained high until she retired to monastic life, perhaps *c.* 1094–5.[34] Theophylact's treatise entitled *Paideia Basilike* written for her son praises her unending study of theology, as well as her care of Constantine and her philanthropy and piety.[35]

In 1094 she seems to have been involved in an intrigue against Alexios masterminded by the rebel Nikephoros Diogenes (a conspiracy which her son refused to aid, though asked to lend Nikephoros his horse to assist his escape).[36] Anna Komnene claims that documents were discovered which revealed that Maria knew about the plot but did her best to dissuade the conspirators; her father kept the references to Maria secret, because of his faith in her and the bond of sympathy between them, dating from even before his accession. If Maria were involved, it must have been in an attempt to recover Constantine's imperial status, and Alexios's affection for her carried her over this crisis. As the palace nursery continued to fill, however, she suffered 'gradual political redundancy',[37] especially after Constantine's death, which may have led to her retirement to a convent, though she was still alive in 1103. A letter written to her by Theophylact, perhaps in 1095, apologising for failing to visit her on the Prince's Islands, may be evidence for her removal there, perhaps to the foundation of the empress Irene.[38] Things had not worked out for her, but at least her motive had been maternal devotion, and her first husband Michael seems to have been as happy as a bishop as he was as an emperor. Maria had had the distinction of appearing on the coinage of two husbands; she had 'legitimated' the accession of one emperor, Nikephoros, and then actively intrigued in orchestrating the coup of another against him. She had seen Constantine, her son by Michael VII, being honoured as the heir-apparent under the new regime, even over the heads of the males of the reigning family, and had herself become the adoptive mother of the new emperor. An active political force in Constantinople for some twenty years, she may even have set the fashion for literary patronage among imperial women. Perhaps unconsciously, she had been following in the steps of her mother-in-law Eudokia Makrembolitissa – or it could have been that Eudokia had been her role-model all along.

ANNA DALASSENE

In the early years of Alexios's reign the new emperor was surrounded by three strong-minded women with the title of empress: his adopted mother Maria, his wife Irene, and his mother Anna Dalassene. Irene had the advantages of youth and her status as consort, and was to emerge the eventual winner, but the contest must have been intense. The predominance of women under the Komnenoi has been noted; they founded monastic institutions, patronised writers and took an active part in politics: even more striking is the acceptance at least by Alexios of the traditional female method of imperial legitimation, for he had been happy to accept Maria of Alania as his adoptive mother and use her support to come to power, along with the more conventional methods employed by his real mother. 'The message of the 1080s was one of family values: if you want to get ahead get a mother: and Alexios had two.'[39] Alexios clearly had no problem working with women: he was a family man, devoted to his mother, and had come to the throne through the ramifications of his family's networks.[40] Anna was to play an important political role in the early years of his reign, as one of the visible women whom the unsettled political conditions of the 1070s had brought to the forefront – women who were well aware of how the kinship system could be manipulated to extend their family's power and influence. Eudokia Makrembolitissa and Anna Dalassene in particular were past masters at the art, and the marriage of Eudokia's daughter Zoe to Anna's son Adrian in 1081 or later signalled a final alliance between the families of two great marriage-brokers.[41]

The ambitions of Anna

Though the daughter of Alexios Charon and a Dalassene, Anna chose to keep her mother's name signifying the illustrious military family with which she was connected, though none of her eight children was to perpetuate the name.[42] She was born around 1030, and was married in 1044 to John Komnenos, the brother of the future emperor Isaac I: their eldest son Manuel was born in 1045. As a young woman, her ambition must have been whetted when her husband's brother became emperor in 1057 and her husband was made *curopalates* and domestic of the *Scholae*: we have seals in which Anna used the titles *curopalatissa* and *domestikissa*.[43] The blow when Isaac was persuaded to abdicate, and, still worse, her husband refused to take over the throne, must have been immense. According to Bryennios, the family historian, she did everything she could – unsuccessfully – to make John change his mind, particularly stressing the advantages to their children.[44] From then on her hostility to the Doukas family, who had won the cherished prize, was unrelenting.[45]

After her husband died on 12 July 1067,[46] she was to keep the family together and protect its fortunes for fourteen years, until her son Alexios's successful coup d'état in 1081 at the age of twenty-four or so. It was during this period that she formed a dexterous network of marriage connections with a number of prominent families, which was to facilitate this coup.[47] As part of her master-plan she supported Eudokia and Romanos Diogenes against the Doukas family, and her eldest son Manuel, despite his youth, was appointed *curopalates* and *strategos autokrator* in the East by Romanos, where he died following an ear infection in spring 1071. Anna rushed from the capital to Bithynia to her son's death-bed, and after performing his funeral rites quickly overcame her anguish and sent Alexios on campaign in his stead.[48] After the battle of Mantzikert in 1071 when the Doukas family returned to power, a letter from her to Romanos, supposedly forged, was intercepted, and after a trial in the palace, at which her stern demeanour and production of an icon from her robe intimidated the more sensitive of her judges, she was declared a rebel. The establishment considered her, like Eudokia, too dangerous to be left at liberty and she was banished to the island of Prinkipo at the beginning of 1072 with her children. If not already a nun, she was tonsured on this occasion, for some of her seals prior to 1081 apparently bear the titles *monache* (nun) and *curopalatissa*.[49]

The throne in transition: Anna Dalassene and Maria of Alania

After Romanos's death Anna was recalled to the imperial court by Michael VII,[50] and continued her matrimonial schemes, her ambitions unabated. It must have seemed likely that the regime of Michael VII would not last, and she ensured that the Komnenoi would be in a position of strength for the next governmental reshuffle. Michael seems to have been anxious to conciliate her and as a sop to her matrimonial ambitions allowed her eldest surviving son Isaac to marry Irene, the cousin of his own wife Maria of Alania.[51] Though this did not extend Komnenian connections among Byzantine aristocratic families, in view of the fact that Maria was later to be the fulcrum for the transference of power in 1081 it was a shrewd move and shows an awareness of the potential influence of the empress consort at times of transition. It may also betray a close knowledge on Anna's part of the character and priorities of Maria of Alania.[52]

In September 1077 John Doukas persuaded Anna to allow the marriage of Irene, his granddaughter, and Alexios, her second surviving son; the marriage probably took place early in the next year when Irene was twelve. Alexios, who was born *c.* 1057, had previously been married to the daughter of one of the Argyros family: the marriage was very brief and perhaps not consummated on account of the girl's age, for no children are recorded.[53] Anna's reaction to the coup of Botaneiates in 1078 was probably disappointment: certainly Alexios had attempted to persuade Constantios Doukas, Eudokia's son, to take the throne, and this step must have represented his mother's views too. Nevertheless Anna immediately took steps to form an alliance with the new regime, betrothing Anna, the only daughter of Manuel, her eldest son (now deceased), to Botaneiates's grandson. This boy was brought up under her care.[54]

The establishment of this connection did not, however, stop her intriguing against the new regime, as she had against that of the Caesar John Doukas and Michael VII. When her sons Isaac and Alexios left Constantinople on 14 February 1081 to form an army to take the field against Botaneiates, Anna organised her family, outwitted the tutor of Botaneiates's grandson who was staying with them, and took refuge in St Sophia, from there negotiating with Botaneiates for the safety of the rest of the family in Constantinople:

> She was allowed to enter [St Sophia]. As if she were weighed down with old age and worn out by grief, she walked slowly (in reality she was pretending to be weary) and when she approached the actual entrance to the sanctuary made two genuflexions; on the third she sank to the floor and taking firm hold of the sacred doors, cried in a loud voice: 'Unless my hands are cut off, I will not leave this holy place, except on one condition: that I receive the emperor's cross as guarantee of safety.'[55]

The cross handed her by her emperor's messenger Straboromanos was not sufficiently visible in her view: it had to be a cross of reasonable size so that any bystanders could witness the oath, and Botaneiates obliged. Significantly, another spokesperson for the women was Irene of Georgia, Isaac's wife and Maria of Alania's cousin, who also spoke forthrightly to the emperor's emissary. Anna in fact appears now to have made the first statement to Botaneiates of the rebels' intentions and justification for their conduct, giving the family line that her sons had left the city, 'not as rebels, but as faithful servants' of the emperor, driven to flight by the jealousy of their enemies at court.[56] After receiving a guarantee of safety, she was relegated to the monastery of Petrion with her daughters and daughters-in-law, all considered to be a potential danger to the regime. The *protovestiaria* Maria, the Bulgarian-born mother of Irene Doukaina, was imprisoned with them too, but their cellars, granaries and store-houses were to be free from interference, and they were allowed to import all the food they needed. Anna still kept up with events: Maria of Bulgaria bribed the guards with the best of their food in exchange for news of current events. And the women also involved George Palaiologos, husband of Irene's sister Anna, in the conspiracy, despite his misgivings: his mother-in-law Maria insisted vehemently on his participation.[57]

On her son's victorious entry into the city on 1 April 1081, Anna may have tried again to remove the Doukas family from power, in this case in the person of her daughter-in-law Irene to prevent her from becoming empress. After all, which of the two brothers – Isaac or Alexios – was to take the throne was not a settled affair until the intervention of John Doukas in favour of Alexios during the course of the revolt: while Anna Komnene obviously stresses her father's pre-eminent claims and support base, there seem to have been two rival factions in favour of Isaac and Alexios respectively, and Alexios came to the fore because of the support of the Doukas family, most notably John Doukas. This may not have been what was planned by Anna; she may have expected Isaac and his Georgian wife to take the throne, and the change of plan would have made her more anxious than ever to dissolve her son's connection with the Doukas family.[58] But Irene's rights were vehemently supported by her grandfather John Doukas, her brother-in-law George Palaiologos and the patriarch Kosmas. The Komnenoi wanted to appoint a new patriarch, the monk Eustratios who was a personal friend and protégé of Anna's and who had forecast Alexios's rise to the throne, as a propagandist for the coup: the implication is that he would have been more pliable than Kosmas. Kosmas, however, refused to resign unless he personally crowned Irene. So Irene was crowned, and any deal which Anna may have done with Maria of Alania was aborted; Kosmas resigned and was replaced with Eustratios, Anna's nominee.[59]

'Mother of the emperor'

Anna's position as mother of the emperor was now assured, a designation which appears on her seals of this period as an official title (Plate 24).[60] Alexios gave her a place in the court hierarchy and awarded her the title *despoina* (empress or mistress), though she was not crowned: Irene was Augusta and senior empress, which may have rankled.[61] But it was Anna who wielded political power. In the early years of Alexios's reign, when he was frequently on campaign, she acted as regent and was given a wide sphere of authority, with control over the entire civil government. In the *chrysobull* of August 1081, in which she was nominated as regent, he declared her decisions to be above all present and future criticism – they were to stand whether justified or unjustified ('κᾶν εὔλογοι κᾶν ἀνεύλογοι'), as were the actions of her ministers and chancellor. The *chrysobull*, which Anna Komnene gives in its entirety, is a statement of Alexios's faith in his mother's capacity to rule and loyalty to the regime, as well as an acknowledgement of her role in the family's success:

> When danger is foreseen or some other dreadful occurrence is expected, there is no safeguard stronger than a mother who is understanding and loves her son, for if she gives counsel, her advice will be reliable; if she offers prayers, they will confer strength and certain protection. Such at any rate has been the experience of myself, your emperor, in the case of my own revered mother, who has taught and guided and sustained me throughout, from my earliest years . . . Never were those cold words, 'mine' and 'yours', uttered between us, and what was even more important, the prayers she poured out during all that time reached the ears of the Lord and have raised me now to the imperial throne.[62]

She is here given an effective *carte blanche*. Alexios speaks of her vast experience of secular matters with respect and she has full powers in matters of promotion, appointment to offices, honours, donations of property, increase of salaries and reduction of taxation. Alexios may have created the

Plate 24 A seal of Anna Dalassene after her son's accession, 1081–*c*. 1100. The four-line inscription reads, 'Lord, help Anna Dalassene, nun, mother of the emperor' (Dumbarton Oaks Byzantine Collection: Washington DC)

position of *logothete ton sekreton* initially as an official to assist his mother, as a 'technical coordinator of services', not as a supervisor of her decisions.[63] Anna was certainly possessed of remarkable administrative skills, gained perhaps through her experience as head and administrator of a large extended family with considerable property. Anna Komnene praises her grandmother for her intellect even as quite a young woman, stating that she was a persuasive and felicitous orator and of great experience and perception in government, and records that she had 'an exceptional grasp of public affairs, with a genius for organisation and administration; she was capable in fact of managing not only the Roman Empire, but every other empire under the sun as well'.[64] The emperor in fact did her bidding like a slave: she was legislator, complete organiser and governor.[65] Despite the element of uncritical adulation here, in an oration delivered perhaps in 1088 Theophylact devotes some time to a eulogy of Anna Dalassene and describes Anna with Alexios as the 'two great suns in the firmament of empire',[66] confirming Anna Komnene's account of how her father shared the government with his mother. It is also evidence for the fact that even in the late 1080s the empress Irene was totally eclipsed by the eminence of her mother-in-law.

Anna's government, in particular her ideas for reform, caused public criticism: her ideas were to the state's detriment, it was whispered. In any case, to the subjects of the empire and members of the court 'rule by mother' must have seemed a little absurd: it had naturally been acceptable for Eudokia Makrembolitissa to rule for Michael, for she was the empress-regent and he – with a little imagination – could still be considered a minor, and was in any case perhaps not wholly competent. For a general of mature years, however, who had come to power by a military coup, to hand over the reins of government to his mother, who had no experience or imperial background either, was an entirely different situation, and it says much for Anna's abilities that it was accepted at all. Even allowing for Anna Komnene's familial *pietas*, there is clear evidence that Anna Dalassene was an exceptional administrator. Nor did her influence stop there: she completely reworked the whole ethos of the palace and the public perception of the imperial family and its womenfolk. In herself she appears to have been a formidable lady: 'her outward serenity, true reflection of character, was respected by angels but terrorised even the demons, and pleasure-loving fools, victims of their own passions, found a single glance from her more than they could bear . . . She knew exactly how to temper reserve and dignity.'[67] Irene Doukaina, Alexios's young bride, was little more than a cipher, and it must have been small comfort that she outranked her mother-in-law for ceremonial purposes. It was Anna who advised her son how to handle the guilt he felt for the looting and crimes committed during his take-over of the city; it was Anna who reorganised life in the palace so that it took on a monastic aura: there were set times for hymns, regular hours for breakfast and a special period for choosing magistrates. At dawn or even earlier Anna could be found attending to the choice of magistrates or answering petitions, with the help of her secretary Genesios, and Anna Komnene makes much of her charitable donations, and especially her hospitality to monks and clerics.[68] It is significant that Anna Komnene in the *Alexiad* perhaps somewhat disingenuously represents her grandmother as longing to spend her remaining years in a monastic institution in contemplation and prayer;[69] only her love for her son and his need for her assistance in ruling dissuaded her from doing so after his accession. In other words, while it was acceptable for a mother to run the empire, she must on no account appear to want to do so.

Apart from the property she controlled belonging to her family, Alexios ensured that his mother had adequate financial backing for her rank and status. Anna Dalassene received the *sekreton* of Myrelaion from her son, the financial prerogatives of which she kept for herself, in the same way as Maria Skleraina had benefited from the *sekreton* of St George at Mangana.[70] Her foundation of the church and convent of the Saviour Pantepoptes ('Who sees all') in Constantinople overlooking the Golden Horn is evidence for her conspicuous spending, though her patronage took the form of government grants of land and exemptions from tax; there are documents detailing her generosity to the monks of the monastery of Docheiariou and St Christodoulos of Patmos.[71]

Retirement

Alexios's reliance on Anna Dalassene was hardly a sign of weakness at the time: he needed a reliable regent, and could hardly have forgotten that he had won the imperial throne largely 'through the unflagging determination and the sedulous intrigues of his mother'.[72] Anna's primary motivations were ambition for her family and concern that it maintain its power, though she must also have had considerable job satisfaction. But the situation was bound not to last – indeed it is remarkable that Anna may have remained in power for nearly twenty years. In the 1090s Alexios was able to spend more time in the capital and perhaps became tired of her hold on the administration; this is recorded by Zonaras and discernible in a Docheiariou document dated to 1089, where he seems to have disapproved of her generosity to the monastery of Docheiariou on Mt Athos.[73] The last decision of hers of which we hear was to send Kymineianos, the *droungarios* of the fleet, to bring the rebel pretending to be Leo Diogenes, Romanos's son, back to Constantinople in 1095, and at some point between 1095 and 1100 she vanishes from the political scene.[74] Zonaras reports that she retired before Alexios took steps to remove her, clearly displaying the sense of timing which had served her so well up to this point, while Anna Komnene is remarkably silent about her disappearance from the centre of power to her own convent, the Pantepoptes, to live in honourable and imperial state for the rest of her life. There have been suspicions that Anna Komnene's silence was due to the fact that her grandmother was involved in something questionable – maybe a heretical sect.[75] She died on 1 November, but we do not know the year: perhaps in 1100.[76]

Whether the charge of heresy was true or not (and it is only supposition), Anna Dalassene was now clearly redundant – and not only from Alexios's point of view. While there is no ground for shifting her removal onto the shoulders of Irene, who was now mature enough to combat opposition from a mother-in-law,[77] two determined women in the palace may have been one too many for Alexios to cope with, and it was certainly easier to get rid of his mother than his wife, if one had to go. By the early 1100s Irene was apparently coming to enjoy Alexios's confidence, or at least had become his constant companion, and Anna Komnene begins to record the doings of her mother: the Anemas conspiracy of 1102 is the first time we hear of her having a direct influence on events.[78] Even if Irene did not engineer her mother-in-law's retirement, she benefited all the same. The stage had already been cleared of Alexios's other 'mother' Maria of Alania, and finally Irene was able to take the place of Anna Dalassene as the first woman of the empire in fact as well as in title.

IRENE DOUKAINA

'The emperor was inhibited by her formidable presence, for she possessed a sharp tongue and was quick to reprimand the slightest insolence': this is how Zonaras characterises Irene Doukaina in her later years as empress.[79] She had come a long way. The eldest daughter of Andronikos Doukas and Maria of Bulgaria (the *protovestiaria*), she was born in 1066,[80] betrothed in September 1077 and married early the next year to Alexios Komnenos, whose domineering mother intensely disliked her family, and disapproved of the marriage, and part of whose large extended household Irene had to become.[81] When she was fourteen her husband came to power through a coup d'état and made it clear that her family connections had served his purpose and he was now prepared to rid himself of her. Only after concerted pressure from her Doukas relatives was she retained as Alexios's wife and crowned.[82] Her first child, Anna Komnene, was to be born on 2 December 1083, to be followed by eight others (the two last of whom died shortly after their births in 1097 and 1098),[83] and at least her first fifteen years as empress were to be overshadowed by the power of her mother-in-law, the virtual ruler, who was responsible for the whole ethos of the court as well as the details of government. Even if she were not as shy as her daughter suggests,[84] presiding over the ceremonies for imperial women must have been daunting when they may well have included the three mature allies, Anna Dalassene, Maria of Alania and perhaps Eudokia Makrembolitissa, none of whom felt entirely well-disposed to young Irene: still more daunting must have been their remarks in private, if these three experienced empresses met at whatever served as the equivalent for coffee mornings in the imperial circles of the capital.[85]

Wife and empress

These first years must have taught Irene survival skills and her tenacity paid off as her position gradually strengthened, while her mother-in-law's influence waned. According to Zonaras, Irene was at first neglected, but later Alexios came to love her and she then had great influence over him.[86] But this was only later. Anna Komnene, their eldest child, naturally presents her parents' marriage as ideal, but even she finds it difficult to say much about Irene's influence at court in the early years, though, when Alexios was trying to collect money after the loss of Dyrrachion to the Normans in October 1081, it was Irene who was the first to contribute from her personal resources: 'all that she had inherited from her father and mother was offered, in the hope that by doing this she might inspire others to follow her example'.[87] Otherwise we hear only of Anna Dalassene. Irene is not singled out for notice either at the time of the flight of the Komnenoi from the city (the other spokesperson for the women of the family was Irene of Georgia, Isaac's wife) or during their incarceration in the convent of Petrion, and when Alexios's conscience troubles him after his coup it is his mother he consults.[88]

After Anna Dalassene's retirement from public life in the late 1090s, Irene comes more to the fore. Another factor in her heightened profile would have been the crowning of her son John as co-emperor in September 1092 – until then the heir to the throne was not even Irene's own son, but Constantine, son of Maria of Alania (the fact that Constantine was her second cousin cannot have made this more palatable).[89] Irene had spent the first seventeen years of her reign carrying nine children, and the first time that we hear of any form of political involvement from her is more than twenty years after her accession, in 1102, when she prevented the blinding of Michael Anemas, at her daughter Anna's instigation.[90] And once her child-bearing days were over and the nursery could safely be left, she even took to accompanying Alexios on campaigns, at his request apparently, both as his nurse (Alexios suffered badly from 'gout', presumably arthritis) and, according to Anna Komnene, as a guardian against conspiracies and poisoning: her eldest son John was already old enough to be left in charge in his father's absence. In September 1105, Alexios, who was in Thessalonika facing an invasion by Bohemond, asked her to join him there and Anna is at pains to make clear that Irene remained hidden from general view and that only her litter pulled by two mules and covered with the imperial canopy showed that she accompanied the army.[91] When Alexios asked for her presence two years later on another campaign against Bohemond in November 1107, she accompanied him, her presence foiling assassins en route. At Mestos Irene wanted to return to the palace, but Alexios insisted she continue. They wintered at Thessalonika, and she returned to the capital in the next spring while Alexios continued westwards.[92]

As Alexios grew older he apparently needed her more: in 1116, dreading a recurrence of his gout and fearing the domestic enemies in his entourage, he decided he needed her tender, loving care and summoned her from Prinkipo to Aer, near Nicomedia, where he was campaigning against the Turks. Two days later at dawn news of a Turkish attack was brought to the couple in bed; when a blood-stained messenger threw himself at Alexios's feet to report that the Turks were at hand, Alexios gave Irene permission to return to Constantinople and she sailed off as far as Helenoupolis on the galley reserved for empresses: she was to rejoin him at Nicomedia when the danger had passed.[93] Empresses had been known on campaign before, most notably the notorious Martina, but it still caused comment: Irene's accompanying of her husband led to jokes and lampoons,[94] and Anna has to make much of the decorum with which she travelled, stressing that it was only her great wifely devotion that enabled her mother to overcome her unwillingness and accompany her husband. In fact, she seems to have been genuinely unwilling, and Alexios's desire for her presence, even in circumstances of some danger, may have had another, less affectionate, motive. In Anna's account of Alexios's last illness, Irene was of course indispensable, summoning the best physicians, holding him up so he could breathe, and being constantly at hand, and even having a special couch made that could be carried around the room to give the emperor some relief.[95] The final stages of his illness are portrayed in poignant terms: in discussing his worsening symptoms, Alexios calls her 'dear heart' (φιλτάτη ψυχή), and her grief at his death is uncontrollable.[96]

A 'breathing monument of harmony'[97]

This portrait of a pattern empress does Anna's heart credit. Her mother as she paints her would have preferred to shun all public duties and remain secluded within the palace, occupying herself in studying Scripture: we should not forget that maternal devotion and piety were the keynotes of the 1080s and 1090s for imperial women.[98] Irene was also immensely beautiful, 'Athena made manifest to the human race', a 'veritable statue of Beauty', like the rest of Anna's female relations.[99] Her generosity and benevolence were beyond measure: after the suppression of the Anemas conspiracy Alexios presented her with the luxurious house of one of the participants, John Solomon. Irene, however, felt sorry for the wife and gave it back to her intact.[100] She allowed all beggars free access to her, and, when she went on campaign with Alexios in 1105 took all her money with her. Her first act wherever they camped was to open her tent to petitioners. No beggar went away empty-handed, while she was also free with good advice: all that were fit to find employment were encouraged to do so and not depend upon charity.[101] She was also responsible for refounding and restoring the convent known as the Theotokos Kecharitomene, though it has been noted that its *typikon*, or charter, is concerned to show favour only to family members: it showed a distinct preference for aristocratic women and the number of nuns was provisionally fixed at twenty-four, with six servants. The convent is bequeathed to several generations of members of her family, and the royal ladies are to have the privileges of luxurious buildings, large courtyards, baths, two servants apiece and unrestricted food and drink of their choice: they can also leave the convent for up to two or three days to visit sick relatives, and receive male visitors.[102]

In addition, Irene cultivated an interest in literature: the court poets Prodromos and Kallikles wrote dedicatory pieces or epitaphs at her request.[103] Like Maria of Alania she was the patron of many scholars and even well-versed in theology, and her daughter notes her taste for the abstruse work of Maximos the confessor.[104] The most notable work dedicated to her was the history of her son-in-law Nikephoros Bryennios,[105] and she was on intimate terms with the teacher of rhetoric Michael Italikos, later archbishop of Philippopolis, and with George Tornikios, metropolitan of Ephesos.[106] It was fitting that Irene should have a daughter like Anna Komnene, who wrote a biography of her father and who played a key role in the revival of Aristotelian scholarship, though not all of Anna's studies seem to have been undertaken with parental approval, and had to be pursued in secret with the palace eunuchs.[107]

It is easy to appear disinterested in power when you are given no choice. Irene seems to have been carefully elbowed from any of the centres of decision-making, even to the extent that she took no part in arranging the marriages of her own children. While later foreign brides of the dynasty took the name Irene, presumably as a compliment to her, Zonaras states that Alexios not only arranged the marriages of his own children, but those of his brother Isaac as well: Irene is not mentioned.[108] In one case, however, she is said to have broken up a marriage, that of her daughter Eudokia, because her son-in-law Iasites was not thought to be treating his wife in a manner suitable for a princess: she took the opportunity of Eudokia's falling ill to have her tonsured, while Iasites was removed from the palace.[109] On occasions when another empress might have been acting as regent in the capital during her husband's absences, Irene was travelling with hers. She was powerful in other ways, especially as part of the extended Doukas kin network, which in itself was central to Komnenian power and possessed great financial resources, but she had no direct say in matters of public policy or family networking.[110] She may have wished for such involvement: in view of events on Alexios's death, it is possible to conjecture that part of Alexios's motivation in taking Irene on campaign may have been to keep her out of the way, so she could not intrigue in the capital and interfere with John. She retained a strong sense of her family connections and her sympathies may have remained with the Doukas family when the chips were down.[111] Despite the fact that she had been the primary reason for Alexios's accession – he would not have had the support of the Doukas family without her[112] – she was little more than a figurehead for her family network, with no part in power for herself. Perhaps this rankled.

Transition and takeover

One of the great omissions in Anna Komnene's history is her failure to tell us that on her father's death she and her mother attempted to divert the succession from her brother John Komnenos to Anna's husband, the Caesar Nikephoros Bryennios.[113] Anna's motivation is clear: she wanted to be empress. Irene's is less so: perhaps she felt that it was her turn to influence events, and Anna seems to have been her favourite. Alexios expected trouble from Irene and exacted an oath from his relatives that they would only accept his son John as emperor; he did this in secret but Irene got to hear of it. John for his part built up an alternative support base.[114] There was clearly a power struggle between John and the imperial women; another brother, Andronikos, seems to have supported his mother's plans.[115] Irene's ploy consisted of broadcasting her bad opinion of John to Alexios in contrast to the virtues of her son-in-law Bryennios, and when Alexios's illness left her in control of government she turned the administration over to him.[116] Her nagging of her husband, now lying near death in the Mangana palace, had no effect: Alexios just pretended not to hear, and her refrain that John was not there because he was trying to steal the throne actually made Alexios smile – it was said that Alexios had connived at John's departure to seize control of the Great Palace and had let him take his ring before he left, on an occasion when Irene was not present.[117] Choniates records her as saying: 'Oh husband, in life you excelled in all kinds of deceits, gilding your tongue with contradictory meaning, and even now as you are departing this life you remain unchanged from your former ways.'[118] Irene appears to have gained the support of the Varangians and certainly built up a faction powerful enough to worry John: he had to gain entrance to the imperial palace by force and was prepared for trouble from his family.[119] His task was made easier by the fact that Bryennios himself made no moves to seize the throne, though John's absence meant that essential duties were not performed. Zonaras notes the shocking neglect of the deceased emperor, who died on 15 August 1118, with no one to bathe the corpse ritually and no imperial dress to attire him ceremonially, while John was too busy consolidating his position to attend the funeral.[120]

Alexios's last remark to Irene in the *Alexiad* seems somewhat enigmatic: 'Instead of surrendering yourself to the flood of woe that has come upon you, why not consider your own position and the dangers that now threaten you?'[121] Anna is here casting aspersions on John's treatment of his mother and sister, following his accession. But Alexios's passing was surely not as peaceful as Anna would like to have us believe. Irene was deliberately trying to upset the transfer of power and install her own candidate and Alexios was well aware of this.

The plot was unsuccessful and John was remarkably forgiving. But later in the year another plot, masterminded by Anna Komnene, centred again around Bryennios. The attempt, a plan to assassinate John while at the palace of Philopation, failed because Bryennios once again took no action at the appropriate time. Anna was furious, but this time Irene disapproved, both of the assassination attempt and of the plans for the coup d'état: she is reported to have said: 'in the absence of a successor it is necessary to seek an emperor, but a reigning monarch must not be removed' – a fine perception of the realities of female legitimation at Byzantium. The conspirators were deprived of their possessions, but many later had them restored, including Anna.[122] Nevertheless, John obviously felt uncomfortable with Irene and Anna around. They were persuaded into semi-retirement at Irene's convent of the Kecharitomene, though not tonsured, where Anna was to write her tale of the golden age when she had imperial status and ambitions. The year of Irene's death is not known: it may have been 19 February 1123 or 1133.[123]

Both Irene and Anna were disappointed that the method of legitimation which had succeeded for Maria of Alania did not work well when they needed it: it would have suited Anna to follow in her mother's, grand-mother's and potential mother-in-law's footsteps and become an empress. Irene and Anna failed, not because women had become less visible and sub-ordinated within the Komnenian family system,[124] but because the times were not propitious. Women did not lose authority under the Komnenoi: they still retained it in periods of transition and crisis, and of disputed succession, which is when they had previously possessed it. At times of stability, when there was an adult legitimate male heir, they had always had little power to influence events. And Komnenian women were their own enemies in this regard for biological reasons: mothers of numerous progeny, they were directly responsible for the firm foundation of the dynasty and there were thus no propitious opportunities for their involvement in the transfer of power. Irene's motives for supporting her daughter's claims over those of her son have to remain obscure, though a desire for authority had obviously lain dormant and frustrated during her years as empress. Irene was more than prepared to influence the transfer of power on her husband's death, and if she, or indeed her daughter Anna, had been left as a widow and regent for a young son, she would no doubt have been quite as capable of ruling the empire as Eudokia Makrembolitissa or Anna Dalassene.

12

MARIA OF ANTIOCH (1161–82/3)

The wives of John II and Manuel I Komnenos were not great political manipulators in the same way as the empresses of Alexios I. Piriska or Piroshka, at least, the Hungarian-born wife of John II, was overshadowed in her early married life by her redoubtable mother-in-law whose name Irene she also adopted, and her foreign birth meant that when she came to the fore she had no power group to support her in any attempts to interfere in political matters, even had she wished to do so.[1] In fact, she seems to have blamelessly devoted herself to her large family of eight children and pious works after her marriage in 1104, and was venerated as a saint after her death; she died, probably on 13 August 1134, under the monastic name Xene, like Anna Dalassene.[2] There is no reason to believe that John and Irene were not well suited; John paid tribute to her assistance in his *typikon* for the monastery of the Pantokrator which they jointly founded, to which was attached a hospital, though she died shortly after it was begun, and his grief at her death is mentioned in a poem of Kallikles.[3] The fact that court poets stress her descent shows that her subjects were conscious of her origins[4] – she was after all only the second foreign-born empress for several centuries. Her portrait in the south gallery of St Sophia (Plate 25) parallels that of Zoe and Constantine IX Monomachos and shows her with luxuriant auburn hair; it is a lasting tribute to her attractions and to the imperial dignity vested in the empress consort.[5] Choniates's history, though beginning with the death of Alexios I, does not mention Piriska or her marriage to John II, which shows that she made little impact on contemporary politics.

Much the same can be said for the first wife of Manuel I, John's successor. John set the fashion for foreign marriages for his four sons, importing, it appears, a number of princesses as imperial brides: the identity of some of these princesses is in doubt,[6] but his youngest son, Manuel, who was to succeed him, married twice, each time to a westerner. His first wife, Bertha of Sulzbach, sister-in-law of the German emperor Conrad III, also known to the Byzantines as Irene, did not have a high profile as empress: Manuel delayed marrying her until 1146, three years after his accession, and she failed to live up to the sartorial standards expected of empresses, instead

Plate 25 Piriska (Irene), wife of John II Komnenos, from the panel in the south gallery of St Sophia depicting her with her husband and eldest son Alexios (photo: Dumbarton Oaks, Washington DC)

devoting herself to literature and good works. She had the natural trait of being unbending and opinionated, and her view that only 'silly women' utilised beauty aids such as eye-liner and face powder must have isolated her among the glamour and frivolity of the court.[7] Manuel was noted for his affairs and taste in women and it was not surprising, therefore, that Bertha was overshadowed by Manuel's mistresses, most notably his niece Theodora who formed part of the imperial retinue.[8] Basil of Ochrid's statement that Bertha did not possess the arrogance and superciliousness one would expect of westerners, but was noted instead for her humility, modesty and piety, is perhaps a pointer to a general distrust of western empresses,[9] and the flattery of her western royal descent by court poets may reflect an awareness of her alien background,[10] which she obviated by trying to study Greek literature, commissioning works such as Tzetzes's *Allegories of the Iliad* in simple Greek verse. In this she was perhaps imitating her sister-in-law, Irene the *sebastokratorissa*, widow of Manuel's elder brother Andronikos, who may also have had western origins.[11] Bertha was the mother of two daughters in the 1150s, Maria and Anna; the latter died at the age of four. In 1147 the patriarch Kosmas had cursed her womb, after he had been accused of heresy, preventing her from bearing a son. Bertha in many ways resembles Piriska; both died before their husbands and were given no chance to make an impact on the Byzantine political scene, though Bertha is recorded by Kinnamos as supporting Manuel's heroic image 'in full senate', and played an important part in the reception of the Second Crusade.[12]

Bertha's death in late 1159 or early 1160 left him only a daughter, Maria. Manuel, while grieving bitterly according to custom ('his lamentation was like the roar of a lion'), was concerned to remarry as soon as possible. His illegitimate son Alexios by his niece Theodora was named *sebastokrator*, and in 1165/6 he fixed the succession on his daughter Maria and her fiancé Béla (Alexios) of Hungary as the future emperor and empress in default of a legitimate male heir.[13] After commencing negotiations for an alliance with Melisend of Tripoli, Manuel married Maria of Antioch, one of the daughters of Raymond of Poitiers and Constance of Antioch, in St Sophia on Christmas Day 1161.

Maria of Antioch and Maria Porphyrogenneta

To contemporary historians Maria was distinguished by exceptional beauty: 'she pulled in everyone as though on a line by the radiance of her appearance, her pearly countenance, her even disposition, candour, and charm of speech.'[14] She is shown as blonde and strikingly attractive in a miniature in a manuscript of the acts of the Council of 1166, which depicts her with Manuel, wearing a sumptuous crown and a blue-patterned red dress with wide sleeves and a high collar decorated with pearls. Her robe is studded with blue and red precious stones and she carries a jewelled sceptre and wears the red imperial shoes (Plate 26).[15] Born in the 1140s, her youth and appearance, linked with her foreign birth, ideal as they were for performing the ceremonial role of an empress consort, were not to prove an advantage, for she became very unpopular in the capital after Manuel's death, as regent for her young son Alexios II. She faced especially vigorous opposition from her stepdaughter Maria (Porphyrogenneta).[16] On Manuel's death, Maria, daughter of Manuel's first wife Bertha of Sulzbach, was nearly thirty and therefore not much younger than her stepmother. She had probably been born in March 1153, being acclaimed empress at her birth, and after waiting in vain for one of the glorious matches negotiated with western rulers to eventuate was finally married in February 1180, at an advanced age for a Byzantine girl, to Renier of Montferrat, who was given the rank of Caesar and was rather younger than his wife at about seventeen years of age. According to Choniates, Maria had now passed her thirtieth year and was said to be as strong as a man, and desperate for marriage.[17] The marriage of Renier and Maria was followed shortly afterwards by the betrothal of the eight-year-old Agnes-Anna of Savoy, daughter of Louis VII of France, to Manuel's son Alexios II.[18] The meeting of the two princesses is depicted in a manuscript

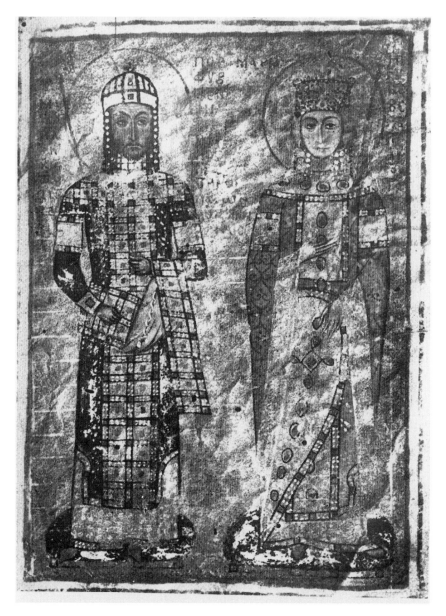

Plate 26 Manuel I Komnenos and Maria of Antioch (Vat. gr. 1176, f. IIr). (Taken from J. Spatharakis (1976) *The Portrait in Byzantine Illustrated Manuscripts*. Published by Brill, Leiden, The Netherlands)

containing verses welcoming Agnes to her new land, which describe how more than seventy ladies of the imperial house are sent to greet her, with one sent ahead to dress her as an Augusta for the occasion; Maria Porphyrogenneta, the *basilissa*, comes out of the city to pay homage to her new sister-in-law in a tent outside the walls.[19] Plate 27 depicts the arrival of Agnes in the capital and her adoption of Byzantine court costume.[20]

Maria and Béla of Hungary had been Manuel's heirs before the birth of her brother Alexios II in 1169, and after her betrothal to Béla was terminated Maria was offered as a bride to William II of Sicily, John Lackland, the youngest son of Henry II of England, and Henry, the son of Frederick Barbarossa.[21] Although her hopes of imperial status in Byzantium or a suitably royal marriage in the West had temporarily been dashed, she had no qualms in interfering in affairs after her father's death, and was one of the independent purple-born Komnenian princesses exemplified by Anna Komnene and Maria, John II's sister, who had foiled her husband's revolt against her brother.[22] Contemporary sources do not hint that Maria Porphyrogenneta had her eye on the throne for herself, but it is very possible that she may have seen herself as at least as suitable for the position of regent as her stepmother.[23] Maria had remained in the palace, still unmarried, for nearly a decade after the birth of her brother, and it is likely that a state of mutual hostility already existed between the two Marias before the regency even commenced: this has been deduced from the poem written by an admirer of the empress to celebrate Agnes's arrival, which emphasises the superiority of the new Latin princess over her sister-in-law.[24]

The new regent

The only involvement in politics by Maria of Antioch during Manuel's reign which has been recorded is when the interpreter Aaron Isaakios advised envoys during an audience not to accede too quickly to the emperor's demands. Maria, who understood what he was saying, later revealed his treachery to Manuel who had him blinded.[25] Clearly Maria was involved in the reception of foreign envoys and must have been a useful figurehead in Manuel's diplomatic relations with western leaders. However, for several years she was childless. Then, after a miscarriage, in September 1169 she became the mother of a long-hoped-for heir, Alexios II, Manuel's only legitimate son.[26] Manuel had been married since 1146 and it was a time of triumph:

> The imperial birth chamber, the Porphyra, was adorned in readiness; the roof was covered with thick purple textiles 'woven in dense hemispheres' by the palace weavers, while the outside walls were hung with silks. Inside was a gilded four-poster maternity bed draped with gold-embroidered curtains and pearl-studded covers.

Plate 27 The reception of the princess Agnes (Anna) of France (Vat. gr. 1851, f. 3v). (Taken from J. Spatharakis (1976) *The Portrait in Byzantine Illustrated Manuscripts*. Published by Brill, Leiden, The Netherlands)

Beside this stood a small couch, also richly covered, for receiving the new-born baby . . .[27]

After the birth, the red, pearl-embroidered slipper of a new-born infant was hung from the gallery above the entrance to the Great Palace, to the accompaniment of a fanfare by Ethiopian and Latin trumpeters with silver trumpets. Choniates adds the detail that the emperor kept anxiously consulting his astrologer.[28]

Manuel was concerned to make provision in case he died while Alexios was still a minor, and on 24 March 1171, eighteen months after Alexios's birth, Manuel had his officials and nobles and the patriarch and synod take an oath of fidelity to himself and his son Alexios: in the case of Manuel dying before Alexios came of age, they swore to accept him as emperor but obey Maria as regent, as long as she became a nun, was canonically tonsured and guarded the honour of the empire and her son.[29] The patriarch Theodosios Boradeiotes appears to have been associated with Maria in the regency: if so, Maria managed to marginalise his role.[30] Maria's reactions to these restrictions can only be imagined, but since the only other empress to have been similarly bound was Eudokia Makrembolitissa, who was not tonsured, it is not difficult to conjecture that she felt mistreated. In taking steps to prevent her remarriage Manuel was legislating against the possibility of a second husband who might endanger Alexios's accession. Maria had ten years in the lax milieu of Manuel's court in which to brood over her future destiny as a nun, and on his death in September 1180 she took the veil under the name 'Xene', the name also used by Anna Dalassene and Piriska. That her tonsure was against her own wishes can be seen by the fact that only a few months later, Maria, now regent for her eleven-year-old son Alexios II, was rumoured as being involved in an affair with Alexios the *protosebastos* and *protovestiarios*, Manuel's nephew, the most senior of the *sebastoi*.[31]

Westerners had become increasingly unpopular during Manuel's reign, and the populace was well aware of Maria's origins,[32] while the policies of her regime were seen to be pro-Latin.[33] She was surrounded by a throng of ambitious or rapacious relations, all of whom had designs on government, and the situation was exacerbated by the fact that Alexios had not actually been crowned. As an empress regent for a minor, especially one who had an older sister and numerous ambitious cousins, Maria was in a difficult and dangerous position. She was young and attractive and Eustathios calls her 'ripe for love': the very hint of the fact that she had bestowed her affections was a tinder-box. Her 'lover' Alexios was a widower,[34] and Choniates records that it was rumoured that the *protosebastos* was planning to seize the throne. He was not her only suitor: some took to curling their hair and using perfume, while others concentrated on appropriating public monies and attempting the throne by more practical means.[35] Alexios the heir was seen merely as a callow youth, and is reported to have been entirely devoted to childish pursuits such as hunting and chariot races, ignored by those who should have been instructing him.[36] Maria was thus at the centre of a power struggle, without the background or family network to cope with events, and she became generally unpopular at court as other bureaucrats saw their perquisites going to the *protosebastos*: still worse they feared that this situation would be perpetuated by her making him emperor. She was, of course, a nun, and a marriage to her husband's nephew would be incestuous, but this and her oath to Manuel could perhaps be circumvented, or she could legitimate his accession without marriage. The gossip reached unacceptable levels: Andronikos Komnenos, Manuel's cousin, whom Manuel had exiled for treasonable practices, argued the need for his return to the capital not merely because the *protosebastos* was a threat to the young emperor, but because of the ugly gossip current about the emperor's mother which was 'being proclaimed from the wall tops and lying in wait at the gates of princes and being echoed throughout the universe'.[37]

The 'holy war'

The *protosebastos* took full advantage of his position, and his combined rapacity and avarice, as well as his arrogance, drove the courtiers whom he had displaced to a state of frenzy, particularly once he had acquired total control of government by having the young emperor sign a decree that every official document had to be ratified by the *protosebastos* himself.[38] As early as February 1181 a number of family members, headed by Manuel's daughter Maria and her husband and Manuel's illegitimate son Alexios the *sebastokrator*, conspired to assassinate the *protosebastos*. The plot miscarried and was betrayed by one of the conspirators. Maria of Antioch herself presided over their trial with her son beside her; her involvement is noted by Eustathios as quite improper, while both Eustathios and Choniates record that it was a summary trial and unfairly conducted. The four principal leaders were imprisoned in the Great Palace; others were set free, went into exile or were secretly executed. Maria Porphyrogenneta and Renier heard they were to be arrested but forestalled this by fleeing to St Sophia and launching a full-scale rebellion.[39]

Maria Porphyrogenneta's revolt was inspired by thwarted ambition, disapproval of her stepmother's illicit affair and now the question of political survival. She had the support and sympathy of the clergy, the patriarch Theodosios, and most of the populace. In St Sophia Maria and Renier were welcomed by the patriarch, and refused the offer of an amnesty, demanding that their fellow conspirators should be released and the *protosebastos* be removed from office. When these demands were not met, St Sophia was turned into a stronghold, despite the patriarch's protests, and foreign mercenaries were enlisted.[40] The populace was securely on the side of 'the Caesars', abusing the *protosebastos* and even Maria of Antioch, both of whom were anathematised by a priest in the hippodrome. When the populace started plundering the city, the *protosebastos* and empress were incited to action and finally mobilised their troops. The patriarch, as a supporter of Maria Porphyrogenneta, had postponed the normal visit to the palace on Easter Sunday for the exchange of the kiss of peace with the emperor till the following Friday, because he feared he would be arrested. He was right to be concerned: the *protosebastos* had him confined in the monastery of Christ Pantepoptes and attempted to depose him, against the empress's wishes it appears, but this failed because there were no convincing charges against him and he was released. The attack on the patriarch allowed Maria Porphyrogenneta to see her cause as a 'holy war' and led to large casualties. The patriarch's release from custody was celebrated as a great popular triumph.[41]

An unpopular regime

The patriarch finally managed to arrange a truce at the beginning of May and under a promise of safe conduct the 'Caesars' agreed to an amnesty engineered by the patriarch: Maria Porphyrogenneta was assured that she would lose no dignities or privileges and there would be no reprisals against her supporters. The empress's popularity had taken a further turn for the worse: Eustathios records that she was hated by the whole community, with few exceptions, and her downfall was now generally canvassed; Andronikos Komnenos, Manuel's cousin, became an entrenched figurehead of opposition. Two of his sons had been involved in the Porphyrogenneta's conspiracy, and he had been invited back from exile by various notables as well as by Maria Porphyrogenneta to assume the protection of the young heir, since his mother had shown herself so unsuitable as a guardian, and to rid the government of the *protosebastos*. He had also written to the patriarch declaring his loyalty to Alexios.[42] Andronikos made his stand on both political and moral issues, accusing Maria of conspiracy against her son, and with the *protosebastos* of 'corrupting the purity of the crown', and demanded the deposition of the *protosebastos* and the retirement of Maria to a convent. He also claimed that Manuel had appointed him as one of the regents responsible for Alexios. Following the defection of the admiral Andronikos Kontostephanos, the *protosebastos* was apprehended in a palace coup and placed in the custody of the Varangian guard; several days later he was taken across the straits to Andronikos and blinded.[43] Choniates comments that had he not been such a weakling, and a 'stammerer spending half the day snoring', he could have barred Andronikos's entry into the city and used the treasury and fleet to defeat him, but that he lost his nerve. Maria's regime may also have had some financial problems: she was unable to establish a convent she had in view, and the 'house of Ioannitzes' was founded by Isaac Angelos instead, though this may simply have been because her plans were overtaken by events.[44] Maria had not just upset the balance of power at court and endangered the succession of her son by placing the government in the hands of one of her in-laws, she had chosen one with feet of clay, and Choniates's criticism of the regime's weakness is an indictment of her ability as well as that of her chief minister.

In April 1182 Andronikos harnessed the populace's anti-Latin sentiments and orchestrated a massacre of the 'Latins' in the city, on the grounds that the empress and the *protosebastos* had been paying for their support by gifts and promises of plundering the city. Some 60,000 are said by Eustathios to have died in the massacre, though the figure is certainly an exaggeration.[45] In the next month the patriarch Theodosios handed the city over to Andronikos, while protecting the interests of the young emperor Alexios, and ensuring he was crowned. The ceremony took place on 16 May 1182, a few days after Andronikos's arrival, and Andronikos carried Alexios into St Sophia on his shoulders and acted like his devoted supporter.[46]

At Andronikos's arrival in the city, Maria of Antioch and Alexios moved to the palace at Philopation, where Andronikos paid his respects to the emperor, though noticeably treating the empress with less courtesy. All the young Alexios's movements were closely guarded, and no one was allowed to discuss anything with him. The empress was now the main barrier to Andronikos's hopes of empire because of the oath that stated that she was to be the head of government until Alexios turned sixteen. In order to separate Alexios from his mother a campaign was orchestrated against Maria, and Andronikos threatened to leave because she was opposed to the good of the state and was conspiring against the emperor: the mob was also encouraged to abuse her. As his next move towards the throne, Andronikos had Maria Porphyrogenneta and Renier poisoned by their attendants. The main obstacle to the empress's removal was now the patriarch, but Andronikos threatened to turn the populace on him unless he cooperated and he was compelled to agree in writing to Maria's expulsion from the palace, later resigning in August 1183 over the issue of the marriage of Andronikos's daughter to Manuel's illegitimate son: Andronikos had gained the support of the populace, which Theodosios had until recently enjoyed.[47]

Then Andronikos turned on the empress: three judges of the *velum* were required to prosecute Maria for treason. When they first wished to ascertain whether the emperor had approved this, Andronikos labelled them supporters of the *protosebastos* and they were roughly handled by the populace. Maria of Antioch had unwisely attempted to enlist the help of her brother-in-law, Béla III of Hungary, by writing to him suggesting he ravage the lands around Branichevo and Belgrade. She was now found guilty of treason before a court composed of judges hostile to her cause and imprisoned in a narrow dungeon near the Golden Gate, where she was subjected to ill-treatment and mockery from her guards. Her son Alexios, now thirteen, signed the document condemning her to death. Her execution was postponed because of the refusal of Andronikos's son Manuel and brother-in-law George to carry it out, but shortly afterwards, perhaps at the end of 1182, she was strangled and buried on the sea-shore. This left the young emperor without protection: Alexios II was strangled with a bowstring, and his body was thrown into the sea encased in lead.[48]

Maria's execution was generally condemned even by her critics: she was after all empress and in charge of the government until her son came of age.[49] She had not been popular, but Andronikos obviously feared a backlash of popular opinion: after her assassination he had all public portraits of her repainted as if she were a wizened old woman, in case they should elicit the populace's sympathy.[50] She had been vulnerable because she had no family network at her back and was without the capacity to rule the empire herself in the same way as Eudokia or Anna Dalassene. In addition she was a vulnerable target for those with anti-Latin sympathies, particularly when they were incited by the porphyrogennete sister of the young emperor, herself married to an Italian. Maria of Antioch's supposed affair with Alexios the *protosebastos* not only disturbed the balance of power at court, it too was used as a means of whipping up popular disapproval and it was easy to portray her activities as endangering the status of her young son, the rightful emperor, and breaking her oath to Manuel that 'she would guard the honour of the empire'. The fact that Alexios was seen as light-minded, even for a young teenager, added additional fuel to criticism of her regency in a milieu where the ideals of motherhood, as embodied in Anna Dalassene for example, were paramount.

By preventing the possibility of her marrying after his death – a restriction she obviously resented – Manuel had tied her hands, robbing her of the choice of securing the dynasty through a second marriage. This, together with the fact that foreign-born women were bound to be at a disadvantage when faced with the realities of imperial power, meant that Maria was vulnerable to ambitious predators. She was unable to call on the necessary support to make her regime viable: her reliance on one of her husband's relatives, like her request for help from her relative Béla, made the situation worse. But this does not mean that imperial women had been marginalised during the twelfth century in terms of their potential for political involvement: Maria had been given the power but not the necessary conditions in which to operate as regent. When, however, Euphrosyne Doukaina comes to the throne as the consort of Alexios Angelos we see once again a dominant imperial woman who had full potential for domination and autocracy even during the reign of her husband.

13

EUPHROSYNE DOUKAINA
(1195–1203)

Euphrosyne Doukaina, the wife of Alexios III Angelos, belonged to the family of the Kamateroi, one of the great bureaucratic families of the empire. Her marriage to Alexios preceded by some years their rise to the throne, which was achieved by deposing and blinding Alexios's younger brother Isaac II Angelos in 1195. Euphrosyne was *par excellence* one of the masterful Byzantine-born women who are seen in the imperial family – a successor of Eudokia Makrembolitissa and Anna Dalassene as well as of Irene Doukaina, all of whom had an eye to their family's advantage and a clear view to their own status and prominence. When Euphrosyne married into the noble but undistinguished family of the Angeloi, she would have had no idea that this would bring her to the purple, but given the opportunity she had no problems in adjusting to imperial rank and prerogatives.

Euphrosyne was descended from the Caesar John Doukas, brother of Constantine X Doukas and grandfather of the empress Irene Doukaina, probably through Irene's brother Michael whose daughter Irene married the *logothete* Gregory Kamateros.[1] Significantly Euphrosyne herself used the name Euphrosyne Doukaina, stressing her imperial connections rather than her descent from the bureaucratic Kamateroi.[2] Euphrosyne's father, Andronikos Doukas Kamateros, had been the eparch of Constantinople and *megas droungarios* (the judge who headed the court of the *velum*). He held the rank of *pansebastos* and as a skilled theologian was one of the ministers close to Manuel I Komnenos, assisting in carrying out ecclesiastical policy: one of his duties was the editing of the transcripts of Manuel's theological debates with papal and Armenian emissaries. In 1161 he had been one of the embassy sent to escort Maria of Antioch to Constantinople to marry Manuel.[3] Choniates, who shows some bias against the Kamateroi for reasons which will become obvious, gives a lively picture of Andronikos's brother John Kamateros, Euphrosyne's uncle, who was *logothete tou dromou* under Manuel I and the emperor Manuel's drinking companion. He describes him as 'of all men the most gluttonous and the hardest drinker': apparently, though this need not be taken literally, Kamateros had a passion for green beans, consuming whole fields, raw when possible, and carrying off what he could not eat.[4]

Euphrosyne's brother John also served as eparch and was imprisoned for opposing Alexios the *protosebastos* in 1181; after Andronikos Komnenos's assassination he may have been made *logothete tou dromou* by Isaac II.[5] A second brother, Basil Kamateros Doukas, who was *logothete tou dromou* under Manuel, was blinded for rebelling against Andronikos Komnenos, but returned to office under Alexios III and Euphrosyne, perhaps as the *logothete tou genikou*.[6] Two of the Kamateroi were patriarchs under the Angeloi brothers: Basil II Kamateros between 1183 and 1186 and John X Kamateros, Euphrosyne's second cousin, from 1198 to 1206, while John Kamateros, the *epi tou kanikleiou* (keeper of the imperial inkstand), became archbishop of Bulgaria.[7] Euphrosyne's brother-in-law, Michael Stryphnos, married to her sister Theodora, became *megas dux* in charge of the fleet.[8] Clearly Euphrosyne's family deserves the title of 'the most powerful bureaucratic dynasty of the late twelfth century',[9] a position to which she herself certainly contributed. While the identity of the first wife of Isaac Angelos is unknown, it is perhaps significant that Isaac's and Alexios's mother, Euphrosyne Kastamonitissa, also came from a family of bureaucrats, and that bureaucrats prospered under the Angeloi brothers.[10]

Isaac and Alexios Angelos

Euphrosyne's brother-in-law Isaac Angelos (1185–95) had himself come to the throne before he was thirty years of age, through killing Stephen Hagiochristophorites, the henchman of Andronikos Komnenos who had come to arrest him, by splitting his head with an axe, and fleeing to St Sophia, where he was proclaimed emperor by the people who rose on his behalf. But the reign of Isaac Angelos was punctuated by revolts – those of Alexios Branas, the pretenders 'Alexios II', Isaac Komnenos and Andronikos Komnenos – and Choniates suggests that these and other leaders of sedition were not only generally inspired to insurrection by Isaac's ineffectual and inconsistent government, but were deliberately trying to copy Isaac's own path to power.[11] Isaac's government was to arouse the jealousy of other aristocratic families connected with the Komnenoi, particularly because he concentrated power within a small clique:[12] however, his downfall was to come from a combination of these and his own family.

During Isaac's reign his elder brother Alexios had enjoyed the rank of *sebastokrator* and in 1192 was governor of the Thrakesion theme. Despite excellent treatment at Isaac's hands, Alexios had long been waiting to seize the throne. Isaac had been warned of this by many, but Alexios was clever at concealing his plans under a pretence of affection and Isaac took no notice of the accusations.[13] Euphrosyne was clearly heavily involved in Alexios's coup in April 1195, and it was supported by a powerful aristocratic faction: Theodore Branas, George Palaiologos, John Petraliphas, Constantine Raoul, Manuel Kantakouzenos 'and many other perverse and weak-minded men, the emperor's kinsmen as well as a swarm of the common herd who for a long time had roamed gaping through the *sebastokrator* [Alexios]'s banqueting hall'.[14] Typically Alexios avoided confrontation and took the opportunity of a hunting expedition of his brother on 8 April, while they were at Kypsella in the Balkans, prior to the commencement of another campaign against the Vlachs, to have him removed from power. Isaac fled when he heard his brother being proclaimed emperor in the imperial tent, but was apprehended and then blinded and incarcerated in a monastery outside of Constantinople. The take-over must have been well planned: as soon as the revolution was noised abroad, all the army, most of the senators, the bureaucracy and Isaac's attendants defected to his brother, and Alexios ascended the throne without factional strife.[15] Alexios and Euphrosyne were clearly using their network of contacts and family connections to good advantage.

While these events took place in Thrace, Euphrosyne was preparing for the new emperor's entry into the city. Alexios, secure in the knowledge that his brother was safely blinded, did not hurry home. His coup was greeted with apathy by the populace in general. There was only violent opposition from one quarter, when some of the 'artisans and rabble' set up a rival candidate Alexios Kontostephanos, while Euphrosyne was on her way to the Great Palace escorted by members of distinguished families. Nevertheless she took over the Great Palace at great risk to herself, the mob was dispersed and Kontostephanos thrown into prison.[16] The patriarch too apparently put up a token resistance but this was only momentary. Even before Alexios arrived or anyone knew what had happened to the last incumbent of the throne everyone slavishly deserted to Euphrosyne:

> They prostrated themselves before the alleged emperor's wife and placed their heads under her feet as footstools, nuzzled their noses against her felt slipper like fawning puppies, and stood timidly at her side, bringing their feet together and joining their hands. Thus these stupid men were ruled by hearsay, while the wily empress, adapting easily to circumstances, gave fitting answers to all queries and put the foolish Byzantines in a good humour, beguiling them with her fair words. Lying on their backs, in the manner of hogs, with their bellies stroked and their ears tickled by her affable greetings, they expressed no righteous anger whatsoever at what had taken place.[17]

Choniates's view of proceedings and of Euphrosyne herself is clearly expressed here in his contempt for the disloyalty of the palace officials and his dislike of the masterful empress. It was not until several days later that Alexios actually entered the city, and his leisurely conduct shows the confidence he had in his wife's ability to manage affairs.[18] Their reign continued in the same way as it had commenced, with Euphrosyne playing a dominant role in imperial politics.

Euphrosyne the 'monstrous evil'

Euphrosyne had three daughters, Irene, Anna and Eudokia, all of whom were married at the time of her accession, and she must have married Alexios not later than 1170.[19] At the time of her accession she need only have been about forty years of age (her husband Alexios was born *c.* 1153). It is inconceivable to imagine that she did not play an important part in her husband's decision to depose his brother, especially since her bureaucratic connections must have been of great assistance in the acceptance of her husband as a suitable ruler. Alexios is invariably shown by Choniates as a weak and malleable emperor and blamed, like his brother, for his devotion to pleasure, his extravagance, and for enriching courtesans and relatives at the state's expense.[20] He rewarded his supporters lavishly, and handed out public money and revenues with abandon; when these were exhausted he granted titles instead, and thus the highest honour became dishonourable and the love of honour a thankless pursuit'; he even signed any document put before him, whatever grant or concession it requested.[21]

Euphrosyne on the other hand was masterful enough for two, and though she was feminine enough to like finery and jewels this may well have been to reinforce her imperial status rather than for reasons of vanity. Choniates, who was *logothete ton sekreton*, in charge of the entire civil administration (at least in name), during the reign of Alexios III and who would thus have known her well,[22] stresses her masculine spirit and love of domination, and commences his account of Alexios's reign following his coronation by depicting Alexios as withdrawing himself from the administration of affairs and spending his time instead wearing golden ornaments and granting the petitions of those who had supported his rise to power. Euphrosyne, in marked contrast to Alexios, he portrays as manly in spirit, as possessor of a graceful and honeyed tongue, and as adept at foretelling the future and managing the present according to her own wishes. Choniates brushes aside discussion of her sartorial splendour, her squandering of the empire's reserves on luxurious living, and her ability to persuade her husband to alter established conventions and create new ones. Instead he concentrates his criticism on the improprieties of behaviour of this 'monstrous evil' and the way in which by publicly dishonouring the 'veil of modesty' by her domineering behaviour she brought reproach upon her husband, who was fully aware of all her improprieties, but preferred to take no notice of them.[23]

Choniates tells us that she loved power so much that she even encroached on the emperor's prerogatives, and held in contempt the conventions of earlier empresses. She issued commands with authority equal to that of Alexios, and when she chose cancelled the emperor's decrees and altered them to suit her wishes. While empresses were accustomed to be present at the reception of important foreign embassies, Euphrosyne used the opportunity to emphasise her collegiality and grasp of power and was seated by the side of the emperor on an equally sumptuous throne. She sat in council with the emperor, dressed majestically, 'her crown embellished with gems and translucent pearls and her neck adorned with costly small necklaces'. She also contravened custom by holding her own separate court, where subjects who had first paid homage to the emperor then paid reverence to her with even deeper prostrations. And the emperor's blood relations, who held the highest offices, would place their shoulders under her splendid throne and carry her as if in a litter.[24]

Alexios's reign was not without its vicissitudes and very real outside threats. Isaac Komnenos, nephew of Manuel I Komnenos, had taken Cyprus in 1184 and, after being captured by Richard Coeur de Lion in 1191, made his way to Kaykhusraw at Ikonion. Euphrosyne encouraged Alexios to recall him and many letters were dispatched to this effect. Isaac firmly refused to return as he had designs on the throne, but was unable to find sufficient support and Kaykhusraw refused to assist him in his plans for an attack on the empire.[25] At Christmas 1196 Henry VI of Germany demanded 5,000 lb of gold or threatened to invade the empire. Alexios was able to have the sum reduced to 1,600 lb, but his proposal of a 'German tax' was strongly resisted by all classes, especially because he had squandered the public wealth among his rapacious relations (all of whom were useless creatures according to Choniates). The emperor was forced to drop the proposal. Enough money was raised, however, by plundering the tombs in the Holy Apostles, the sum amounting to 7,000 lb of silver.[26]

Bureaucracy and corruption

It was under the Angeloi that bureaucrats once again came back to real power at court.[27] Euphrosyne's connections were among the great bureaucratic families and thanks to her, and to his general apathy, Alexios tended to leave the bureaucracy to itself as the controlling power in the empire. All the emperor's relatives, and notably his in-laws, were avaricious and grasping, according to Choniates, and the turnover of officials taught them to steal and loot, purloin public taxes and amass immense wealth. They despoiled the petitioners who came to them to use their interest with the emperor, and appropriated the monies involved, which surpassed any private fortune. As a result, ministries were offered for sale; anyone who wished could become governor of a province or receive high rank, and Choniates blames for this the light-mindedness of the emperor and his inability to govern, the greed of his connections and the desire to amass money by which 'the affairs of state became the sport of the women's apartments and the emperor's near male relations. Alexios had no more idea of what was going on in the empire than the inhabitants of "ultima Thule" [the British Isles].'[28]

Euphrosyne, however, was better informed of the state of affairs and it was in these circumstances that she decided to interfere openly in government, even though some of the worst perpetrators were her own relatives and Alexios himself. This was perhaps in late 1195. 'As nothing could escape her inquisitiveness and her love for money, she decided she could not voluntarily keep quiet for long; either the appointments were not to be sold by the command of her husband or the monies collected must be stored in the imperial treasury.'[29] There was to be no more large-scale pilfering or sale of offices for personal enrichment, and to effect this she had Constantine Mesopotamites reappointed to office: Mesopotamites had previously served under Isaac II. She managed to reconcile Alexios and Mesopotamites, even though Mesopotamites had disapproved of Alexios's coup and Alexios had dismissed him. This move by Euphrosyne changed the dynamics of government, as administration was in the hands of Mesopotamites, who in the emperor's eyes was now 'the horn of plenty, the mixing-bowl of many virtues, or the herbage of Job's field . . . light was shed from his eyes, and life-giving air poured into his nostrils; he was the genuine pearl of Perez, ever hanging from the emperor's ears, considered worth the entire realm'.[30] Considering that earlier Alexios had looked on him with contempt, this shows the power of Euphrosyne's influence in politics and Alexios's unrivalled ability to change his mind. On the other hand the description of Mesopotamites as 'Briareus the hundred-handed' implies that far too much power was put into Mesopotamites's hands and that he took full advantage of the fact, which redounds to Euphrosyne's discredit, though his depredations were far more restrained and far less dangerous than those of Euphrosyne's relatives.

The effectiveness of these measures in controlling the rapacity of her family was to cause Euphrosyne's temporary downfall. Her own son-in-law, her daughter Irene's husband Andronikos Kontostephanos, and her brother Basil Kamateros Doukas, after considerable thought and conspiratorial deliberation, countered the move and took revenge for this appointment of Mesopotamites by laying a charge of adultery against her in 1196.[31] Pretending that their loyalty and affection to the emperor outweighed their relationship to Euphrosyne, they asserted that Euphrosyne had taken a young man, Alexios's adopted son Vatatzes, as her lover, further suggesting that this might mean a threat to Alexios's throne, the implication being that as Euphrosyne's choice he was sure of becoming emperor. They reported to Alexios:

Your wife, O Despot, with unveiled hand perpetrates the most loathsome acts, and as she betrays you, her husband, in the marriage bed as a wanton, we fear lest she soon instigate rebellion. The confidant with whom she rejoices licentiously to lie, she has likely chosen to become emperor and is bent upon achieving this end. It is necessary, therefore, that she be deprived of all power and divested of her great wealth.[32]

They suggested that Vatatzes be immediately dealt with, while Euphrosyne could wait until after the conclusion of Alexios's campaign in Thrace which was due to commence. Their appeal to Alexios's avarice and desire to be rid of Euphrosyne succeeded. Delighted with the pretext he listened to them as though they were a 'rare and welcome treasure'. Vatatzes, who was on campaign against Alexios the Cilician, a pretender to the throne, was executed by Vastralites, one of Alexios's bodyguards. His head was taken back to the emperor, who kicked it and 'addressed it in terms wholly unfit to be included in this history'.[33] However, he set out for Thrace without taking further action against Euphrosyne.[34] On Alexios's return two months later, he moved first into the palace at Aphameia and then into the Philopation. Euphrosyne in the meantime had realised the danger which faced her of being expelled in disgrace from the palace and even of losing her life. She appealed to all who had the emperor's confidence to assist her, and was pitied by the majority. One faction roundly informed the emperor to take no notice of the charges against her by such untrustworthy accusers, 'prickly in manner, stitchers of falsehood, crooked in speech, and even captious and querulous'. Another faction warned him that, if he dismissed Euphrosyne now, he could hardly recall her later without disgrace.[35]

Alexios finally entered the palace of Blachernai and allowed Euphrosyne to have dinner with him for one last time, but was unable to disguise his anger. In a forthright manner she demanded to be placed on trial and begged the emperor to give her a fair hearing rather than be swayed by the falsehoods of her relatives. But instead Alexios tortured some of the women of the bedchamber, learning the precise details of affairs from the eunuchs. Whatever was revealed in these sessions, a few days later Euphrosyne was divested of her imperial robes and removed from the palace, through a little-known passageway. Dressed in a common work-woman's frock she was taken in a two-oared fishing boat to Nematarea, a convent near the mouth of the Black Sea. Her escort comprised two handmaids, who spoke only broken Greek.[36]

The emperor's display of his ultimate power caused Euphrosyne's relations some discomfort. They had not expected such drastic measures and were rather taken by surprise. They had after all neatly undercut their own power base and caused themselves some distress, 'though they were not as distressed as they should have been', and were publicly reproached by the populace for their behaviour.[37] Euphrosyne remained banished from October 1196 to March 1197, and would have remained so had her relatives not had enough. They had not achieved the removal of Mesopotamites, and were harassed by public criticism for their behaviour in having disgraced the empress who had honoured them. She was therefore reinstated and became more powerful than ever before. With consummate diplomacy, she avoided expressing her anger against her opponents, took no revenge and insinuated herself back into her husband's affections: 'since it was a long time since he had shown her any affection, nor had he gone to bed with her, she cleverly insinuated herself into his good graces, choosing to wheedle him with cunning. In this way, she took over almost the complete administration of the empire.'[38]

Despite continual attempts by her relatives to topple Mesopotamites, Euphrosyne successfully retained him in power. But he, delighted by the empress's return, then overreached himself, considering the office of *epi tou kanikleiou*, keeper of the imperial inkstand, not suited to his abilities. He chose to enter the church as well, and was appointed archbishop of Thessalonika, thinking any situation intolerable except that in which he controlled both palace and church. He inserted his two brothers into government 'like wedges or hoops', or hung them 'like earrings on both the emperor's ears so that should he ever be attending a church synod nothing should be done or said without his knowledge'.[39] He soon returned to direct affairs in the palace, including the conduct of campaigns, but his opponents had had enough. Under the leadership of Michael Stryphnos, *megas dux* of the fleet and Euphrosyne's brother-in-law, a case was presented to the emperor, which had Mesopotamites expelled from the palace, 'like a well-rounded missile propelled from a mighty siege engine'. He was also expelled from holy orders. The decision of the synod was made without due examination and as a result of unjust accusations. When the charges brought against him were not thought to be substantial enough, the patriarch George Xiphilinos added others, and Mesopotamites was dismissed. On this occasion it appears that Euphrosyne's relatives outmanoeuvred her. Choniates even speaks of the 'extreme stupidity of those responsible' which implies that this was done without her involvement. Mesopotamites was replaced as *epi tou kanikleiou* by the urbane and rhetorically minded Theodore Eirenikos and 'a second individual', who learnt from Mesopotamites's downfall, and both relied on intrigue to minimise their own overt power for fear of the consequences.[40]

Michael Stryphnos, who was so instrumental in having Mesopotamites expelled from the palace, was another of Euphrosyne's grasping relatives (Plate 28). He was particularly concerned to oppose the influence wielded by the *epi tou kanikleiou*, because Mesopotamites had, quite justifiably, prosecuted him for his depredations as admiral. Stryphnos survived Mesopotamites in power and was one of the prime examples of the maladministration which was so prevalent under Alexios. According to Choniates, he 'beyond all men, was greedy of gain and appropriated and eagerly gulped down the public revenues'; he even used his position as admiral to sell the ships' nails, anchors, ropes and sails, and, because of his depredations, by the time of the Fourth Crusade only twenty rotting and worm-eaten ships were available for active service.[41] The Fourth Crusade thus met no opposition from the Byzantine navy when it sailed into Constantinople. Being a member of the imperial family under Alexios was a profitable business, but it is to

217

Plate 28 A seal of Michael Stryphnos, showing St Theodore with a spear and shield and St Hyakinthos with an axe (he suffered martyrdom for cutting down an elm tree venerated by pagans). The inscription reads, 'St Theodore, St Hyakinthos. The seal of Michael, *megas dux* and husband of Theodora, sister of the empress' (Dumbarton Oaks Byzantine Collection: Washington DC)

Euphrosyne's credit that she attempted to remedy some of the drain on the state's revenues. On the other hand little was achieved in actual terms. Alexios himself was involved in some of the worst manifestations of criminal maladministration, and actually commissioned Constantine Phrangopoulos with six triremes to plunder foreign merchant shipping in the Black Sea. Those who survived came to Constantinople entreating recompense from the emperor, but he had sold the merchandise and placed the revenues in his treasury and so dismissed their appeal. Choniates's indictment of the poor administration under the Angeloi brothers is damning for their government,[42] though it should be noted that Euphrosyne herself was extremely wealthy, with estates in southern Thessaly and Epiros, and had gained considerable financial independence from her husband's rise to power.[43]

Her influence remained paramount. Alexios suffered from inflammation in the joints, resulting in immobility and high fevers, as well as a virulent discharge from his feet. The consequences of an attempt to cauterise his feet himself caused alarm: his physicians were all summoned and his relatives feared for the worst. Purgatives, mixed almost day by day, worked wonders. Nevertheless Euphrosyne made contingency plans for the future:

> With her close friends she took counsel over hidden portents and disclosed the secrets hidden in her breast pertaining to the successor to the throne, so that he should not be hostile and hateful towards her but well pleased . . . Various choices were proposed and votes taken on possible future emperors, all with the purpose of benefiting their promoters; no thought whatsoever was given as to who would be a worthy emperor of the Romans and an excellent administrator of

public affairs, and so infants at the breast and wrapped in swaddling clothes were picked by the dolts to rule.[44]

The emperor's three brothers and his brother-in-law had been blinded by Andronikos Komnenos, he had no male issue, and his daughters Anna and Irene were recently widowed. The main contenders for the throne, therefore, appear to have been Alexios's uncle the *sebastokrator* John Doukas and his nephew the *protostrator* Manuel Kamytzes, and the emperor's nephews, who were canvassed as possibilities. This wheeling and dealing inspires Choniates to a diatribe on the departed glory of the empire and those who coveted it, ravishing her like lustful lovers. As it turned out the emperor recovered, but Choniates felt that negotiations which offered the possibility of a 'job lot' of nephews hardly redounded to the credit of the empire.[45]

Euphrosyne continued to keep an eye on affairs in the capital during her husband's absences. She seems to have played a part in 1201 in foiling the rebellion of John 'the Fat', and when Alexios returned in the summer of 1200 after a campaign in the Balkans against Ivanko, he found Euphrosyne not content with 'keeping within doors but playing the man against seditionists and demagogues and unravelling the machinations woven by a certain Kontostephanos'.[46] This rebellion in the capital seems to have been a symbol of general discontent,[47] possibly centring on the same Alexios Kontostephanos who was proclaimed emperor in 1195. Choniates implies moderate approval: 'these things would not have been held in contempt, nor would they have excited wonderment from afar, had they been bound by limitations.' Her involvement in government was not only beneficial but even expected, but apparently Euphrosyne had developed a passionate interest in fortune-telling and divination, and her 'mad delusions and excessive zeal' led her to believe that she could dispel coming misfortunes. Her attempts to foretell the future involved unspeakable rituals and divinations and she even cut off the snout of the Kalydonian boar in the hippodrome and proposed to have one of the statues there flogged in the belief that this would affect events. Other statues had their limbs and heads removed, which disgusted the populace and gave rise to popular taunts and reproaches, though it should be noted that she was not the only member of the imperial family to believe in such methods of divination: Isaac II, after his return to the throne in 1203, removed the Kalydonian boar from its pedestal, brushed up the hair on its body and placed it in the Great Palace, in the hope that this would control the populace. Parrots were especially trained to repeat in the streets and crossroads 'πολιτικὴ τὸ δίκαιον' ('whore, set a fair price') to mock Euphrosyne's behaviour and remind her of the 'adultery' episode three years earlier.[48]

Furthermore, Euphrosyne was given to falconry, and obviously took it seriously, wearing a properly fitted leather glove, shot through with gold, on which she held a bird trained to hunt game. She even 'clucked and shouted out commands and was followed by a considerable number of those who attend to and care about such things' – Choniates's scorn is obvious from his phraseology and Euphroysne clearly displayed contempt for the conventions of behaviour adhered to by Irene Doukaina and other Komnenian empresses.[49] The celebrations held by Alexios and Euphrosyne in 1199 to mark the second marriages of their daughters Irene and Anna to members of the Byzantine nobility is further evidence for the imperial family's taste for vulgar pastimes, the entertainment revolving essentially around the buffoonery and humiliation of one of the court's high-ranking eunuchs.[50]

Euphrosyne's public face

Euphrosyne was a nonconformist in behaviour – she was too masterful, too masculine and unconventional,[51] while her behaviour was totally inappropriate for an empress consort. Not only did she publicly parade her mastery and love of majesty but she let the side down in other ways, such as her involvement in sorcery and divination. But a very different impression of Euphrosyne is given in Choniates's public speeches, where he portrays her as a fitting consort for Alexios. The fact that he praises her political wisdom, her actions against dissidents and revolutionaries, and her guardianship of the empire in Alexios's absence on campaign, shows that these qualities were part of her public image and suitable grounds on which to flatter the empress. While Alexios combats weapons of war among the barbarian tribes, Euphrosyne is compared to the wise woman of Solomon's *Proverbs* and praised for protecting his throne at home. Rather than just emphasising her appearance in the kind of flattery that would do for any woman, and passing by her stature, complexion and standing as a 'Fourth Grace', Choniates also stresses her royal descent, and the fact that she is Byzantine-born.[52] But she was clearly not above praise of her appearance; in another speech in which he describes Euphrosyne as co-ruling with Alexios, he also pays tribute to her beauty, which surpasses that of all other woman, as her virtues surpass those of all other empresses.[53] Nikolaos Mesarites also praised Euphrosyne for her resourcefulness in the context of the revolution of John Komnenos 'the Fat', implicitly contrasting her with other women whose concern was only with items of rich clothing, while Euphrosyne is instead beautified by her wisdom and counsel.[54]

With regard to her immediate family, Euphrosyne demonstrated her skill at strengthening the family's influence and connections in the advantageous marriages of her daughters to members of the Byzantine aristocracy. All three of them married at least twice, and one was to become empress as wife of Theodore Laskaris, while another became the ancestress of the Palaiologue dynasty. Irene, the eldest, married first Andronikos Kontostephanos who died *c.* 1197, and then Alexios Palaiologos, who had first to divorce his existing wife. He received the title despot and his wife Irene was proclaimed empress, as the designated heirs. Irene was to be the grandmother of Michael

VIII Palaiologos through her daughter Theodora. Anna, the beautiful one, was married first to Isaac Komnenos Vatatzes the *sebastokrator*, who was taken prisoner by the Bulgars in 1196 and died in captivity, and then to Theodore Laskaris, the first emperor of Nicaea.[55] Their sister Eudokia was married first to Stephen I Nemanja of Serbia, a match presumably arranged by her uncle Isaac II, but Stephen threw her out on the grounds of adultery in 1198, and she then had an affair with Alexios V Doukas Mourtzouphlos (so called because of his heavy eyebrows) who fell passionately in love with her and may not have married her until after the fall of the city to the Latins in 1204. Her third husband was Leo Sgouros of Corinth.[56]

The crusaders and the empire

In the autumn of 1201 Isaac Angelos's son Alexios managed to escape from the capital and flee to the West, first to Sicily and then to his brother-in-law Philip of Swabia. He was able to enlist the help of the leader of the Fourth Crusade, now in preparation, Boniface of Montferrat. This was to have fatal consequences for the empire and provided an excuse to divert its destination to the Byzantine capital. When the crusade fleet reached the city in June 1203 the young Alexios was with them. Even the news that the crusaders were besieging Zara in November 1202, and might well prove a threat to the empire, saw the emperor disposed to inaction, despite the fact that he had had advance information about the Latins' plans:

> When it was proposed that he make provisions for an abundance of weapons, undertake the preparation of suitable war engines, and, above all, begin the construction of warships, it was as though his advisers were talking to a corpse. He indulged in after-dinner repartee and in wilful neglect of the reports on the Latins; he busied himself with building lavish bathhouses, levelling hills to plant vineyards, and filling in ravines, wasting his time in these and other activities. Those who wanted to cut timber for ships were threatened with the gravest danger by the eunuchs who guarded the thickly wooded mountains, that were reserved for the imperial hunts . . .[57]

Alexios III's failure to deal with the arrival of the Fourth Crusade was masterly in its inactivity. After one ignominious attempt at meeting the newcomers, and faced with the crusaders outside the city and an increasingly vocal and hostile populace inside it, his reaction in mid-July 1203 was to run away to Develtos, just south of Anchialos on the Black Sea. He communicated his scheme, to which he had clearly given some thought, to several of his female chamberlains and relatives and his daughter Irene, and he took with him 1,000 lb of gold and other imperial ornaments of jewels and pearls. Euphrosyne was left behind, and presumably was not informed of his plans because they would have incurred her extreme disapproval.[58] All Alexios's relatives and friends, including Euphrosyne, were immediately under suspicion of treason. Hence the finance minister, Constantine Philoxenites, assured of the backing of a faction that would support the blinded ex-emperor Isaac II, had him brought out of prison and set on the throne again on 17–18 July. On 1 August Isaac crowned his son Alexios IV co-emperor, even though this meant that the crusaders would expect the immense sum of 200,000 marks that Alexios had promised for their help.

That Euphrosyne was a considerable threat to any opposing regime was clearly shown by the fact that, when Alexios fled the capital in July 1203, one of the first actions of the new government was to seize and imprison Euphrosyne and her close relatives. The new emperor, the reinstated Isaac II, also appropriated their funds, which Choniates implies were immense, to use to conciliate the crusader leaders who were pressing heavily for payment.[59] The young Alexios IV was soon murdered and replaced by his cousin's lover, Alexios V Doukas Mourtzouphlos, who came to power to combat the crusaders. Alexios IV's deposition and murder triggered the crusaders' attack on the city on 9 April 1204, followed by a second attack on 12 April which was successful. When Mourtzouphlos was sure that the city was lost, he took Euphrosyne and her daughters, including his beloved Eudokia, and sailed away after a two-month reign.[60] Choniates suggests that Mourtzouphlos and Eudokia were married after their escape and Villehardouin also implies that Mourtzouphlos asked for Eudokia's hand only when he heard that Alexios III was at Mosynoupolis.[61]

After Develtos, Alexios III made for Adrianople, where he proclaimed himself emperor – but not for long. He was soon forced to flee again before the approach of a crusader force, and Mourtzouphlos and the women met up with him at Mosynoupolis in the summer of 1204. Mourtzouphlos was invited by Alexios for dinner, but Alexios had a grudge against him, perhaps because of his affair with Eudokia or his time as emperor. Instead of entertaining him in a manner befitting a family member he had his son-in-law's eyes put out in the bathroom.[62] Mourtzouphlos was later captured by the Latins and sentenced to death for killing his 'lord' Alexios IV: the crusaders dispatched him in novel fashion by throwing him down from a column at the Forum Tauri.[63] Alexios III and Euphrosyne then moved to Thessalonika where they were welcomed by Isaac II's widow Margaret-Maria of Hungary, now wife of one of the crusade leaders, Boniface of Montferrat, who was absent campaigning in northern Greece. Alexios III and Euphrosyne were expelled after being discovered in a conspiracy, and they then moved to Corinth, where Eudokia was married to Leo Sgouros, the ruler of Corinth and the surrounding region. Once again they were forced to move on when Corinth's capture by the Latins was imminent. Late in 1204, while making their way to Michael I Komnenos Doukas of Epiros, a cousin of Alexios, they fell into the hands of Boniface, and after being confined at Halmyros, where their imperial trappings were exchanged for a ration of bread and wine, the couple were carried off to Montferrat.[64]

In 1209 or 1210, however, Alexios and Euphrosyne were ransomed by Michael of Epiros. Leaving Euphrosyne at Arta, Alexios made his way to the sultan Kaykhusraw I, at Konion. Kaykhusraw had received kindness at Alexios's hands prior to his accession and welcomed him, intending to use him as a pretext for making war on Nicaea, his rationale being an attempt to replace the 'rightful' sovereign, Alexios III, on the Nicene throne. When Theodore I, Alexios's son-in-law, defeated the sultan in spring 1211 Alexios was captured and placed in a monastery at Nicaea. Euphrosyne was to pass the rest of her life at Arta. The date of her death is unknown, though it may have been *c.* 1211: the fact that she still had considerable possessions in the region of Epiros at least meant that she could live comfortably in her retirement,[65] while she also had the satisfaction of knowing that the Nicene throne was in the hands of her family.

Euphrosyne was not liked by Choniates, but he appreciated her abilities, however misplaced. She was unusual in the fact that rather than being satisfied with the informal exercise of power open to empresses she chose to display her love of domination openly: Choniates speaks of her as a co-emperor, even in his oration to Alexios. Her *de facto* assumption of power may well have been because of the nature both of her husband and of the government of the time, where the bureaucracy had reached a new level of corruption and nepotism, to a great extent due to the inroads of her own family. Euphrosyne was one of the strong-minded and ambitious imperial women whom historians were unable to refrain from criticising: Euprepia (Constantine Monomachos's sister), Eudokia Makrembolitissa, Irene Doukaina, Anna Komnene and Maria Porphyrogenneta are all targeted for their domineering tendencies.[66] Such women were not a feature merely of the early Komnenian period, and while it is possible that the Komnenian system disadvantaged women to the extent that power was kept in the hands of the males of the family,[67] Euphrosyne is proof that women were not subordinated under this system, or, if they were, that this attempt at subordination was not always successful.

Piriska, Bertha and Maria of Antioch may not have shown any aptitude for government, but there were two factors involved in this. Foreign-born women were bound to be at a disadvantage. Not only did they lack the training and appreciation of the way the establishment worked, they lacked the family networking which could provide them with material resources and an official support group in times of crisis. In any case, Piriska and Bertha had no chance to put their skills to the test. Maria of Antioch was put in a position of responsibility at a time of transition, and failed, not because she was not given the requisite authority, but because she was constitutionally unable to wield it and additionally was hampered by her foreign birth at a time when westerners were extremely unpopular and becoming more so.

Euphrosyne, however, demonstrates that in a time of crisis, or imperial weakness, a woman was still able to dominate events: she had great authority and the spending power to match and used it to interfere in matters of government. Moreover the principle of legitimation, which gave widowed empresses their chance to wield power, was also still at work: Euphrosyne clearly felt that if Alexios were to die she had the right to nominate a successor. Furthermore, when Boniface of Montferrat and Baldwin fell out over who was to take possession of Thessalonika in 1204, Boniface to win Byzantine support proclaimed Manuel, the eldest son of his wife Margaret-Maria of Hungary and Isaac II, emperor of the *Romaioi*, 'ceding him the form, name, and mask by way of pretext', campaigning successfully in Manuel's name in northern Greece. Maria had originally come from Hungary to marry Isaac at the tender age of nine in 1185 or 1186 and after the fall of the city she married Boniface.[68] Boniface was not serious in his claim, but clearly it was respected by the inhabitants of the empire, who felt that his title had been legitimated by his marriage to the widow of Isaac II and mother of his son.

As the last 'pre-crusade' empress, and as an empress whose power devolved solely from her relationship with her husband, Euphrosyne was a worthy successor of Justinian's wife Theodora. In fact, since much of her authority was wielded in the teeth of Alexios's indifference or ignorance, Euphrosyne was essentially the most independent of empress consorts of this period, just as she was one of the most wealthy. While she has to be held at least partially responsible for condoning much of the corruption of her husband's reign, Euphrosyne did attempt to halt its most extreme manifestations and helped to counter Alexios's indifference to the more practical aspects of government. She was one of the major protagonists in Alexios's bid for the throne, and certainly did not condone his flight in the face of the crusaders. It is arguable that had Alexios not run away, the city would not have fallen to the Fourth Crusade, and certainly, had Euphrosyne been given the chance, she like Justinian's Theodora would have encouraged the emperor to ride out his difficulties and so have prevented the disastrous events of 1204.

EPILOGUE

Following the Palaiologue restoration in 1261, a number of empresses had a chance to interfere in Byzantine politics and the succession, but almost invariably without success. A number of factors were here at work: most notably the foreign birth of Palaiologue empresses, which left them without a family network or an awareness of the niceties of Byzantine institutions and politics; another is the fact that the Palaiologue dynasty lasted until the fall of the empire to the Turks and accordingly there were few opportunites for involvement in the transfer of power, though there was considerable internal dissension during this period within the dynasty itself, which disadvantaged rather than empowered the empresses of the time. Those who had the chance to be involved in politics were almost invariably in opposition to the establishment, rather than in government.

The most notable players in Palaiologue politics were the empresses Yolanda-Irene of Montferrat and Anna of Savoy, and on the whole their record is woeful: Yolanda-Irene of Montferrat, second wife of Andronikos II, was unable to comprehend the succession rights of her eldest stepson, Michael IX, and since her husband remained obstinately unmoved by her representations she flounced off with her three sons to Thessalonika where she kept a separate court for many years from 1303 to her death in 1317. From her own domain she issued her own decrees, conducted her own foreign policy and plotted against her husband with the Serbs and Catalans: in miti-gation, she had seen her five-year-old daughter married off to the middle-aged Serbian lecher Milutin, and considered that her eldest son John had been married beneath him to a Byzantine aristocrat, Irene Choumnaina. She died embittered and extremely wealthy.[1]

When Yolanda's grandson Andronikos III died early, leaving a nine-year-old son John V and no arrangements for a regent, the empress Anna of Savoy assumed the regency. In so doing she provoked a civil war with her husband's best friend John Kantakouzenos, and devastated the empire financially, bringing it to bankruptcy and pawning the crown jewels to Venice, as well as employing Turkish mercenaries and, it appears, offering to have her son convert to the church of Rome. Gregoras specifically blames her for the civil war, though he admits that she should not be criticised too heavily since she was a woman and a foreigner.[2] Her mismanagement was not compensated for by her later negotiations in 1351 between John VI Kantakouzenos and her son in Thessalonika, who was planning a rebellion with the help of Stephen Dushan of Serbia. In 1351 Anna too settled in Thessalonika and reigned over it as her own portion of the empire until her death in c. 1365, even minting her own coinage.[3] Thessalonika was a useful haven for dissatisfied empresses: Rita-Maria, an Armenian princess who had married Michael IX and who was the mother of Andronikos III, had also found it politic to retire there. When her son was disinherited by his grandfather as responsible for the murder of his younger brother, Maria moved to Thessalonika and sided with her son in his civil war against the emperor, remaining there as a nun from 1320 to 1333.[4]

These women were powerful and domineering ladies *par excellence*, but with the proviso that their political influence was virtually minimal. Despite their outspokenness and love of dominion they were not successful politicians: Anna of Savoy, the only one in whose hands government was placed, was compared to a weaver's shuttle that ripped the purple cloth of empire.[5] But there were of course exceptions. Civil wars ensured that not all empresses were foreigners and more than one woman of Byzantine descent reached the throne and was given quasi-imperial functions by her husband. Theodora Doukaina Komnene Palaiologina, wife of Michael VIII, herself had imperial connections as the great-niece of John III Vatatzes, and issued acts concerning disputes over monastic properties during her husband's reign, even addressing the emperor's officials on occasion and confirming her husband's decisions. Nevertheless, unlike other women of Michael's family who went into exile over the issue, she was forced to support her husband's policy of church union with Rome, a stance which she seems to have spent the rest of her life regretting. She was also humiliated when he wished to divorce her to marry Constance-Anna of Hohenstaufen, the widow of John III Vatatzes.[6] Another supportive empress consort can be seen in Irene Kantakouzene Asenina, whose martial spirit came to the fore during the civil war against Anna of Savoy and the Palaiologue 'faction'. Irene in 1342 was put in charge of Didymoteichos by her husband John VI Kantakouzenos; she also organised the defence of Constantinople against the Genoese in April 1348 and against John Palaiologos in March 1353, being one of the very few Byzantine empresses who took command in military affairs. But like Theodora, Irene seems to have conformed to her husband's wishes in matters of policy and agreed with his decisions concerning the exclusion of their sons from the succession and their eventual abdication in 1354.[7]

Irene and her daughter Helena Kantakouzene, wife of John V Palaiologos, were both torn by conflicting loyalties between different family members, and Helena in particular was forced to mediate between her ineffectual husband and the ambitions of her son and grandson. She is supposed to have organised the escape of her husband and two younger sons from prison in 1379 and was promptly taken hostage with her father and two sisters by her eldest son Andronikos IV and imprisoned until 1381; her release was celebrated with popular rejoicing in the capital. According to Demetrios Kydones she was involved in political life under both her husband and son, Manuel II, but her main role was in mediating between the different members of her family.[8] In a final success story, the last Byzantine emperor, Constantine XI, owed his throne to his mother. The Serbian princess Helena Dragash, wife of Manuel II Palaiologos, in the last legitimating political manoeuvre by a Byzantine empress, successfully managed to keep the throne for her son Constantine and fend off the claims of his brother Demetrios. She arranged for Constantine's proclamation as emperor in the Peloponnese and asserted her right to act as regent until his arrival in the capital from Mistra in 1449.[9]

Despite the general lack of opportunity for them to play a role in politics, Palaiologue imperial women in the thirteenth century found outlets for their independent spirit and considerable financial resources in other ways. They were noted for their foundation or restoration of monastic establishments and for their patronage of the arts. Theodora Palaiologina restored the foundation of Constantine Lips as a convent for fifty nuns, with a small hospital for laywomen attached, as well as refounding a smaller convent of Sts Kosmas and Damian. She was also an active patron of the arts, commissioning the production of manuscripts like Theodora Raoulaina, her husband's niece. Her *typikon* displays the pride she felt in her family and position, an attitude typically found amongst aristocratic women.[10] Clearly, like empresses prior to 1204, she had considerable wealth in her own hands both as empress and dowager. She had been granted the island of Kos as her private property by Michael, while she had also inherited land from her family and been given properties by her son Andronikos. Other women of the family also display the power of conspicuous spending: Theodora Raoulaina used her money to refound St Andrew of Crete as a convent where she pursued her scholarly interests.[11] Theodora Palaiologina Angelina Kantakouzene, John Kantakouzenos's mother, was arguably the richest woman of the period and financed Andronikos III's bid for power in the civil war against his grandfather.[12] Irene Choumnaina Palaiologina, in name at least an empress, who had been married to Andronikos II's son John and widowed at sixteen, used her immense wealth, against the wishes of her parents, to rebuild the convent of Philanthropos Soter, where she championed the cause of 'orthodoxy' against Gregory Palamas and his hesychast followers.[13] Helena Kantakouzene, too, wife of John V, was a patron of the arts. She had been classically educated and was the benefactor of scholars, notably of Demetrios Kydones who dedicated to her a translation of one of the works of St Augustine.[14]

The woman who actually holds power in this period, Anna of Savoy, does her sex little credit: like Yolanda she appears to have been both headstrong and greedy, and, still worse, incompetent. In contrast, empresses such as Irene Kantakouzene Asenina reflect the abilities of their predecessors: they were educated to be managers, possessed of great resources, patrons of art and monastic foundations, and, given the right circumstances, capable of significant political involvement in religious controversies and the running of the empire. Unfortunately they generally had to show their competence in opposition to official state positions.[15] While they may have wished to emulate earlier regent empresses, they were not given the chance: the women who, proud of their class and family, played a public and influential part in the running of the empire belonged to an earlier age.[16]

TABLES

Table 1 Byzantine emperors and empresses

na = name not known
pn = previous name
* = not given the title Augusta

Byzantine rulers	Spouses
Constantine I (324–37)	(1. Minervina), 2. Flavia Maxima Fausta; mother: Flavia Julia Helena; ?daughter: Constantia
Constantius II (337–61)	1. daughter of Julius Constantius,* 2. Eusebia,* 3. Faustina*
Julian (361–3)	Helena,* daughter of Constantine
Jovian (363–4)	Charito*
Valens (364–78)	Domnica*
Theodosios I (379–95)	1. Aelia Flavia Flaccilla, 2. Galla,* sister of Valentinian II; daughter: Aelia Galla Placidia, wife of Constantios III
Arkadios (395–408)	Aelia Eudoxia
Theodosios II (408–50)	Aelia Eudokia (pn Athenais); sister: Aelia Pulcheria; daughter: Licinia Eudoxia, wife of Valentinian III
Marcian (450–7)	1. na, 2. Aelia Pulcheria, daughter of Arkadios
Leo I (457–74)	Aelia Verina
Leo II (474)	—
Zeno (474–91)	Aelia Ariadne
Basiliskos (475–6)	Aelia Zenonis
Anastasios I (491–518)	Ariadne, widow of Zeno
Justin (518–27)	Euphemia (pn Lupicina)
Justinian I (527–65)	Theodora
Justin II (565–78)	Aelia Sophia
Tiberios Constantine (578–82)	Aelia Anastasia (pn Ino)
Maurice (582–602)	Aelia Constantina, daughter of Tiberios
Phokas (602–10)	Leontia
Herakleios (610–41)	1. Eudokia (pn Fabia), 2. Martina; daughters: Eudokia (pn Epiphaneia), Augustina, Martina
Constantine III (641)	Gregoria
Heraklonas (641)	—

Byzantine rulers	Spouses
Constans II (641–68)	Fausta
Constantine IV (668–85)	Anastasia
Justinian II (685–95)	1. Eudokia, 2. Theodora, sister of the Khazar khagan
Leontios (695–8)	na
Tiberios II Apsimar (698–705)	na
Justinian II (again) (705–11)	—
Philippikos Bardanes (711–13)	na
Anastasios II (713–15)	Irene
Theodosios III (715–17)	na
Leo III (717–41)	Maria
Constantine V (741–75)	1. Irene the Khazar, 2. Maria, 3. Eudokia
Leo IV (775–80)	Irene
Constantine VI (780–97)	1. Maria of Amnia,* 2. Theodote
Irene (797–802)	Leo IV
Nikephoros I (802–11)	na
Staurakios (811)	Theophano
Michael I Rangabe (811–13)	Prokopia, daughter of Nikephoros I
Leo V (813–20)	Theodosia
Michael II (820–9)	1. Thekla, 2. Euphrosyne, daughter of Constantine VI
Theophilos (829–42)	Theodora; daughters: Thekla, Anna, Anastasia
Michael III (842–67)	Eudokia Dekapolitissa
Basil I (867–86)	1. Maria, 2. Eudokia Ingerina
Leo VI (886–912)	1. Theophano, 2. Zoe Zaoutzaina, 3. Eudokia Baiane, 4. Zoe Karbounopsina; daughter: Anna
Alexander (912–13)	na
Constantine VII (913–59)	Helena, daughter of Romanos Lekapenos
Romanos I Lekapenos (920–44)	Theodora; daughter-in-law: Sophia
Romanos II (959–63)	1. Eudokia (pn Bertha), 2. Theophano (pn Anastaso)
Nikephoros II Phokas (963–9)	1. na Pleustaina, 2. Theophano
John I Tzimiskes (969–76)	1. Maria Skleraina, 2. Theodora, daughter of Constantine VII
Basil II (976–1025)	—
Constantine VIII (1025–8)	Helena Alypia
Romanos III Argyros (1028–34)	1. Helena, *sebaste*, 2. Zoe Porphyrogenneta
Michael IV Paphlagon (1034–41)	Zoe Porphyrogenneta
Michael V Kalaphates (1041–2)	—
Zoe and Theodora (1042)	Zoe married 1. Romanos (III) Argyros, 2. Michael (IV) Paphlagon, 3. Constantine (IX) Monomachos
Constantine IX Monomachos (1042–55)	1. na, 2. na Skleraina, 3. Zoe Porphyrogenneta; mistresses: Maria Skleraina, *sebaste**, Alan princess, *sebaste**
Theodora (again) (1055–6)	—
Michael VI Stratiotikos (1056–7)	na
Isaac I Komnenos (1057–9)	Aikaterina, daughter of John Vladislav of Bulgaria
Constantine X Doukas (1059–67)	1. daughter of Constantine Dalassenos, 2. Eudokia Makrembolitissa

Byzantine rulers	Spouses
Eudokia Makrembolitissa (1067)	1. Constantine (X) Doukas, 2. Romanos (IV) Diogenes
Romanos IV Diogenes (1068–71)	Eudokia Makrembolitissa
Eudokia Makrembolitissa (again) (1071)	
Michael VII Doukas (1071–8)	Maria of Alania (Georgia) (pn Martha)
Nikephoros III Botaneiates (1078–81)	1. na, 2. Vevdene, 3. Maria of Alania
Alexios I Komnenos (1081–1118)	1. na Argyropoulina, 2. Irene Doukaina; mother: Anna Dalassene,* *despoina*
John II Komnenos (1118–43)	Irene of Hungary (pn Piriska)
Manuel I Komnenos (1143–80)	1. Irene of Sulzbach (pn Bertha), 2. Maria of Antioch (pn Marguerite-Constance); daughter: Maria Porphyrogenneta
Alexios II Komnenos (1180–3)	Anna of Savoy (pn Agnes)
Andronikos I Komnenos (1183–5)	1. na, 2. Anna of Savoy (pn Agnes)
Isaac II Angelos (1185–95)	1. na, 2. Maria of Hungary (pn Margaret)
Alexios III Angelos (1195–1203)	Euphrosyne Doukaina; daughter: Irene*
Isaac II Angelos (again) and Alexios IV Angelos (1203–4)	—
Alexios V Doukas Mourtzouphlos (1204)	1. na, 2. Eudokia, daughter of Alexios III
Theodore I Laskaris (1204–21)	1. Anna, daughter of Alexios III, 2. Philippa, 3. Maria of Courtenay
John III Vatatzes (1221–54)	1. Irene, daughter of Theodore I, 2. Anna of Hohenstaufen (pn Constance)
Theodore II Laskaris (1254–8)	Helena, daughter of John Asen II
John IV Laskaris (1258–61)	—
Michael VIII Palaiologos (1259–82)	Theodora Doukaina Komnene Palaiologina, great-niece of John III (Doukas) Vatatzes
Andronikos II Palaiologos (1282–1328)	1. Anna of Hungary, 2. Irene of Montferrat (pn Yolanda); daughter-in-law: Irene Choumnaina*
(Michael IX Palaiologos (1294–1320)	Maria of Armenia (pn Rita))
Andronikos III Palaiologos (1328–41)	1. Irene of Brunswick (pn Adelheid), 2. Anna of Savoy (pn Giovanna)
John V Palaiologos (1341–91)	Helena, daughter of John VI Kantakouzenos
John VI Kantakouzenos (1347–54)	Irene Asenina
(Andronikos IV Palaiologos (1376–9)	Maria, daughter of Ivan Alexander (pn Kyratza))
(John VII Palaiologos (1390)	Eugenia, daughter of Francesco II Gattilusio)
Manuel II Palaiologos (1391–1425)	Helena, daughter of Constantine Dragash of Serbia
John VIII Palaiologos (1425–48)	1. Anna, daughter of Basil I of Moscow, 2. Sophia of Montferrat, 3. Maria Komnene of Trebizond
Constantine XI Palaiologos (1449–53)	1. Theodora, daughter of Leonardo II Tocco (pn Maddelena), 2. Caterina, daughter of Dorino Gattilusio. Constantine XI was a widower at his accession, and died unmarried.

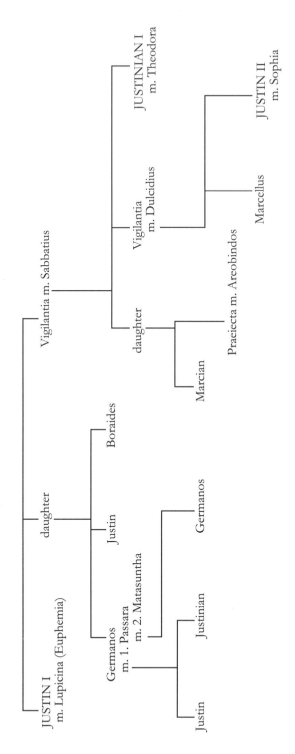

Table 2 The family of Justinian I

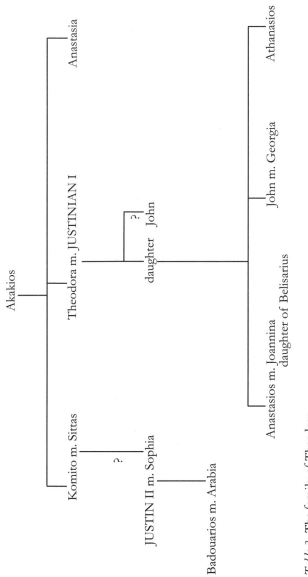

Table 3 The family of Theodora

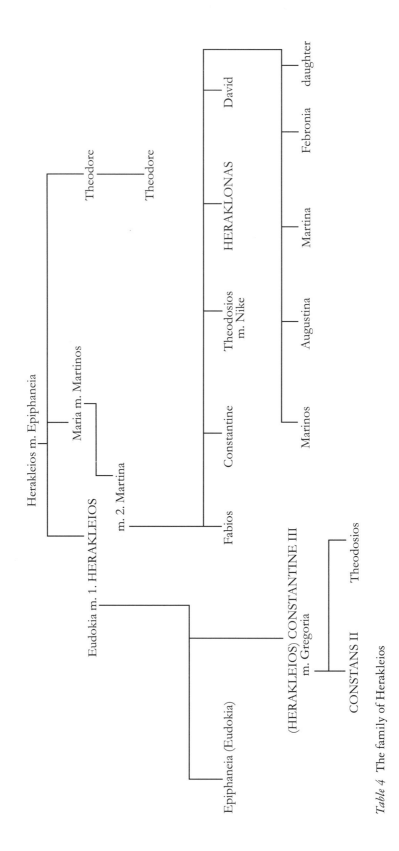

Table 4 The family of Herakleios

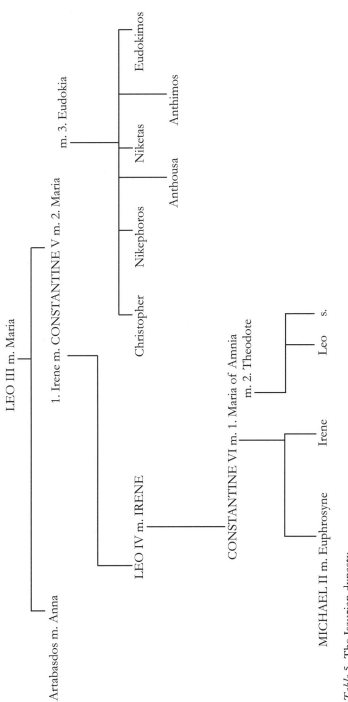

Table 5 The Isaurian dynasty

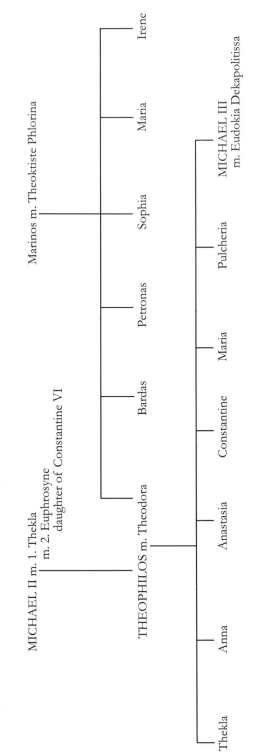

MICHAEL II m. 1. Thekla
m. 2. Euphrosyne
daughter of Constantine VI

Marinos m. Theoktiste Phlorina

THEOPHILOS m. Theodora

Thekla   Anna   Anastasia   Constantine   Bardas   Maria   Petronas   Pulcheria   Sophia   Maria   Irene

MICHAEL III
m. Eudokia Dekapolitissa

Table 6 The Amorian dynasty

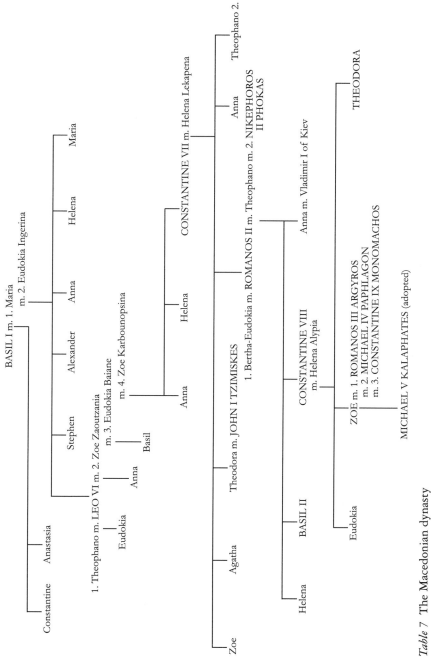

Table 7 The Macedonian dynasty

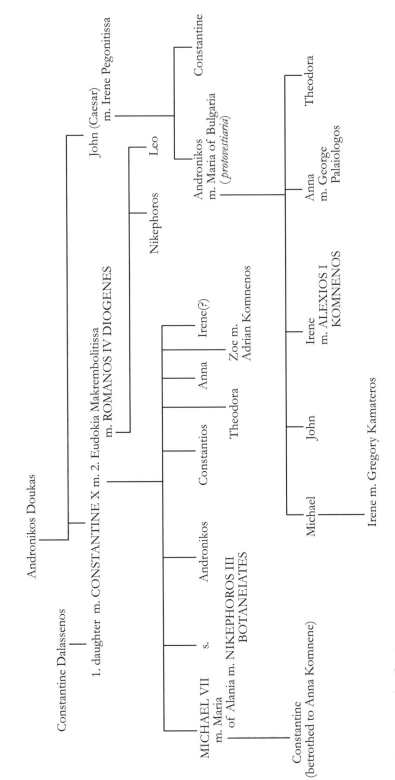

Table 8 The Doukas family

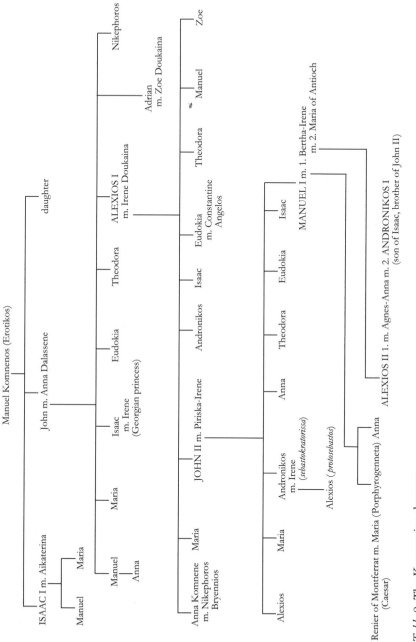

Table 9 The Komnenian dynasty

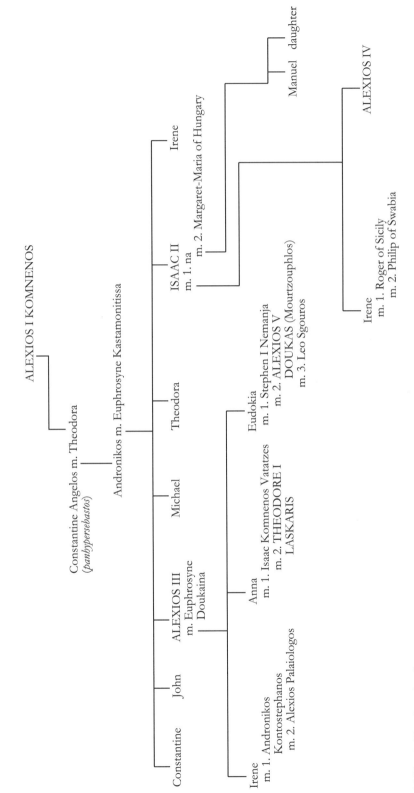

Table 10 The Angelos dynasty

GLOSSARY

Aphthartodocetism   An extreme form of **monophysitism**, which stated that Christ's flesh was incorruptible.

Archimandrite   The head of a region or federation of monasteries.

Asekretis   An imperial secretary.

Augusta   A title of honour given to some empresses.

Autokrator   The official Greek translation of Latin *imperator*, emperor. From the ninth century it designates the senior emperor.

Basileus   Classical Greek word for 'king'; the main title used of an emperor.

Basilis, basilissa   Classical Greek word for 'queen'; the main title used of an empress. It appears as an official title on coins from the eighth century.

Blakhernai   A residential palace in the north-eastern quarter of the capital.

Boukoleon   The harbour attached to the Great Palace in Constantinople.

Caesar   A high honorary title, until the eleventh century the highest title below that of emperor. In the eleventh century one of the three highest honours, with *curopalates* and *nobilissimos*. Under the Komnenoi, the title ranked after *sebastokrator* and was reserved for members of the imperial family, particularly the husband of one of the emperor's daughters.

Chalcedonian   Orthodox in belief, as defined by the Council of Chalcedon in 451, particularly in respect of the dual nature of Christ (that Christ's nature was both divine and human).

Chalke   The main entrance hallway of the Great Palace in Constantinople, over which stood a famous icon of Christ.

Charistikion   The gift, for a restricted period, of a monastery to an individual or institution, by which the beneficiary administered the properties of the monastery.

Chartoularios   The keeper of records. The *chartoularios epi tou kanikleiou*, keeper of the inkstand, was an important imperial adviser who kept the pen and ink used for signing imperial documents.

Chelandion, pl. *chelandia*   A transport ship.

Chlamys   The imperial purple mantle, which was fastened with a fibula (a brooch with three pendants) at the right shoulder.

Chrysobull   An official document with a gold seal (*bulla*), signed by the emperor in red ink.

City Prefect (eparch)   The civil governor of Constantinople.

Comes (sacrarum) largitionum   Count of the Sacred Largesse, a high-ranking official in charge of finances.

Consistorium   The body of imperial officials who advised on matters of legislation, foreign affairs, and policy. A session of the *consistorium* was known as a *silentium*.

Count, *comes*   A military officer, a title given to various imperial officials.

Cubicularia   A lady-in-waiting at court.

Cubicularius, pl. *cubicularii*   A chamberlain, or official who served the 'sacred bedchamber' of the emperor.

Curopalates   The palace official in charge of construction and organisation in the Great Palace, 'major-domo' of the imperial palace; later a high honorary title.

Curopalatissa   The wife of the *curopalates*.

Despoina (also *despotis*)   Literally 'mistress'. Used officially as a title by the empress from the eighth century.

Diptychs   Lists of the names of living and dead emperors, popes and bishops.

Domestic of the East (West)   A military commander-in-chief.

Domestic of the Schools, *Scholae*   The commander of the corps of *Scholae*.

Domestikos   A term designating a wide range of officials.

Dromon, pl. *dromones*   A warship.

Droungarios   An officer commanding a *droungos*, an infantry troop of 1,000 men, or an admiral.

Dux   A general, military commander.

Eparch   See **City Prefect**.

Epi tou kanikleiou   See *Chartoularios*.

Exarch   The governor of Byzantine Africa or Italy (his province was known as an exarchate).

Excubitors   An elite corps of imperial guards.

Faction   One of the two circus factions of the empire, the Blues and the Greens.

Follis   The largest denomination of copper coin, initially worth 40 *nummi*.

Globus cruciger   An orb, surmounted by a cross, which appears on Byzantine coinage as a symbol of sovereignty; the globe (*globus*) represents the world.

Gynaikonitis   The women's quarters in the palace or in an aristocratic household.

Hegoumenos   The superior of a monastic institution.

Hetaireiarch   The commander of the *hetaireia* (a unit of the emperor's bodyguard), responsible for the security of the imperial palace.

Hippodrome   A facility for horse-racing and popular entertainment. In

Constantinople the hippodrome adjoined the Great Palace, and the emperor had his own box, the *kathisma*, which was entered from the palace.

Histamenon, pl. *histamena*   Gold coinage of full weight introduced by Nikephoros II Phokas.

Horos   The definition or resolution of a church council.

Iconophiles, iconodules   Those who defended the holiness of icons and their veneration (literally, 'lovers of icons', 'servants of icons').

Illustris   The highest title awarded to senators.

Kommerkia   Trade duties, normally 10 per cent of the value of the merchandise.

Labarum   A standard or sceptre which appears on Byantine coinage; the original *labarum*, introduced by Constantine the Great, bore a Christogram, but the term comes to be used of various types of sceptre or standard.

Logothete   A government minister.

Logothete tou dromou   The official responsible for the postal system, ceremonial, security and foreign affairs.

Logothete tou genikou   The chief finance minister, head of the treasury.

Logothete tou stratiotikou, military *logothete*.   The official responsible for the pay of the army and navy.

Loros   The elaborately decorated consular robe, which in the Byzantine period had the form of a long jewelled scarf wrapped round the body. In the ninth century, the scarf came to be replaced by a simplified *loros* put on over the head.

Magister, magistros   A high-ranking court official.

Magister militum   The master of soldiers, high-ranking military official.

Magnaura   A ceremonial hall, part of the complex of the Great Palace.

Megas dux   The grand admiral of the imperial navy.

Miliaresion   The basic silver coin before the eleventh century, reckoned at 12 to the *solidus*.

Monophysite   An adherent of **monophysitism**.

Monophysitism   A widespread religious sect, teaching that Christ had only one nature, which was divine.

Monostrategos   A *strategos* commanding more than one theme.

Monothelete   An adherent of **monotheletism**.

Monotheletism   A doctrine promulgated by the emperor Herakleios, that Christ had two natures, but only one will.

Mystikos   An imperial private secretary.

Nimbus (adj. **nimbate**)   A halo encircling the head of Christ, saints or the emperor in artistic representations.

Nobilissimos, pl. *nobilissimi*   A very high-ranking dignity reserved for members of the imperial family; prior to the Komnenoi, one of the three highest honours.

Nomisma, pl. *nomismata*   A gold coin, usually referring to the late Roman *solidus*, struck at 72 to the Roman pound of gold (6 to the ounce), and equivalent to 12 *miliaresia* (silver coins) or 288 *folles* (copper coins).

Notarios   A secretary, especially one responsible for the preparation of official documents.

Oikonomia   Literally 'economy'. A principle of concession by which ecclesiastical law could be relaxed in certain circumstances.

Oikonomos   A cleric given the management of a see or religious foundation.

Orphanotrophos   The administrator of imperial orphanages in Constantinople.

Pansebastos   An honorific epithet, conferred on the nobility, especially the relations of the Komnenoi.

Papias   The eunuch in charge of the gates and buildings of the palace.

Parakoimomenos   The eunuch who guarded the imperial bedchamber and supervised the staff of the emperor's personal apartments.

Patriarch   The incumbent of one of the five major sees: Rome, Alexandria, Antioch, Jerusalem and Constantinople.

Patrician   A high-ranking dignitary.

Pendilia (also *prependulia*)   The pendants hanging down on either side of the imperial crown.

Porphyrogennetos (fem. **porphryogenneta**)   A child born to a reigning emperor in the Porphyra (purple chamber) of the Great Palace.

Praetorium   The public prison.

Primikerios   Senior member of any group of functionaries. Many *primikerioi* were eunuchs.

Proedros   A high senatorial dignitary.

Protoasekretis   The head of the college of *asekretis*, concerned with drafting and keeping imperial records.

Protospatharios   Initially the commander of the sword-bearers (*spatharii*); later a high-ranking dignitary. One group of the *protospatharii* were eunuchs.

Protostrator   The keeper of the emperor's stable, master of the horse.

Protovestiaria   The wife of the *protovestiarios*.

Protovestiarios   The custodian of the imperial wardrobe and the emperor's private treasury.

Quaestor sacri palati   An imperial official concerned with legal matters.

Romaioi   A term used by the Byzantines of themselves: literally 'Romans'.

Sakellarios   An imperial fiscal official.

Satrap   An ancient Persian title for a provincial governor.

Scholastikos   A title given to lawyers.

Schools, Scholae   A corps of guards of the imperial palace. The highest ranking *tagma*, together with the **excubitors**, forming a mobile strike-force of cavalry.

Sebastokrator Under the Komnenoi, the highest honorary title after that of emperor.

Sebastokratorissa The wife of a *sebastokrator*.

Sebastos, pl. *sebastoi* An epithet denoting high rank, generally reserved for the emperor's relatives; literally 'venerable'.

Sekreton, pl. *sekreta* A bureau or government department; a *sekreton* could be set up to administer the revenues of a religious foundation.

Senate A group of officials and dignitaries, having mainly a ceremonial role.

Silentium A meeting of the *consistorium* to consider issues of state.

Solidus A gold coin (in Greek known as a *nomisma*).

Spatharios A bodyguard of the emperor, later an honorific title.

Strategos, pl. *strategoi* Originally Greek for a general, later a military governor and commander of a **theme**.

Synkellos The adviser and chief assistant of a **patriarch**.

Tagma, pl. *tagmata* A unit of soldiers (*c.* 3,000 men), primarily a mobile army unit based in or near Constantinople.

Tetarteron, pl. *tetartera* Gold coinage of lighter weight introduced by Nikephoros II Phokas, which circulated along with coins of full weight (*histamena*).

Theme, *thema*, pl. *themata* A military division and administrative unit governed by a *strategos*.

Theotokos The Mother of God, the Virgin Mary.

Triklinos of Justinian A hall constructed by Justinian II and decorated by Theophilos with mosaics.

Tritheism A heresy which emphasised the distinction between the three persons of the Trinity.

Typikon The foundation charter for a monastic institution.

Velum Literally 'curtain'. The judges of the *velum* were one of the highest tribunals from the tenth century until 1204.

Xenodocheion A guest-house for travellers, and for the sick.

Watch (*vigla*) A cavalry *tagma*, usually stationed in Constantinople to serve as a police force and garrison.

Zoste patrikia The principal lady-in-waiting at the court, 'mistress of the girdle'.

NOTES

INTRODUCTION

1 *de cer.* 1.39–41, 49, 50.
2 Theoph. Cont. 78.
3 Nicholas, *Ep.* 32.77–84.
4 Kazhdan and McCormick (1997) 176–7.
5 *de cer.* 1.49 (40).
6 Nicol (1968) no. 9.
7 Herrin (1995) 78–9.

1 THEODORA, WIFE OF JUSTINIAN (527–48)

1 *SH* 9.33, 10.15–18; for Justinian's support of the Blues, cf. *SH* 7.1; Evagr. 4.32; Malalas 425. All translations from the *SH* are taken from G.A. Williamson, *Procopius: Secret History*, Harmondsworth: Penguin, 1966.
2 *SH* 9.13, 10, 16, 27–8, 19. According to the *SH* Antonina was skilful in magic and the mother of many illegitimate children (1.11–12), and malignant and revengeful (1.27); she dominated her husband (4.29–30) and had an affair with his adopted son (1.14–18). Procopius attacks Theodora through Antonina, as they are said to have been intimate friends and collaborators (*SH* 1.13, 4.18); cf. *Wars* 1.25.13–30; *Lib. Pont.* 61 (Vigilius).
3 For Procopius as the author of both the *Wars* and the *SH*, see Greatrex (1995) 10, with n. 26, who considers there to be a close relationship between the *Wars* and the *SH*; cf. Cameron (1985) 50. On the nature of Malalas's *Chronicle* as Justinianic propaganda, see Scott (1985) 99–109.
4 Evans (1996a) 5 suggests it to be an underground commentary which must have found appreciative readers; cf. *idem* (1996b) 308. *ODB* 1732 s.v. *Prokopios of Caesarea*, calls it 'vicious, indeed ludicrous, invective . . . it can have circulated only clandestinely'.
5 *Souda* (Adler: 2479) s.v. *Procopius* treats it as the last book of the *Wars* and states that it contains 'ψόγους καὶ κωμῳδίαν' ('invective and comedy') against the imperial couple and Belisarius and his wife.
6 *SH* 18.33, 23.1; 24.29; 24.33. On this, see most recently Greatrex (1994) 101–14; cf. Evans (1996b) 308–12, who believes it was composed after *Wars* 1–7, i.e., after 551.
7 Cameron (1985) 53; *SH* 5.23, 27 refer to her death; cf. 30.34.
8 Mallet (1887) 9; Barker (1966) 68: 'probably the most infamous and scurrilous

piece of sustained character assassination in all of literature'; for the tradition of the repentant saint, see Ward (1987).

9 See esp. Fisher (1973) 252–79, who sees (275) these portraits as intending to discredit Belisarius and Justinian, who are the primary targets of the *SH*; cf. Beck (1986) 89–158.

10 Mich. Syr. 11.6 (ed. Chabot 2.419–20).

11 For example, *Wars*, 3.12.2–3, 13.24, 20.1.

12 Allen (1992) 93–103; cf. Cameron (1985) 81–3.

13 John Eph., *Lives*, *PO* 17.188–9 (quoted below, n. 70); cf. *SH* 9.10: 'she acted as a sort of male prostitute . . . and for some considerable time remained in a brothel, given up to this unnatural bodily commerce.'

14 *SH* 9.11; contra Allen (1992) 95, 'It does appear, in fact, that Theodora had been both an actress and a prostitute before she met Justinian'.

15 Cf. Evans (1996a) 98; Roueché (1993) 26–8. The *ODB* 1741 s.v. *prostitution* distinguishes between poor girls working for pimps (*pornai* or *hetairai*) and more professional theatrical performers (*skenikai*), both of whom provided sexual services.

16 *SH* 4.37, 5.18, 5.20, 5.23 for Anastasios; John Eph., *HE* 2.11, 'the illustrious John, who was descended from King Anastasius, and the son moreover of Queen Theodora's daughter'. Cf. *ibid.* 5.1 for Athanasios, 'son of Queen Theodora's daughter'; Mich. Syr. 9.30, 10.1 (Chabot 2.253, 285). See Alan Cameron (1978) 269–73.

17 *SH* 17.16–23. Evans (1996a) 102 suggests that this John may have been an imposter.

18 It is even possible that an ordinary freeborn citizen was forbidden to marry an actress, though not her child: D. 23.2.44; Ulpian, *Reg.* 13.1, 16.2 (cited by Daube (1967) 381 n. 5).

19 *SH* 6.17, 9.47; Vasiliev (1950) 91.

20 Daube (1967) 385–6.

21 Honoré (1978) 9–10 with n. 80; Clark (1993) 30 dates the law to Justinian's reign, *c.* 530, but this dating is untenable.

22 For Justinian's role in policy and government during Justin's reign, see Vasiliev (1950) 121.

23 Tr. Honoré (1978) 10.

24 *CJ* 5.4.23 (1b): 'neque differentiam aliquam eas habere cum his, quae nihil simile peccaverunt.'

25 *CJ* 5.4.23(4).

26 Daube (1967) 392–3, citing D. 23.2.43.4 (Ulpian), 'not only she who practises prostitution but also she who has practised it, though she has now ceased to do so, is marked by this statute: for her vileness is not abolished by discontinuance'; cf. D. 23.2.44. Justinian never relieved repentant prostitutes of their disabilities: cf. *Nov. J.* 14 pr.

27 Daube (1967) 393; cf. Beauchamp (1990) 1.207–8.

28 *SH* 9.51.

29 On this see esp. Daube (1967) 380–81; Alan Cameron (1978) 270–71.

30 Evans (1996a) 209: 'Justin's constitution, which smoothed the way for Justinian's marriage to Theodora, set the tone' (of women's rights).

31 Evans (1996a) 207; Honoré (1978) 19 n. 178.

32 Cf. *Nov. J.* 21 pr. (AD 536) on the inheritance rights of women in Armenia; *Nov. J.* 18.4 (AD 536); 89.12.5 (AD 539).

33 *Nov. J.* 127.4 (AD 548); cf. *CJ* 6.58.14.5 (AD 531).

34 *Nov. J.* 22 (AD 535); 117.8–9 (AD 542): Moorhead (1994) 37 points out that in some respects the law improved the position of women.

35 Cf. *CJ* 5.4.29: if however (§ 8) they wish to return to the stage after marrying, their privileges are revoked.
36 *CTh.* 9.7.1 (Constantine, AD 326); Gardner (1986) 124; Clark (1993) 29–30.
37 Evagr. 4.30.
38 § 2: 'nec ad fragilitatem muliebrem respicientes nec quod et corpore et substantia et omni vita sua marito fungitur'; tr. Clark (1993) 58.
39 Daube (1967) 397.
40 Note *CJ* 11.41.7 (Leo I, AD 460), which tried to ban prostitution entirely; cf. Beauchamp (1990) 1.121–32, esp. 127–9.
41 Evagr. 4.30.
42 *Buildings* 1.9.2–10. (The passage quoted is 1.9.4–6.)
43 *SH* 17.5–6; Baldwin (1992) 255–7.
44 *SH* 20.9–10; Malalas 440–41 (Jeffreys *et al.* (1986) 255–6).
45 *Wars* 7.31.14; cf. John Lyd. 3.69, on her help towards 'those wronged'.
46 *Wars* 7.31.2–6, 11–16; see Alan Cameron (1978) 268.
47 Malalas 439–40 (Jeffreys *et al.* (1986) 255). The strict veracity of this account may be questioned.
48 Note Cameron (1985) 68: measures to help girls in distress and prostitutes were traditional actions of great ladies, not attempts to improve the status of women.
49 John of Nikiu 93.3 (tr. Charles (1916) 147).
50 For Justin's origins, see *SH* 6.18; cf. 10.2 for the qualities of a suitable imperial bride: noble birth, excellent upbringing, modesty and virginity.
51 *SH* 10.4; Zon. 3.151.
52 Harrison (1989) 137–9; Milner (1994) 73–81; for the dating, see Mango and Shevchenko (1961) 244–5.
53 *Anth. Gr.* 1.10, 42–9.
54 Theophanes AM 6005 [AD 512/13].
55 Gregory of Tours, *De Gloria Martyrum* (*On the Glory of the Martyrs*), *PL* 71, 793–5 (tr. van Dam (1988) 125–6).
56 S. Runciman, foreword to Harrison (1989) 9.
57 *SH* 16.11; 30.21–6; 10.6–9; on the ceremony of prostration, see Guilland (1967).
58 *SH* 15.24–35, cf. 17.7–14 (Theodora married off young aristocratic girls to loutish husbands).
59 *SH* 15.13–16, cf. 30.30–1; 15.36–7. For her self-indulgence and luxurious lifestyle (contrasted to Justinian's austerity and spartan lifestyle), see 15.6–9; 13.28–30.
60 Malalas 441 (Jeffreys *et al.* (1986) 256); cf. Theophanes AM 6025, who misdates this to AD 532/3. For the spa at Pythia, see *Buildings* 5.3.16–17.
61 Malalas 423 (Jeffreys *et al.* (1986) 243).
62 *Buildings* 1.2.17; 1.9.5; 1.11.27; 5.3.14; *Wars* 4.9.13–14.
63 *SH* 9.31; cf. *Nov. J.* 28.5.1, cf. 29.4, 30.6.1; Honoré (1978) 11.
64 *SH* 10.11.
65 For a discussion of this portrait, see Clark (1993) 106–10; Barber (1990) esp. 35–40; MacCormack (1981) 262–4.
66 Procopius, *Buildings* 1.10.17–19; cf. *Wars* 4.9.3–12.
67 John of Nikiu 90.87 (tr. Charles (1916) 144). John, however, must be wrong in stating that Theodora persuaded Justinian to make Timothy patriarch (in 517). Her monophysitism does not seem to have come from her Green background: see Alan Cameron (1976) 126–56, dismissing the idea that factions had religious allegiances.
68 *V. Sabas* (*Life of St Sabas*) 71 (Schwartz (1939) 173).
69 Evagr. 4.10; *SH* 10.15.

70 John Eph., *Lives*, PO 17.189: 'God . . . directed the virtuous Stephen to Theodora who came from the brothel, who was at that time a patrician, but eventually became queen also with King Justinian. She . . . made entreaty to Justinian her husband, who was master of the soldiers (στρατηλάτης) and also a patrician and the king's nephew, that he would inform his uncle, and he might order relief to be given to these distressed men, making this entreaty even with tears.'

71 *V. Sabas*, 71 (Schwartz (1939) 173–4).

72 John Eph., *Lives*, PO 18.529. According to John Eph., *HE* 5.1, John was himself later in charge of the administration of all monophysite revenues.

73 Zach. Rhet. 9.19 (tr. Hamilton and Brooks (1899) 265), 'Severus . . . was received in a friendly manner in the palace by the king, who was disposed and incited thereto by Theodora the queen, who was devoted to Severus, and he was honourable and venerable in her eyes'. The ecclesiastical history of Zacharias actually ended in 491 and has been continued by a Syriac annalist.

74 Severos, *Letters* 1.63, AD 537 (tr. Brooks (1903) 2.197–9); Hardy (1968) 31.

75 Theodosios of Alexandria, 'Tome to Empress Theodora', and Constantine of Laodiceia, 'Address to the Empress Theodora', in *Monophysite Texts* 16–56, 66–71.

76 For Justinian's edict against heretics in 527 (*CJ* 1.1.5) and his wavering position with regard to monophysitism between 527 and 536, see Frend (1972) 255–73.

77 *Buildings* 1.4.1–2, 10.4; Mango (1972b) 189–90.

78 John Eph., *Lives*, PO 18.680–81; 17.v–vi; Mango (1972b) 191; John was also archimandrite of the 'Monastery of the Syrians' which he established at Sykai in the suburbs (*HE* 2.41).

79 Tr. Mango (1972a) 190; see also Mango (1975).

80 *CJ* 1.1.6 (AD 533).

81 See Theophanes AM 6029 [AD 536/7]; Zon. 3.166, who notes that this was contrary to the canon forbidding the transfer of bishops from one see to another.

82 Evagr. 4.10.

83 See *Lib. Pont.* 60 cited below, p. 36.

84 Liberatus, *Brev.* 20; Frend (1972) 270.

85 'History of the Patriarchs of the Coptic Church of Alexandria', 1.13 (*PO* 1.459–60); Liberatus, *Brev.* 20; interestingly the 'History' claims Alexandria as Theodora's place of origin (*ibid.* 459).

86 Theophanes AM 6033 [AD 540/1]; Mich. Syr. 9.21 (Chabot 2.193–4); John of Nikiu, 92.1–4; 'History of the Patriarchs of the Coptic Church of Alexandria', 1.13 (*PO* 1.456–60).

87 Frend (1972) 273.

88 Zach. Rhet. 9.20 (tr. Hamilton and Brooks (1899) 270).

89 John Eph., *Lives*, PO 18.528–9; Severos, *Letters* 1.63 (tr. Brooks (1903) 2.196).

90 John Eph., *Lives*, PO 18.680, cf. 683–4.

91 John Eph., *Lives*, PO 18.686–7; *HE*, 1.42, however, written twenty years later in 585/6, has Anthimos more correctly as patriarch for only a year and leaving the capital on his deposition. Cf. Mich. Syr. 9.21 (Chabot 2.195).

92 John Eph., *Lives*, PO 18.679–80; 18.676–9.

93 John Eph., *Lives*, PO 18.677, 681–3.

94 John Eph., *HE* 1.10.

95 John Eph., *Lives*, PO 18.531, cf. 600 and 532–5 for John's wholesale ordinations, which caused Theodora to request that he make no more priests in Constantinople.

96 John Eph., *Lives*, PO 19.154; Mich. Syr. 9.29 (Chabot 2.245–6).

97 Evans (1996a) 185; John Eph., *Lives*, PO 19.153–4.

 98 John Eph., *Lives*, *PO* 18.690–97, 19.154–8; Frend (1972) 285–7.
 99 Frend (1972) 299; John Eph, *HE* 4.6.
100 See Hardy (1968) 36.
101 John Eph., *Lives*, *PO* 18.681; cf. *HE* 3.37.
102 Alan Cameron's statement (1976) 127, that 'her [Theodora's] devotion to the monophysite case was notorious, a serious embarrassment to her orthodox husband' is overstated, and perhaps reflects what the couple wanted to have thought about them rather than the reality.
103 *SH* 10.13; cf. 13.9.
104 *SH* 13.19, 15.10.
105 *SH* 22.28, 32; cf. 9.32, 'his love burned up the Roman state'; 12.14.
106 *Wars* 1.25.4; 4.9.13; *Buildings* 1.2.17; 1.9.5; 1.11.27; 5.3.14.
107 John Lyd. 3.69 (with n. at 339), 'ἡ ὁμόζυγος γυνή'; cf. Zon. 3.152.
108 *SH* 3.19, 17.13, 22.5; 14.8; 15.10; 17.27; 15.21.
109 *SH* 16.14; 4.6–8, 3.19; 16.23–8, 17.38–45; 3.9–11, 21–2, 4.7–12, 16.25–6. Allen (1992) 100: 'for Procopius, at least, Theodora's power and influence, chiefly exercised though they were within the bounds of contemporary and political norms, were only too threatening and real.'
110 *SH* 16.7–10.
111 Malalas 449 (tr. Jeffreys *et al.* (1986) 263), who dates this to 529.
112 Constantine Porphyrogennetos, 'Excerpta de insidiis', 3.171–2; see Malalas, tr. Jeffreys *et al.* (1986) xxxiii; Theophanes AM 6026 [AD 533/4].
113 The *SH*'s portrait of Antonina's son Photios (1.32) is also confirmed by John Eph., *HE* 1.32; cf. Theophanes AM 6058 [AD 565/6].
114 *SH* 4.6–12.
115 *Wars* 1.24.33–8.
116 *Chron. Pasch.* 625.
117 *Wars* 1.24.54; 35,000: Malalas 476 and *Chron. Pasch.* 627; 50,000: John Lyd. 3.70; 80,000: Zach. Rhet. 9.14.
118 Cameron (1985) 69.
119 Theodora misquotes Isokrates: the citation should be 'tyranny is a good burial shroud' (Isok., *Archidamos* 45); Evans (1984) 382.
120 *Wars* 1.24.11–15; 3.13.12–20; cf. the comments of John Lyd. 3.58–61, on his extortionate measures in Lydia; Tsirpanlis (1974).
121 *Wars* 3.10.7: 'the boldest and cleverest man of the time'; cf. 1.24.13. Honoré (1978) 13 comments that most of the administrative measures of the decade 531–41 bear his mark.
122 Ironically the Cappadocian had been responsible for driving villagers off the land to swell the mob: John Lyd. 3.70.
123 For Phokas, who was far more acceptable to the public service, see John Lyd. 3.73–5.
124 *Wars* 3.10.7–18; 1.25.4; *SH* 17.38.
125 *Wars* 1.25.7–8 (tr. Dewing).
126 John Lyd. 3.69 (tr. Bandy (1983) 243). Lydus's comment on Justinian's lack of action and inability to 'dislodge the wrecker of the government' is a clear indictment of his rule.
127 *Wars* 1.25.13–30.
128 *Wars* 1.25.37–44. According to Malalas 480–81 this was by the emperor's command.
129 *SH* 17.40–45; Malalas 483, who names them as Andreas and John Dandax.
130 *Wars* 2.30.49–54; Malalas 481.
131 Cameron (1985) 70. Greatrex (1995) has recently suggested that this section of

the *Wars* (1.25) was originally intended for the *SH* and dates the composition of this chapter to 546.

132 *SH* 22.5, 22–7.
133 For Procopius's portrait of Amalasuintha, see Fisher (1973) 264–5.
134 *Wars* 5.4.22–30.
135 *SH* 16.1–5.
136 Evans (1996a) 138.
137 *Wars* 5.6.12, 15–26.
138 Cass. *Variae* 10.20, 10.21. *Letters* 10.10, 10.23 and 10.24 are also addressed to Theodora (from Amalasuintha (534), Theodahad (535) and Gudeliva (535)).
139 Cass. *Variae* 10.20 (?May 535) (tr. Barnish (1992) 137–8).
140 Cass. *Variae* 10.21.2.
141 *PLRE* 3b.994–8, s.v. *Petrus* 6: Peter received the title of patrician soon afterwards, perhaps as a reward for his diplomatic services.
142 *Wars* 5.25.13; cf. *SH* 1.13, 27.
143 Liberatus, *Brev.* 22; cf. *Lib. Pont.* 60 (Silverius); Vict. Tonn., s.a. 542: 'Theodorae factione Augustae … Silverius romanus episcopus exilio mittitur et pro eo Vigilius ordinatur.'
144 *Lib. Pont.* 60 (Silverius) (Davis (1989) 55).
145 *Wars* 5.25.13; cf. *Lib. Pont.* 60 (tr. Davis (1989) 55).
146 *Lib. Pont.* 61 (Vigilius) (tr. Davis (1989) 57).
147 Theophanes AM 6039 [AD 546/7]: ironically Vigilius sought sanctuary in St Sergios's in the monastery of Hormisdas; Frend (1972) 281.
148 Malalas 430 (tr. Jeffreys *et al.* (1986) 249), under 528/9; cf. Theophanes AM 6020 [AD 527/8].
149 Cameron (1985) 81 notes that both marriages united 'a self-made general with an actress'.
150 *SH* 4.37, 5.18–22; Alan Cameron (1978) 269–70.
151 John Eph., *HE* 5.7; cf. Alan Cameron (1978) 273–5.
152 John Eph., *HE* 5.1: 'Athanasius, the son of queen Theodora's daughter, who increased and multiplied the heresy [of tritheism] by a liberal expenditure of gold'; cf. 5.7; Mich. Syr. 10.1, cf. 9.30 (Chabot 2.285, 253); Frend (1972) 290–91.
153 John Eph., *HE* 2.11.
154 John Eph., *HE* 2.12; cf. Mich. Syr. 10.7 (Chabot 2.306).
155 Theophanes AM 6054 [AD 561/2]; Alan Cameron (1978) 270.
156 Cameron (1985) 81.
157 *SH* 5.8–15.
158 Downey (1959) 27–51, esp. 30–44. For Justinian's reconstruction of this church, see *Buildings* 1.4.9–18; Evagr. 4.31; Theophanes AM 6042 [AD 549/50].
159 Vict. Tonn. s.a. 549: 'Theodora Augusta Calchedonensis synodi inimica canceris plaga corpore toto perfusa vitam prodigiose finivit'; see Fitton (1976) 119, who suggests gangrene as a possible translation for 'cancer'; *SH* 15.7.
160 *SH* 8.3, 28; 13.10–11; 22.30–31; Barker (1966) 185–93.
161 *de cer.* 1, append. 14.

2 SOPHIA (565–601+)

1 John Eph., *HE* 3.22 (tr. Payne Smith (1860) 202): 'when the king Tiberius was but a youth … we both of us, together with the rest of the court, were constantly in one another's company, in attendance upon his late majesty Justin'; cf. 3.5 (AD 574), 'for a long time he [Tiberius] had been Justin's keeper'.

2 Evagr. 5.1, cf. 5.11.
3 John Eph., *HE* 2.10, 3.4 (tr. Payne Smith (1860) 171); cf. Vict. Tonn. s.a. 567: 'huius {Iustini} coniunx Sophia Theodorae Augustae neptis asseritur.'
4 Cameron (1976b) 51; contrast Frend (1972) 317, who calls Sophia a woman of 'similar character but with less ability than her aunt Theodora'.
5 Cf. Cameron (1975b) 21.
6 Malalas 430; Theophanes AM 6020 [AD 527/8].
7 For Corippus's praises of Arabia, see Corippus, *Iust.* 2.72–83: 'Her eyes blaze with fire, like her mother's: her name and her age were different, but the grace of her noble form was not different'; *Iust.* 2.285; cf. Theophanes AM 6065 [AD 572/3]. For a possible daughter of Arabia who died young, see Cameron (1980) 73. All translations from Corippus in this chapter are taken from *Flavius Cresconius Corippus in Laudem Iustini Augusti Minoris Libri IV*, ed. and tr. Averil Cameron, University of London: Athlone Press, 1976.
8 Theophanes AM 6061 [AD 568/9].
9 Corippus, *Iust.* 2.84–298; Evagr. 5.1; Cameron (1975b) 8.
10 Corippus, *Iust.* 2.172.
11 Corippus, *Iust.* 1.8–9.
12 Corippus, *Iust.* 3.147–9; 1.10–11: 'You are enough for me in place of all the Muses in composing my song, you tell me all the hidden secrets'; cf. *ibid.* 127.
13 Corippus, *Iust.* 2.198–200; 2.52–69; cf. Cameron (1980) 78.
14 Corippus, *Iust.* 4.263–91; 1.208–10, 4.270–71.
15 Corippus, *Iust.* 1.272–90, 291.
16 Cameron (1975b) 8; *V. Eutychii* (*Life of Eutychios*) 66, *PG* 86: 349 (Eutychios saw the couple depicted in imperial costume in a dream); *V. Symeoni Iun.* (*Life of St Symeon the Younger*), 203.
17 John Biclar. s.a. 568, 'Justin son of Germanos was killed in Alexandria by the supporters (*factione*) of Augusta Sophia'; Evagr. 5.1–2; cf. Agathias 4.22.
18 Theophanes AM 6059 [AD 566/7]; Evagr. 5.3; cf. Corippus, *Iust.* 1.60–61.
19 Corippus, *Iust.* 2.361–406.
20 For Justin's coronation speech which contained a bizarre emphasis on the treasury as the stomach of the state, see Cameron (1980) 80; Corippus, *Iust.* 2.178–274, esp. 249–54.
21 *Nov. J.* 148 pr. (AD 566): 'we found the treasury burdened with many debts and reduced to utter exhaustion' (tr. Mango and Scott (1997) 358), who also note that there may have been a possible connection with the bankers' revolt of 562/3.
22 Theophanes AM 6059 [AD 566/7]; AM 6055 [AD 562/3]; Evagr. 5.3; Corippus, *Iust.* 1.60–61.
23 Corippus, *Iust.* 2.389–91, 395–7.
24 Theophanes AM 6060 [AD 567/8]; cf. Zon. 3.175. Theophanes's account actually places this in the wrong year. Mango and Scott (1997) 358 n. 1, suggest that perhaps in Theophanes's source Sophia's action balanced Justin's consular largesse (AM 5059), which Theophanes has dated a year late.
25 Corippus, *Iust.* 3.308–401; John Eph., *HE* 6.24; Jones (1964) 1.307.
26 Evagr. 5.1; John Eph., *HE* 5.20; Greg. Tur., *HF* 4.40; Paul Diac., *HL* 3.11.
27 Cameron (1979) 13; Corippus, *Iust.* 2.351–2, 357–8; 4.10–12, 100–104; Theophanes AM 6059 [AD 566/7].
28 Jones (1964) 1.306; John Eph., *HE* 3.14.
29 Theophanes AM 6060 [AD 567/8].
30 John Eph., *HE* 2.10 (tr. Payne Smith (1860) 105): 'and when he [Andrew] was reserving the consecrated elements, she used to tell him to put by one pearl, – for

so they called the pieces of bread, – and place it upon the patten under the cloth; and . . . it was supposed by every one that it was the merciful Justin himself who took it in secret'; according to the monophysite Mich. Syr. 10.7 (Chabot 2.306) Sophia continued to practise monophysitism after her accession, and had a vision of the Theotokos warning her against tritheism.

31 John Eph., *HE* 2.10.
32 Cameron (1976) 62.
33 John Eph., *HE* 5.7, who gives the will in detail; Mich. Syr. 10.1 (Chabot 2.283).
34 Corippus, *Iust.* 2.52–69; *ibid.* 152; cf. Cameron (1978) 82–3.
35 John Eph., *HE* 1.19, 2.29; Corippus, *Iust.*, ed. Cameron, 123.
36 Evagr. 5.1; Theophanes AM 6058 [AD 565/6]; Zon. 3.174.
37 Mich. Syr. 10.1 (Chabot 2.283).
38 *V. Symeoni Iun.* 207–8; a letter of Symeon to Justin is preserved: *PG* 86 (2): 3216–20 (but cf. van den Ven, *V. Symeoni Iun.* 2.204 n. who considers it to have been addressed to Justinian).
39 Cameron (1976) 62; *V. Symeoni Iun.* 203, 207–9.
40 Theophanes AM 6058 [AD 565/6]; cf. John Eph., *HE* 1.32. Mango and Scott (1997) 356 suggest that he may also have been assigned the task of removing Justin, the emperor's cousin.
41 Mich. Syr. 10.2 (Chabot 2.285–90). The clearest discussion of Justin's edicts against the monophysites can be found in Allen (1981) 22–5, 212–14.
42 Evagr. 5.4; cf. John Eph., *HE* 1.19–20; Mich. Syr. 10.4 (Chabot 2.295–9).
43 John Eph., *HE* 1.24–5.
44 Note the statement of the imperial couple to recalcitrant bishops: John Eph., *HE* 1.26 (tr. Payne Smith (1860) 44), 'Cheer up, and be comforted: for we purpose in God to content you, and unite you to us in perfect unity'.
45 John Eph., *HE* 1.5, 2.17 (tr. Payne Smith (1860) 117); *ibid.* 1.10. John may here be overstating the patriarch's anti-monophysite stance (see *ODB* 1047 s.v. *John III Scholastikos*), especially as John was prepared to acquiesce in Justinian's edict of aphthartodocetism (*Syn. Vetus* 124).
46 John Eph., *HE* 2.3 (Stephen of Cyprus); Cameron (1977) 6–7.
47 John Eph., *HE* 1.11 (tr. Payne Smith (1860) 9).
48 *HE* 1.22, 2.4–7.
49 John Eph., *HE* 2.11, 12; cf. Mich. Syr. 10.7 (Chabot 2.306).
50 See Moorhead (1981).
51 *Anth. Gr.* 9.779, 810, 812–13; cf. the 'θεσπείη συνωρίς' (sacred pair) of 16.41 (= *Planudean Anthology*), though this epigram may be from the reign of Justinian and Theodora; cf. *Anth. Gr.* 1.2, 1.11.
52 Zon. 3.174.
53 See Cameron (1968) 11–20.
54 Theophanes AM 6062 [AD 569/70].
55 John Eph., *HE* 3.24; Theophanes AM 6061–2 [AD 568–70].
56 *HE* 3.24.
57 See Cameron (1980) 70–71.
58 Theophanes AM 6058 [AD 565/6]; AM 6068 [AD 575/6]; Zon. 3.174; Cameron (1980) 76–7.
59 Cameron (1979) 17.
60 Venantius Fortunatus, *Appendix Carminum* 2: 'Ad Iustinum et Sophiam Augustos' (tr. George (1995) 111–15); for discussion, see Cameron (1976) 58–9; Brennan (1995) esp. 12–13.
61 Beckwith (1968) fig. 55; MacCormack (1981) 84–5, pl. 24.

62 As suggested by Cameron (1976) 61.

63 Evagr. 5.8–9; cf. Theoph. Sim. 3.9.8–11.

64 Paul Diac., *HL* 2.5; cf. *DAI* 27.

65 Cf. *Lib. Pont.* 63 (Life of John III, AD 579–90). Narses finally died in Rome in 572 or 573.

66 Jones (1964) 1.306 calls the renewal of the war 'megalomaniac and irresponsible'. See Turtledove (1983) 292–301.

67 John Eph., *HE* 6.2–5 recounts that the fall of Dara was partially due to 'the unbusinesslike habits of the king himself, who allowed the underhand dealings of the weak court of Constantinople to come to light by a carelessness as indefensible as the treachery it disclosed was base' – two letters were missent to the wrong addressees (6.2; tr. Payne Smith (1860) 369–70).

68 Theophanes AM 6065 [AD 572/3] (Mango and Scott (1997) 364). Theophanes mistakenly calls Badouarios Justin's brother-in-law.

69 John Eph., *HE* 3.2–3. For Justin's illness and his final operation for gallstones, see Kislinger (1986) 39–44.

70 See Bellinger (1966) 204–17, 221–5, 226–39, 243–50, 254–8; Wroth (1908) xix, 77–102. Justin and Sophia also appear together on bronze weights: Vikan (1990) 152.

71 Corippus, *Iust.*, ed. Cameron, 121.

72 *V. Symeoni Iun.* 207–9; for ventriloquism, see Greenfield (1988) 128–9, 293.

73 John Eph., *HE* 3.5; for the recurrence of lucid intervals in which he was well enough to give audiences and appear in the hippodrome, see also 3.6. *Ibid.*, 3.2; he was ill for five years.

74 Corippus, *Iust.*, ed. Cameron, 138.

75 John Eph., *HE* 3.5; cf. Evagr. 5.13; Greg. Tur., *HF* 5.19 (tr. Dalton (1927) 193), 'the empire fell under the sole rule of the empress Sophia'.

76 Evagr. 5.12, 'urging the unseemliness of trampling upon a widowed female, a prostrate monarch, and a desolate empire . . .'; John Eph., *HE* 6.8.

77 Men. Prot. 18.1–2 (*FHG* 4.240–41, fr. 37–8; Blockley (1985) 156–8); see Blockley (1980) 91–4; John Eph., *HE* 1.19.

78 Men. Prot. 18.1 (tr. Blockley (1985) 158): 'Jacob was given an audience, not with Justin, who was sick, but with the empress, who at this time managed everything with Tiberius. When she read the letter she said that she herself would send an envoy to the Persian king to discuss all the points at dispute.'

79 Theophanes AM 6071 [AD 578/9].

80 John Eph., *HE* 3.7.

81 John Eph., *HE* 3.11.

82 John Eph., *HE* 5.20; cf. Paul Diac., *HL* 3.11.

83 John Eph., *HE* 3.14 (tr. Payne Smith (1860) 190); cf. Evagr. 5.13.

84 Greg. Tur., *HF* 5.19; cf. Paul Diac., *HL* 3.11. For Gregory (d. 594) as a valuable source, see Cameron (1975a).

85 John Eph., *HE* 3.8.

86 *HE* 3.7 (tr. Payne Smith (1860) 179); cf. Mich. Syr. 10.17 (Chabot 2.343).

87 John Eph., *HE* 3.4 (quoted above, p. 40).

88 Their names are given by Theophanes AM 6071 [AD 578/9].

89 John Eph., *HE* 3.8.

90 Theophanes AM 6071.

91 John Eph., *HE* 3.7; cf. Mich. Syr. 10.17 (Chabot 2.343) who states that when Tiberios refused the patriarch's request Sophia allowed Ino to come to the palace with full honours. Michael misnames Ino as Helena (not Anastasia), and his account is suspect.

92 Badouarios had died in the tenth year of the reign in Italy fighting the Lombards: John Biclar. s.a. 576.

93 John Eph., *HE* 3.7.

94 John Eph., *HE* 3.9 (the Greens wanted her to be called Helena); Theophanes AM 6071 [AD 578/9].

95 John Eph., *HE* 3.6; Theophanes AM 6070 [AD 577/8].

96 Theophanes AM 6070 [AD 577/8] (Mango and Scott (1997) 368); cf. Theoph. Sim. 3.11.5–13. Evagr. 5.13 and John Eph., *HE* 3.5, give this speech more correctly upon Tiberios's proclamation as Caesar. See Cameron (1986).

97 Greg. Tur., *HF* 5.30; cf. Paul Diac., *HL* 3.12.

98 *HE* 3.10 (tr. Payne Smith (1860) 183–4).

99 John Eph., *HE* 3.10 (tr. Payne Smith (1860) 185).

100 Bellinger (1966) 277; Wroth (1908) 112, 114.

101 John Eph., *HE* 3.23.

102 John Eph., *HE* 3.24, 23 (tr. Payne Smith (1860) 204).

103 Theophanes AM 6072 [AD 579/80]; John Eph., *HE* 3.23, cf. 3.10. Mango and Scott (1997) 371 n. 2 suggest that Theophanes may be referring to Tiberios's remodelling operations; neither John's nor Theophanes's account supports Cameron's statement ((1975b) 20; cf. *PLRE* 3.179) that Sophia was established in the palace of Sophiai in virtual custody.

104 Greg. Tur., *HF* 6.30; cf. John Eph., *HE* 5.13.

105 Greg. Tur., *HF* 6.30; John Eph., *HE* 5.13; Theophanes AM 6074 [AD 581/2], according to whom Tiberios at the same time married his other daughter Charito to the general Germanos. Constantina and Maurice were to have three daughters and six sons: *Chron. Pasch.* 693; after the accession of Phokas and murder of Maurice, Constantina was put in a monastery and later beheaded for attempting a rebellion: *Chron. Pasch.* 695–6.

106 Theophanes AM 6093 [AD 600/601]; AM 6085 [AD 592/3]; Grierson (1962) 47.

107 It may have been this crown which Leo IV (husband of Irene) coveted, and the wearing of which caused him to break out into carbuncles causing a violent fever and early death: Theophanes AM 6272 [AD 779/80]; cf. *DAI* 13; *V. Irenes* 9.

3 MARTINA (?615/16–41)

1 Nikephoros 1; Theophanes AM 6102 [AD 609/10]; *Chron. Pasch.* 699–701; Olster (1993) 117–18, 127–8. On Phokas's 'tyranny', see Rösch (1979).

2 See esp. Kaegi (1982) 109–33.

3 Note Theophanes's comments, AM 6121 [AD 628/9].

4 For a discussion, see Herrin (1987) 207–10, 213–14, 217–19.

5 Theophanes AM 6104 [AD 611/12]; *Chron. Pasch.* 703: after being crowned in the palace, the infant Epiphaneia was seated in a chariot and escorted to St Sophia. She was to be married in 629 to T'ong Yabghu Kaghan, lord of the western Turks: Zuckerman (1995) 113; cf. Nikephoros 18.

6 *Chron. Pasch.* 702–4; Theophanes AM 6102, 6103 [AD 609/10, 610/11]; Nikephoros 3.

7 Such marriages were banned by Constantine the Great: *CTh.* 3.12.1 (AD 342).

8 Theophanes AM 6105 [AD 612/13].

9 Nikephoros 11. AD 624 is the *terminus ante quem*: see Nikephoros, ed. Mango 179–80; *Chron. Pasch.* 714. *Ibid.* append. 4, Whitby argues for a date of 614, considering that Nikephoros is here arranging his material thematically not chronologically.

10 Grierson (1968–73) 3.1, 216–17, 288, 292 (no. 99a.1, AD 624/5). Zuckerman's

suggestion (1995) 113–26 that the female figure is Epiphaneia relies on the assumption that Herakleios and Martina did not marry until 623 and fails to explain why Epiphaneia only began to be represented in 615/16: Epiphaneia would also have been the first daughter of an emperor to appear on the coinage, the next being the daughters of Theophilos.

11 Grierson (1982) 88, 107–8, who notes that as the mother of an heir to the throne she had as good a title to being represented as any of her predecessors.

12 Grumel (1989) 284; van Dieten (1972) 6; Zon. 3.205.

13 Nikephoros 11.

14 Nikephoros 20: Theodore may have been removed from his command after a defeat at Gabitha in 634; Theophanes AM 6125 [AD 632/3]; cf. Mich. Syr. 11.5 (Chabot 2.418); Kaegi (1992) 100.

15 Nikephoros 11; John of Nikiu 120.54 (John was a late seventh-century Egyptian bishop). For Theodosios's marriage to Nike daughter of Shahrvaraz in 629/30, see Nikephoros 17; Mango (1985) 105–17. Their eldest child is often said to have been called Flavios, but see Mango, note on Nikephoros 11, where the reading Fabios should be preferred. Herakleios and Martina seem to have had ten children in total, but the names of some are much debated: see the family tree in *ODB* 916; Stratos 1.358.

16 Chron. Pasch. 714; Theophanes AM 6105 [AD 612/13]; Nikephoros 12. She was with him at Antioch (with a child), when the news was received of the serious defeat by the Arabs at the river Yarmuk in August 636: Nikephoros 23. For an exchange of gifts between Caliph 'Umar's wife, Umm Kulthum, and Martina (Martina sent a necklace in exchange for perfume), see Kaegi (1992) 250.

17 Nikephoros 18.

18 Theoph. Sim. 8.11.9–10. Of course, control of some of these regions was by now purely nominal.

19 Nikephoros 19; Theophanes AM 6108 [AD 615/16].

20 Spain (1977) esp. 298–304 considers that the 'Relics Ivory' from Trier represents Herakleios and Martina and their role in the return of the True Cross, with Martina intended to be seen as the new Helena in an attempt to counter condemnation over their illegal marriage.

21 Nikephoros 24; Stratos 2.137, 3.231.

22 Nikephoros 25, 27 (who says that Marinos was also made Caesar: cf. *de cer.* 2.29); Stratos 2.140.

23 Nikephoros 27. Herrin (1987) 215 notes that the title implies considerably greater power than the senate was likely to accord a female regent.

24 Stratos 1.7.

25 Nikephoros 30; Leo Gramm. 156, who tells us the gruesome detail that part of the skull broke away as the crown was removed.

26 Grierson (1962) 48. For his condition in which he had to place a board against his abdomen while urinating to stop his urine discharging in his face, see Nikephoros 27; Leo Gramm. 155; Geo. Mon. 673. The authors believe that his condition was due to his trangression in marrying his niece; cf. Theophanes AM 6132 [AD 639/40].

27 Nikephoros 28 (tr. Mango (1990) 77–9).

28 See Mango (1990) 8 for the possible date of Nikephoros's work.

29 Nikephoros 29, with note (correcting the 50,000 *solidi* of Stratos 3.192); cf. John of Nikiu 120.3. The crown of Herakleios recovered from his grave by Constantine was worth approximately 5,000 *solidi*.

30 See Grierson (1962) 48–9; Stratos 2.184–5, 3.196–7; Kaegi (1992) 184, 261 for the date of his death.

31 Nikephoros 29; John of Nikiu 116.9; Leo Gramm. 156; Kedr. 1.753; Stratos 2.178.
32 Theophanes AM 6121 [AD 628/9], AM 6132 [AD 639/40]; Leo Gramm. 155; cf. Mich. Syr. 11.7, 8 (Chabot 2.426, 430); Geo. Mon. 673; Kedr. 1.753; Zon. 3.216.
33 Psellos, *HS* 66 records that Constantine apparently 'adhered to the true and faultless orthodoxy'; cf. Zon. 3.216.
34 Nikephoros 30; on Martina's regency, see Christophilopoulou (1970) 15–20.
35 John of Nikiu 120.2; cf. Leo Gramm. 156, who calls Heraklonas a bastard.
36 Nikephoros 30; Kedr. 1.753.
37 John of Nikiu 119.24; Stratos 2.188, 3.59–60.
38 Nikephoros 30; John of Nikiu 119.17–22. Herakleios had exiled Cyrus for supposedly betraying the interests of the empire in his negotiations with the Arabs: cf. Nikephoros 23, 26.
39 For Valentinos, see Kaegi (1981) 154–8; Stratos 2.200–202; Haldon (1986) 180.
40 John of Nikiu 120.5; Stratos 2.189.
41 Nikephoros 30; John of Nikiu 119.23, 120.41–3.
42 Nikephoros 31; cf. John of Nikiu 120.44, who states that it was Valentinos who crowned the young Herakleios.
43 Nikephoros 32; Theophanes AM 6133 [AD 640/41]; Kedr. 1.754; Mich. Syr. 11.7 (Chabot, 2.427); van Dieten (1972) 76.
44 Nikephoros 31; Stratos 2.197–8 (1976) 11–19.
45 Nikephoros 32; John of Nikiu 120.61–2.
46 John of Nikiu 120.63.
47 John of Nikiu 120.45–6, 50–53.
48 Stratos 2.203.
49 Theophanes AM 6133 [AD 640/41]; John of Nikiu 120.52; Zon. 3.217. John's account is unreliable: Marinos was the youngest, and it is unclear whether his nose was slit or he was castrated. The seventh-century Armenian source, Sebeos 31 (tr. Bedrosian (1985) 134), states that Martina's tongue was cut out and then she and her sons were killed.
50 Theophanes AM 6134 [AD 641/2] (tr. Mango and Scott (1997) 475).
51 Nikephoros 1, 17. See Mango (1985) 105–18.
52 Herrin (1987) 216.
53 Their son Herakleios was born in November 630: Theophanes AM 6122 [AD 629/30].
54 Mango (1985) 114; cf. Laiou (1992b) 169.
55 Kaegi (1992) 213–18.
56 Theophanes AM 6160 [AD 667/8]; Mich. Syr. 11.11, 12 (Chabot 2.446, 450–51).

4 IRENE (769–802)

1 *ODB* 1008 s.v. *Irene* suggests that she was born *c.* 752.
2 Theophanes AM 6295, 6269, 6300 [AD 802/3, 776/7, 807/8]; Lilie (1996) 36–41; Herrin (1995) 66 sees Irene as specifically chosen because of her family's importance.
3 Theophanes AM 6291 [AD 798/9].
4 Speck (1978) 1.203–8 and Rydén (1985) argue, unnecessarily, against the historicity of bride-shows: Karlin-Hayter (1991) 100; Mango and Scott (1997) 664 n. 4. See esp. Hunger (1965); Treadgold (1979); Schreiner (1984); Hans (1988).
5 For her marriage, see Theophanes AM 6224 [AD 731/2]; her original name may

have been Chichek: she is said to have introduced the garment called the *tzitzakion* to court (Mango and Scott (1997) 568n. 1).

6 Theophanes AM 6261, 6262 [AD 768/9, 769/70]; Nikephoros 88; Leo Gramm. 188, 190.

7 Theophanes AM 6267 [AD 774/5] (tr. Mango and Scott (1997) 619); cf. Nikephoros 80–81, 83–4.

8 Theophanes AM 6224 [AD 731/2]; *Syn. CP* 848–52 (*BHG* Auct. 2029h); Mango (1982) 409; Morris (1995) 13. For the question of the authorship of Theophanes's *Chronicle*, and the degree to which Theophanes contributed to the draft of George Synkellos, see Mango and Scott (1997) xliii–lxiii; George was *synkellos* under Tarasios and still writing in 810; Theophanes died in 818.

9 See Anastos (1955) for the Christological arguments of the iconoclastic Council of Hiereia in 754; its *horos* is given in Mansi 13.204–364. The council essentially argued that God is uncircumscribable, hence a material depiction confuses or separates his two inseparable natures. It did, however, acknowledge Mary as Theotokos, and higher than all creation, and her power of intercession with God (Anastos (1955) 185–6).

10 Theophanes AM 6268, 6272 [AD 775/6, 779/80]; Leo Gramm. 190–91; for Constantine V's persecution, see Alexander (1977); Gero (1977). For Constantine V's crowning of his third wife Eudokia as Augusta and his lavish patrimony for Eudokia's five sons (50,000 lb of gold) and the ranks bestowed on them, see Theophanes AM 6260 [AD 767/8]; Kedr. 2.18; Treadgold (1982a) 67, (1988) 9.

11 Kedr. 2.19–20 (tr. Mango and Scott (1997) 626 n. 9). The chronicle of Symeon the Logothete tells us that Irene was persuaded to worship icons by Theophanes and three *cubicularii* and that Leo from now on had nothing to do with her: Leo Gramm. 192.

12 Theophanes AM 6273 [AD 780/81]; Leo Gramm. 193. See Treadgold (1988) 6 for the suggestion that Leo may not have died a natural death and that Irene and her supporters 'probably connived at her husband's murder': Treadgold accepts Kedrenos's version of events.

13 Theophanes AM 6273 [AD 781/81]; Leo Gramm. 192–3. The other brothers were the Caesar Christopher and the *nobilissimi* Niketas, Anthimos and Eudokimos: all five were the sons of Constantine V's third wife Eudokia.

14 Kaegi (1966) 63–5 notes that a characteristic feature of the years 787–815 was the persistent attempt of the Armeniac theme to overthrow imperial authority, irrespective of the religious stance of the ruler.

15 Mango (1982) 401–9; *Syn. CP* 613–14; Bosch (1966) 24–9. Anthousa was born in 756–7 and died in 808 or 809 (Mango 408).

16 Runciman (1978) 104: Leo III's legislation had laid down that a widow was to be sole guardian of children not of age.

17 Grierson (1968–73) 3.1, 337–8; Grierson (1982) 158; Treadgold (1988) 60.

18 McCormick (1995) 365; Herrin (1987) 381.

19 Theophanes AM 6274 [AD 781/2]. See Herrin (1987) 412–13; Grierson (1981) 902–5.

20 Theophanes AM 6273 [AD 780/81].

21 Theophanes AM 6274 [AD 781/2].

22 Mich. Syr. 12.3 (Chabot 3.9).

23 Theophanes AM 6274 [AD 781/2].

24 Arvites (1983) 225; Theophanes AM 6274 [AD 781/2]; the tribute may have been 70,000 or 90,000 dinars per year for three years: see Tabari, tr. Williams 2.100; Treadgold (1988) 69. *ODB* 902 s.v. *Harun al-Rashid* states that it was an annual tribute of 70,000 dinars and commercial concessions.

25 Arvites (1983) 225; Tritle (1977).

26 Theophanes AM 6275 [AD 782/3]; Leo Gramm. 194; Shepard (1995a) 234; Treadgold (1988) 73: the Asiatic *themata* were operating there in 786 (Theophanes AM 6279 [AD 786/7]); Lilie (1996) 169–79.

27 Theophanes AM 6295 [AD 802/3]; Treadgold (1982b) 243–51; cf. *V. Irenes* 25–7.

28 *AASS* Nov 3.880BC; Cormack (1977) 40; Mango (1972a) 156–7.

29 Theophanes AM 6273 [AD 780/81] (tr. Mango and Scott (1997) 627); Mich. Syr. 12.3 (Chabot 3.10–11); Mango (1963) 201–7.

30 Theophanes AM 6276 [AD 783/4]; Leo Gramm. 194–5.

31 *V. Taras.* 397–8.

32 Theophanes AM 6276 [AD 783/4]; cf. AM 6272.

33 Theophanes AM 6277 [AD 784/5]; Leo Gramm. 195 calls him *asekretis* (imperial secretary); cf. *V. Irenes* 12; *V. Taras.* 397, 398 calls him *protoasekretis* (head of the college of *asekretis*).

34 Thomas (1987) 124; cf. Every (1962) 95.

35 Theophanes AM 6277, 6278 [AD 784/5, 785/6]; Mansi 12.990–1, 999–1002; *V. Taras.* 404; Alexander (1958a) 18–19.

36 For the Byzantine army and iconoclasm, see Kaegi (1966), esp. 53–61, who argues that not all Byzantine troops in Asia were iconoclast and that Constantine V had consciously indoctrinated the *tagmata* with his iconoclastic beliefs: Theophanes AM 6259 [AD 766/7].

37 Theophanes AM 6283 [AD 790/91]; Arvites (1983) 227; Haldon (1975) 206–11, (1984) 236–45.

38 Theophanes AM 6279 [AD 786/7]; Runciman (1978) 108.

39 Theophanes AM 6280 [AD 787/8]; Dumeige (1978) 101–42; Herrin (1987) 417–24. Darrouzès (1975) 5–76 lists the bishops who attended.

40 Mansi 13.377DE (tr. Alexander (1958a) 21).

41 Theophanes AM 6281 [AD 788/9]; Leo Gramm. 193; Treadgold (1979) 395–413, (1988) 89–90, 92; McCormick (1995) 366–7.

42 Theophanes AM 6300 [AD 807/8].

43 *V. Philareti* 135–43; *V. Irenes* 16; for the *V. Philareti*, written *c.* 822, as a non-iconodule text, see Shevchenko (1977) 18–19. The *lauraton* has generally been taken to mean an ideal portrait against which the candidates were compared: Kazhdan and Sherry (1996) 353 n. 7 suggest instead that it measured the girls' waists.

44 Theophanes AM 6281 [AD 788/9]; McCormick (1995) 367.

45 Theophanes AM 6282 [AD 789/90]; cf. *V. Irenes* 16.

46 Theophanes AM 6259, 6282 [AD 766/7, 789/90].

47 Arvites (1983) 221.

48 Theophanes AM 6283 [AD 790/91]; Leo Gramm. 196–7; Kaegi (1966) 63–5.

49 See Theophanes AM 6258 [AD 765/6]: *strategos* of the Thrakesians; AM 6262 [AD 769/70]: he took part in the persecution of iconophiles, forcing monks and nuns to marry; AM 6263 [AD 770/71]: he sold off monasteries and their possessions, burnt books, and killed and tortured monks.

50 Grierson (1968–73) 3.1, 336–8.

51 Theophanes AM 6284 [AD 791/2]; Leo Gramm. 197 is more positive about Constantine's military achievements. Grierson (1968–73) 3.2, 338–9: Irene's name is in the dative, as the object of an acclamation.

52 Theophanes AM 6284 [AD 791/2].

53 Theophanes AM 6285 [AD 792/3]. Failing to receive the reward they had hoped for the Armenians then went over to the Arabs.

54 Psellos, *HS* 80–82.

55 Theophanes AM 6287 [AD 794/5] (tr. Mango and Scott (1997) 645); Leo Gramm. 198–9; *V. Taras.* 408–12.

56 *V. Taras.* 409; 'De Sanctis Patriarchis Tarasio et Nicephoro', *PG* 99:1852D; cf. Theod. Stoud., *Ep.* 36.

57 Cheynet and Flusin (1990) 195 n. 21.

58 Theophanes AM 6288 [AD 795/6]. Maria was one of Theodore the Stoudite's correspondents: Theod. Stoud., *Epp.* 227, 309, 514.

59 Treadgold (1988) 105.

60 Theod. Stoud., *Eulogy of Platon* 832B–3A; *Epp.* 1–3; Theophanes AM 6288 [AD 795/6]. Theodore's letters frequently refer to Constantine as a 'second Herod': *Epp.* 22, 28, 31, 443; Lilie (1996) 71–8.

61 Theophanes AM 6288 [AD 795/6].

62 Theophanes AM 6258 [AD 765/6]; 'L'histoires des reliques d'Euphémie par Constantin de Tios' (*BHG*³ 621) in Halkin (1965) 99–104 (Constantine of Tios accuses Leo III not Constantine); Mango (1966) 485–8; Kountoura-Galake (1987).

63 Theophanes AM 6258 [AD 765/6]; Halkin (1965) 97–8 (Constantine of Tios); *Patria* 3.9 (Preger 217) dates the rebuilding to her sole rule.

64 Wortley (1982) esp. 270–79, who considers the story of the desecration of St Euphemia's by Constantine V 'pious fiction' (277): anathema 15 of the iconoclast Council of 754 cursed anyone who 'does not confess that all the saints . . . are honourable in his sight in soul and body, and if he does not entreat their prayers . . .' (Mansi 13.348DE), a vindication of relics, as well as of the practice of intercession.

65 Theophanes AM 6289 [AD 796/7].

66 Theophanes AM 6289 [AD 796/7] (Mango and Scott (1997) 649); Leo Gramm. 199–200. Theophanes says that 15 August was a Saturday: it was in fact a Tuesday; cf. Grierson (1962) 54–5.

67 See Brooks (1900) 654–7. He seems to have died shortly afterwards: Genesios 25, but cf. Kedr. 2.31. Theodote went to a monastery, where she bore a posthumous son: Ps-Symeon 809: Theod. Stoud., *Ep.* 31.

68 Grierson (1968–73) 3.1, 347–51; Zepos, *JGR* 1.45–50; Dölger (1936) 129–31; Dölger (1924–65) 358, 359; cf. Hiestand (1990) 274–81. For her seals, see Zacos and Veglery (1972) 1.1, nos. 40–41.

69 Grierson (1968–73) 3.1, 347–8; Grierson (1982) 158; Wroth (1908) 1.xxxix.

70 Theophanes AM 6289 [AD 796/7]; Herrin (1987) 454–7, 464. Cf. Brown (1995) 331: 'One possible motive for Charles may have been to win support in the "Roman areas" of Italy such as the Exarchate and Rome by exploiting vestigial nostalgia for the Roman imperial title.'

71 Theophanes AM 6290, 6291 [AD 797/8, 798/9].

72 Theophanes AM 6298 [AD 805/6]; Theod. Stoud., *Eulogy of Platon* 833A–D.

73 Theophanes AM 6290, 6291 [AD 797/8, 798/9].

74 Theophanes AM 6291, 6292 [AD 798/9, 799/800]; Leo Gramm. 200.

75 Theophanes AM 6293 [AD 800/1], cf. AM 6289 [AD 796/7]; Arvites (1983) 230; Treadgold (1988) 119.

76 Theophanes AM 6294, 6295 [AD 801/2, 802/3] (tr. Mango and Scott (1997) 654); cf. Geo. Mon. Cont. 771–2.

77 Kaegi (1981) 242 notes that the support of the *tagmata* was 'critical in the intrigues that led to the deposition of Irene' and that in the conspiracies and seditions of the early ninth century their actions were frequently determined by material considerations.

78 Theophanes AM 6294 (AD 801/2).

79 Mich. Syr. 12.4 (Chabot 3.12–13). Mango and Scott (1997) 658 n. 11 note that Theophanes mentions no measures taken against Aetios, a possible rival, or indeed his brother Leo.

80 *Syn. Vetus* 153; cf. Genesios 6–8.

81 Theophanes AM 6300 [AD 807/8].

82 Theophanes AM 6295 [AD 802/3]; *de cer.* 2.42 mentions her tomb in the list of imperial tombs in the Holy Apostles.

83 See Herrin (1983a) 171: they dominated the personal activity of the imperial couple as wardrobe officials, chamberlains and treasurers, and played a similar role in wealthy households: Guilland (1943), (1944), (1945); Ringrose (1994).

84 Theophanes AM 6291 [AD 798/9]; Tabari, tr. Williams (1989) 2.222; Arvites (1983) 230.

85 Theophanes AM 6293 [AD 800/801]. Cf. Theod. Stoud., *Ep.* 7; Oikonomides (1991a) 2.242. Treadgold (1988) 118 states that this would have reduced prices by at least a tenth.

86 Anastos (1966) 89.

87 Theod. Stoud., *Ep.* 7.31–2; Theophanes AM 6302 [AD 809/10]; Thomas (1987) 128; Treadgold (1988) 151; Haldon (1993) 23–4, 37.

88 Mango (1959) 121; cf. *Patria* 3.20 (Preger 219).

89 Herrin (1987) 429.

90 *Patria* 3.20, 77, 85, 154 (Preger 219, 243, 246, 265).

91 Cormack (1977) 38, 40.

92 *Patria* 3.202 (Preger 278).

93 *Patria* 3.85 (Preger 246); Constantelos (1991) 100, citing *V. S Niketae Confessoris, AASS* 1 April, App. 24.30. For Irene's public bakeries, installed in a disused ancient hippodrome near the Amastrianon (*Patria* 3.85, 173; Preger 246, 269), see Herrin (1987) 449; Striker (1986) 7–11.

94 Theophanes AM 6303 [AD 810/11]; Leo Gramm. 198–9; Browning (1975) 49–50.

95 *V. Irenes* 16–17, 21. Herrin (1983b) 73 even suggests that Irene adopted the iconophile position for purely political reasons: 'the latter cannot be ruled out, for we are dealing with an untypical woman, who did not stop at the blinding of her own son, when he stood in the way of her ambition'; see also Whittow (1996) 149–50.

96 Theophanes AM 6363 [AD 810/11]; see Genesios 5 for her rancour against Prokopia the new empress.

97 Jenkins (1966) 90; cf. Diehl (1938–9) 1.77–109.

5 THEODORA, RESTORER OF ORTHODOXY (830–67+)

1 Herrin (1987) 466–7.

2 Theophanes AM 6305 [AD 812/13]; Alexander (1958a) 111–25.

3 Herrin (1983b) 68–75. Pope Gregory the Great considered: 'what writing presents to readers, this a picture presents to the unlearned who behold, since in it even the ignorant see what they ought to follow: in it the illiterate read. Hence . . . a picture is instead of reading' (tr. Herrin (1983b) 56).

4 See esp. Cameron (1978) 79–108, (1979) 42–56.

5 Kazhdan and Talbot (1991/2) 396–400; Hatlie (1996) 40–44.

6 Theod. Stoud., *Ep.* 538; Kazhdan and Talbot (1991/2) 399.

7 Topping (1982/3) 98–111.

8 Theoph. Cont. 89; Charanis (1961) 207–8; *ODB* 2037 s.v. *Theodora.*

9 Treadgold (1975) 325–41; cf. Brooks (1901) 540–45, who dates it to 12 May 821.

10 Ps-Symeon 628–9; cf. Theoph. Cont. 89–91; Kazhdan and Talbot (1991/2) 391.

11 Leo. Gramm. 213 (tr. Treadgold (1979) 403); Treadgold (1988) 268–9.

12 On the date of the marriage, see Treadgold (1975). For a variant version of the bride-show, see *V. Theodorae*, ed. Markopoulos, 258–60: in this version Theophilos gives each of the girls an apple. When they are summoned again on the next day, only Theodora has not eaten hers. For a survey of female influence on Theophilos, see Nikolaou (1994).

13 Leo Gramm. 214; Theoph. Cont. 86.

14 *V. Theodorae*, ed. Markopoulos, 260.

15 Treadgold (1988) 276–7 with n. 383.

16 Grierson (1982) 175, 178; *idem* (1968–73) 3.1, 407, 415–16.

17 Theoph. Cont. 95, 139–40, 144, 160; Ps-Symeon 653; Treadgold (1988) 310; Skyl. 56.

18 Ps-Symeon 628–9; cf. Theoph. Cont. 89–91; Skyl. 52 (who have Theoktiste, Theodora's mother, rather than Euphrosyne, as the protagonist); Kazhdan and Talbot (1991/2) 391. On Euphrosyne, see Genesios 35. Plate 8, from the Madrid manuscript of Skylitzes, shows Theodora's five daughters – Thekla, Anastasia, Anna, Pulcheria and Maria – being taught to venerate an icon of Christ by their grandmother Theoktiste in her convent.

19 Theoph. Cont. 91–2; Skyl. 53; Ps-Symeon 629–30; Bonner (1952) suggests that Denderis's posture is intended to resemble that of a magical amulet.

20 Leo Gramm. 228.

21 Leo Gramm. 226; Skyl. 61–3; for an extended, if inaccurate, account, see *V. Michaelis Syncelli* (*The Life of Michael the Synkellos*), 73–97.

22 Theoph. Cont. 103; Skyl. 61.

23 Genesios 55; Theoph. Cont. 148; Skyl. 81; Mango (1977) 134; Bury (1912) 144, 476.

24 Genesios 53; Theoph. Cont. 88–9, who adds that he threatened to put her to death if she repeated the offence. Treadgold (1988) 289 with n. 394 notes that the version of Theoph. Cont. dates the incident to after 835. For aristocratic women as shop-owners in Constantinople, see Herrin (1983a) 170; Oikonomides (1972) 345–6.

25 Mango (1967).

26 Geo. Mon. Cont. 811; Genesios 56; Theoph. Cont. 148–50 gives the credit to Manuel.

27 Bury (1912) 147; *V. Methodii*, *PG* 100: 1252C.

28 Whittow (1996) 158–9.

29 Mango (1977) 135; Gouillard (1961) 387–401; Dvornik (1953).

30 *V. Theodorae*, ed. Halkin, 32–3; Mango (1959) 131–2, who notes that the story contains an anachronism as the Chalke image would not have been restored until after the return to orthodoxy.

31 *V. Theodorae*, ed. Halkin, 33–4. Karlin-Hayter (1971) 495–6 notes the legendary qualities in the biography of Theodora; cf. Angold (1995) 432 for praise of Theodora from the thirteenth-century patriarch Germanos II.

32 Genesios 56–8; Theoph. Cont. 148; Geo. Mon. Cont. 811; Skyl. 83–4.

33 Genesios 57–8; Theoph. Cont. 149–50; Geo. Mon. Cont. 802. On the chronology, see Dölger (1924–65) 416, 425; Grumel (1989) 416.

34 Genesios 58; Theoph. Cont. 150–51; Bury (1912) 147 n. 4.

35 Theoph. Cont. 152–3 (she stated that she held an icon to his lips before he passed away); cf. *V. Theodorae*, ed. Markopoulos, 264–5; Dvornik (1953) 73.

36 *Patria* 3.155 (Preger 265); cf. Theoph. Cont. 109; Ps-Symeon 632 for the monastery erected by her son-in-law Alexios Mousele (fiancé of Maria), which she also

helped endow. She built a church of St Anna during Theophilos's lifetime: *Patria* 3.41 (Preger 232–3); this foundation was associated with one of her pregnancies, but cf. 107 (251) where a similar anecdote is told of the wife of Leo III. For her donations by *chrysobull* to the church of the Theotokos at Pege, where Thekla was cured of a serious fever, see *AASS* Nov. 3.880CD.

37 Genesios 59–60; Theoph. Cont. 158–60.
38 Genesios 58–9; Skyl. 84; cf. Theoph. Cont. 151, where he was banished to his suburban house, perhaps a more probable version.
39 Dvornik (1953); Mango (1977) 135.
40 Grierson (1968–73) 3.1, 454–5; (1982) 178; Zacos and Veglery (1972) 1.1, no. 54, cf. 55 (dated to shortly before Theodora's removal from power), where she appears on the reverse with the title 'Theodora despoina'.
41 *The Homilies of Photius*, no. 17, 286–96; Mango (1977) 140 attributes much of the church decoration of this period to Photios (between 858 and 867).
42 Jenkins and Mango (1955/6) 139–40. For the inscription round the ceiling of the Chrysotriklinos, see *Anth. Gr.* 1.106.
43 *Patria* 2.20 (Preger 219); Theoph. Cont. 103; Skyl. 60–61.
44 Mango (1959) 125–8.
45 Lines 2–10, 19–29 (tr. Mango (1959) 127–8).
46 Genesios 61; Ps-Symeon 816.
47 Charanis (1961) 207–8. But there was no favouritism shown to Theodora's family; when her brother Petronas built a palace which overshadowed his neighbour's house, Theophilos had him flogged and the palace demolished and the site handed over to the neighbour, a woman: Leo Gramm. 215–16.
48 *de cer.* 1.50; Skyl. 52; Herrin (1995) 74; cf. Sayre (1986) 230–31.
49 Theoph. Cont. 175; Bury (1912) 155.
50 Grumel (1989) 435.
51 Theoph. Cont. 165–6.
52 Leo Gramm. 229; Vasiliev (1935) 194–218; Grégoire (1966) 106–7.
53 Bury (1912) 291–4; *DAI* 50.9–25; cf. Leo Gramm. 229, 235.
54 Genesios 64; Theoph. Cont. 172; Treadgold (1988) 453 n. 460: 'between 842 and 856 Theodora saved 864,000 nomismata for an annual average surplus of *c*. 61,000 nomismata.' Karlin-Hayter (1989) 8, however, suggests that the figure has been inflated to stress the profligacy of Michael III, who emptied the treasury.
55 For the date, see Halkin (1954) 11–14.
56 Geo. Mon. Cont. 816; Leo Gramm. 229–30; cf. Ps-Symeon 655.
57 Leo Gramm. 229–30; Mango (1973).
58 *AASS* July 6.603–4; Leo VI, 'Oraison funèbre de Basile I', 54; Treadgold (1979) 404–5; Mango (1973) 19–20.
59 Geo. Mon. Cont. 816; Leo Gramm. 229–30; cf. Ps-Symeon 655.
60 Leo Gramm. 235; Theoph. Cont. 169; Genesios 61–2; Geo. Mon. Cont. 821; cf. Guilland (1971) 49.
61 Genesios 62; Leo Gramm. 235. The fact that Kalomaria sided with Bardas rather than with Theodora might imply that she had not enjoyed her role in the palace; alternatively she may have genuinely considered that Theoktistos was blocking Michael's rightful role in government.
62 For a discussion, see Karlin-Hayter (1971) 460–74.
63 Genesios 62–4; Leo Gramm. 235–6; Theoph. Cont. 169–70; Ps-Symeon 658; Geo. Mon. Cont. 823; Skyl. 94–5.
64 Theoph. Cont. 171; cf. Leo Gramm. 236; Skyl. 95.
65 Leo Gramm. 236–7; Genesios 64; *V. Theodorae*, ed. Markopoulos, 268; *V. Ignatii* 504–5; Skyl. 97.

66 Leo Gramm. 237. On the chronology of the fall of Theodora, see Bury (1912) appendix VII, 469–71 and Karlin-Hayter (1971) 469–74.

67 Theoph. Cont. 179–83; cf. Grégoire (1966) 109. On Bulgaria, see Shepard (1995a) 238–42; Browning (1975) 145–7.

68 Theoph. Cont. 227–8; Skyl. 122–3. Danielis was given the title *basileometer*, 'mother of the emperor': Theoph. Cont. 318.

69 Leo Gramm. 230; Ps-Symeon 816; an alternative version has Basil's skills as a wrestler bringing him to Michael's notice: Theoph. Cont. (*V. Basilii*) 229–30; Skyl. 193–4; Genesios 78.

70 Genesios 89.

71 Leo Gramm. 234–5; Genesios 78; Theoph. Cont. 233; Geo. Mon. Cont. 821; Skyl. 126.

72 Leo Gramm. 245; Genesios 4.23 (who does not mention Basil's involvement, but who states that Bardas's genitals were paraded on a pole); Theoph. Cont. (*V. Basilii*) 235–8.

73 Leo Gramm. 238 tells us that Michael married Bardas's son to a woman 'who had a bad reputation' but this is not sufficient grounds on which to identify her with Eudokia Ingerina, especially as Leo mentions Eudokia by name elsewhere on numerous occasions and would surely have made the identification; cf. Kislinger (1983) 123–5; Dvornik (1966) 19; Jenkins (1965c) 246–7 for *V. Ignatii* 508, as aimed by Niketas at Leo VI and his patriarch Nicholas.

74 Leo Gramm. 240; Ps-Symeon 665, 667; Theoph. Cont. 193; Geo. Mon. Cont. 824; *V. Ignatii* 504–8; cf. Genesios 99; Kislinger (1983). Bardas was certainly excommunicated in 858 by Ignatios for his relationship with his daughter-in-law, for whom he had abandoned his wife.

75 Leo Gramm. 242; Mango (1973) 22–3. Thekla is said later to have had an affair with Neatokomites, who was tonsured by Basil: Leo Gramm. 256.

76 Leo Gramm. 249, cf. 255; Geo. Mon. Cont. 835; Mango (1973) 23; cf. Karlin-Hayter (1991) 85–111.

77 Leo Gramm. 249–50; Geo. Mon. Cont. 835–6; Theoph. Cont. (*Vita Basilii*) 249 mentions an attempt made on Basil's life while hunting; cf. Leo Gramm. 248. Grierson (1968–73) 3.1, 453 notes that Michael 'ostentatiously denied him [Basil] the place on the gold and silver coinage of the capital to which as co-Augustus he could reasonably aspire'. Michael's willingness to be rid of Basil may have been connected with an insurrection in the army in 866, attesting Basil's unpopularity: Grégoire (1966) 115.

78 Leo Gramm. 250; Geo. Mon. Cont. 836.

79 Theoph. Cont. 210; Geo. Mon. Cont. 836–7. See Karlin-Hayter (1991) 85–111.

80 Leo Gramm. 252; Geo. Mon. Cont. 838. After Michael's murder Eudokia may also have been given the high-ranking title *zoste patrikia*: Sayre (1986) 231. The title, however, belonged to the chief attendant of the empress, and could not have been held by Eudokia as empress.

81 Leo Gramm. 250, 252.

82 Grierson (1962) 57; Leo Gramm. 252; according to Theoph. Cont. 174 she died before Michael.

83 Leo Gramm. 257. For Eudokia Ingerina portrayed in a MS illustration (Paris. gr. 510) of the Homilies of Gregory Nazianzus, with the description of Eudokia as 'the well-branched vine bearing the grapes of the Empire', see Kalavrezou-Maxeiner (1977) 317 n. 58; for her appearance on Basil's coinage, see Grierson (1968–73) 3.3, 489–90.

84 See esp. Karlin-Hayter (1971); Jenkins (1948a) 71–7; Tinnefeld (1971) 98–101.

For the section of Theoph. Cont. known as the *Vita Basilii*, written by Constantine VII Porphyrogennetos, see esp. Alexander (1940).

85 Jenkins (1948a) 73: 'the Michael of the *Vita Basilii* is a quite unconvincing compound of vulgarity, reckless extravagance, drunkenness, impiety, hippomania and cruelty'; Jenkins and Mango (1955/6).

86 Theoph. Cont. 200–1, 244–5; cf. *V. Ignatii* 528. As told by Theoph. Cont. the incident has to be apocryphal: the *V. Ignatii* only mentions Michael's profanation of the eucharist and not this encounter, which it certainly would have done, had it occurred.

87 Theoph. Cont. 172, 253–4.

88 Theoph. Cont. 251–2.

89 Theoph. Cont. (*V. Basilii*) 243. For his 'profanations' of religious sanctity, see Theoph. Cont. (*V. Basilii*) 244–6 and *V. Ignatii* 528. For the incident where his jester Gryllos dresses up as the patriarch and farts in Theodora's face when she comes for his blessing, see Theoph. Cont. 201–2; *V. Basilii* 246–7; cf. Skyl. 110, where she responds by tearing her hair, weeping and cursing Michael.

90 Genesios 70: his devotion to the 'theatre' and horse-racing; Theoph. Cont. (*V. Basilii*) 243. According to Geo. Mon. Cont. 835 he had a private track at the palace of St Mamas; Theoph. Cont. 197–8: he discontinued fire signals from Asia Minor because they interfered with his sport. See Kislinger (1987); Karlin-Hayter (1987).

91 Leo Gramm. 229, 239.

92 Jenkins and Mango (1955/6) 129–30, 135–40; for his settlement with Bulgaria, see Theoph. Cont. 162–5; Geo. Mon. Cont. 824; Genesios 69; Browning (1975) 54–5. For Michael's personal successes over the Arabs in 859, see Huxley (1975); Grégoire (1966) 110; cf. Vasiliev (1935) 234–40.

93 Theoph. Cont. 199–200; Scott (1985) 100–101.

94 *V. Ignatii* 528: 'ἐμοὶ μὲν πατριάρχης ὁ Θεόφιλος, ὁ Φώτιος δὲ τῷ Καίσαρι, καὶ τοῖς Χριστιανοῖς ὁ Ἰγνάτιος καθέστηκεν.'

95 Scott (1985) 100–101.

96 Theoph. Cont. 171.

6 THE WIVES OF LEO VI (886–919)

1 Boojamra (1974) 113.

2 Mango (1973); cf. Kislinger (1983); Jenkins (1966) 198. Leo Gramm. 249 specifically tells us that Leo was Michael's child.

3 Leo Gramm. 262.

4 Leo's younger brother Stephen, the patriarch, died in 893; Basil I had also confined his three daughters by Eudokia in a convent: Theoph. Cont. 264; Alexander was suspected of a plot to murder Leo in 903. Tougher (1996) points out that during Leo's three-year incarceration (883–6) Alexander would have expected to have been Basil's successor. Alexander's reputation has been at least partially rehabilitated by Karlin-Hayter (1969a).

5 *V. Theophanous* 2; for Eudokia, see Mango (1973) 20; Theoph. Cont. 121; Skyl. 127–8; Genesios 70 (apparently referring to Eudokia Ingerina).

6 *V. Theophanous* 3; Herrin (1995) 77, who notes that she was obviously literate, even if not well read in secular literature.

7 *V. Theophanous* 4; Leo Gramm. 259. For the date, see Vogt (1934) 415. *ODB* 2064 s.v. *Theophano* has her born *c.* 875 (an error for 865).

8 *V. Theophanous* 5–6 (tr. Treadgold (1979) 407).

9 *V. Euthymii* 41.

10 *V. Euthymii* 39–41.
11 Leo VI, 'Oraison funèbre', 54.
12 For his popularity on his release, see *V. Theophanous* 13; Leo Gramm. 260. Karlin-Hayter (1991) 102 asks whether they were applauding the son of the popular Michael III.
13 *V. Euthymii* 3–5.
14 *V. Euthymii* 5, with note; cf. Jenkins (1966) 197; for different versions of Basil's death, cf. Leo Gramm. 262; Theoph. Cont. 352; Genesios 128; *V. Theophanous* 11–12.
15 Jenkins (1965a) 103; Mango (1973) 26; Vogt (1934) 426–8.
16 *V. Euthymii* 5: Basil on his death-bed entrusted to Zaoutzes the direction of all affairs, ecclesiastical and political.
17 *V. Euthymii* 11; Leo Gramm. 263; Hussey (1937) 135.
18 *V. Euthymii* 21, 25; 11–21, 31, cf. 149–52.
19 *V. Theophanous* 8. Eudokia Ingerina seems to have died shortly after Leo's marriage: *V. Theophanous* 7. Theophano would then have been sole Augusta. The little Eudokia was entombed with her mother: Downey (1959) 30; Grierson (1962) 22.
20 *V. Euthymii* 37–8.
21 Leo Gramm. 270, 274. For the date of her death, see Karlin-Hayter (1969b) 14. For her foundation of the convent of St Constantine, see Majeska (1977) 19–21.
22 Leo Gramm. 274; *V. Theophanous* 17–23; Skyl. 180; *Patria* 3.209 (Preger 281); Majeska (1977) 14: there was apparently some opposition to her informal canonisation and the name of the church was changed to 'All Saints'; cf. Dagron (1994b); Downey (1956). For popular clamour to have her proclaimed a saint, see Alexakis (1995) 46–7.
23 *V. Euthymii* 5.
24 *V. Theophanous* 11–13, where he is also called *protospatharios*; Leo Gramm. 260. According to Geo. Mon. Cont. 846–7, Zaoutzes and Photios together persuaded Basil not to blind Leo; Majeska (1977) 20 points out that in the *Life of Constantine of Synada* the reconciliation of Basil and Leo is attributed to the saint.
25 *V. Euthymii* 3–5; Ps-Symeon 700.
26 Theoph. Cont. 324; Skyl. 172; Leo. Gramm. 263.
27 *V. Euthymii* 7; *V. Theophanous* 14; Theoph. Cont. 357 (stating that Leo created the title); Skyl. 175; Leo Gramm. 266.
28 Leo Gramm. 266–7; Theoph. Cont. 357; Skyl. 175–6. Karlin-Hayter (*V. Euthymii* 151) notes Leo's words to Euthymios in 899: 'I am not going to have you for another Zaoutzes, giving me orders and instructions' (*V. Euthymii* 55).
29 *V. Euthymii* 43; Theoph. Cont. 362; Leo Gramm. 271; Oikonomides (1976b) 183.
30 Skyl. 175.
31 Theoph. Cont. 361; Skyl. 172; while the *V. Theophanous* does not mention Leo's relationship with Zoe, it is perhaps hinted at by the statement that Theophano was *not* jealous: *ibid*. 15.
32 Theoph. Cont. 360; Leo Gramm. 270; Skyl. 178–9; cf. *V. Euthymii* 37.
33 Leo Gramm. 269–70; Theoph. Cont. 360–61.
34 *V. Euthymii* 45; according to Symeon the *logothete* (Leo Gramm. 266) Gouzouniates died first and the chronicler suggests (incorrectly) that the relationship between Leo and Zoe started after Gouzouniates's death; cf. Skyl. 175.
35 *V. Euthymii* 45.
36 *V. Euthymii* 47.
37 Leo Gramm. 270; Theoph. Cont. 361; Ps-Symeon 703; Geo. Mon. Cont. 856–7.

Karlin-Hayter (1969b) 13 suggests that Zoe died not before March 900 and was crowned in July 898.

38 *V. Euthymii* 49; earlier in her reign, she had been miraculously cured of an unclean spirit when Euthymios opened the casket preserving the girdle of the Virgin and unfolded it over her: *Syn. CP* 936.25; *V. Euthymii* 172.

39 'Θυγάτηρ Βαβυλῶνος ἡ ταλαίπωρος': Leo Gramm. 270–71; Theoph. Cont. 361; Skyl. 179.

40 Ps-Symeon 703; Leo Gramm. 274; Theoph. Cont. 364; Skyl. 180. According to *V. Euthymii* 55, Leo took away his brother Alexander's wife at this time, presumably removing her to a convent, and hence she was unavailable to act as Augusta; this was perhaps because Alexander had been plotting against him; see Grumel (1936) 32–4.

41 Herrin (1995) 67; Previté Orton (1914) (Anna may have died on giving birth to Charles, for in 915 Louis appears married to Adelaide); cf. Macrides (1992b) 267.

42 Basil, *Canons* 80, 4, 50: *PG* 32: 805, 673, 732.

43 Zepos, *JGR* 1.49–50 (there is some doubt as to the attribution of this novel to Irene); Oikonomides (1976a) 162; (1976b) 182–3. On previous legislation concerning subsequent marriages, see Oikonomides (1976b) 174–93, esp. 181–3. For a French translation of Leo's *Novels* 90 and 91 on concubinage and third marriages, see Noailles and Dain (1944) 296–300.

44 Oikonomides (1976b) esp. 186–7 considers this as a later interpolation; *Procheiros Nomos* 4.25 (Zepos, *JGR* 2.127–8; tr. Jenkins (1966) 218): 'Let it now be absolutely clear to all, that if any shall dare to proceed to a fourth marriage, which is no marriage, not merely shall such a pretended marriage be of no validity and the offspring of it be illegitimate, but it shall be subject to the punishment of those who are soiled with the filthiness of fornication, it being understood that the persons who have indulged in it shall be separated from one another.'

45 Nicholas, *Ep.* 32.77–84.

46 Leo Gramm. 274; Theoph. Cont. 364; Skyl. 180.

47 *de cer.* 2.42: the boy was christened Basil; cf. *V. Euthymii* 63.

48 *V. Euthymii* 63–5. Gerstel (1997) 704–7 suggests that Leo dedicated a church to Eudokia, as he had to his two previous wives.

49 Leo Gramm. 277; Theoph. Cont. 367, 76; *DAI* 22; Jenkins (1966) 203, 209–10, 215.

50 On the question of whether Zoe had other children, see *de cer.* 2.42; Ohnsorge (1958) 78–81, who considers that Zoe gave birth to Anna and Helena in 903 and 904: cf. *DAI* 26 (Eudokia).

51 Leo Gramm. 275–6; Theoph. Cont. 366. At some point in his reign, Leo had a bathhouse built in the palace, which was adorned with statues and portraits of himself and an empress, possibly Zoe: see Magdalino (1988), esp. 114, 117.

52 Leo Gramm. 279; Theoph. Cont. 370; Skyl. 184–5; *AASS* Nov. 3.885E.

53 *V. Euthymii* 81: 'When you ordered prayers of propitiation to be made in the Great Church for seven days, and with your own hands blessed our wife's womb . . . you said and gave assurance that it was a male she bore in her womb. At that time you daily addressed her as a bride when you sat down to table and ate with her.'

54 Nicholas was born in Italy; for his possibly servile origins, see Jenkins (1963) 145–7. *V. Euthymii* 11 speaks of Nicholas as Leo's school-fellow and adopted brother. Nicholas was appointed prior to the death of Eudokia Baiane, when the question of a fourth marriage had not yet arisen. On the *mystikos*, see Magdalino (1984b).

55 *V. Euthymii* 71; Leo Gramm. 279; Theoph. Cont. 370; Skyl. 185.

56 Boojamra (1974) 118; Grumel (1989) 600.
57 Leo Gramm. 279; Theoph. Cont. 370; Skyl. 182.
58 Nicholas, *Ep.* 32 (tr. Jenkins and Westerink (1973) 219).
59 *V. Euthymii* 113; Grumel (1989) 606.
60 Grumel (1989) 601a. For a poem on Leo's marriage, see Shevchenko (1969/70) 201.
61 Boojamra (1974) 119; cf. Arethas, in Jenkins and Laourdas (1956) 343; *V. Euthymii* 71–3. Nicholas's willingness to please Leo may have been connected with his possible involvement in the conspiracy of Andronikos Doukas in 904 or 906/7: *V. Euthymii* 69–71; Karlin-Hayter (1966); Polemis (1968) 16–21.
62 Nicholas, *Ep.* 32.123–7; Grumel (1989) 602.
63 *Arethae Scripta Minora*, 2.169 (Niketas Paphlagon), 67–8 (tr. Oikonomides (1976a) 164).
64 Nicholas, *Ep.* 32.27–35 (tr. Jenkins and Westerink (1973) 217).
65 *V. Euthymii* 75–9, 87–9.
66 Oikonomides (1976a) 165.
67 Nicholas, *Ep.* 32.164–76: Nicholas is eloquent about his want of creature comforts, including lack of a shirt, book, servant and mattress; Grumel (1989) 603–5.
68 *V. Euthymii* 19.
69 Leo Gramm. 280; Theoph. Cont. 371; Ps-Symeon 709; *V. Euthymii* 97.
70 Boojamra (1974) 114–15; on Nicholas, see esp. Karlin-Hayter (1970) 74–101.
71 Leo Gramm. 283; Theoph. Cont. 375; Grierson and Jenkins (1962) 132–8.
72 *V. Euthymii* 109; Grumel (1989) 607, 607a; Leo Gramm. 284; Theoph. Cont. 376; Ps-Symeon 712; Geo. Mon. Cont. 869; Oikonomides (1976b) 181.
73 *V. Euthymii* 109.
74 *V. Euthymii* 111; Grumel (1989) 608–9.
75 *V. Euthymii* 113; Grumel (1989) 610.
76 Leo Gramm. 285; Theoph. Cont. 377; Jenkins (1966) 210. His illness was exacerbated by a serious defeat suffered by the Byzantine fleet off Chios.
77 Leo Gramm. 285; Theoph. Cont. 377; *V. Euthymii* 112–14; cf. Jenkins (1966) 227.
78 Nicholas, *Ep.* 32.499–503; on the genuineness of the will written by Leo condemning his fourth marriage and restoring Nicholas, see Oikonomides (1963a) 46–52, esp. n. 15; *idem* (1976a) 166–7. If Leo did write this will, which is doubtful, it undercut all his work for the legitimacy of his son since 905.
79 Leo Gramm. 292; Theoph. Cont. 386; Ps-Symeon 721; Geo. Mon. Cont. 878; Arethas, *Epitaphios for Euthymios* (= *Arethae Scripta Minora* 1.90).
80 Leo Gramm. 283; Theoph. Cont. 375–6; Skyl. 190. For Samonas and his career, see Jenkins (1948b).
81 *V. Euthymii* 125.
82 Leo Gramm. 286; Theoph. Cont. 378; *V. Euthymii* 121; Jenkins (1966) 228. Karlin-Hayter (1969a) 588 points out that this episode 'is more genuinely shocking to the modern reader than it was to contemporaries', and that such incidents were fairly frequent. Nicholas's vengeance even extended to Euthymios's donkey: Nicholas wanted to have it drowned, but instead a note was hung round its neck forbidding anyone to give it food or water as it wandered the city (one of the poor, however, had pity on it and appropriated it): *V. Euthymii* 125.
83 Jenkins (1966) 229.
84 Leo Gramm. 285; Theoph Cont. 377: Ἴδε, ὁ κακὸς καιρὸς μετὰ τοὺς δεκατρεῖς μῆνας.' Karlin-Hayter (1969a) 590 n. 13 suggests this may have been a reference to the fact that Alexander was already ill and not likely to rule for long.

85 *V. Euthymii* 129; Leo Gramm. 286–8; Theoph. Cont. 378–9; Arethas, *Epitaphios for Euthymios* (*Arethae Scripta Minora* 1.91).

86 *V. Euthymii* 127–9: Alexander's wife was tonsured by Nicholas and sent with her mother to the convent of Mesokapilou.

87 Leo Gramm. 286; Theoph. Cont. 379; Arethas, *Epitaphios for Euthymios* (*Arethae Scripta Minora* 1.90).

88 Karlin-Hayter (1969a) 589–90 proves that the tradition that he died after a polo game is erroneous.

89 Leo Gramm. 286, 288; Theoph. Cont. 380. The regents were Nicholas, Stephen the *magistros*, John Eladas the *magistros*, John the rector, Euthymios (not the patriarch), Basilitzes and Gabrilopoulos; *V. Euthymii* 130 omits Basilitzes and Gabrilopoulos. See Christophilopoulou (1970) 43–5.

90 *V. Euthymii* 131, 133. She was tonsured at this point according to the *Vita Euthymii*, which places her removal to a convent after the revolt of Constantine Doukas.

91 Leo Gramm. 290; Theoph. Cont. 383; Grumel (1989) 619.

92 *V. Euthymii* 131, 133: 'all the government of the empire was ordered by his lips, so that he was universally hated, not only by others but by those who were held for his own familiars'; Leo Gramm. 290–91; Theoph. Cont. 384–5.

93 Leo Gramm. 292; Theoph. Cont. 385. Browning (1975) 61–2; Whittow (1996) 288–9.

94 Nicholas, *Epp.* 16.73–5 to Symeon (December 920) speaks of Symeon previously having demanded a marriage alliance, which was 'rejected by those who saw fit to do so'.

95 Leo Gramm. 292; Skyl. 201; Theoph. Cont. 386: 'αὐτὴ οὖν περικρατὴς γενομένη τῆς βασιλείας'.

96 Leo Gramm. 296; Theoph. Cont. 390–91; Skyl. 233; Nicholas, *Ep.* 47.

97 Theoph. Cont. 386, 395; Leo Gramm. 292, 301; Skyl. 201. She also made the eunuch Damianos *droungarios* of the Watch.

98 Nicholas, *Epp.* 18.54 (to Symeon): 'your letter also mentioned the "eunuchs" as the cause of evils from our side: and this is obvious and notorious to everybody'; cf. 18.76.

99 Leo Gramm. 292; Theoph. Cont. 386.

100 *V. Euthymii* 73; Theoph. Cont. 386, who tells us that Zoe deposed Nicholas on the advice of the hetaireiarch Dominikos, angrily telling him to confine himself to looking after the church; Skyl. 201.

101 *V. Euthymii* 139.

102 *V. Euthymii* 133–7; Grumel (1989) 643.

103 Runciman (1929) 53, 'though it was her views rather than his own that he was obliged to express'; examples of such letters are *Epp.* 8–13 (to Symeon of Bulgaria, his archbishop and an official); *Epp.* 144 (to the military governor of Longibardia).

104 See esp. *Epp.* 40, 45.

105 *Epp.* 35 (to the military governor of Strymon); the draft status of clergy: *Epp.* 37, 150, 164; levy of money: *Ep.* 58, 72 and 183.

106 Nicholas, *Epp.* 138.7–10 (tr. Jenkins and Westerink (1973) 447); cf. *Epp.* 151.1–7, 189.1–8.

107 Grierson (1968–73) 3.1, 12; cf. Christophilopoulou (1970) 55–7. For the imperial seals of the regency, see Zacos and Veglery (1972) 1.1, nos. 62–4.

108 Nicholas, *Epp.* 8; Georg. Mon. Cont. 879–80; Whittow (1996) 289.

109 Jenkins (1966) 233; Runciman (1929) 53, 184–5. See Vasiliev (1968) 2.1, 223–44. Grégoire (1966) 136: 'In contemplating this double military effort on the

part of Byzantium at this period . . . it is impossible not to admire the energy, self-confidence and resolution of the Empress Zoe and of the forces of legitimism of which she was the embodiment.'

110 Leo Gramm. 294 (Theoph. Cont. 388) speaks of it as her personal decision; cf. Leo Gramm. 293 (Theoph. Cont. 387); Skyl. 202–3. The success of Zoe's handling of military affairs in the east can be seen by the fact that in the exchange of prisoners, which was part of the treaty with the Arabs, the Moslems had to buy back 120,000 dinars' worth of prisoners: Vasiliev (1968) 2.1, 243.

111 Nicholas, *Ep.* 183.35–9.

112 Nicholas, *Ep.* 66 (AD 915/16); cf. Leo Gramm. 293; Theoph. Cont. 387.

113 Leo Diac. 124; Leo Gramm. 295; Theoph. Cont. 389; Nicholas, *Ep.* 9; Skyl. 202–4. Cf. Browning (1975) 63.

114 Leo Gramm. 296; Theoph. Cont. 390; Vasiliev (1968) 2.1, 244.

115 Nicholas, *Ep.* 9: Nicholas apologises for neglecting to write and inform Symeon, as he had been requested to do by those in power, of the invasion plans (lines 121–31).

116 Leo Gramm. 296; Theoph. Cont. 390.

117 Nicholas, *Ep.* 47; Runciman (1929) 57–8. Constantine could, of course, have had more than one sister.

118 Jenkins (1965b) 164–5, with n. 4; however, Nicholas, who married Alexander and his concubine, was not noted for the rigorousness of his principles.

119 Leo Gramm. 296; Theoph. Cont. 390; Skyl. 205, 233 considers Phokas to have been aiming at the throne.

120 Leo Gramm. 296–8; Theoph. Cont. 390–2; Skyl. 207.

121 Leo Gramm. 298: 'let my mother stay with me'; Theoph. Cont. 392; Skyl. 207.

122 Leo Gramm. 299–301; Theoph. Cont. 393–4. Thus, instead of marrying Helena, daughter of Symeon of Bulgaria, Constantine had married Helena, daughter of Lekapenos.

123 Leo Gramm. 301–3; Theoph. Cont. 395–7; Skyl. 209–11.

124 Grumel (1989) 715; Zepos, *JGR* 1.192–7.

125 Jenkins (1966) 239.

126 Leo Gramm. 303; Theoph. Cont. 397; Skyl. 211; cf. Runciman (1929) 61.

127 Arethas, *Epitaphios for Euthymios* (*Arethae Scripta Minora*, 1.90).

7 THEOPHANO (*c.* 955–76+)

1 Theoph. Cont. 458; Skyl. 240.

2 Liudprand of Cremona, *Antapodosis* 5.14, 20.

3 Leo Diac. 31; cf. Skyl. 240: 'she was not of distinguished family, but born of common people, who plied the trade of innkeepers', cf. 246; Psellos, *HS* 94. Herrin (1995) 68 n. 12 deduces that 'his bride was an internal candidate, who would need to be trained for her position'; cf. Schreiner (1991) 191; contra McCormick (1997) 243: 'Romanos II had been bewitched by a tavern keeper's daughter who took the name of Theophano when she climbed out of bed and into the throne.' For a discussion of Theophano, see Diehl (1938–9) 1.217–43; Jenkins (1966) 276–93.

4 *de cer.* 2.15; Whittow (1996) 257–9; Toynbee (1973) 504–5.

5 For Constantine's promotion of members of the Phokas family, see Whittow (1996) 347–8. On Nikephoros, see esp. Schlumberger (1923); Morris (1988).

6 Skyl. 248; Leo Diac. 31.

7 Leo Diac. 9–16, 27–30; Skyl. 249–50, 252–3. For the celebration of Nikephoros's triumphs, see McCormick (1986) 162, 167–70.

8 Skyl. 246–7; cf. Zon. 3.488–9.

9 Skyl. 252; Theoph. Cont. 471. Jenkins (1966) 270.

10 For her brothers' plot, see Skyl. 236; Zon. 3.481; Theoph. Cont. 436–7.

11 Skyl. 237; Zon. 3.483, cf. 487. For Basil the Nothos, see Brokkarr (1972).

12 Theoph. Cont. 459: Agatha is described as his μεσῖτις (prime minister); Herrin (1995) 77.

13 Skyl. 254, 314 (Constantine was three years younger than Basil); for Helena, born in ?955, see Poppé (1976) 230 n. 114.

14 Leo Diac. 31; cf. Skyl. 253, who does not mention the accusation. Zon. 3.493–4 states that he was either poisoned or died exhausted by his pleasure-loving lifestyle.

15 Leo Diac. 31; Christophilopoulou (1970) 62–4. The seal depicting the bust of Theophano on the reverse (the observe shows a bust of the Virgin) may have been issued during her regency: Zacos and Veglery (1972) 1.1, no. 72.

16 Skyl. 248–9; Leo Diac. 31.

17 Leo Diac. 33–4; Skyl. 254–5. According to Yahya of Antioch 788, Theophano entrusted her two sons and the empire to Nikephoros in the presence of Polyeuktos.

18 Leo Diac. 39–40; Skyl. 256.

19 Skyl. 257; cf. Zon. 3.497–8.

20 Leo Diac. 40–41, 44–5, 47–8; Skyl. 256–60. Bringas was banished to Paphlagonia and then to the monastery of the Asekretis near Nicomedia. For Nikephoros and his family, see Cheynet (1986) esp. 299–301; Cheynet (1990) 268 for a family tree.

21 Psellos, *HS* 98.

22 Zon. 3.494.

23 Skyl. 255; cf. Zon. 3.495.

24 Leo Diac. 49; Skyl. 260; Zon. 3.498–9.

25 Leo Diac. 50; Skyl. 261, who makes it clear that the explanation was untrue and that the patriarch was aware of this. See Macrides (1987) esp. 159–60.

26 Leo Diac. 50; Matthew of Edessa 1.7 (Dostorian 1.6).

27 Skyl. 268.

28 Leo Diac. 83; cf. Skyl. 255.

29 Liudprand of Cremona, *Relatio de Legatione Constantinopolitana* 3, cf. 23; compare the favourable description of Nikephoros at Leo Diac. 48.

30 Note, for example, the 'Armenian frenzy', when fighting took place between Byzantines and Armenians in the capital: Leo Diac. 64–5; cf. the riot caused by military exercises in the hippodrome: Leo Diac. 63; Skyl. 275–6; for Nikephoros's taxation, see Leo Diac. 63, Skyl. 274. For his debasement of the coinage, see Skyl. 275; Grégoire (1966) 155; Hendy (1985) 507; for the hatred felt for him, see Skyl. 271, 273; Tinnefeld (1971) 115–17; Whittow (1996) 350–53.

31 See Morris (1988) *passim* for a discussion.

32 On this cycle, see Morris (1994) 213–14.

33 Leo Diac. 83.

34 Leo Diac. 88; Skyl. 279; Whittow (1996) 353; Cheynet (1990) 270, 327. According to Zon. 3.516 he was compensated by being given the office of *logothete tou dromou*; cf. Psellos, *HS* 102.

35 Leo Diac. 84–5.

36 Zon. 3.516; Skyl. 279; Psellos, *HS* 100 states that Nikephoros from his youth had no sexual intercourse with women, and never slept with the empress, which 'provided her with fuel for hatred'.

37 Skyl. 279; Zon. 3.516–17; Psellos, *HS* 102; the *Chronicle of Salerno*, *MGH* SS 3,

467–561, see 556, knows of the affair between John and Theophano, Nike-phoros's 'crudelissima sua uxor' ('his most cruel wife').

38 Leo Diac. 85; cf. Skyl. 279, who states that one conspirator was hidden by Theophano.

39 See Guilland (1953).

40 Cheynet (1990) 23; on Bourtzes and Brachamios, see Cheynet and Vannier (1986) 18–24, 58–9.

41 Leo Diac. 86–9; Skyl. 279–81; Psellos, *HS* 102 has Theophano's maidens ready to hoist up the basket containing the conspirators; cf. Zon. 3.517–18.

42 Mich. Syr. 13.4 (Chabot 3.129); Matthew of Edessa 1.8 (Dostourian 1.8), who reports that on his accession John removed Basil and Constantine to Armenia because he feared that their mother might give them poison and thus kill them; Morris (1994) 207–8 sees this as a variant of pro-Tzimiskes propaganda.

43 Leo Diac. 94; cf. Skyl. 284–5; Zon. 3.520.

44 Leo Diac. 98–9; Skyl. 285–6; Zon. 3.520–1. According to Leo, Nikephoros named Leo Abalantes, while Skylitzes says that he put the blame on both Aba-lantes and Atzupotheodoros and that they acted 'ἐπιτροπῇ τῆς δεσποίνης' ('on the instructions of the empress'). Leo has Theophano banished to the island of Prote, one of the Prince's Islands (perhaps a more probable destination than the Sea of Marmora), Skylitzes to Prokonnesos.

45 Leo Diac. 89.

46 Leo Diac. 90–1, 96–8.

47 Skyl. 255, 280; Leo Diac. 83 (who calls it a cloak); Morris (1988) 100–7; Morris (1995) 46, 80.

48 Leo Diac. 85; cf. Skyl. 279; Zon. 3.516; Psellos, *HS* 100.

49 Psellos, *HS* 100; Bar Hebraeus 192 (tr. Wallis Budge (1932) 1.173); Yahya of Antioch 827–8.

50 Grumel (1989) 794; for Polyeuktos, see Leo Diac. 32. For John's regained popularity, see Tinnefeld (1971) 118.

51 Skyl. 285.

52 Leo Diac. 127; Skyl. 294; Zon. 3.527.

53 Skyl. 279 (μοιχαλίς, adulteress); cf. Zon. 3.517 (τὴν μαχλάδα, wanton).

54 Skyl. 283; cf. Grégoire (1966) 151.

55 John Geometres 41, *PG* 106: 927; Morris (1988) 93.

56 Morgan (1954). For a late medieval Slavic poem on the episode, see Turdeanu (1985).

57 Skyl. 314; Zon. 3.539; Kedr. 2.416; Yahya of Antioch 831.

58 Constantine's eldest daughter Eudokia was born in 976/7, and his second, Zoe, *c.* 978: Psellos 2.5, 6.160 (Renauld 1.27, 2.50). We have no information as to whether Theophano or Basil the *parakoimomenos* arranged the match between Constantine VIII and Helena.

59 'Vie des SS. Jean et Euthyme' 9, tr. P. Peeters (in Latin), *AB* 36–7 (1917–19) 20; see also Martin-Hisard (1991) 89; J. Lefort *et al.* (1985) 22; Schlumberger (1932) 1.348 n. 1, 419 n. 3, 430 n. 2; the monastery was founded by two disciples of St Athanasios, a friend of Nikephoros, and their relative John Tornik: see Morris (1995) 46–7.

60 Jenkins (1966) 302.

8 ZOE PORPHYROGENNETA (1028–50)

1 Contemporaries noticed the parallel: see Laiou (1992b) 171 with n. 41.

2 Psellos 2.5 (Renauld 1.27): Eudokia was unlike the rest of the family in being of a

tranquil disposition and gentle in spirit; Zon. 3.570; Garland (1994) 27. All translations from Psellos's *Chronographia* in this chapter are taken from Sewter (1966).

3 Psellos 5.34, cf. 46 (Renauld 1.107, 113); Skyl. 375–7, 385, 422; cf. Attal. 18; Zon. 3.613 ('she [Zoe] was excessively jealous of her'), cf. *ibid.* 574–5.

4 According to Psellos 6.160 (Renauld 2.50) Zoe was seventy-two when she died in 1050; Zon. 3.647 says that she had passed her seventieth year.

5 The millennium of the death in 991 of Theophano, empress of the West, was commemorated by a number of publications and conference proceedings in 1991; the most useful are Wolf (1991a); von Euw and Schreiner (1991); and Davids (1995a). For a discussion of the marriages of Byzantine princesses with foreigners, see esp. Macrides (1992b); Shepard (1995a); Herrin (1995) 67–70.

6 Dölger (1924–65) 784, 787; Davids (1995b) 109 with n. 36; Johnson (1982) 222–3; Wolf (1991b) 212–22 argues that Theodora not Zoe was the intended bride.

7 Note the advice given to Basil by Bardas Skleros, 'admit no woman to the imperial councils' (Psellos 1.28 (Renauld 1.17). For the suggestion that Basil's celibacy was due to a monastic vow, see Crostini (1996) 76–80.

8 Psellos 2.7–9 (Renauld 1.29–30); but cf. Johnson (1982).

9 Psellos 6.15 (Renauld 1.125).

10 Skyl. 343; Dölger (1924–65) 794; Davids (1995b) 110–11; Ciggaar (1995) 56. Peter Damian's diatribe (*Institutio Moniales* 11 (*PL* 145:744)) against a Greek '*dogaressa*' (?Maria) criticises her use of rose-water, forks and incense. Similar accusations of a luxurious lifestyle were made against the Ottonian empress Theophano, niece of John Tzimiskes: see esp. Ciggaar (1995) 54–6. For further foreign matches negotiated for ladies of Romanos Argyros's family, see Davids (1995b) 110 with n. 38; Vannier (1975) 43–4, 47–9. A request by Conrad II in 1028 for a princess for his son Henry may have been answered by Romanos Argyros offering him one of his sisters: Vannier (1975) 34 n. 2; Wolf (1991b) 219–20; Davids (1995b) 110; cf. Dölger (1924–65) 830.

11 Psellos 3.5 (Renauld 1.35) states that he was more than ten years older than Zoe.

12 Skyl. 386; Vannier (1975) 37; for the title *sebastos/sebaste*, see Stiernon (1965) 222–32. For her epitaph, in which she is called the *sebaste* Maria, see Sola (1916) 152–3; on divorce and tonsure, see Laiou (1992c) 113–36.

13 Psellos 2.10 (Renauld 1.30–31); cf. Skyl. 374; Zon. 3.572–3, who says Theodora had heard that Romanos's wife was divorced unwillingly; Laiou (1992b) 167–9. Romanos and Zoe were cousins in the seventh degree, but a synod convened to consider the question considered this no impediment (this degree of relationship was not declared an impediment to marriage until 1038): Laiou (1992b) 169; Kalavrezou (1994) 245–6; Grumel (1989) 836; Skyl. 374.

14 Psellos 2.5 (Renauld 1.27) states that she was very regal in her ways and able to command respect; cf. 6.157 (Renauld 2.49).

15 Skyl. 385; cf. Zon. 3.574–5, 579; Psellos 5.34–5 (Renauld 1.107–8): Romanos, however, still treated Theodora with courtesy and granted her certain imperial favours; Skyl. 375, 376–7, 384.

16 Psellos 3.5, 17 (Renauld 1.34–5, 44); Zon. 3.581. As in the case of Theophano, Romanos's denial of sexual relations is seen to be the catalyst that causes Zoe's hatred.

17 Psellos 3.6 (Renauld 1.35). One of the keynotes of Zoe's tenure of power is her uncontrolled extravagance; Basil II had left 200,000 talents in the treasury: Psellos 1.31 (Renauld 1.19).

18 Psellos 3.18–20 (Renauld 1.46–8); Skyl. 390, who calls her passion 'a demonic and manic love'; Zon. 3.582.

19 Psellos 3.19 (Renauld 1.46): Michael suffered her attentions, 'thinking in his heart of the glory that power would bring him'.

20 Psellos 6.13, 16 (Renauld 1.123, 125–6); cf. Skyl. 422–3; Zon. 3.583, who says that Romanos asked Michael on oath if he were sleeping with Zoe, and that Michael's epilepsy stemmed from his perjury.

21 Psellos 3.21, 23 (Renauld 1.47–9); Zon. 3.583. For the affair, see Garland (1995/6) 28–33.

22 Psellos 3.26, 4.1 (Renauld 1.50–52); Skyl. 390–91, who says specifically that Zoe was poisoning Romanos; Zon. 3.584–5; Cheynet (1990) 44–5.

23 Psellos 4.1–2 (Renauld 1.53–4); Laiou (1992b) 169–70, who also notes that a charge of adultery, if proved in court, would have made the marriage invalid; cf. Kalavrezou (1994) 247–8. Alexios the Stoudite left behind him no less than 2,500 lb of gold, which after his death was appropriated by Constantine Monomachos: Skyl. 391, 429; Zon. 3.586; Morris (1976) 15.

24 Psellos 4.2 (Renauld 1.54); cf. Zon. 3.586.

25 Psellos 4.9 (Renauld 1.57).

26 Psellos tells us that 'saintly men' advised Michael to abstain from all intercourse, even with his wife Zoe, presumably as a penance: 4.17 (Renauld 1.63); cf. Skyl. 397–8; Zon. 3.596–7.

27 Psellos 4.6, 16–17 (Renauld 1.56, 61–2); Skyl. 392; Zon. 3.586–7. Psellos also suggests (4.17) that Michael may have distanced himself from Zoe, not wanting her to see him suffering an epileptic fit.

28 Skyl. 403; cf. Zon. 3.595. *Protospatharioi* (a dignity in the imperial hierarchy) were divided into two groups, one of which was reserved for eunuchs: Constantine was doubtless one of these.

29 Psellos 4.22 (Renauld 1.67): 'the empire belongs by inheritance to Zoe, and the whole nation owes greater allegiance to her, because she is a woman and heir to the throne.' Hill, James and Smythe (1994) 226 note that 'this text is a clear statement of Zoe's right to rule'; cf. Gamillscheg (1991); Hiestand (1990).

30 Psellos 4.22–3 (Renauld 1.66–8); Skyl. 416; cf. Zon. 3.605; on adoption, see Macrides (1990) esp. 117.

31 Psellos 4.28 (Renauld 1.70).

32 Psellos 4.31, 36 (Renauld 1.71–2, 74–5).

33 Psellos 4.53 (Renauld 1.84); cf. Zon. 3.604.

34 Psellos 5.4 (Renauld 1.87–8); cf. Zon. 3.605–6. Cf. Hill, James and Smythe (1994), who argue persuasively for Zoe as ruler in her own right, as well as for her role in 'imperial renewal'.

35 Psellos 5.5 (Renauld 1.88); Skyl. 416–17; cf. Attal. 10–11. Psellos 5.14 (Renauld 1.94) has John exiled by Michael V.

36 One has the figure of Christ Antiphonetes on the obverse (for Zoe's devotion to Christ Antiphonetes, see p. 156); another appears to have Zoe on the obverse and her father Constantine VIII on the reverse: Grierson (1968–73) 3.2, 722, 727–30.

37 Psellos 5.17 (Renauld 1.96); cf. Skyl. 417, where John advises him by letter, as does his uncle Constantine the *nobilissimos* (who had been recalled by Michael), not to trust Zoe but to watch her in case she plotted against him as she had against Romanos and Michael IV.

38 Psellos 5.21 (Renauld 1.98): Skyl. 417; Zon. 3.609; cf. Attal. 13.

39 Psellos 5.22 (Renauld 1.99). Psellos has presumably forgotten here that he wrote earlier that the responsibility for their training devolved on their father: 2.4 (Renauld 1.27); cf. Herrin (1995).

40 Psellos 5.23 (Renauld 1.100).

41 Psellos 5.23, 25–6 (Renauld 1.100–2); Zon. 3.610; cf. Skyl. 418.
42 Skyl. 418; cf. Attal. 14.
43 Psellos 5.26 (Renauld 1.102); cf. Laiou (1986) 118–19.
44 Psellos 5.28–9 (Renauld 1.103–4); Zon. 3.610: cf. Attal. 15.
45 Psellos 5.31–2 (Renauld 1.105–6).
46 Psellos 5.32 (Renauld 1.106); Skyl. 419 (who says that she was dressed again in imperial robes); Zon. 3.611; Garland (1994) 306–7.
47 Psellos 5.36–7 (Renauld 1.108–9); Skyl. 418; Attal. 16; Zon. 3.611–12.
48 Skyl. 419; Psellos 5.38 (Renauld 1.109); cf. Zon. 3.611. On the popular uprising, see Cheynet (1990) 54–5; Garland (1992) 22–4.
49 Attal. 16: 'καὶ τὸ κράτος τῆς βασιλείας δεξιῶς περιεζωσμένη' ('skilfully assuming control of the empire').
50 Psellos 5.44, 46 (Renauld 1.112–13); Skyl. 420; Attal. 17. According to Zon. 3.612, Theodora's supporters were afraid on her behalf that Zoe would recall Michael, and therefore ordered the blinding.
51 Psellos 5.51 (Renauld 1.116).
52 Skyl. 420, 422; Zon. 3.613.
53 Attal. 18: his epithet θαυμασίως ('amazingly') presumably denotes astonishment at two women rulers.
54 For their coinage, see Grierson (1968–73) 3.2, 731–2; Plate 17 depicts one of their *histamena*.
55 Psellos 6.5, 3 (Renauld 1.118–19); he states that neither one had the intelligence to rule (this was later proved wrong by Theodora, even by his own account); cf. Zon. 3.613–14.
56 Skyl. 422; according to Attal. 11 the appointment of Maniakes was made by Michael V.
57 Psellos 6.1, 3, 5 (Renauld 1.117–19); cf. Zon. 3.614.
58 Psellos 6.4, 5, 7–8 (Renauld 1.119, 120–1).
59 Psellos 6.10 (Renauld 1.122).
60 Psellos 6.11 (Renauld 1.122); Zon. 3.614.
61 Psellos 6.12–13, 18 (Renauld 1.122–3, 126); Skyl. 422–3; Zon. 3.614.
62 Psellos 6.16–18 (Renauld 1.125–6); Skyl. 422–3; cf. Zon. 3.614–15; Attal. 18. For beauty as an imperial attribute, see Garland (1994); cf. Laiou (1992c) 95–6; it was also, of course, a factor which weighed heavily with Zoe. On Dalassenos, see Cheynet and Vannier (1986) 80–2.
63 Psellos 6.16–18 (Renauld 1.125–6); Zon. 3.615; for Constantine's second wife, see Seibt (1976) 70–1.
64 Psellos 6.17 (Renauld 1.125–6); Skyl. 423; Attal. 18; Zon. 3.615.
65 Psellos 6.21 (Renauld 1.127); cf. Zon. 3.616.
66 Grierson (1968–73) 3.2, 731. The legend on the coins reads 'Θεοτόκε βοήθει τὰς βασιλίσις Ζωὴν καὶ Θεοδώραν (Mother of God, help the Empresses Zoe and Theodora)'.
67 For Skleraina, see Seibt (1976) 71–6; Spadaro (1975); Garland (1995/6) 33–6.
68 Psellos 6.20 (Renauld 1.127); Skyl. 423; Zon. 3.617. Kalavrezou (1994) 252–9; Laiou (1992b) 172: although Zoe at sixty-four was well over the canonical limit for third marriages, she was childless and thus technically the marriage was permissible (though it carried a penance of five years without communion).
69 *Peira* 15.16 (in Zepos, *JGR* 5.54); Kazhdan and Epstein (1985) 147.
70 Seibt (1976) 69; cf. Zon. 3.618 (ἀνεψιά).
71 Psellos 6.51 (Renauld 1.142). On the whole the evidence does not support the statement of Kazhdan and Constable (1982) 113, that 'Sklerena . . . was praised

for her beauty and for her mildness, but Psellos did not mention her political ambitions'.

72 Psellos 6.52–3 (Renauld 1.142–3); Zon. 3.619; Dölger (1924–65) 854 (12 June 1042).

73 Psellos 6.54–6 (Renauld 1.143–4). For the church at Mangana, see Janin (1969) 70–6.

74 For the *sekreton tou Tropaiophorou*, see Oikonomides (1980/81) 241–2.

75 Psellos 1.147 (Renauld 1.144): 'he wasted the imperial treasures in satisfying her every whim'; cf. Zon. 3.620; *AASS* Nov. 3.584. For a further estate, which may have been owned by Skleraina, see 'Le typicon du Christ Sauveur Pantocrator', ed. Gautier, 123, and 122 n. 37.

76 Psellos 6.58–9 (Renauld 1.145); cf. Zon. 3.620.

77 Psellos 6.61 (Renauld 1.146); Psellos, 'On Skleraina', line 214; Zon. 3.620 states that the title was a new one, but incorrectly: it was given to Romanos Argyros's first wife, for which see n. 12 above. See Plate 14 and Oikonomides (1980/81) 239–42 for a seal giving her the titles '*hyperperilampros* and *eutychestate sebaste*'. For the title *despotis/despoina*, see Bensammar (1976) 284–8.

78 Psellos 6.59, 63 (Renauld 1.145, 147); Zon. 3.620–21.

79 Skyl. 427, 434; cf. Zon. 3.621, who states that Romanos Skleros, brother of the emperor's mistress, was made *magistros* and *protostrator*. For praise of Romanos in Psellos's epitaph for Skleraina, see 'On Skleraina', esp. lines 408–10. Romanos Skleros and George Maniakes had a long-standing feud (Skyl. 427), and Skleraina may have played a part in having the general recalled – which led to his rebellion.

80 Psellos 6.61–2, cf. 63 (Renauld 1.146–7).

81 For the identity of this bride, see Vannier (1975) 35 n. 5; Poppé (1971) 267 n. 181, who believes her to be Skleraina's daughter; Seibt (1976) 71 n. 250; Kazhdan (1988/89) 416–17. Psellos does not mention her, even in his epitaph for Skleraina; but there are many things which Psellos does not mention, including illegitimate children, which one might expect him to. It is, however, not entirely sure that the girl in question was even Monomachos's daughter by either his second wife or Skleraina, though if she were, the date of her marriage (between 1046 and 1050) would perhaps suggest Skleraina to be the mother, as Constantine's second wife died before 1034.

82 Psellos 6.60–1 (Renauld 1.146–7); cf. 6.50 (Renauld 1.142) where Skleraina is described as beautiful and discreet; Zon. 3. 618; Garland (1994) 294–5.

83 Skyl. 434; Garland (1992) 26–7; Cheynet (1990) 59. Kedr. 2.556 records that Constantine was repeatedly criticised by the Stoudite monk Niketas Stethatos over the liaison.

84 Psellos 6.159 (Renauld 2.49).

85 Psellos 6.59 (Renauld 1.145).

86 John Mauropous, *Ep.* 26; cf. his epigram (54) to the two empresses, where they are also linked with Monomachos (*PG* 120: 1169–70).

87 Psellos 6.88 (Renauld 2.7); McCormick (1986) 204.

88 Psellos 6.69 (Renauld 1.150).

89 Oikonomides (1980/81) 240; Seibt (1976) 75; Chon. 614.

90 Psellos 6.69–70, 182 (Renauld 1.150–1, 2.60); cf. Zon. 3.621; Skyl. 478; Kedr. 2.610.

91 *AASS*, Nov. 3.584; Spadaro (1975) 353; Seibt (1976) 75.

92 'On Skleraina', esp. 423–48; Skleraina's death was also commemorated by Christopher of Mytilene, no. 70; cf. Follieri (1964) 137–8.

93 Psellos 6.65, 68 (Renauld 1.148, 150).

94 Psellos 6.159, 157 (Renauld 2.49, 48).

95 Psellos 6.62–7, 144, 157–61 (Renauld 1.147–50, 2.40–1, 48–50). Hill, James and Smythe (1994) 223 with n. 29 point out that the evidence for her vanity has been generally taken out of context. For the ornaments pertaining to imperial women, see Garland (1994) 299–302.

96 Psellos 6.6, 158 (Renauld 1.120, 2.49); Garland (1994) 32–3.

97 While the mosaic originally dates to the reign of Romanos III, all three heads (those of Zoe and Christ as well as Romanos) have been changed: Whittemore (1942) 19–20. The debate as to why is not yet ended: see esp. Teteriatnikov (1996) esp. 54–64 (who thinks the mosaic originally depicted Michael); Kalavrezou (1994) 252–9; Hill, James and Smythe (1994) 223–5; Oikonomides (1978) 221; Cormack (1981) 141–4.

98 Psellos 6.64 (Renauld 1.148).

99 Psellos 6.64, 158 (Renauld 1.148, 2.49).

100 Psellos 6.6, 6.159 (Renauld 1.120, 2.49); Duffy (1995) 88–90.

101 For the appearance of Christ Antiphonetes on Zoe's coinage, see Grierson (1968–73) 3.2, 162–3, 722, 727–30.

102 Psellos 6.66–7 (Renauld 1.149–50).

103 Psellos 6.159 (Renauld 2.49).

104 Duffy (1995) 90. Note, for example, a case reported by Theodore Balsamon which took place between 1134 and 1143, when Zoe, a member of the imperial family, fell ill due to the magical use of wax images by her relatives and servants: Greenfield (1993) 73, 82.

105 Psellos 6.160 (Renauld 2.50).

106 *Alexiad* 6.3.5 (Leib 2.48); Sathas, *MB* 7.163.

107 Psellos, 6.183 (Renauld 2.60–61), *Scr. Min.* 1.29; Chamberlain (1986) 25–7; cf. Zon. 3.647–8.

108 Hill, James and Smythe (1994) 218; cf. Gamillscheg (1991).

109 Kazhdan and Epstein (1985) 101.

110 See esp. Garland (1988); Laiou (1985).

9 THEODORA, THE LAST MACEDONIAN (1042–56)

1 Psellos 2.5 (Renauld 1.27). All translations from Psellos's *Chronographia* in this chapter are taken from Sewter (1966).

2 Psellos 6.4, 6 (Renauld 1.119, 120): she was taller than Zoe, but her head was too small and out of proportion with the rest of her body, but she was a ready talker and quicker in her movements, cheerful and smiling and anxious to talk; cf. Garland (1994) 34–5.

3 Psellos 6.4, 62 (Renauld 1.119, 147).

4 Psellos 5.34–5 (Renauld 1.107–8).

5 Skyl. 375, 376–7, 384; cf. Zon. 3.574; Cheynet (1990) 41–3; Vannier (1975) 49.

6 Skyl. 385; Zon. 3.575, 579; Psellos 7(Romanos).10 (Renauld 2.157); Cheynet (1990) 43–4.

7 Psellos 5.35 (Renauld 1.107).

8 Skyl. 420, 422, 429 ('the emperor being unwilling'); cf. Zon. 3.624.

9 Zon. 3.614 states that Zoe's coup was inspired by whispers that Theodora should rule and not Zoe, because Theodora had removed Michael V; cf. Psellos 6.11 (Renauld 1.122).

10 See esp. Psellos 6.61, 88 (Renauld 1.146, 2.7). On the crown of Monomachos she is shown with black hair in the ornate robes and red shoes of an empress, while her coinage shows her in full regalia: Hunt (1984) 139–41; see Oikonomides

(1994) for the suggestion that the crown may be a nineteenth-century fake. For Codex Sinait. gr. 364, see Spatharakis (1976) 99–102.

11 Psellos 6.15 (Renauld 2.79).

12 Psellos 6.49 (Renauld 1.141).

13 Psellos 6.138 (Renauld 2.37–8).

14 Psellos 6.144 (Renauld 2.40–1).

15 Psellos 6.151–3 (Renauld 2.45–6); Zon. 3.648; Zepos, *JGR* 1.637 (a *chrysobull* of 1054 stating that the properties of the Alan *sebaste* were distinct from those of the *sekreton tou Tropaiophorou*); Oikonomides (1980/81) 241; cf. Garland (1995/6) 36.

16 Psellos 6.140, 150 (Renauld 2.38, 44); Zon. 3.645; Skyl. 473–4. For a more serious view of the conspiracy, see Psellos 6.145; Zon. 3.644–6; Kedr. 2.605; Cheynet (1990) 62–3; Savvidis (1995). Constantine's strong-minded younger sister Euprepia played an important role in the revolt of Tornikios, and Constantine exiled her, at least temporarily: see Psellos 6.100, 116 (Renauld 2.15, 25); Garland (1994) 295; *eadem* (1995/6) 37.

17 Psellos 6.202–3 (Renauld 2.70–1); Skyl. 477–8 (who says he was suffering from his accustomed gout); Attal. 51; Zon. 3.650; Kedr. 2.610.

18 Skyl. 478; cf. Zon. 3.651.

19 Psellos 6 (Theodora).1–2 (Renauld 2.72): ʽἑαυτὴν παρρησιαστικώτερον ἀρρενώσασα'; cf. Gamillscheg (1991); Hiestand (1990).

20 Psellos 6 (Theodora).2 (Renauld 2.72); cf. Zon. 3.652.

21 Grierson (1968–73) 3.2, 748 notes that this would have been of considerable advantage to the treasury (which must have felt the strain of Zoe's extravagance). For Theodora's coinage, see *ibid.* 748–53.

22 Psellos 6 (Theodora).3, 17 (Renauld 2.73, 80).

23 Psellos 6 (Theodora).6–7, 9 (Renauld 2.74–5, 76); Attal. 51–2.

24 Psellos 6 (Theodora).13–14 (Renauld 2.78–9).

25 Skyl. 479–80; Zon. 3.657–8; cf. Attal. 52; Cheynet (1990) 66–7.

26 Psellos 6 (Theodora).5 (Renauld 2.73); Zon. 3.652. For her determination and tenacity of purpose, see Psellos 6.15 (Renauld 2.78–9).

27 Psellos 6 (Theodora).4 (Renauld 2.73); cf. 7(Michael VI).14 (Renauld 2.91) where he implicitly criticises her appointment of the eunuch Theodore to the command of the eastern armies. Theodore appears to have been competent but treacherous.

28 Psellos 6 (Theodora).15, 18–19 (Renauld 2.79, 81).

29 Psellos 6 (Theodora).20–1 (Renauld 2.81–2); Skyl. 480; Zon. 652–3. Jenkins (1966) 363: 'of all their choices [of emperor] during this fateful half-century, this may fairly lay claim to being the worst . . . It was a sign of the times that this idiotic old man should have been put in the seat of Basil II.'

30 Grierson (1968–73) 3.1, 180, 3.2, 753; the other two were Constantine VII and Basil II, her uncle.

10 EUDOKIA MAKREMBOLITISSA (1059–78+)

1 Attal. 56.

2 Psellos 7(Eudokia).1 (Renauld 2.152); see 7.3–4 (Renauld 2.153–4), for example, for Psellos as an intimate adviser of Eudokia. All translations from Psellos in this chapter are taken from Sewter (1966).

3 Rambaud (1877) 273. She appears to have been the authoress of a poem on Ariadne and of a number of instructive works. Par. gr. 3057, f. 2r, a MS of the sixteenth century, contains the *Ionia*, or *Violarium*, a dictionary of gods, heroes and curiosities from the ancient Greek world, ascribed to Eudokia herself: Spatharakis (1976) 105 n. 33.

4 See Polemis (1968) 34; Oikonomides (1963b) 79 n. 3 for the probable number and names of their children; Oikonomides includes an eighth child, Irene.

5 Psellos 7(Isaac).79–82, 89 (Renauld 2.131–3, 137); Skyl. Cont. 111; for Aikaterina, see Garland (1994) 37.

6 Bryen. 81–3. On the career of John Doukas, see Leib (1950a); Polemis (1968) 34–41.

7 Angold (1984b) 48: 'after his victory over Constantine Monomachos in 1054 Michael Keroularios was the most powerful figure in Constantinople'; he even adopted red shoes, as a sign that the patriarch was equal in authority to the emperor. See Tinnefeld (1989).

8 Psellos 7(Constantine).20, 26 (Renauld 2.147, 151).

9 Zon. 3.681.

10 Psellos 7(Michael VII).1 (Renauld 2.173).

11 Psellos 7(Eudokia).4 (Renauld 2.154); cf. 2.142, for Psellos's friendship with Constantine X, whose house Psellos moved into when Monomachos gave Constantine a more splendid mansion.

12 Sathas, MB 5.347; cf. 284 and 377 for letters possibly written to Eudokia by Psellos.

13 Psellos, Scr. Min. 2.46–9, 254–6.

14 'Quelques lettres de Psellos inédits ou déjà édités', ed. Gautier, 192–4 (no. 35).

15 Psellos 7(Constantine).6 (Renauld 2.141).

16 Psellos 7(Eudokia).1 (Renauld 2.152); he also cites her own statement (made to him personally) that she hoped she would not die an empress, as evidence for her piety and lack of ambition: Psellos 7.4 (Renauld 2.154).

17 Psellos 7(Constantine).27 (Renauld 2.151); cf. Zon. 3.681; Skyl. Cont. 118.

18 Attal. 92; Skyl. Cont. 118; Zon. 3.682; Grumel (1989) 898. The text of Eudokia's oath is given by Oikonomides (1963b) 105–8.

19 Sathas, MB 4.351, 5.513–23 (a letter 'On Friendship' written to them by Psellos); cf. Kedr. 2.635; Oikonomides (1963b) 119. For Constantine Keroularios's career apparently as logothete tou genikou (Sathas, MB 5.363, 441), proedros, grand droungarios, sebastos and epi ton kriseon (judge), see Oikonomides (1963b) 119–20.

20 Grierson (1968–73) 3.2, 765–6; cf. 3.1, 110, noting that the view that Eudokia is depicted on one follis in the place of honour is a misinterpretation: the labarum which they flank is considered as representing the standing figure of Christ, in which case the order of precedence is correct.

21 Grierson (1968–73) 3.2, 771, 774.

22 Kalavrezou-Maxeiner (1977) 312; cf. ibid. 311–12 for an MS belonging to Eudokia (Paris. gr. 922), which depicts the Virgin placing her hands on the heads of Constantine X and Eudokia. On either side stand the two co-emperors, both receiving crowns from angels.

23 Psellos 7(Eudokia).2 (Renauld 2.153).

24 The same term is used by Zon. 3.651 of Theodora in 1055.

25 Psellos 7(Constantine).21 (Renauld 2.148).

26 See Christophilopoulou (1970) 65–75, esp. 67 citing Attal. 181, 'after the emperor died, the Augusta embraced for herself the power like an emperor', but this could be taken as implying a de facto rather than de iure position; cf. Attal. 92. See Oikonomides (1963b) 123–4; Grierson (1968–73) 3.2, 781–2.

27 Psellos 7(Eudokia).1 (Renauld 2.152–3); cf. Zon. 3. 682–3; Attal. 92; Skyl. Cont. 119; Bryen. 85.

28 Attal. 180 calls him 'old among the young'; cf. Skyl. Cont. 156, who blames Psellos for his lack of capacity. Psellos gives a eulogistic description of his pedantic literary interests: 7(Michael VII).4 (Renauld 2.174–5). We should perhaps

remember that his father wanted to be known as a great orator rather than as a great emperor: Skyl. Cont. 112.

29 Psellos 7(Eudokia).3 (Renauld 2.153): 'she [Eudokia] frequently handed him over to me and suggested that I should instruct him in the functions of his office and give him advice'; Polemis (1968) 44–5.
30 Psellos 7(Eudokia).2–3 (Renauld 2.153).
31 Grierson (1968–73) 3.2, 781–2.
32 Kalavrezou-Maxeiner (1977) 313; cf. Zon. 3.682.
33 Zacos and Veglery (1972) 1.1, nos. 89–91.
34 Oikonomides (1963b) 123–4; Grierson (1968–73) 3.2, 782 comments that while she may not have been fully *autokrator*, 'the distinction is one that would have passed unnoticed by most of her subjects and probably by most of her court. She was as nearly emperor as made no matter'.
35 Psellos 7(Eudokia).4, 5 (Renauld 2.154–5).
36 Psellos 7(Eudokia).5–6 (Renauld 2.155). Another candidate envisaged was apparently the *dux* of Antioch Nikephoros Botaneiates, who became emperor in 1078: Skyl. Cont. 121; Attal. 96.
37 Psellos 7(Eudokia).4–6 (Renauld 2.154–5); cf. Zon. 3.683–4.
38 Psellos 7(Eudokia).10 (Renauld 2.157); cf. Attal. 97–8; Skyl. Cont. 122; Zon. 3.684–5; Cheynet (1990) 74–5.
39 Attal. 99–100; Skyl. Cont. 122; Zon. 3.685.
40 Skyl. Cont. 123; Zon. 3.686–7; Attal. 100. Oikonomides (1963b) 126 n. 118 notes how the accounts differ in their details, suggesting that the story was a fabrication by the Doukas family to damage the reputation of the empress and patriarch.
41 Psellos 7(Eudokia).7–8 (Renauld 2.156).
42 Psellos 7(Eudokia).6 (Renauld 2.155).
43 Psellos 7(Eudokia).9 (Renauld 2.156–7); cf. Zon. 3.687.
44 Skyl. Cont. 124, according to whom Eudokia's sons did not know about the marriage until afterwards.
45 Psellos 7(Eudokia).8 (Renauld 2.156).
46 Psellos 7(Romanos).10 (Renauld 2.157); cf. Zon. 3.687–8, 'When Romanos Diogenes took hold of the rule of the Romans, he succeeded in establishing himself against the expectations of Eudokia who was ruling'.
47 Psellos 7(Romanos).14, 18 (Renauld 2.159–61).
48 Attal. 101–2; Skyl. Cont. 124.
49 Attal. 106; Skyl. Cont. 127.
50 Attal. 101–2; Skyl. 124.
51 Grierson (1968–73) 3.2, 785–92.
52 Grierson (1968–73) 3.1, 181; Kalavrezou-Maxeiner (1977) 309–10, who notes that the only example besides the Romanos ivory of the singular title *basilis Romaion* is the silver reliquary in Moscow portraying Constantine X and Eudokia Makrembolitissa.
53 Zacos and Veglery (1972) 1.1 nos. 92–3(b–d); 92 depicts Christ on one side crowning Romanos and Eudokia, and the Virgin on the other crowning Michael and Constantios.
54 Kalavrezou-Maxeiner (1977) esp. 307, who suggests (*ibid.* 317) that 'Eudokia expressed in the official iconography of their reign her wish to maintain the position she had enjoyed under Constantine X.' The ivory has also been considered, less convincingly, to depict Romanos II and Bertha-Eudokia.
55 *Alexiad* 9.6.1 (Leib 2.172–3); Sathas, *MB* 7.167–8.
56 Bryen. 119; Psellos 7(Romanos).18 (Renauld 2.161): on a number of occasions

Romanos considered putting John to death, but instead forced him and his sons to take an oath of loyalty; Attal. 106; Skyl. Cont. 127.

57 Cheynet (1990) 75–6; Angold (1984b) 22–3.

58 Psellos 7(Romanos).23–4 (Renauld 2.163); cf. Bryen. 119–21.

59 Psellos 7(Romanos).25 (Renauld 2.163–4). Michael did blush easily: Psellos 7(Michael VII).3, 6 (Renauld 2.174, 175). The anecdote is not so unbelievable as might be thought: a similar story is told of Edward VII of Great Britain (then Prince of Wales) at the age of fifty-eight hiding behind a pillar and afraid of meeting his mother Queen Victoria because he was late for dinner at Osborne.

60 Psellos 7(Romanos).25 (Renauld 2.164); Attal. 168; Bryen. 119–21.

61 Psellos 7(Romanos).26–7 (Renauld 2.164); Bryen. 123; Tinnefeld (1971) 128–30.

62 Attal. 168; Skyl. Cont. 152; Zon. 3.704.

63 Attal. 168–9; Skyl. Cont. 152; Zon. 3.704; Bryen. 123–5; *Alexiad* 9.6.1 (Leib 2.172).

64 Psellos 7(Romanos).28–9 (Renauld 2.165–6).

65 Psellos 7(Romanos).30–31 (Renauld 2.166). Both Skyl. Cont. 152 and Zon. 3.704 say that Psellos was among the foremost in having Eudokia deposed and tonsured and Romanos declared a rebel.

66 Bryen. 131.

67 Attal. 169–79; Zon. 3.704–6; Skyl. Cont. 153–4; Psellos 7(Romanos).32–42 (Renauld 2.167–72); Bryen. 131–41; Cheynet (1990) 76–7. For the date of his blinding, see Polemis (1965) 65–6, 76.

68 Bryen. 139; Zon. 3.707; Skyl. Cont. 155; Psellos 7(Romanos).42–3 (Renauld 2.171–2).

69 Attal. 200. On Nikephoritzes's government, see Angold (1984b) 98–102.

70 Bryen. 253–5; *Alexiad* 3.2.3 (Leib 1.107); Skyl. Cont. 181; Zon. 3.722–3. Bryen. 221–3: Zoe, whom her brother Constantios had offered to Alexios Komnenos in 1077, was to marry Adrian, Alexios's brother. The eldest daughter (Anna) became a nun; Theodora married the Venetian doge Domenico Silvio: Polemis (1968) 18–20.

71 Laiou (1992b) 173; Skyl. Cont. 181–2; Zon. 3.722; Bryen. 255. *Alexiad* 3.2.5 (Leib 1.108–9) also hints that there would have been a scandal if Eudokia married Botaneiates. The fact that Eudokia had been a nun (though by compulsion: Attal. 168–9, Skyl. Cont. 152) and her vow to Constantine X that she would not remarry may have been considered difficulties.

72 Bryen. 247–51, cf. 57–9.

73 Attal. 304; Skyl. Cont. 184 (he gave her a very generous *pronoia*, a grant of tax revenues from a particular region). For some verses, supposedly written on her death, see Lampros *NE* 16 (1922) 41.

74 Spatharakis (1976) 102–6, with fig. 68. A further portrait of Eudokia, in fifteenth-century Italian style, can be seen in Par. gr. 3057, f. 2r, in which she is shown as having blond hair and is seated on a lyre-backed throne in her palace: Spatharakis (1976) 105 n. 33; Bordier (1883) 290–91; Lampros (1930) pl. 61.

75 Tr. Spatharakis (1976) 104.

76 Oikonomides (1963b) 128.

11 THE EMPRESSES OF ALEXIOS I KOMNENOS (1081–1118)

1 Polemis (1968) 46 n. 43; cf. Tzetzes, *Chiliades* 5.590–91, 'Maria from Abasgia, whom most people inaccurately call from Alania'; Kazhdan and Epstein (1985)

168–9 note the anachronistic nature of Byzantine nomenclature. For Maria, I have been unable to consult Nodia (1978). All translations from the *Alexiad* in this chapter are taken from Sewter (1979).

2 Kazhdan and Epstein (1985) 177; cf. Macrides (1992b) esp. 266–71.

3 Vannier (1975) 47–8; Skyl. 377; Thomson (1996) 377–8; Rapp (1997) 618–19; Alexidze (1991) 204–12, esp. 205; Brosset (1849) 314–15, 329–30. Bagrat's mother had also visited Constantinople to arrange for the marriage of her son. The Georgian sources state that it was Theodora who originally invited Martha to Constantinople in 1056 and that she returned to Georgia and was married to Michael after Theodora's death: perhaps Maria was resident in the capital before her marriage.

4 Leib (1956); Zon. 3.714; *Alexiad* 3.1.3 (Leib 1.104); Psellos 7(Michael VII).12 (Renauld 2.178).

5 Skyl. Cont. 720, 724; *Alexiad* 1.10.2, 1.12.11 (Leib 1.37, 46); Dölger (1924–65) 1003. The proposal was put forward in a *chrysobull* written by Psellos himself: *Scr. Min.* 1.329–34; on Olympias, see Shepard (1988) 100–102; von Falkenhausen (1982) 56–72.

6 *Alexiad* 3.2.4 (Leib 1.107–8); Psellos 7(Michael VII).9 (Renauld 2.177); Laiou (1992c) 94–5; Garland (1994) 261–2. For a portrait of Maria and Michael (retouched as Nikephoros III), see Plate 22; cf. Spatharakis (1976) pls 9–11, 70, 74; Kalavrezou (1994) 249–51.

7 Skyl. Cont. 181–2.

8 *Alexiad* 3.2.3–5 (Leib 1.107–8); Bryen. 253–5; Skyl. Cont. 181; Zon. 3.722.

9 Hill (1996a) 44.

10 Ostrogorsky (1968) 348.

11 Skyl. Cont. 177–8, 181–2; Zon. 3.722; Bryen. 253–5; Mich. Syr. 15.5 (Chabot 3.176); Leib (1950); Laiou (1992b) 172–3, (1992c) 123; Kalavrezou (1994) 249. Bryennios mentions that the marriage was illegal (a third marriage was only permissible by canon law if one were childless) and recounts that John Doukas was afraid that even at the eleventh hour Botaneiates would change his mind and marry Eudokia instead. The historian Attaleiates, who is concerned to show Botaneiates's reign in a good light, does not mention the marriage, which is in itself evidence for its illegality.

12 Matthew of Edessa 1.64 (Dostourian 1.248).

13 Skyl. Cont. 182; Zon. 3.722; Grumel (1989) 910; Laiou (1992b) 173.

14 *Alexiad* 2.2.1, 3.4.5 (Leib 1.66, 115): Constantine was allowed to wear silk shoes of various colours (but not the imperial purple).

15 Busts of the two appear on the reverse of a *miliaresion* whose obverse bears the inscription 'Nikephoros and Maria, faithful *basileis* of the Romaioi' (Grierson (1968–73) 3.2, 829).

16 *Alexiad* 2.2.2–3, 3.1.2, cf. 3.2.3 (Leib 1.67–8, 104, 107).

17 *Alexiad* 2.1.4–6, 2.2.2–3 (Leib 1.64–8); cf. Bryen. 259. On the adoption, see Macrides (1990) 117.

18 *Alexiad* 2.3.4, 2.2.3 (Leib 1.70, 68).

19 Hill (1996a) 38–9.

20 *Alexiad* 2.1.4, 2.3.4 (Leib 1.64, 70).

21 *Alexiad* 2.4.5 (Leib 1.72–3).

22 *Alexiad* 2.10.4, 3.1.1 (Leib 1.94, 102).

23 Maria's marriage to Alexios would also have been illegal because his brother Isaac was married to her cousin: Laiou (1992c) 49. In addition, Michael VII was still alive (he died *c.* 1090).

24 *Alexiad* 3.1.4–5, 3.2.1 (Leib 1.105–6); Bryen. 221.

25 *Alexiad* 3.2.1, 3.2.6–7 (Leib 1.106, 109–10).

26 Zon. 3.747; Mullett (1984b) 208 suggests that here Zonaras is casting Maria in the role of imperial mistress until Irene grew up enough to be able to shake off the competition.

27 *Alexiad* 3.4.6 (Leib 1.115–16); Zon. 3.733; cf. Dölger (1924–65) 1064. Theophylact in his *Paideia Basilike*, perhaps delivered in 1085/6, addresses Constantine as *basileus* (*Or.* 4, ed. Gautier 1.179).

28 Bryen. 65–7; Zon. 3.738; *Alexiad* 6.8.3 (Leib 2.62).

29 *Alexiad* 3.1.4 (Leib 1.105), where Anna says she was put in Maria's care before she was eight years old; the engagement was therefore still in place in 1090 or 1091.

30 Mullett (1984b) 208; cf. *eadem* (1994) 262: 'the women [Maria and Anna] come over as very similar, embodiments of the new piety and orthodoxy of the 1080s.'

31 Theophylact, *Or.* 4 (ed. Gautier 1.187); Zon. 3.723, cf. 3.733 where he suggests there may have been an element of coercion.

32 *Alexiad* 6.8.3 (Leib 2.62); Polemis (1968) 62 n. 17; Bryen. 65–7; Zon. 3.738. Bryennios is first mentioned as Alexios's *gambros* (son-in-law) in 1097: Bryen. 225.

33 *Alexiad* 9.5.5 (Leib 2.171–2), where Alexios's affection for Constantine is described.

34 Zon. 3.733; cf. *Alexiad* 3.4.5 (Leib 1.115); Mullett (1984b) 205–6; Alexidze (1991). For her role as literary patroness, see Mullett (1984a) 177–8, (1984b) 205–6.

35 Theophylact, *Or.* 4 (ed. Gautier 1.179–211, esp. 185–93).

36 *Alexiad* 9.5.5, 9.7.2, 9.8.2 (Leib 2.171, 175, 178–9); Cheynet (1990) 98; cf. Mullett (1984b).

37 Mullett (1984b) 211.

38 Theophylact, *Ep.* 4, cf. 107 (ed. Gautier 2.137–41, 525); Mullett (1984b) 206–7; Alexidze (1991) 212.

39 Mullett (1994) 262; *Alexiad* 2.1.5 (Leib 1.65); cf. Hill (1996a) 37; Macrides (1990) esp. 116–17.

40 Lemerle (1977) 298 describes him, perhaps not very fairly, as 'faible devant les femmes'.

41 *Alexiad* 9.7.4 (Leib 2.176); Hill (1996a) 44; Magdalino (1996) 150–1. The date of Eudokia's death is not known, but she seems not to have been alive at this point as her son Nikephoros Diogenes is said to have arranged the match. Eudokia's son, Constantios Doukas, had wanted in 1077 to see his sister Zoe married to Alexios: Bryen. 221–3. Instead Zoe was betrothed to Nikephoros Synadenos, who was to be Botaneiates's heir-elect, and Alexios to Irene Doukaina.

42 Cheynet and Vannier (1986) 95–9; Varzos (1984) 1.51–7; Diehl (1938–9) 1.317–42.

43 Cheynet and Vannier (1986) 97; Zacos and Veglery (1972) 1.3, 2695.

44 Psellos 7(Isaac).83, 89 (Renauld 2.133–4, 136–7); Bryen. 81–5. There seems, however, to have been no serious rival to Constantine Doukas.

45 Bryen. 221 speaks of her 'ancient hatred' towards the Caesar and his family; cf. *Alexiad* 3.2.1, 3 (Leib 1. 106, 107).

46 Bryen. 85; 'L'obituaire du typikon du Pantocrator', ed. Gautier, 248.

47 Hill (1996a) 42; Magdalino (1996) 150–1; Angold (1995) 45. For Anna's children and their marriages, see Bryen. 85–7; Varzos (1984) 1.61–120: both Manuel and Theodora married into the Diogenes family.

48 Bryen. 101–5; Attal. 138; Skyl. Cont. 139; Zon. 3.694.

49 Bryen. 129–31; Cheynet and Vannier (1986) 97; Zacos and Veglery (1972) 1.3, 2695.

50 Bryen. 143.

51 Bryen. 143; Hill (1996a) 43; cf. Angold (1984b) 100.

52 It was Anna who suggested a pretext to Isaac for visiting Maria with Alexios and persuading her to discuss her concerns over the succession: *Alexiad* 2.2.2 (Leib. 1.67).

53 Bryen. 221; Vannier (1975) 52.

54 *Alexiad* 2.5.1 (Leib 1.75); Bryen. 247–51; Varzos (1984) 1.122–3. The marriage may have taken place in 1085.

55 *Alexiad* 2.5.6 (Leib 1.78). For the freedom of movement allowed to ladies of the aristocracy and imperial family at this period, see Garland (1988) esp. 381–3.

56 *Alexiad* 2.5.5 (Leib 1.77).

57 *Alexiad* 2.5.7–9 (Leib 1.78–9). For Maria's beauty and learning, see *Alexiad* 2.6.3, 15.9.1 (Leib 1.80–81, 3.223); Bryen. 219–21; Polemis (1968) 58.

58 *Alexiad* 2.7.1–7 (Leib 1.84–7).

59 *Alexiad* 2.6.2, 3.2.7, 3.4.4 (Leib 1.80, 109–10, 115); Zon. 3.734; Angold (1995) 46.

60 Cheynet and Vannier (1986) 98; Zacos and Veglery (1972) 2.2696 and Plate 24. There are a large number of seals with this inscription, and these were the ones Anna used for governmental purposes; cf. Danielis, who adopted Basil (I) as her son and was given the title *basileometer*, mother of the emperor, by him: Theoph. Cont. 318.

61 *Alexiad* 3.6.4 (Leib 1.121); Zon. 3.731. For Maria Skleraina, given the title *despoina* by Constantine Monomachos, see Psellos 6.58–9 (Renauld 1.145); Zon. 3.620.

62 *Alexiad* 3.6.3–8 (Leib 1.120–22); Dölger (1924–65) 1073; cf. Bosch (1979) 89–90.

63 Hill (1996a) 50; Magdalino (1996) 152–3, who notes that Alexios set the precedent for the formula 'justified or unjustified'. For the *logothete ton sekreton*, see Oikonomides (1976c) esp. 132–3.

64 *Alexiad* 3.7.2–3 (Leib 1.123–4); cf. Bryen. 81–3.

65 *Alexiad* 3.7.5 (Leib 1.124–5).

66 Theophylact, *Or.* 5 (Gautier 1.241); Irene by contrast is mentioned only as 'the most beautiful of women, a consort worthy of empire': *ibid.* 235.

67 *Alexiad* 3.8.3 (Leib 1.126). See also Theophylact, *Or.* 5 (Gautier 1.237–9), for her piety and reorganisation of the palace. See Hill (1996c) esp. 49–50 for Anna's characterisation of her grandmother.

68 *Alexiad* 3.5.4, 3.8.3–4 (Leib 1.118, 126). For the visit of St Cyril the Phileote to Anna *c.* 1071, see *La vie de St Cyrille* (Sargologos (1964), 90–94 (ch. 17)). When Alexios was on campaign before his accession, he always travelled with a monk as his tent companion on his mother's insistence: *Alexiad* 1.8.2 (Leib 1.32); Bryen. 289; *La vie de St Cyrille* ch. 47, 233–4. Angold (1995) 283 notes that 'Anna Dalassena had a string of holy men in her pocket', including Cyril Phileotes.

69 *Alexiad* 3.6.2 (Leib 1.119–20); she had perhaps become a nun during her exile in 1072.

70 Oikonomides (1980/81) 245 n. 58; *MM* 6.27, 28, 33.

71 Janin (1969) 1.517–29; Hill (1996a) 49; *MM* 6.32–3, 34–44; Docheiariou 2 (Oikonomides (1984) 54–9). The church of the Saviour Pantepoptes is generally identified with the Eski Imaret Camii.

72 Runciman (1949) 517.

73 Magdalino (1996) 155; Docheiariou 2 (Oikonomides (1984) 57). On the other hand, this should not be overstated: it would be unusual if he had not occasionally disagreed with one of her decisions in over a decade of collaboration.

74 *Alexiad* 10.4.5 (Leib 2.201).

75 *Alexiad* 6.7.5 (Leib 2.59); Zon. 3.731–2, 746; Matthew of Edessa 1.91 (Dostourian 1.277–8) records under 1089 that a Latin monk (accompanied by a dog to whom he offered his prayers) corrupted large numbers, including the emperor's mother; Runciman (1949) 521–2, who suggests that the heretic was Blachernites, who was condemned *c.* 1094 (*Alexiad* 10.1.6; Leib 2.189); cf. Leib (1958) for what Anna does not tell us.

76 See 'L'obituaire du typikon du Pantocrator', ed. Gautier, 244–5; According to Zon. 3.746 she died a little more than a year before her son Isaac, who died in 1102–4.

77 Hill (1996a) 53.

78 *Alexiad* 12.5.7, 12.3.2 (Leib. 3.60, 74); Zon. 3.747.

79 Zon. 3.766; tr. Angold (1984b) 150; for Irene, see Polemis (1968) 70–4; Varzos (1984) 1.99–106; Diehl (1938–9) 2.53–85.

80 *Alexiad* 3.1.5, 3.3.3 (Leib 1.105, 111).

81 Bryen. 221; cf. *Alexiad* 2.5.1–2 (Leib 1.75–6). For her marriage, see Polemis (1965) 68–9.

82 See esp. *Alexiad* 3.1.5, 3.2.1, 3.2.7 (Leib 1.105–6, 109–10); Zon. 3.733.

83 *Alexiad* 6.8.1 (Leib 2.60); for Irene's children see Varzos (1984) 1.176–265.

84 *Alexiad* 12.3.2–3 (Leib 3.60): 'Whenever she had to appear in public as empress at some important ceremony, she was overcome with modesty and a blush at once suffused her cheeks.' For conventions regarding women's behaviour, see Garland (1988) 371–4, cf. 388–9.

85 Kazhdan and McCormick (1997) 183 cite *Vita Basilii Iunioris* (*BHG*[3] 263) for the wives of nobles frequently congregating at the house of the *zoste patrikia* to meet a holy man.

86 Zon. 3.747.

87 *Alexiad* 5.2.1 (Leib 2.10).

88 *Alexiad* 2.5.8, 3.5.4 (Leib 1.78–9, 118).

89 For a commemorative issue depicting John II crowned by Christ, and showing Alexios I and Irene on the reverse (the only time Irene appears on the coinage), presumably minted for this occasion, see Hendy (1969) 40–41.

90 *Alexiad* 12.6.7 (Leib 3.74).

91 *Alexiad* 12.3.2, 12.3.4–6 (Leib 3.59–62); she was of course accompanied by her retinue: *Alexiad* 13.1.8 (Leib 3.90).

92 *Alexiad* 13.1.4, 13.4.1 (Leib 3.88, 100); cf. 14.4.1, where Alexios wintered at Chrysopolis with the empress, 14.5.1 (Leib 3.159, 164).

93 *Alexiad* 15.1.6, 15.2.1–2, 15.2.4, 15.3.1 (Leib 3.190–2, 194–5).

94 *Alexiad* 13.1.7 (Leib 3.89): according to Anna the 'famosa' and lampoons were the work of criminals who wanted to frighten away Irene and assassinate Alexios; see Garland (1992) 30–31.

95 *Alexiad* 15.11.4, 8, 9 (Leib 3.231, 233–4). For his arthritis (gout), see *Alexiad* 14.4.8–9, 14.5.1 (Leib 3.163–4).

96 *Alexiad* 15.11.4, 17–20 (Leib 3.231, 238–40).

97 *Alexiad* 3.3.4 (Leib 1.112).

98 *Alexiad* 12.3.2–3; cf. 3.3.4 (Leib 3.59–60, 1.112).

99 *Alexiad* 3.3.3–4 (Leib 1.111–12); so were Maria of Alania and Maria the *protovestiaria*, Anna's maternal grandmother: see Garland (1994) 264–8. The only portrait which may be of Irene is an enamel on the pala d'oro in St Mark's Venice: Lampros (1930) pl. 66.

100 *Alexiad* 12.6.4 (Leib 3.72).

101 *Alexiad* 12.3.9 (Leib 3.63).

102 *MM* 5.327–91; *PG* 127:985–1128; 'Le typikon de la Théotokos Kéchari-toméné', ed. Gautier 5–165; Janin (1969) 539–41; Galatariotou (1988) esp. 264–71, 280–1, (1987) 103; Angold (1995) 274, 295–6, 304, 306; Magdalino (1996) 151. Laiou (1981) 242 notes that it is evidence for her experience in managing a large economic concern.

103 Kallikles 81, 120–21 (nos. 6, 35); Prodromos, ed. Horandner no. 2, cf. nos. 39, 42, 43; Garland (1994) 268–9.

104 *Alexiad* 5.9.3 (Leib 2.38). Anna's grandmother Maria also knew Euthymios Zigabenos, author of the *Dogmatike Panoplia*: *Alexiad* 15.9.1 (Leib 3.223).

105 *Alexiad* pref. 3.2 (Leib 1.5); Bryen. 71; cf. Polemis (1968) 72.

106 Mullett (1984a) 175–9; Polemis (1968) 72–3; for Italikos's oration for Irene, see Hill (1996b) 13–16.

107 Browning (1962); see Tornikios, ed. Darrouzès, 220–323, esp. 243–5. For Anna's account of her education see *Alexiad* pref. 1.2, 15.7.9 (Leib 1.3–4, 3.218); cf. Zon. 3.754 for Anna's and Bryennios's scholarship.

108 Zon. 3.739–40, 746–7; Hill (1996a) 45–6. On Alexios's marriage policy, see Magdalino (1993) 202–6.

109 Zon. 3.739.

110 Hill (1996a) 47.

111 Unlike Eudokia Makrembolitissa, Irene retained her family name on her seals, which read, 'Lord, help Irene Doukaina, Augusta': Zacos and Veglery (1972) 1.103. Euphrosyne Doukaina was to do the same.

112 *Alexiad* 3.2.1 (Leib 1.106): George Palaiologos tells the Komnenoi when they try to silence the acclamations 'Alexios and Irene', 'it was not for your sakes that I won so great a victory, but because of that Irene you speak of'; cf. Magdalino (1993) 201.

113 Chon. 8–11; Zon. 3.762–5.

114 Chon. 5; Zon. 3.748.

115 Zon. 3.748; Mullett (1994) 263.

116 Chon. 5; Zon. 3.754.

117 Zon. 3.762; Chon. 5–7.

118 Chon. 7.

119 Chon. 7–8; Zon. 3.763–4.

120 Chon. 6, 8; Zon. 3.764–5; Cheynet (1990) 103.

121 *Alexiad* 15.11.14 (Leib 3.237).

122 Chon. 10–12; Cheynet (1990) 103.

123 'L'obituaire du typikon du Pantocrator', ed. Gautier, 245–7. On the possible dating of Anna's death to 1153–5, see Browning (1962) 4; Anna was tonsured on her death-bed, *ibid.* 12.

124 Hill (1996a) 40, 54; Mullett (1994) 267 n. 61: 'what remains to be analysed is how the smooth "Macedonian female" takeover in 1081 and the imposition of "Comnene female" values in the 1080s came to be superseded in 1118 by a male Comnene victory.'

12 MARIA OF ANTIOCH (1161–82/3)

1 She was the daughter of St Ladislas of Hungary and Adelheid of Rheinfelden, or of Koloman: Makk (1989) 127; Varzos (1984) 1.219–22; Kinnamos 1.4.

2 Kinnamos 1.4 ; *Syn. CP* Nov. 887–90; 'L'obituaire du typikon du Pantocrator', ed. Gautier, 247–8; Angold (1995) 76.

3 See Chon. 46 for his fidelity as a husband; Kallikles nos. 2, 28, 31; Prodromos, ed. Horandner, no. 8; Epstein (1981) 385–400; 'Le typicon du Christ Sauveur

Pantocrator', ed. Gautier, 5–165. All translations from Choniates *Historia* in this chapter are taken from Magoulias (1984).

4 Prodromos, ed. Horandner, no. 1, lines 47–113, cf. no. 7; Kallikles no. 28.

5 For the portrait (Plate 25), probably dated to 1122 or shortly afterwards, see Whittemore (1942) 21–8; Cormack (1981) 145. For praise of her appearance, see Laiou (1992c) 95; Prodromos, ed. Horandner, no. 1.

6 Kazhdan (1988/9) 419–20, 422–3; Magdalino (1993) 206–7; Jeffreys (1994); Varzos (1984) 1.339–476.

7 Chon. 53–4; cf. Kinnamos 2.4. For the official view of their marriage, see *Fontes Rerum Byzantinarum* 311–30; Hill (1996b) 8 notes that the speech tells us more about Manuel than Bertha; cf. Laiou (1992c) 95; Irmscher (1996).

8 For Manuel's illegitimate children and many affairs, especially that of long standing with his niece Theodora, see esp. Chon. 54, 204; Garland (1995/6) 39–42. For an anonymous poem mentioning enemies of the empress, see Varzos (1984) 1.456. These may have been connected with one of the emperor's ladies: Manuel's niece Theodora tried to murder a rival in a fit of jealousy: Chalandon (1971) 205–6; Angold (1995) 438.

9 *Fontes Rerum Byzantinarum*, 316–25; cf. Kinnamos 5.1.

10 Prodromos, ed. Horandner, no. 20; *Codex Marc.* no. 233.

11 Jeffreys (1980) 472–3; M. Jeffreys (1974) 151. She seems to have had difficulty paying Tzetzes: see *Ep.* 57. On Irene the *sebastokratorissa*, see esp. Jeffreys (1982), (1984), (1994).

12 Chon. 81; Kinnamos 3.5, 3.11, 5.1; Odo of Deuil, ed. Berry, 56.

13 Chon. 115: Bertha was buried in the Pantokrator; 137, 425.

14 Chon. 244; cf. Chon. 116, 269, 332–3; Kinnamos 5.4; Eustathios 14; Constantine Manasses, ed. Horna, 330; Garland (1994) 278–81.

15 Spatharakis (1976) 209–10; Magdalino and Nelson (1982) 139–40.

16 For Maria, see Varzos (1984) 2.439–52.

17 Chon. 170–71; Kinnamos 3.11; Eustathios 14 calls her 'that holy child born to the emperor Manuel'; William of Tyre 22.4: William himself was present at the festivities. For the date of Maria's birth, see Magdalino (1993) 198, 243 (1152).

18 William of Tyre 22.4; cf. Chon. 275; *Fontes Rerum Byzantinarum* 80–92; Magdalino (1993) 100. The date of the MS has been disputed. Agnes was later to marry her husband's successor, Andronikos, and then a nobleman Branas, and at the time of the Fourth Crusade was living in the capital. She had acclimatised in Byzantium, because according to Robert of Clari she refused to talk French to the crusaders: Chon. 275–6; Eustathios 44; Robert of Clari 20, 53 (Lauer, 19, 54); Villehardouin 403, 423.

19 M. J. Jeffreys (1981) 101–2; Spatharakis (1976) 213–14, 216–18; Magdalino (1993) 245.

20 In the upper left-hand corner she faces a group of Byzantine court ladies, who wear wide-sleeved purple robes and large fan-shaped headdresses; behind her are her western court ladies; at this point she is simply dressed with her hair in a plait. In the upper right corner she is clothed in Byzantine costume, a purple robe with rich gold decoration. The lower zone shows her flanked by Byzantine ladies paying her court: Spatharakis (1976) 229.

21 Chon. 112, 128, 137, 170; Magdalino (1993) 89, 92; on Manuel's marriage policy, see Magdalino (1993) 209–17.

22 On Maria, wife of the Caesar John Roger, and other Komnenian princesses, see Garland (1994) 286–8, (1995) 103–4.

23 Mich. Syr. 21.1 (Chabot 3.381), however, states that she had imperial ambitions.

24 M. J. Jeffreys (1981) 108: 'The obeisance performed by Maria to Agnes marked the

formal acceptance, by one of the chief symbols of the anti-Latin cause, of a marriage which seemed to set the seal on the success of pro-Latin policy.'

25 Chon. 146–7.

26 Chon. 168–9. For the date of his birth, see Wirth (1956); Jones (1988), note on Eustathios 14. For Manuel's desire for a legitimate son, see Chon. 81–2; Kinnamos 6.2.

27 Magdalino (1993) 243 (unpublished sermon by Samuel Mauropous).

28 Chon. 169.

29 Grumel (1989) 1120; Chon. 169–70, 228; Angold (1995) 116.

30 Eustathios 14; Chon. 253–4.

31 Chon. 224–5, cf. 229–30; Eustathios 14; cf. William of Tyre 22.11.

32 Chon., *Orationes* 40; Constantine Manasses, ed. Horna, 330–31, lines 185–6; *Codex Marc.* nos. 98, 100, 109, 221, 335, 336; cf. M. J. Jeffreys (1981).

33 William of Tyre 22.11; Eustathios 28; Chon. 247; cf. Chon. 204–5; Brand (1968) 28–32, 45–7; Angold (1984b) 203–5.

34 For Alexios, see Varzos (1984) 2.189–218; his wife had been Maria Doukaina: Polemis (1968) 191; cf. *Codex Marc.* no. 70. For the reaction against the ascendancy of Alexios the *protosebastos* which changed the existing equilibrium at court, see Magdalino (1993) 224–5.

35 Chon. 224–5, 227–8, 230; Eustathios 14. On Maria's regency, see Christophilopoulou (1970) 75–83; Angold (1995) 116–18; Garland (1997) 270–84.

36 Chon. 223, cf. 227, 229, 257; Eustathios 14.

37 Chon. 228; Laiou (1992c) 50 n. 147.

38 William of Tyre 22.11; Chon. 229–30; Eustathios 14. See Brand (1968) 31–4 for the *protosebastos's* unpopularity with the bureaucracy and populace. For a poem accompanying the gift of a crown to the young emperor by the *protosebastos*, see *Codex Marc.* no. 108.

39 Eustathios 14–15; Chon. 231–2. William of Tyre 22.5 dates the discovery of the conspiracy to 1 March 1181.

40 Chon. 232–3; Eustathios 16–17, 20–1; Grumel (1989) 1156.

41 Eustathios 18–20, 23; Chon. 235–43; Angold (1995) 116–17 with n. 5; cf. Mich. Syr. 21.1 (Chabot 3.381–2).

42 Chon. 228, 230–1, 240–1; Eustathios 21–2; William of Tyre 22.5.

43 Chon. 247–9: he was ill-treated by his guards in not being allowed to sleep; Eustathios 24, cf. 31; William of Tyre 22.12 says he was blinded and horribly mutilated. The Latin mercenaries of the palace guard had already defected to Andronikos: Brand (1968) 41, 325–6.

44 Chon. 250, cf. 244; cf. Eustathios 27 for the unimpressive nature of Andronikos's forces at close quarters. For the 'house of Ioannitzes', see Chon. 419.

45 Chon. 250–51; Eustathios 28–30. Four thousand who survived the slaughter were sold to the Turks as slaves. See also William of Tyre 22.12–13; Nicol (1988) 107–8; Brand (1968) esp. 41–2, cf. 204–6; Angold (1984b) 196, 264–5.

46 Chon. 264–5; cf. Eustathios 31.

47 Chon. 255, 257, 259–60, 265; Eustathios 34–5; Grumel (1989) 1158.

48 Chon. 265–6, 267–9, 274; cf. Eustathios 35, 43.

49 Chon. 269; cf. Eustathios 35–6.

50 Chon. 332–3.

13 EUPHROSYNE DOUKAINA (1195–1203)

1 Polemis (1968) nos. 32, 101.

2 Chon. 455; for her seal as *sebastokratorissa* and sister-in-law (*nymphe*) of Isaac II

Angelos, see Zacos and Veglery (1972) 1.3, no. 2746, cf. 2744; for a suggestion that *nymphe* should be translated as 'lady-in-waiting', see Sayre (1986) 237–8; for Euphrosyne's family connections, see also Garland (1997) 283–4.

3 Kinnamos 5. 4; Dölger (1924–65) 1442; Polemis (1968) no. 98; Magdalino (1993) 259–60, 350, 507–8. All translations from Choniates *Historia* in this chapter are taken from Magoulias (1984).

4 Chon. 112–15; Magdalino (1993) 255, 259. Polemis (1968) no. 99 appears to be a conflation of several figures including this John Kamateros: see Garland (1997) 284 n. 106; cf. Magdalino (1993) 255–6; Eustathios 39 for an unflattering picture of Basil Kamateros.

5 Chon. 231; Eustathios, *Capture of Thessalonike*, 14–15; Polemis (1968) no. 99.

6 Chon. 266–7, 485; Polemis (1968) no. 100, who notes that he was on friendly terms with the brothers, Michael and Niketas Choniates, who addressed several of their letters to him.

7 Chon. 262, 514, 274; Eustathios 39; Varzos (1984) 2.747 n. 88.

8 Chon. 491; Varzos (1984) 1.309; Brand (1968) 142; Zacos and Veglery (1972) 1.3, no. 2749; for a seal belonging to Stryphnos, see Plate 28.

9 Magdalino (1993) 255.

10 For Euphrosyne Kastamonitissa, see Chon. 282–3: Andronikos I Komnenos during the siege of Isaac in Nicaea attached Euphrosyne to a battering-ram, but she was later rescued by the defenders of the city; for Gregory of Antioch's speech on her death, see *Fontes Rerum Byzantinarum* 300–4.

11 Chon. 405–8, 420–24, 428, 444–6; cf. 399–401, 435–6 for the rebellions of Theodore Manganas and Constantine Angelos. For the four pretenders styling themselves Alexios II (son of Manuel Komnenos) during the reigns of the Angeloi, see also Brand (1968) 86–7, 161–2, 135–6; Cheynet (1990) 434–40. For Isaac's reign, see Brand (1968) 113–16; Angold (1984b) 271–4.

12 Angold (1984b) 271.

13 Chon. 448, 450. Brand (1968) 111 cites Alberic de Tre Fontane as recording that Alexios was given the Boukoleon Palace and 4,000 lb of silver a day.

14 Chon. 451; Angold (1984b) 279: 'they agreed that Isaac had both failed the Empire and themselves. They expected Alexius Angelos to rule in their interests.' See Polemis (1968) no. 180 for Raoul.

15 Chon. 451–2, 455; Cheynet (1990) 440–2; Garland (1992) 41–2.

16 Chon. 455–6.

17 Chon. 456–7.

18 Chon. 457.

19 For Euphrosyne and her daughters Irene, Anna and Eudokia, see Polemis (1968) no. 101; *ODB* 749 s.v. *Euphrosyne Doukaina Kamatera*. Irene was born *c.* 1170, Anna *c.* 1171 or 1173 and Eudokia *c.* 1172 or 1174.

20 Chon. 459, 537, 540, cf. 529.

21 Chon. 454.

22 Niketas Choniates became *logothete ton sekreton* in 1195. He stayed in office until Alexios V Mourtzouphlos replaced him as *logothete* and head of the senate with his father-in-law Philokales in 1204: Chon. 565.

23 Chon. 460; Garland (1988) *passim*, (1990) 308.

24 Chon. 460–1.

25 Chon. 463–4; Polemis (1968) no. 103.

26 Chon. 475–9.

27 Angold (1984b) 270; Chon. 444 criticises Isaac II for putting offices up for sale

like a street trader with a barrow load of fruit. For the bureaucracy under Alexios III, see Brand (1968) 142–3; cf. Magdalino (1993) 228–315.

28 Chon. 483–4.

29 Chon. 484.

30 Chon. 484–5; cf. ibid. 439–41 for Mesopotamites's role under Isaac II, where Choniates stresses his indispensability, aptitude and rapacity.

31 Brand (1968) 144–6 places Euphrosyne's period of disgrace in 1196–7, and Constantine Mesopotamites's downfall in 1197, noting that he had been succeeded by Theodore Eirenikos as *epi tou kanikleiou* by November 1197 (*MM* 6.139, no. 33); Grumel (1989) 1187 dates Mesopotamites's disgrace to 1198, the dating accepted by van Dieten in his edition and by Garland (1995/6) 53–4.

32 Chon. 486.

33 Chon. 486, cf. 497.

34 Chon. 484–6.

35 Chon. 487–8. For the political implications of Euphrosyne's banishment, see Garland (1995/6) 53–4, (1997) 284–93.

36 Chon. 488. Compare the banishment of Euphrosyne's youngest daughter Eudokia on a charge of adultery by her husband Stephen I Nemanja of Serbia: Chon. 531–2; Garland (1995/6) 55.

37 Chon. 488–9.

38 Chon. 489.

39 Chon. 490; Angold (1995) 126, 196; Grumel (1989) 1186 (dated to 1198). See Garland (1990) 18–20 for examples of Choniates's satire against bureaucrats.

40 Chon. 492–3; Grumel (1989) 1187.

41 Chon. 491, 541; Brand (1968) 147.

42 Chon. 528, 537.

43 Cheynet (1990) 442; *TT* 1.487 (*Partitio Romanie*): 'pertinentia imperatricis scilicet Vesna, Fersala, Domocos, Revenica, duo Almiri, cum Demetriadi'; *TT* 1.278–9 for possessions of the empress and her daughters in the province of Nikopolis in Epiros; for her daughter Irene's possessions in the Peloponnese, see also *TT* 1.470; cf. Chon. 551, 486 for Euphrosyne's wealth.

44 Chon. 497–8.

45 Chon. 498: 'the proposal made in common was far worse than that made by the individual.'

46 Chon. 519; cf. Chon., *Orationes* 67.

47 Chon. 519. For revolts in Alexios III's reign, see esp. Cheynet (1990) 445–58; Garland (1992) 41–4.

48 Chon. 519–20, 557–8, cf. 530; Garland (1992) 42. Women were constantly criticised by churchmen for dabbling in magic and fortune-telling: Greenfield (1993) 73–85; cf. *V. Euthymii* 129, for the similar activities of the emperor Alexander (912–13).

49 Chon. 520.

50 Chon. 508–9.

51 Chon. 460; cf. his description of Maria Kaisarissa (*ibid.* 171). For his conventional view of women's intelligence, see 105, where he describes Eudokia, mistress of Andronikos Komnenos, as 'quick-witted and gifted with sagacity, contrary to the nature of women'.

52 Chon., *Orationes* 67–8. See also Garland (1994) 292–3.

53 Chon., *Orationes* 105, 'συνάρχοι δέ σοι καὶ συνδεσπόζοι ἡ φερώνυμος τῷ ὄντι βασίλισσα' ('may the aptly named empress co-rule and co-govern with you'). The name Euphrosyne means joy or good cheer. Euthymios Tornikes also refers in a speech to Euphrosyne's beauty: see Darrouzès (1968) 64, 72.

54 Nikolaos Mesarites, ed. Heisenberg, 41–2; cf. Nikephoros Chrysoberges, ed. Treu, 21–2, where in her role as imperial helpmate she is compared to Athena and the woman of Solomon's *Proverbs*.

55 Chon. 508; Cheynet (1990) 443; Varzos (1984) 2.742–3; Chon. 497, 473, cf. 534–5. For seals belonging to Alexios Palaiologos and Theodore Laskaris, see Zacos and Veglery (1972) 1.3, nos. 2752, 2753.

56 Chon. 531–2, 571, 608–9; Akropolites 5, 8; Villehardouin 270, 272. On Sgouros, see Angold (1995) 205–6; Cheynet (1990) 455–8: he may have been associated with Euphrosyne's family before their downfall, for Michael Choniates complained to Constantine Tornikes that Sgouros had the support of the emperor's in-laws in his depredations around Athens.

57 Chon. 540. It was only when Alexios IV was proclaimed emperor at Epidamnos that Alexios started to feel enough concern to begin to repair the fleet, which then consisted of twenty rotting skiffs (*ibid.* 541).

58 Chon. 547–8.

59 Chon. 497–8, 549–50, 551.

60 Chon. 571, 608. For Mourtzouphlos, see Hendrickx and Matzukis (1979).

61 Chon. 608; Villehardouin 266, 270. Akropolites 5, on the other hand, specifically states that Eudokia and Mourtzouphlos were married before the fall of the city.

62 Chon. 608; Villehardouin 271; cf. Akropolites 5, who states that Eudokia was shocked at what occurred and Alexios thereupon reproached her for 'her shameful and licentious love'.

63 Chon. 608–9; Akropolites 5; Villehardouin 307.

64 Chon. 612, 620: 'the wretched emperor Alexios and his wife Euphrosyne were sent across the sea to the ruler of the Germans. Alas and alack! Such a novel and extraordinary thing was unheard-of among the Romans!'; cf. Akropolites 8; Villehardouin 309.

65 Akropolites 8–10; Angold (1995) 300; *TT* 1.1278–9; Loernertz (1973) 370–76.

66 See Garland (1988) esp. 385–93.

67 See Hill (1996a) 40, who sees the 'subordination of women as women' under the Komnenoi.

68 Chon. 598–9, 368, cf. 601. For Margaret-Maria, cf. Akropolites 8, 11; Villehardouin, 185–6, 212; Robert of Clari 51; Chon., *Orationes* 35–46.

EPILOGUE

1 See esp. Nicol (1994) 48–58; *PLP* 9.21361. Yolanda-Irene and Anna of Savoy are the only two Palaiologue empresses given entries in the *ODB*.

2 Nicol (1994) 82–95; *PLP* 9.21437; Gregoras 2.761.

3 Nicol (1968) 44–63; Grierson (1982) 287–8, cf. 299–300.

4 Nicol (1994) 92.

5 Doukas, *Istoria Turco-Bizantina*, ed. Grecu, 47.

6 Talbot (1992) 296–8, 303; *PLP* 9.21380.

7 Nicol (1968) no. 23; *PLP* 5.10935; see esp. Gregoras 2.625. Note too the praise for John's mother Theodora (Nicol (1968) no. 21; *PLP* 5.10492) by John and Gregoras for her administrative ability and resourcefulness. She was put in charge of the city of Didymoteichos by Andronikos III, with his first wife Irene, in 1321–2 and 1327, and it was her decision to finance Andronikos III's rebellion against his grandfather. She was imprisoned by Anna of Savoy and died in prison in 1342.

8 Nicol (1968) no. 30; for her father's praise of her, see Kant. 3.253–4. For Manuel

II's letter to his mother, see his *Letters*, ed. Dennis, no. 1; for Kydones's letters to her, see Demetrios Kydones, ed. Loenertz, nos. 25, 134, 143, 222, 256, 389, esp. 222.

9 Nicol (1993) 369–70.
10 Talbot (1992) 298–302; Galatariotou (1987) 89; for Theodora, see Nicol (1994) 33–47, esp. 40–41.
11 Nicol (1994) 40–46.
12 Laiou (1981) 242–3; Nicol (1968) no. 21; Kant. 1.28, 52, 138, 2.137–8.
13 Nicol (1994) 59–70; Hero (1985) esp. 121–2, 144–5.
14 Nicol (1968) 136.
15 Laiou (1981) 251.
16 Contra Nicol (1994) 4.

BIBLIOGRAPHY

Primary sources and collections of sources

Acta Sanctorum Bollandiana, Brussels, 1643–1779; Paris and Rome, 1866–87; Brussels, 1965–70, 68 vols.

Actes de Docheiariou, ed. N. Oikonomides, Paris: Lethielleux, 1984.

Agathias, *Agathiae Myrinaei Historiarum Libri Quinque*, ed. R. Keydell, Berlin: de Gruyter, 1967; English translation by J.D. Frendo, *Agathias: The Histories*, Berlin: de Gruyter, 1975. References are by book and chapter.

Akropolites, *Georgii Akropolitae Opera*, ed. A. Heisenberg, rev. P. Wirth, 2 vols, Stuttgart: Teubner, 1978. References are by chapter.

Anna Komnene, *Anne Comnène: Alexiade*, ed. and tr. B. Leib, 3 vols, Paris: Budé, 1937–45, repr. 1967; English translation by E.R.A. Sewter, *The Alexiad of Anna Comnena*, Harmondsworth: Penguin, 1979. References are by book and chapter, and by volume and page.

Anthologia Graeca, ed. H. Beckby, 4 vols, 2nd edn, Munich: Heimeran, 1957–8; English translation by W.R. Paton, *The Greek Anthology*, 5 vols, London and New York: Loeb, repr. 1960.

Arethas, *Arethae Scripta Minora*, ed. L.G. Westerink, 2 vols, Leipzig: Teubner, 1968–9. References are by page.

Attaleiates, *Michaelis Attaliotae Historia*, ed. E. Bekker, Bonn: *CSHB*, 1853. References are by page.

Bar Hebraeus, tr. E.A. Wallis Budge, *The Chronography of Gregory Abu'l Faraj, Commonly Known as Bar Hebraeus*, London: Oxford University Press, 1932.

Bibliotheca Hagiographica Graeca, ed. F. Halkin, 3rd edn, Brussels: Société des Bollandistes, 1957.

Bryennios, Nikephoros, *Histoire*, ed. P. Gautier, Brussels: *CFHB*, 1975. References are by page.

Cassiodorus, *Variae*, ed. Th. Mommsen, *MGH* AA 12, Berlin: Weidmann, 1894; English translation by S.J.B. Barnish, *The Variae of Magnus Aurelius Cassiodorus Senator*, Liverpool: Liverpool University Press, 1992.

Choniates, Niketas, Χρονικὴ διήγησις, ed. J.-L. van Dieten, Berlin and New York: *CFHB*, 1975; English translation by H.J. Magoulias, *O City of Byzantium: Annals of Niketas Choniates*, Detroit: Wayne State University Press, 1984. References are by page.

Choniates, Niketas, *Orationes et Epistulae*, ed. J.-L. van Dieten, Berlin and New York: *CFHB*, 1972. References are by page.

Christopher of Mytilene, *Die Gedichte des Christophoros Mitylenaios*, ed. E. Kurtz, Leipzig: Neumann, 1903.

Chronicle Paschale [Easter Chronicle], ed. L. Dindorf, Bonn: *CSHB*, 1832; English translation by M. and M. Whitby, *Chronicon Paschale 284–628 AD*, Liverpool: Liverpool University Press, 1989. References are by page.

Chrysoberges, Nikephoros, 'Λόγος ἕτερος εἰς 'Αλέξιον', in *Ad Angelos Orationes Tres*, ed. M. Treu, Breslau, 1892.

Codex Justinianus, Corpus Iuris Civilis, ed. P. Krueger, vol. 2, Berlin: Weidmann, 1929.

Codex Marcianus 524, ''Ο Μαρκιανὸς Κῶδιξ 524', ed. S. Lampros, *NE* 8 (1911) 3–59, 113–92.

Codex Theodosianus, ed. Th. Mommsen, 3rd edn, Berlin: Weidmann, 1962: English translation by C. Pharr, *The Theodosian Code and Novels and the Sirmondian Constitutions*, Princeton: Princeton University Press, 1952.

Constantine Manasses, 'Das Hodoiporikon des Konstantin Manasses', ed. K. Horna, *BZ* 13 (1904) 313–55.

Constantine Porphyrogennetos, *De Administrando Imperio*, ed. and tr. Gy. Moravcsik and R.J.H. Jenkins, Washington, DC: Dumbarton Oaks, rev. edn 1967. References are by page.

Constantine Porphyrogennetos, *De Cerimoniis Aulae Byzantinae*, ed. J.J. Reiske, 2 vols, Bonn: *CSHB*, 1829; partial French translation by A. Vogt, *Constantin Porphyrogénète: Le livre des cérémonies*, 2 vols, Paris: Budé, 1935–40. References are by book and chapter.

Constantine Porphyrogennetos, 'Excerpta de insidiis', in *Excerpta Historica*, vol. 3, ed. C. de Boor, Berlin: Weidmann, 1905, 151–76. References are by page.

Corippus, *Flavius Cresconius Corippus in Laudem Iustini Augusti Minoris Libri IV*, ed. and tr. Averil Cameron, University of London: Athlone Press, 1976; also ed. U. Stache, Berlin: Mielke, 1976.

Doukas, *Istoria Turco-Bizantina*, ed. V. Grecu, Bucharest: Editura Academiei Republicii Populaire Romine, 1958; English translation by H.J. Magoulias, *The Decline and Fall of Byzantium to the Ottoman Turks*, Detroit: University of Michigan Press, 1975.

Eustathios of Thessaloniki: The Capture of Thessaloniki, tr. J.R. Melville Jones, Canberra: Byzantina Australiensia 8, 1988; ed. B.G. Niebuhr, *De Thessalonica Capta*, Bonn: *CSHB*, 1842.

Evagrios, *The Ecclesiastical History of Evagrius*, ed. J. Bidez and L. Parmentier, London: Methuen, 1898, repr. Amsterdam: Hakkert, 1964; French translation by A.J. Festugière, 'Évagre, Histoire Ecclésiastique', *Byzantion* 45(2), 1975: 187–488. References are by book and chapter.

Fontes Rerum Byzantinarum: Rhetorum Saeculi XII Orationes Politicae, I (1–2), ed. V.E. Regel and N.I. Novosadskij, St Petersburg, 1892; repr. Leipzig: Zentralantiquariat der Deutsches Demokratischen Republik, 1982. References are by page.

Fragmenta Historicorum Graecorum, ed. C. Müller, vol. 4, Paris: Didot, 1851. References are by page.

Gautier, P. (ed.), 'L'obituaire du typikon du Pantocrator', *REB* 27 (1969) 235–62.

Gautier, P. (ed.), 'Le typicon du Christ Sauveur Pantocrator', *REB* 32 (1974) 1–145.

Gautier, P. (ed.), 'Le typikon de la Théotokos Kécharitoméné', *REB* 43 (1985) 5–165.

Gautier, P. (ed.), 'Quelques lettres de Psellos inédités ou déjà édités', *REB* 44 (1986) 111–97.

Genesios, *Iosephi Genesii Regum Libri Quattuor*, ed. A. Lesmueller-Werner and I. Thurn, Berlin: de Gruyter, 1978. References are by page.

Georgius Monachus, *Chronicon*, ed. C. de Boor, rev. P. Wirth, vol. 2, Stuttgart: Teubner, 1978. References are by page.

Georgius Monachus, *Vitae Recentiorum Imperatorum*, in Theophanes Continuatus, ed. I. Bekker, Bonn: *CSHB*, 1838, 761–924. References are by page.

Gregoras, Nikephoros, *Byzantina Historia*, ed. L. Schopen, 3 vols, Bonn: *CSHB*, 1829–55. References are by volume and page.

Gregory of Tours, 'De gloria martyrum', *PL* 71: 828–912; English translation by R. van Dam, *Gregory of Tours: Glory of the Martyrs*, Liverpool: Liverpool University Press, 1988.

Gregory of Tours, *Historia Francorum*, ed. W. Arndt and B. Krusch, *MGH*, Scriptores Rerum Merovingicarum 1, Hanover: Impensis Bibliopolii Hahniani, 1951; English translation by O.M. Dalton, *History of the Franks*, vol. 2, Oxford: Clarendon Press, 1927, repr. 1971; and by L. Thorpe, *Gregory of Tours: The History of the Franks*, Harmondsworth: Penguin, 1974. References are by book and chapter.

History of the Patriarchs of the Coptic Church of Alexandria, tr. B. Evetts, *PO* 1 (1907) 381–518. References are by page.

John of Biclaro, *Chronicle*, ed. Th. Mommsen, *MGH* AA 11, Berlin, 1894, 207–20; tr. K.B. Wolf, *Conquerors and Chroniclers of Early Medieval Spain*, Liverpool: Liverpool University Press, 1990.

John of Ephesus, *Iohannis Ephesini Historiae Ecclesiasticae Pars Tertia*, ed. E.W. Brooks, *CSCO* 106, Scr. Syr. 54–5, Louvain: L. Durbecq, 1935–6, repr. 1952; English translation by R. Payne Smith, *The Third Part of the Ecclesiastical History of John Bishop of Ephesus*, Oxford: Oxford University Press, 1860. References are by book and chapter.

John of Ephesus, *The Lives of the Eastern Saints*, *PO* 17 (1923) 1–307, 18 (1924) 513–698, 19 (1926) 153–285. References are by page.

John Geometres, *Versus Iambici*, *PG* 120: 1119–1200.

John Lydus, *Ioannes Lydus: On Powers or the Magistracies of the Roman State*, ed. and tr. A.C. Bandy, Philadelphia: American Philosophical Society, 1983. References are by book and chapter.

John of Nikiu, tr. R.H. Charles, *The Chronicle of John, Coptic Bishop of Nikiu*, London: Williams and Norgate, 1916. References are by book and section.

Justinian, *Novellae*, in *Corpus Juris Civilis*, ed. R. Schoell and W. Kroll, vol. 3, 6th edn, Berlin: Weidmann, 1954.

Kallikles, *Nicola Callicle: Carmi*, ed. R. Romano, Naples: Bibliopolis, 1980.

Kantakouzenos, John (VI), *Ioannis Cantacuzeni Eximperatoris Historiarum Libri IV*, ed. L. Schopen, 3 vols, Bonn: *CSHB*, 1828–32. References are by volume and page.

Kedrenos, George, *Compendium Historiarum*, ed. I. Bekker, 2 vols, Bonn: *CSHB*, 1838–9. References are by page.

Kekaumenos, *Cecaumeni Strategicon et Incerti Scriptoris de Officiis Regiis Libellus*, ed. B. Wassiliewsky and V. Jernstedt, St Petersburg, 1896; repr. Amsterdam: Hakkert, 1965.

Kinnamos, John, *Ioannis Cinnami Epitome Rerum ab Ioanne et Manuele Comnenis Gestarum*, ed. A. Meineke, Bonn: *CSHB*, 1836; English translation by C.M. Brand, *Deeds of John and Manuel Comnenus by John Kinnamos*, New York: Columbia University Press, 1976. References are by book and chapter.

Kydones, Demetrios, *Démétrius Cydonès: Correspondance*, ed. R.-J. Loenertz, Vatican: Biblioteca Apostolica Vaticana, 1960.

Leo VI (the Wise), *Les Novelles de Léon VI le Sage*, ed. P. Noailles and A. Dain, Paris: Les Belles Lettres, 1944.

Leo VI (the Wise), 'Oraison funèbre de Basile I', ed. A. Vogt and I. Housherr, *OCP* 26 (1932) 1–79. References are by page.

Leo the Deacon, *Historiae*, ed. C.B. Hase, Bonn: *CSHB*, 1828. References are by page.

Leo Grammaticus, *Leonis Grammatici Chronographia*, ed. I. Bekker, Bonn: *CSHB*, 1842. References are by page.

Le Liber Pontificalis, ed. L. Duchesne, 2 vols, 2nd edn, Paris: de Boccard, 1955–7; English translation by R. Davis, *The Book of Pontiffs (Liber Pontificalis): The Ancient Biographies of the First Ninety Roman Bishops to AD 715*, Liverpool: Liverpool University Press, 1989; *idem, The Lives of the Eighth-century Popes*, Liverpool: Liverpool University Press, 1992. References are by chapter.

Liberatus, *Breviarium Causae Nestorianorum et Eutychianorum*, ed. E. Schwartz, *ACO* 2.5, Berlin and Leipzig: de Gruyter, 1932, 98–141. References are by page.

Liudprand of Cremona, *Antapodosis*, ed. J. Becker, Hanover: Hahnsche Buchhandlung, 1908. References are by book and chapter.

Liudprand of Cremona, *Relatio de Legatione Constantinopolitana*, ed. and tr. B. Scott, Bristol: Bristol Classical Press, 1993. References are by chapter.

Malalas, John, *Chronographia*, ed. L. Dindorf, Bonn: *CSHB*, 1831; English translation by E. Jeffreys, M. Jeffreys and R. Scott, *John Malalas: The Chronicle*, Melbourne: Australian Association for Byzantine Studies, 1986. References are by page.

Mansi, G.D. (ed.), *Sacrorum Conciliorum Nova et Amplissima Collectio*, Florence, 1759–98, repr. Paris: Welter, 1901–27. References are by page.

Manuel II Palaiologos, *The Letters of Manuel II Palaeologus*, ed. and tr. G.T. Dennis, Washington DC: Dumbarton Oaks, 1977.

Marcellinus Comes, *Chronicon*, ed. Th. Mommsen, *MGH* AA 11, Berlin: Weidmann, 1894, 37–109; English translation by B. Croke, *The Chronicle of Marcellinus*, Sydney: Australian Association for Byzantine Studies, 1995.

Matthew of Edessa, *The Chronicle of Matthew of Edessa*, ed. and tr. A.E. Dostourian, 2 vols, unpublished PhD thesis, Rutgers University, 1972. References are by part and chapter.

Matranga, P. (ed.), *Anecdota Graeca*, Rome: Bertinelli, 1850; repr. Hildesheim/New York, 1971.

Mauropous, John, *The Letters of Ioannes Mauropous, Metropolitan of Euchaita*, ed. and tr. A. Karpozilos, Thessalonika: Association for Byzantine Research, 1990.

Menander Protector, *The History of Menander the Guardsman*, ed. and tr. R. C. Blockley, Liverpool: Francis Cairns, 1985; also in *FHG* 4.200–269. References are by book and section.

Mesarites, Nikolaos, ed. A. Heisenberg, *Die Palasrevolution des Johannes Komnenos*, Würzburg, 1907.

Michael the Syrian, tr. J.-B. Chabot, *Chronique de Michel le Syrien, Patriarche Jacobite d'Antioche*, 4 vols, Paris: Ernest Leroux, 1899–1924. References are by book and chapter.

Miklosich, F. and J. Müller, *Acta et Diplomata Graeca Medii Aevi Sacra et Profana*, 6 vols, Vienna: Gerold, 1860–90.

Narratio de Sanctis Patriarchis Tarasio et Nicephoro, PG 99: 1849–54.

Nicholas I Patriarch of Constantinople: Letters, ed. and tr. R. Jenkins and L. Westerink, Washington DC: Dumbarton Oaks, 1973.

Nikephoros, Patriarch of Constantinople: Short History, ed. and tr. C. Mango, Washington DC: *CFHB*, 1990. References are by chapter.

Odo of Deuil, *De Profectione Ludovici VII in Orientem*, ed. and tr. V.G. Berry, New York: Norton, 1948.

Patria Constantinopoleos, ed. Th. Preger, in *Scriptores Originum Constantinopolitanarum*, vol. 2, Leipzig: Teubner, 1907.

Paul the Deacon, *Historiae Langobardorum*, ed. L. Bethmann and G. Waitz, *MGH*, Scriptores Rerum Langobard. et Ital. Saec. VI–IX, Hanover, 1878; English translation by W.D. Foulke, *History of the Lombards*, Philadelphia: University of Pennsylvania Press, 1974. References are by book and chapter.

Photios, *The Homilies of Photius Patriarch of Constantinople*, tr. C. Mango, Cambridge, Mass.: Harvard University Press, 1958.

Procopius of Caesarea, *Opera*, ed. J. Haury, rev. G. Wirth, 4 vols, Leipzig: Teubner, 1962–4; ed. and tr. H.B. Dewing, 7 vols, Cambridge, Mass.: Loeb, 1914–40; and by G.A. Williamson, *Procopius: The Secret History*, Harmondsworth: Penguin, 1966 (original edn, reprinted several times).

Prodromos, Theodore, *Theodoros Prodromos: Historische Gedichte*, ed. W. Horandner, Vienna: Österreichischen Akademie der Wissenschaften, 1974.

Psellos, Michael, *Chronographia*, ed. and tr. E. Renauld, 2 vols, Paris: Budé, 1926–8; English translation by E.R.A. Sewter, *Michael Psellus: Fourteen Byzantine Rulers*, Harmondsworth: Penguin, 1966. References are by book and chapter, and by volume and page.

Psellos, 'Εἰς τὴν τελευτὴν τῆς Σκληραίνας', ed. M.D. Spadaro, *In Mariam Sclerenam: Testo critico, introduzione e commentario*, Catania: University of Catania, 1984.

Psellos, *Michaeli Pselli Historia Syntomos*, ed. and tr. W.J. Aerts, Berlin and New York: *CFHB*, 1990. References are by page.

Psellos, Michael, *Michaelis Pselli Scripta Minora*, 2 vols, ed. E. Kurtz and F. Drexl, Milan: Vita e Pensiero, 1936–41. References are by page.

Pseudo-Symeon, *Chronographia*, in Theophanes Continuatus, ed. I. Bekker, Bonn: *CSHB*, 1838, 601–760. References are by page.

Robert of Clari, *La conquête de Constantinople*, ed. P. Lauer, Paris: Budé, 1924; English translation by E.H. McNeal, *The Conquest of Constantinople*, New York: Columbia University Press, 1936. References are by chapter.

Sathas, K.N. (ed.), Μεσαιωνικὴ βιβλιοθήκη (*Bibliotheca graeca medii aevi*), 7 vols, Venice and Paris: Gregoriades, 1872–94. References are by page.

Sebeos, *Histoire d'Héraclius par l'évêque Sebêos*, tr. F. Macler, Paris: Leroux, 1904; English translation by R. Bedrosian, *Sebeos' History*, New York: Sources of the Armenian Tradition, 1985. References are by page.

Severos, *The Sixth Book of the Select Letters of Severus Patriarch of Antioch*, ed. and tr. E.W. Brooks, 2 vols, London: Williams and Norgate, 1903.

Skylitzes, John, *Ioannis Scylitae Synopsis Historiarum*, ed. I. Thurn, Berlin and New York: *CFHB*, 1973.

Skylitzes Continuatus, Ἡ συνέχεια τῆς χρονογραφίας τοῦ Ἰωάννου Σκυλίτζη, ed. E. Tsolakes, Thessalonika: Ἵδρυμα μελετῶν Χερσονήσου τοῦ Αἵμου, 1968. References are by page.

Souda, *Suidae Lexicon*, ed. A. Adler, 5 vols, Leipzig: Teubner, 1928–38.

Synaxarium Ecclesiae Constantinopolitanae, ed. H. Delehaye, *Propylaeum ad AASS Nov.*, Brussels: Société des Bollandistes, 1902.

The Synodicon Vetus, ed. and tr. J. Duffy and J. Parker, Washington DC: Dumbarton Oaks, 1979. References are by chapter.

Tabari, *Annales*, translated by J.A. Williams, *The Early 'Abbasi Empire*, 2 vols, Cambridge: Cambridge University Press, 1988–9; also trans. E.W. Brooks, 'The Byzantines and Arabs in the Time of the Early Abbasids', *EHR* 15 (1900) 728–47. References are by page.

G.L.F. Tafel and G.M. Thomas, *Urkunden zur älteren Handels- und Staatsgeschichte der Republik Venedig*, 3 vols, Vienna: Hof- und Staatsdruckerei, 1856–7.

Theodore of Stoudios (the Stoudite), *Theodori Studitae Epistulae*, ed. G. Fatouros, 2 vols, Berlin and New York: *CFHB*, 1992.

Theodore of Stoudios, 'Eulogy of his Mother', *PG* 99: 883–902.

Theodore of Stoudios, 'Eulogy of Platon', *PG* 99: 803–49.

Theophanes, *Chronographia*, ed. C. de Boor, Leipzig: *CSHB*, 1883–5; English translation by C. Mango and R. Scott, with the assistance of G. Greatrex, *The Chronicle of Theophanes Confessor: Byzantine and Near Eastern History AD 284–813*, Oxford: Clarendon Press, 1997. References are by year.

Theophanes Continuatus, *Chronographia*, ed. I. Bekker, Bonn: *CSHB*, 1838.

Theophylact of Ochrid, *Théophylacte d'Achride*, vol. 1: *Discours, traités, poésies*, ed. P. Gautier, Thessalonika: *CFHB*, 1980; vol. 2: *Lettres*, Thessalonika: *CFHB*, 1986. References are by page.

Theophylact Simocatta, *History*, ed. C. de Boor, rev. P. Wirth, Stuttgart: Teubner, 1972; English translation by M. and M. Whitby, *The History of Theophylact Simocatta: An English Translation with Introduction and Notes*, Oxford: Clarendon Press, 1986. References are by page.

Thomson, R.W., *Rewriting Caucasian History: The Medieval Armenian Adaptation of the Georgian Chronicles. The Original Georgian Texts and the Armenian Adaptation*, Oxford: Clarendon Press, 1996.

Tornikios, George and Demetrios, *Georges et Démétrius Tornikès: Lettres et discours*, ed. J. Darrouzès, Paris: Éditions du Centre National de la Recherche Scientifique, 1970.

Tzetzes, John, *Ioannis Tzetzae Historiarum Variarum Chiliades*, ed. Th. Kiessling, Leipzig: Georg Olms Verlagsbuchhandlung, 1826.

Tzetzes, John, *Epistulae*, ed. P.A.M. Leone, Leipzig: Teubner, 1972.

Tzetzes, John, *Historiae*, ed. P.A.M. Leone, Leipzig: Teubner, 1968.

van Roey, A. and P. Allen, Syriac ed. and Latin tr., *Monophysite Texts of the Sixth Century*, Leuven: Peeters, 1994.

Venantius Fortunatus, *Opera Poetica*, ed. F. Leo, *MGH AA* 4, Berlin, 1881; English translation by J. George, *Venantius Fortunatus: Personal and Political Poems*, Liverpool: Liverpool University Press, 1995.

Victor Tonnenensis, *Chronicle*, ed. Th. Mommsen, *MGH AA* 11, Berlin, 1894, 178–206.

La vie de St Cyrille le Philéote Moine Byzantin, ed. and tr. E. Sargologos, Brussels: Société des Bollandistes, 1964.

Vie de St Sabas, by Cyril of Skythopolis, ed. E. Schwartz, Leipzig: Hinrichs, 1939. References are by chapter.

Villehardouin Geoffrey of, *La conquête de Constantinople*, 2 vols, ed. E. Faral, Paris: Budé, 1938–9; English translation by M.R.B. Shaw, *Joinville and Villehardouin: Chronicles of the Crusades*, Harmondsworth: Penguin, 1963, 29–160. References are by chapter.

Vita Euthymii Patriarchae Cp., ed. and tr. P. Karlin-Hayter, Brussels: Éditions de Byzantion, 1970. References are by page.

Vita Eutychii, *PG* 86: 2273–390.

Vita Ignatii, *PG* 105: 487–574.

Vita Irenes, 'La vie de l'impératrice Sainte Irène', ed. F. Halkin, *AB* 106 (1988) 5–27; see also W.T. Treadgold, 'The Unpublished Saint's Life of the Empress Irene', *BF* 7 (1982) 237–51. References are by page.

Vita Methodii, *PG* 100: 1244–61.

Vita Michaelis Syncelli, The Life of Michael the Synkellos, ed. M.B. Cunningham, Belfast: Belfast Byzantine Enterprises, 1991.

Vita Philareti, 'La vie de S. Philarète, ed. M.-H. Fourmy and M. Leroy, *Byzantion* 9 (1934) 113–67. References are by page.

Vita S. Symeoni Iunioris, La vie ancienne de Syméon Stylite le jeune, ed. and tr. P. van den Ven, 2 vols, Brussels: Société des Bollandistes, 1962–70. References are by chapter.

Vita Tarasii, 'Ignatii Diaconi Vita Tarasii Archiepiscopi Constantinopolitani', ed. I.A. Heikel, *Acta Societatis Scientiarum Fennicae*, 17 (1891) 395–423.

Vita Theodorae, 'Βίος τῆς αὐτοκράτειρας Θεοδώρας (*BHG* 1731)', ed. A. Markopoulos, *Symmeikta* 5 (1983) 249–85; 'L'impératrice Sainte Theodora († 867)', ed. F. Halkin, *AB* 106 (1988) 28–34. References are by page.

Vita Theophanous, 'Zwie griechische Texte über die Hl. Theophano, die Gemahlin Kaisers Leo VI.', ed. E. Kurtz, *Zapiski Imp. Akad. Nauk*, 8th ser., *Hist.-phil. otdel*, 3.2, St Petersburg, 1898, 1–24. References are by page.

William, Archbishop of Tyre, *Guillaume de Tyr: Chronique*, ed. R.B.C. Huygens, 2 vols, Corpus Christianorum: Continuatio Mediaevalis, 63, 63a, Turnhout: Brepols, 1986; also in *Recueil des historiens des croisades: Historiens occidentaux*, I (1 and 2), Paris: Imprimerie Royal, 1844; English translation by Emily Atwater Babcock and A.C. Krey, *A History of Deeds Done Beyond the Sea*, 2 vols, New York: Columbia University Press, 1943. References are by book and chapter.

Yahya of Antioch, 'Histoire de Yahya-ibn-Saʿïd d'Antioche', ed. and tr. I. Kratchkovsky and A. Vasiliev, *PO* 18 (1924), 701–833.

Zachariah of Mytilene, tr. J.F. Hamilton and E.W. Brooks, *Zacharias of Mytilene: The Syrian Chronicle known as that of Zachariah of Mytilene*, London: Methuen, 1899. References are by book and chapter.

Zepos, J. and P. (eds), *Ius Graecoromanum*, 8 vols, Athens: Phexe, 1931, repr. Aalen: Scientia, 1962.

Zonaras, John, *Epitome Historiarum*, ed. T. Büttner-Wobst, vol. 3, Bonn: *CSHB*, 1897. References are by page.

Modern works

Abrahamse, D. de F. (1985) 'Women's Monasticism in the Middle Byzantine Period: Problems and Prospects', *BF* 9: 35–58.

Adshead, K. (1993) 'The Secret History of Procopius and its Genesis', *Byzantion* 63: 5–28.

Alexakis, A. (1995) 'Leo VI, Theophano, a Magistros Called Slokakas, and the Vita Theophano (*BHG* 1794)', *BF* 21: 45–56.

Alexander, P.J. (1940) 'Secular Biography at Byzantium', *Speculum*, 15: 194–209.

Alexander, P.J. (1958a) *The Patriarch Nicephorus of Constantinople: Ecclesiastical Policy and Image in the Byzantine Empire*, Oxford: Clarendon Press.

Alexander, P.J. (1958b) 'Church Councils and Patristic Authority: The Iconoclastic Councils of Hiereia (754) and St. Sophia (815)', *Harvard Studies in Classical Philology* 63: 493–505.

Alexander, P.J. (1977) 'Religious Persecution and Resistance in the Byzantine Empire of the Eighth and Ninth Centuries: Methods and Justifications', *Speculum* 52: 238–64.

Alexidze, A. (1991) 'Martha-Maria: A Striking Figure in the Cultural History of Georgia and Byzantium', in *The Greeks in the Black Sea from the Bronze Age to the Early Twentieth Century*, ed. M. Koromila, Athens: Panorama, 204–12.

Allen, P. (1981) *Evagrius Scholasticus the Church Historian*, Leuven: Spicilegium Sacrum Lovaniense.

Allen, P. (1992) 'Contemporary Portrayals of the Empress Theodora (A.D. 527–548)', in *Stereotypes of Women in Power: Historical Perspectives and Revisionist Views*, ed. B. Garlick, S. Dixon and P. Allen, New York: Greenwood, 93–103.

Anastos, M.V. (1954) 'The Ethical Theory of Images Formulated by the Iconoclasts in 754 and 815', *DOP* 8: 153–60.

Anastos, M.V. (1955) 'The Argument for Iconoclasm as Presented by the Iconoclastic Council of 754', in *Late Classical and Medieval Studies in Honor of Albert Mathias Friend Jr*, ed. K. Weitzmann, Princeton: Princeton University Press, 177–88 (= *Studies in Byzantine Intellectual History*, London: Variorum, 1979, X).

Anastos, M.V. (1966) 'Iconoclasm and Imperial Rule 717–842', in *The Cambridge Medieval History*, vol. 4.1, ed. J.M. Hussey, Cambridge: Cambridge University Press, 61–104.

Anastos, M.V. (1975) '*Vox populi voluntas Dei* and the Election of the Byzantine Emperor,' in *Christianity, Judaism and other Greco-Roman Cults: Studies for Morton Smith*, ed. J. Neusner, Leiden: Brill, 181–207 (= *Studies in Byzantine Intellectual History*, London: Variorum, 1979, III).

Anastos, M.V. (1993) 'The Coronation of Emperor Michael IV in 1034 by Empress Zoe and its Significance', in *To Ellenikon: Studies in Honor of Speros Vryonis Jr*, vol. 1, ed. J.S. Langdon *et al.*, New Rochelle, N.Y.: Caratzas, 23–43.

Angold, M., ed. (1984a) *The Byzantine Aristocracy IX to XIII Centuries*, Oxford: British Archaeological Reports.

Angold, M. (1984b) *The Byzantine Empire: A Political History*, London and New York: Longman.

Angold, M. (1995) *Church and Society in Byzantium under the Comneni, 1081–1261*, Cambridge, Cambridge University Press.

Arvites, J. (1983) 'The Defense of Byzantine Anatolia during the Reign of Irene

(780–802)', in *Armies and Frontiers in Roman and Byzantine Anatolia*, ed. S. Mitchell, Oxford: British Archaeological Reports, 219–37.

Baldwin, B. (1992) 'Three-obol Girls in Procopius', *Hermes* 120: 255–7.

Barber, C. (1990) 'The Imperial Panels at San Vitale: A Reconsideration', *BMGS* 14: 19–42.

Barker, J.W. (1966) *Justinian and the Later Roman Empire*, Madison: University of Wisconsin Press.

Beaton, R. and C. Roueché, eds (1993) *The Making of Byzantine History: Studies Dedicated to Donald M. Nicol on his 70th Birthday*, Aldershot: Variorum.

Beauchamp, J. (1977) 'La situation juridique de la femme à Byzance', *Cahiers de civilisation médiévale* 20: 145–76.

Beauchamp, J. (1982) 'L'allaitement: mère ou nourrice?', *JÖB* 32(2): 549–58.

Beauchamp, J. (1990) *Le statut de la femme à Byzance (4e–7e siècle)*, 2 vols, Paris: de Boccard.

Beck, H.-G. (1959) *Kirche und theologische Literatur im byzantinischen Reich*, Munich: Beck.

Beck, H.-G. (1986) *Kaiserin Theodora und Prokop: Der historiker und sein Opfer*, Munich: Piper.

Beckwith, J. (1968) *The Art of Constantinople*, 2nd edn, London and New York: Phaidon.

Bellinger, A.R. (1966) *Catalogue of the Byzantine Coins in the Dumbarton Oaks Collection and in the Whittemore Collection*, vol. 1: *Anastasius to Maurice 491–602*, Washington DC: Dumbarton Oaks.

Bensammar, E. (1976) 'La titulature de l'impératrice et sa signification: Recherches sur les sources byzantines de la fin du VIIIe siècle à la fin du XIIe siècle', *Byzantion* 46: 243–91.

Blockley, R.C. (1980) 'Doctors as Diplomats in the Sixth Century A.D.', *Florilegium* 2: 89–100.

Bonner, C. (1952) 'A Story of Iconoclastic Times', *Byzantion* 22: 237–41.

Boojamra, J.L. (1974) 'The Eastern Schism of 907 and the Affair of the Tetragamia', *Journal of Ecclesiastical History* 25: 113–33.

Bordier, H. (1883) *Description des peintures et autres ornements contenus dans les manuscrits grecs de la Bibliothèque Nationale*, Paris: Champion.

Bosch, U.V. (1966) 'Anthusa, ein Beitrag zum Kaisertum der Eirene', *Polychordia. Festschrift Franz Dölger, BF* 1: 24–9.

Bosch, U.V. (1979) 'Einige Bemerkungen zum Kanzleiwesen der byzantinischen Kaiserin', in *Byzance et les Slaves: Mélanges Ivan Dujchev*, Paris: Association des Amis des Études Archéologiques, 83–102.

Brand, C.M. (1968) *Byzantium Confronts the West 1180–1204*, Cambridge, Mass.: Harvard University Press.

Brand, C.M. (1993) 'Some Women of Thebes – and Elsewhere', in *To Hellenikon: Studies in Honor of Speros Vryonis*, vol. 1, New Rochelle, N.Y.: Caratzas, 59–68.

Brennan, B. (1995) 'Venantius Fortunatus: Byzantine Agent?', *Byzantion* 65: 7–16.

Brokkarr, W.G. (1972) 'Basil Lacapenu, Byzantium in the Tenth Century', in *Studia Byzantina et Neohellenica Neerlandia*, ed. W.F. Bakker *et al.*, Leiden: Brill, 199–234.

Brooks, E.W. (1900) 'On the Date of the Death of Constantine the Son of Irene', *BZ* 9: 654–7.

Brooks, E.W. (1901) 'The Marriage of the Emperor Theophilus', *BZ* 10: 540–45.

Brosset, M. (1849) *Historie de la Géorgie depuis l'antiquité jusqu'au XIXe siècle*, vol. 1, St Petersberg: Académie Impériale des Sciences.

Brown, P. (1973) 'A Dark Age Crisis: Aspects of the Iconoclastic Controversy', *EHR* 88: 1–34.

Brown, P. (1982) *Society and the Holy in Late Antiquity*, Berkeley: University of California Press.

Brown, T.S. (1995) 'Byzantine Italy, c. 680–c. 876', in *The New Cambridge Medieval History*, vol. 2: *c. 700–c. 900*, ed. R. McKitterick, Cambridge: Cambridge University Press, 320–48.

Browning, R. (1962) 'An Unpublished Funeral Oration on Anna Comnena', *Proceedings of the Cambridge Philosophical Society* 188, n.s. 8: 1–12.

Browning, R. (1965) 'Notes on the "Scriptor Incertus de Leone Armenio"', *Byzantion* 35: 389–411.

Browning, R. (1975) *Byzantium and Bulgaria: A Comparative Study across the Early Medieval Frontier*, Berkeley and Los Angeles: University of California Press.

Brubaker, L. (1989) 'Byzantine Art in the Ninth Century: Theory, Practice and Culture', *BMGS* 13: 23–94.

Bryer, A. and J. Herrin, eds (1977) *Iconoclasm: Papers given at the Ninth Spring Symposium of Byzantine Studies, University of Birmingham (1975)*, Birmingham: University of Birmingham.

Buckler, G. (1936) 'Women in Byzantine Law about 1100 A.D.', *Byzantion* 11: 391–416.

Bury, J.B. (1889a) *A History of the Later Roman Empire from Arcadius to Irene (395–800)*, 2 vols, London: Macmillan.

Bury, J.B. (1889b) 'Roman Emperors from Basil II to Issac Komnenos', *EHR* 4: 41–64, 251–85.

Bury, J.B. (1912) *A History of the Eastern Roman Empire from the Fall of Irene to the Accession of Basil I*, London: Macmillan.

Cameron, Alan (1976) *Circus Factions: The Blues and Greens in Rome and Byzantium*, Oxford: Clarendon Press.

Cameron, Alan (1978) 'The House of Anastasius', *GRBS* 19: 259–76.

Cameron, Averil (1968) 'Notes on the Sophiae, the Sophianae, and the Harbour of Sophia', *Byzantion* 37: 11–20.

Cameron, Averil (1975a) 'The Byzantine Sources of Gregory of Tours', *JTS* 26: 421–6.

Cameron, Averil (1975b) 'The Empress Sophia', *Byzantion* 45: 5–21.

Cameron, Averil (1976), 'The Early Religious Policies of Justin II', in *The Orthodox Churches and the West* (Studies in Church History 13), ed. D. Baker, Oxford: Blackwell, 51–67.

Cameron, Averil (1977) 'Early Byzantine *Kaiserkritik*: Two Case Histories', *BMGS* 3: 1–17.

Cameron, Averil (1978) 'The Theotokos in Sixth-century Constantinople', *JTS* n.s. 29: 79–108.

Cameron, Averil (1979) 'Images of Authority: Elites and Icons in Late Sixth-century Byzantium', *PP* 84: 3–35.

Cameron, Averil (1980) 'The Artistic Patronage of Justin II', *Byzantion* 50: 62–84.

Cameron, Averil (1985) *Procopius*, Berkeley and Los Angeles: University of California Press.

Cameron, Averil (1986) 'An Emperor's Abdication', *BS* 37: 161–7.

Cameron, A. and A. Kuhrt, eds (1983) *Images of Women in Antiquity*, London: Croom Helm.

Chalandon, F. (1971) *Jean II Comnène (1118–1143) et Manuel I Comnène (1143–1180)* Paris: Picard, 1912; repr. New York: Burt Franklin.

Chamberlain, C. (1986) 'The Theory and Practice of Imperial Panegyric in Michael Psellos: The Tension between History and Rhetoric', *Byzantion* 56: 16–27.

Charanis, P. (1961) 'The Armenians in the Byzantine Empire', *BS* 22: 196–240.

Charanis, P. (1974) *Church and State in the Later Roman Empire*, 2nd edn, Thessalonika: Kentron Vyzantinon Ereunon.

Cheynet, J.-C. (1986) 'Les Phocas', in *Le traité sur la guerilla de l'empereur Nicéphore Phocas (963–969)*, ed. G. Dagron and H. Mihaescu, Paris: Éditions de Centre National de la Recherche Scientifique, 289–315.

Cheynet, J.-C. (1990) *Pouvoir et contestations à Byzance (963–1210)*, Paris: Sorbonne.

Cheynet, J.-C. and B. Flusin (1990) 'Du monastère ta Kathara à Thessalonique: Théodore Stoudite sur la route de l'éxil', *REB* 48: 193–211.

Cheynet, J.-C. and J.-F. Vannier (1986) *Études prosopographiques*, Paris: Sorbonne.

Christophilopoulou, A. (1970) Ἡ ἀντιβασιλεία εἰς τὸ Βυζάντιον', *Symmeikta* 2: 1–144.

Chrysostomides, J. (1982) 'Italian Women in Greece in the Late Fourteenth and Early Fifteenth Centuries', *RSBS* 2: 119–32.

Ciggaar, K. (1995) 'Theophano: An Empress Reconsidered', in *The Empress Theophano: Byzantium and the West at the Turn of the First Millennium*, ed. A. Davids, Cambridge: Cambridge University Press, 49–63.

Clark, G. (1993) *Women in Late Antiquity: Pagan and Christian Lifestyles*, Oxford: Clarendon Press.

Clucas, L. (1981) *The Trial of John Italos and the Crisis of Intellectual Values in the Eleventh Century*, Munich: Institut für Byzantinistik.

Congourdeau, M.-H. (1993) 'Regardes sur l'enfant nouveau-né à Byzance', *REB* 51: 161–76.

Constantelos, D.J. (1991) *Byzantine Philanthropy and Social Welfare*, 2nd edn, New Rochelle: Caratzas.

Constantinidi-Bibikou, H. (1950) 'Yolande de Montferrat impératrice de Byzance', *L'hellénisme contemporain*, series 2, 4: 425–42.

Cormack, R. (1977) 'The Arts During the Age of Iconoclasm', in *Iconoclasm*, ed. A. Bryer and J. Herrin, Birmingham: University of Birmingham, 35–44.

Cormack, R. (1981) 'Interpreting the Mosaics of S. Sophia at Istanbul', *Art History* 4: 131–49.

Crostini, B. (1996) 'The Emperor Basil II's Cultural Life', *Byzantion* 66: 55–80.

da Costa-Luillet, G. (1954) 'Saints de Constantinople aux VIIIe, IXe et Xe siècles', *Byzantion* 24: 179–263.

Dagron, G. (1994a) 'Nés dans la Pourpre', *TM* 12: 105–42.

Dagron, G. (1994b) 'Théophanô, les Saints-Apôtres et l'église de Tous-les-Saints', *Symmeikta* 11: 201–17.

Darrouzès, J. (1968) 'Les discours d'Euthyme Tornikès (1200–1205)', *REB* 26: 49–121.

Darrouzès, J. (1975) 'Listes épiscopales du concile de Nicée (787)', *REB* 33: 5–76.

Daube, D. (1967) 'The Marriage of Justinian and Theodora: Legal and Theological Reflections', *Catholic University Law Review*, 16: 380–99.

Davids, A., ed. (1995a) *The Empress Theophano: Byzantium and the West at the Turn of the First Millennium*, Cambridge: Cambridge University Press.

Davids, A. (1995b) 'Marriage Negotiations between Byzantium and the West and the Name of Theophano in Byzantium (Eighth to Tenth Centuries)', in *The Empress Theophano: Byzantium and the West at the Turn of the First Millennium*, ed. A. Davids, Cambridge: Cambridge University Press, 99–120.

Diehl, C. (1938–9) *Figures byzantines*, 2nd edn, 2 vols, Paris: Armand Colin.

Diehl, C. (1964) *Byzantine Empresses*, tr. H. Bell and T. de Kerpley, London: Elek.

Dieten, J.L. van (1972) *Geschichte der Patriarchen von Sergios I. bis Johannes VI. (610–715)*, Amsterdam: Hakkert.

Diethart, J. and E. Kislinger (1991) 'Papyrologisches zur Prostitution im byzantinischen Ägypten', *JÖB* 41: 15–23.

Dölger, F. (1924–65) *Regesten der Kaiserkunden des oströmischen Reiches*, 5 vols, Munich and Berlin: Beck.

Dölger, F. (1936) Review of E. Stein, 'Postconsulat et αὐτοκρατορία' (*AIPHOS* 2 (1933/4)), *BZ* 36: 123–45.

Dölger, F. (1961) 'Zum Kaisertum des Anna von Savoyen', in F. Dölger, *Paraspora: 30 Aufsätze zur Geschichte, Kultur und Sprache des byzantinischen Reiches*, Munich: Buch-Kunstverlag Ettal, 208–21.

Downey, G. (1956) 'The Church of All Saints (Church of St Theophano) near the Church of the Holy Apostles at Constantinople', *DOP* 9–10: 301–5.

Downey, G. (1959) 'The Tombs of the Byzantine Emperors at the Church of the Holy Apostles in Constantinople', *JHS* 79: 27–51.

Duffy, J. (1995) 'Reactions of Two Byzantine Intellectuals to the Theory and Practice of Magic: Michael Psellos and Michael Italikos', in *Byzantine Magic*, ed. H. Maguire, Washington DC: Dumbarton Oaks, 83–97.

Dumeige, G. (1978) *Nicée II*, Histoire des conciles oecuméniques 4, Paris: de l'Orante.

Dvornik, F. (1953) 'The Patriarch Photius and Iconoclasm', *DOP* 7: 69–97.

Dvornik, F. (1966) 'Patriarch Ignatius and the Caesar Bardas', *BS* 27: 7–22.

Epstein, A.W. (1981) 'Formulas for Salvation: A Comparison of Two Byzantine Monasteries and their Founders', *Church History* 50: 385–400.

Euw, A. von and P. Schreiner (1991) *Kaiserin Theophanu: Begegnung des Ostens und Westens um die Wende des ersten Jahrtausends*, 2 vols, Cologne.

Evans, J.A.S. (1975) 'The Secret History and the Art of Procopius', *Prudentia* 7(2): 105–9.

Evans, J.A.S. (1982) 'The Holy Women of the Monophysites', *JÖB* 32.2: 525–8.

Evans, J.A.S. (1984) 'The "Nika" Rebellion and the Empress Theodora', *Byzantion* 54: 381–3.

Evans, J.A.S. (1996a) *The Age of Justinian: The Circumstances of Imperial Power*, London and New York: Routledge and Kegan Paul.

Evans, J.A.S. (1996b) 'The Dates of Procopius' Works: A Recapitulation of the Evidence', *GRBS* 37: 301–13.

Every, G. (1962) *The Byzantine Patriarchate 451–1204*, 2nd edn, London: SPCK.

Falkenhausen, V. von (1982) 'Olympias, eine normannische Prinzessin in Konstantinopel,' in *Bisanzio e l'Italia: Raccolta di studi in memoria di Agostino Pertusi*, Milan: Vita e Pensiero, 56–72.

Fisher, E.A. (1973) 'Theodora and Antonina in the Historia Arcana: History and/or Fiction?' *Arethusa* 11: 253–79.

Fitton, J. (1976) 'The Death of Theodora', *Byzantion* 46: 119.

Follieri, E. (1964) 'Le poesie di Cristoforo Mitileneo come fonte storica', *ZRVI* 8(2): 133–48.

Frazee, C. (1981) 'St Theodore of Studius and Ninth-century Monasticism in Constantinople', *Studia Monastica* 23: 27–58.

Frend, W.H.C. (1972) *The Rise of the Monophysite Movement*, Cambridge: Cambridge University Press.

Galatariotou, C. (1984/5) 'Holy Women and Witches: Aspects of Byzantine Conceptions of Gender', *BMGS* 9: 55–94.

Galatariotou, C. (1987) 'Byzantine Ktetorika Typika: A Comparative Study', *REB* 45: 77–138.

Galatariotou, C. (1988) 'Byzantine Women's Monastic Communities: The Evidence of the Typika', *JÖB* 38: 263–90.

Galatariotou, C. (1989) '*Eros* and *Thanatos*: A Byzantine Hermit's conception of Sexuality', *BMGS* 13: 95–137.

Gamillscheg, E. (1991) 'Zoe und Theodora als Träger dynastischer Vorstellungen in den Geschichtsquellen ihrer Epoche', in *Kaiserin Theophanu: Begegnung des Ostens und Westens um die Wende des ersten Jahrtausends*, ed. A. von Euw and P. Schreiner, vol. 2, Cologne: Kölner Schnütgen Museum, 397–401.

Gardner, J. (1986) *Women in Roman Law and Society*, London: Croom Helm.

Garland, L. (1988) 'The Life and Ideology of Byzantine Women: A Further Note on Conventions of Behaviour and Social Reality as Reflected in Eleventh and Twelfth Century Historical Sources', *Byzantion* 58: 361–93.

Garland, L. (1990) ' "And his Bald Head Shone Like a Full Moon . . .": An Appreciation of the Byzantine Sense of Humour as Recorded in Historical Sources of the Eleventh and Twelfth Centuries', *Parergon*, n.s. 8: 1–31.

Garland, L. (1992) 'Political Power and the Populace in Byzantium Prior to the Fourth Crusade', *BS* 53: 17–52.

Garland, L. (1994) ' "The Eye of the Beholder": Byzantine Imperial Women and their Public Image from Zoe Porphyrogenita to Euphrosyne Kamaterissa Doukaina (1028–1203)', *Byzantion* 64: 19–39, 261–313.

Garland, L. (1995) 'Conformity and Licence at the Byzantine Court in the Eleventh and Twelfth Centuries', *BF* 21: 101–15.

Garland, L. (1995/6) ' "How Different, How Very Different from the Home Life of Our Own Dear Queen": Sexual Morality at the Late Byzantine Court, with Especial Reference to the Eleventh and Twelfth Centuries', *BS/EB* n.s. 1/2: 1–62.

Garland, L. (1997) 'Morality versus Politics at the Byzantine Court: The Charges against Marie of Antioch and Euphrosyne', *BF* 24: 259–95.

Geanakoplos, D.J. (1966) *Byzantine East and Latin West: Two Worlds of Christendom in the Middle Ages and Renaissance*, Oxford: Barnes and Noble, 55–83.

Gero, S. (1977) *Byzantine Iconoclasm during the Reign of Constantine V, with Particular Attention to the Oriental Sources*, Louvain: Corpusso.

Gerstel, S.E.J. (1997) 'Saint Eudokia and the Imperial Household of Leo VI', *Art Bulletin* 79: 699–707.

Gill, J. (1985) 'Matrons and Brides of Fourteenth-century Byzantium', *BF* 9: 39–56.

Gouillard, J. (1961) 'Deux figures mal connues du second iconoclasme', *Byzantion* 21: 371–401.

Grabar, A. (1971) *L'empereur dans l'art byzantine*, London: Variorum.

Grabar, A. and M. Manoussacas (1979) *L'illustration du manuscrit de Skylitzès de la Bibliothèque Nationale de Madrid*, Venice: Institut Hellenique d'Études Byzantines.

Greatrex, G. (1994) 'The Dates of Procopius' Works', *BMGS* 18: 101–14.

Greatrex, G. (1995) 'The Composition of Procopius' *Persian Wars* and John the Cappadocian', *Prudentia* 27: 1–13.

Greenfield, R.P.H. (1988) *Traditions of Belief in Late Byzantine Demonology*, Amsterdam: Hakkert.

Greenfield, R.P.H. (1993) 'Sorcery and Politics at the Byzantine Court in the Twelfth Century: Interpretations of History', in *The Making of Byzantine History*, ed. R. Beaton and C. Roueché, Aldershot: Variorum, 73–85.

Grégoire, H. (1966) 'The Amorians and Macedonians 842–1025', in *The Cambridge Medieval History*, vol. 4.1, ed. J.M. Hussey, Cambridge: Cambridge University Press, 105–92.

Grierson, P. (1962) 'The Tombs and Obits of the Byzantine Emperors (337–1042)', *DOP* 16: 1–63.

Grierson, P. (1968–73) *Catalogue of the Byzantine Coins in the Dumbarton Oaks Collection and in the Whittemore Collection*, vols 2.1–2, 3.1–2, Washington DC: Dumbarton Oaks.

Grierson, P. (1981) 'The Carolingian Empire in the Eyes of Byzantium', *Settimane di studio del centro italiano di studi sull'alto medievo* 27: 885–916.

Grierson, P. (1982) *Byzantine Coins*, London: Methuen.

Grierson, P. and R. Jenkins (1962) 'The Date of Constantine VII's Coronation', *Byzantion* 32: 132–8.

Grumel, V. (1936) 'La chronologie des événements du regne de Léon VI', *EO* 35: 5–42.

Grumel, V. (1989) *Les regestes des actes du patriarchat de Constantinople*, vol. 1 (fasc. 2 and 3), revised edn, Paris: Institut Français d'Études Byzantines.

Guilland, A. and J. Durand, eds (1994) *Byzance et les images*, Paris: La Documentation française.

Guilland, R. (1943) 'Les eunuques dans l'empire byzantine', *REB* 1: 196–238.

Guilland, R. (1944) 'Fonctions et dignités des eunuques, I', *REB* 2: 185–225.

Guilland, R. (1945) 'Fonctions et dignités des eunuques, II', *REB* 3: 179–214.

Guilland, R. (1953) 'Le palais du Boukoléon: l'assassinat de Nicéphore II Phokas', *BS* 13: 101–36.

Guilland, R. (1967) 'La cérémonial de la προσκύνησις', in *Recherches sur les institutions byzantines*, ed. R. Guilland, vol. 1, Amsterdam: Hakkert, 144–50.

Guilland, R. (1971) 'Les logothètes', *REB* 29: 1–115.

Hackel, S., ed. (1981) *The Byzantine Saint*, London: Fellowship of St Alban and St Sergius.

Haldon, J. (1975) *Aspects of Byzantine Military Administration: The Elite Corps, the Opsikion, and the Imperial Tagmata from the Sixth to the Ninth Century*, Birmingham: University of Birmingham.

Haldon, J. (1984) *Byzantine Praetorians: An Administrative, Institutional and Social Survey of the Opsikion and Tagmata, c. 580–900*, Bonn: Habelt.

Haldon, J. (1986) 'Ideology and Social Change in the Seventh Century: Military Discontent as a Barometer', *Klio* 68: 139–90.

Haldon, J. (1990) *Byzantium in the Seventh Century*, Cambridge: Cambridge University Press.

Haldon, J.F. (1993) 'Military Service, Military Lands, and the Status of Soldiers: Current Problems and Interpretations', *DOP* 47: 1–67.

Halkin, F. (1954) 'Trois dates historiques précisées grace au Synaxaire', *Byzantion* 24: 7–17.

Halkin, F., ed. (1965) *Euphémie de Chalcédoine: Légendes byzantines*, Brussels: Société des Bollandistes.

Hans, L.M. (1988) 'Der Kaiser als Märchenprinz: Brautschau und Heiratspolitik in Konstantinopel 395–882', *JÖB* 38: 33–52.

Hardy, E.R. (1968) 'The Egyptian Policy of Justinian', *DOP* 22: 23–41.

Harrison, M. (1989), with foreword by S. Runciman, *A Temple for Byzantium: The Discovery and Excavation of Anicia Juliana's Palace Church in Istanbul*, London: Harvey Miller.

Harvey, A. (1989) *Economic Expansion in the Byzantine Empire 900–1200*, Cambridge: Cambridge University Press.

Hatlie, P. (1996) 'Women of Discipline During the Second Iconoclast Age', *BZ* 89: 37–44.

Hendrickx, B. and C. Matzukis (1979) 'Alexios V Doukas Mourtzouphlos: His Life, Reign and Death', *Hellenika* 31: 108–32.

Hendy, M.F. (1969) *Coinage and Money in the Byzantine Empire 1081–1261*, Washington DC: Dumbarton Oaks.

Hendy, M. (1985) *Studies in the Byzantine Monetary Economy, c. 300–1450*, Cambridge.

Henry, P. (1969) 'The Moechian Controversy and the Constantinopolitan Synod of Jan., AD 809', *JTS* 20: 495–522.

Henry, P. (1976) 'What was the Iconoclastic Controversy About?', *Church History* 45: 16–31.

Hero, A.C. (1985) 'Irene-Eulogia Choumnaina Palaiologina Abbess of the Convent of Philanthropos Soter in Constantinople', *BF* 9: 119–47.

Hero, A.C. (1986) *A Woman's Quest for Spiritual Guidance: The Correspondence of Princess Irene Eulogia Choumnaina Palaiologina*, Brookline, Mass.: Hellenic College Press.

Herrin, J. (1983a) 'In Search of Byzantine Women: Three Avenues of Approach', in *Images of Women in Antiquity*, ed. A. Cameron and A. Kuhrt, Detroit: Wayne State University Press, 167–89.

Herrin, J. (1983b) 'Women and the Faith in Icons in Early Christianity', in *Culture, Ideology and Politics: Essays for Eric Hobsbawm*, ed. R. Samuel and G. Stedman Jones, London: Routledge and Kegan Paul, 56–83.

Herrin, J. (1987) *The Formation of Christendom*, Princeton: Princeton University Press.

Herrin, J. (1995) 'Theophano: Considerations on the Education of a Byzantine Princess', in *The Empress Theophano: Byzantium and the West at the Turn of the First Millennium*, ed. A. Davids, Cambridge: Cambridge University Press, 64–85.

Hiestand, R. (1990) 'Eirene Basileus: die Frau als Herrscherin im Mittelalter', in *Der Herrscher: Leitbild und Abbild im Mittelalter und Renaissance*, ed. H. Hecker, Düsseldorf: Droste, 253–83.

Hill, B. (1996a) 'Alexios I Komnenos and the Imperial Women', in *Alexios I Komnenos*, vol. 1: *Papers*, ed. M. Mullett and D. Smythe, Belfast: Belfast Byzantine Enterprises, 37–54.

Hill, B. (1996b) 'The Ideal Imperial Komnenian Woman', *BF* 23: 7–17.

Hill, B. (1996c) 'A Vindication of the Rights of Women to Power by Anna Komnene', *BF* 23: 45–53.

Hill, B., L. James and D. Smythe (1994) 'Zoe: The Rhythm Method of Imperial Renewal', in *New Constantines: The Rhythm of Imperial Renewal in Byzantium, 4th–13th Centuries*, ed. P. Magdalino, Aldershot: Variorum, 215–29.

Holum, K.G. (1982) *Theodosian Empresses: Women and Imperial Domination in Late Antiquity*, Berkeley and Los Angeles: University of California Press.

Honoré, T. (1978) *Tribonian*, London: Duckworth.

Hunger, H. (1965) 'Die Schönheitskonkurrenz in "Belthandros und Chrysantza" und die Brautschau am byzantinischen Kaiserhof', *Byzantion* 35: 150–58.

Hunt, L.-A. (1984) 'Comnenian Aristocratic Palace Decorations: Descriptions and Islamic Connections', in *The Byzantine Aristocracy IX to XIII Centuries*, ed. M. Angold, Oxford: British Archaeological Reports, 138–57.

Hussey, J.M. (1937) *Church and Learning in the Byzantine Empire 867–1185*, London: Oxford University Press.

Hussey, J.M. (1986) *The Orthodox Church in the Byzantine Empire*, Oxford: Clarendon Press.

Huxley, G. (1975) 'The Emperor Michael III and the Battle of Bishops' Meadow', *GRBS* 16: 443–50.

Irmscher, J. (1989) 'Ἡ πορνεία στὸ Βυζάντιο', in *Ἡ καθημερινὴ ζωὴ στὸ Βυζάντιο: Πρακτικὰ τοῦ Α´ διεθνοῦς συμποσίου*, 15–17 September 1988, Athens: Κέντρο Βυζαντινῶν Ἐρευνῶν, 253–8.

Irmscher, J. (1996) 'Bertha von Sulzbach, Gemahlin Manuels I', *BF* 22: 279–90.

Janin, R. (1964) *Constantinople byzantine: Développement urbain et répertoire topographique*, 2nd edn, Paris: Institut Français d'Études Byzantines.

Janin, R. (1969) *La géographie ecclésiastique de l'Empire byzantin*, 1: *Le siège de Constantinople et le patriarchat oecuménique*, 3: *Les églises et les monastères*, 2nd edn, Paris: Institut Français d'Études Byzantines.

Jeffreys, E.M. (1980) 'The Comnenian Background to the "romans d'antiquité"', *Byzantion* 50: 455–86.

Jeffreys, E.M. (1982) 'The Sevastokratorissa Eirene as Literary Patroness: The Monk Iakovos', *JÖB* 32.3: 63–71.

Jeffreys, E.M. (1984) 'Western Infiltration of the Byzantine Aristocracy: Some Suggestions', in *The Byzantine Aristocracy IX to XIII Centuries*, ed. M. Angold, Oxford: British Archaeological Reports, 202–10.

Jeffreys, E.M. and M.J. (1994) 'Who was Eirene the Sevastokratorissa?' *Byzantion* 64: 40–68.

Jeffreys, M.J. (1974) 'The Nature and Origins of the Political Verse', *DOP* 28: 141–95.

Jeffreys, M.J. (1981) 'The Vernacular εἰσιτήριοι for Agnes of France', *Byzantine Papers: Proceedings of the First Australian Byzantine Studies Conference, Canberra, 17–19 May 1978*, ed. E. Jeffreys, M. Jeffreys and A. Moffatt, Canberra: Australian Association for Byzantine Studies, 101–15.

Jeffreys, M.J. (1987) 'The Comnenian Prokypsis', *Parergon* n.s. 5: 38–53.

Jenkins, R.J.H. (1948a) 'Constantine VII's Portrait of Michael III', *Bulletin de la classe des lettres et des sciences morales et politiques, Académie Royale de Belgique (5e série)*, 34: 71–7 (= *Studies on Byzantine History of the Ninth and Tenth Centuries*, London: Variorum, 1970, I).

Jenkins, R.J.H. (1948b) 'The Flight of Samonas', *Speculum* 23(2): 217–35.

Jenkins, R.J.H. (1962) 'Three Documents Concerning the Tetragamy', *DOP* 16:

231–41 (= *Studies on Byzantine History of the Ninth and Tenth Centuries*, London: Variorum, 1970, VIII).

Jenkins, R.J.H. (1963) 'A Note on the Patriarch Nicholas Mysticus', *Acta Antiqua Academiae Scientiarum Hungaricae*, 2: 145–7.

Jenkins, R.J.H. (1965a) 'The Chronological Accuracy of the "*logothete*" for the Years A.D. 867–913', *DOP* 19: 91–112.

Jenkins, R.J.H (1965b) 'A "Consolatio" of the Patriarch Nicholas Mysticus', *Byzantion* 35: 159–66.

Jenkins, R.J.H. (1965c) 'A Note on Nicetas David Paphlago and the *Vita Ignatii*', *DOP* 19: 241–7.

Jenkins, R.J.H. (1966) *Byzantium: The Imperial Centuries AD 610–1071*, London: Weidenfeld and Nicolson.

Jenkins, R.J.H. (1970) *Studies on Byzantine History of the Ninth and Tenth Centuries*, London: Variorum.

Jenkins, R.J.H. and B. Laourdas (1956) 'Eight Letters of Arethas on the Fourth Marriage of Leo the Wise', *Hellenika* 14: 293–370 (= *Studies on Byzantine History of the Ninth and Tenth Centuries*, London: Variorum, 1970, VII).

Jenkins, R.J.H. and C.A. Mango (1955/6) 'The Date and Significance of the Xth Homily of Photius', *DOP* 9/10: 125–40.

Johnson, G.J. (1982) 'Constantine VIII and Michael Psellos: Rhetoric, Reality and the Decline of Byzantium, A.D. 1025–28', *BS/EB* 9(2): 220–32.

Jones, A.H.M. (1964) *The Later Roman Empire 284–602: A Social, Economic and Administrative Survey*, 2 vols, Oxford: Blackwell.

Kaegi, W.E. (1966) 'The Byzantine Armies and Iconoclasm', *BS* 27: 48–70.

Kaegi, W.E. (1981) *Byzantine Military Unrest 471–843: An Interpretation*, Amsterdam: Hakkert.

Kaegi, W.E. (1982) 'Heraclius and the Arabs', *GOTR* 27: 109–33.

Kaegi, W.E. (1992) *Byzantium and the Early Islamic Conquests*, Cambridge: Cambridge University Press.

Kalavrezou-Maxeiner, I. (1977) 'Eudokia Makrembolitissa and the Romanos Ivory', *DOP* 31: 305–25.

Kalavrezou, I. (1994) 'Irregular Marriages in the Eleventh Century and the Zoe and Constantine Mosaic in Hagia Sophia', in *Law and Society in Byzantium, Ninth to Twelfth Centuries*, ed. A.E. Laiou and D. Simon, Washington DC: Dumbarton Oaks, 241–59.

Karlin-Hayter, P. (1966) 'The Revolt of Andronicus Ducas', *BS* 27: 23–5.

Karlin-Hayter, P. (1969a) 'The Emperor Alexander's Bad Name', *Speculum* 44: 585–96.

Karlin-Hayter, P. (1969b) 'La mort de Théophano (10.11.896 ou 895)', *BZ* 62: 13–19.

Karlin-Hayter, P. (1970) 'Le synode à Constantinople de 886 à 912 et le role de Nicolas le Mystique dans l'affaire de la tétragamie', *JÖB* 19: 59–101.

Karlin-Hayter, P. (1971) 'Études sur les deux histoires du règne de Michel III', *Byzantion* 41: 452–96.

Karlin-Hayter, P. (1987) 'Imperial Charioteers Seen by the Senate or by the Plebs', *Byzantion* 57: 326–35.

Karlin-Hayter, P. (1989) 'Michael III and Money', *BS* 50(1): 1–8.

Karlin-Hayter, P. (1991) 'L'enjeu d'une rumeur: Opinion et imaginaire à Byzance au IXe siècle', *JÖB* 14: 85–111.

Kazhdan, A. (1988/9) 'Rus'-Byzantine Princely Marriages in the Eleventh and Twelfth Centuries', *HUS* 12–13: 414–29.

Kazhdan, A. (1990) 'Byzantine Hagiography and Sex in the Fifth–Twelfth Centuries', *DOP* 44: 131–43.

Kazhdan, A. and G. Constable (1982) *People and Power in Byzantium: An Introduction to Modern Byzantine Studies*, Washington DC: Dumbarton Oaks.

Kazhdan, A.P. and A.W. Epstein (1985) *Change in Byzantine Culture in the Eleventh and Twelfth Centuries*, Berkeley, Los Angeles, and London: University of California Press.

Kazhdan, A. (with S. Franklin) (1984) *Studies on Byzantine Literature of the Eleventh and Twelfth Centuries*, Cambridge: Cambridge University Press.

Kazhdan, A.P. and M. McCormick (1997) 'The Social World of the Byzantine Court', in *Byzantine Court Culture from 829 to 1204*, ed. H. Maguire, Washington DC: Dumbarton Oaks, 167–97.

Kazhdan, A. and L.F. Sherry (1996) 'The Tale of a Happy Fool: The *Vita* of St. Philaretos the Merciful (*BHG* 1511z–1512b)', *Byzantion* 66: 351–62.

Kazhdan, A.P. and A.-M. Talbot (1991/2) 'Women and Iconoclasm', *BZ* 84/5: 391–408.

Kislinger, E. (1983) 'Eudokia Ingerina, Basileios I., und Michael III.', *JÖB* 33: 119–36.

Kislinger, E. (1986) 'Der kranke Justin II. und die ärztliche Haftung bei Operationem in Byzanz', *JÖB* 36: 39–44.

Kislinger, E. (1987) 'Michael III: Image und Realität', *Eos* 75: 389–400.

Kitzinger, E. (1954) 'The Cult of Images before Iconoclasm', *DOP* 8: 83–150.

Kountoura-Galake, E.S. (1987) Ἡ ἁγία Εὐφημία στὶς σχέσεις παπῶν καὶ αὐτοκρατόρων', *Symmeikta* 7: 59–75.

Kravari, V., J. Lefort and C. Morrisson, eds (1991) *Hommes et richesses dans l'empire byzantin, vol. 2: VIIIe–XVe siècle*, Paris: Lethielleux.

Kyriakis, M.J. (1977) 'Medieval European Society as Seen in Two Eleventh-century Texts of Michael Psellos', *BS/EB* 4: 67–80, 157–88.

Kyrris, C.P. (1982) 'Le rôle de femme dans la société byzantine pendant les derniers siècles', *JÖB* 32.2: 463–72.

Laiou, A.E. (1981) 'The Role of Women in Byzantine Society', *JÖB* 31(1): 233–60.

Laiou, A.E. (1982) 'Addendum to the Report on the Role of Women in Byzantine Society', *JÖB* 32(1): 198–203.

Laiou, A.E. (1985) 'Observations on the Life and Ideology of Byzantine Women', *BF* 9: 59–102.

Laiou, A.E. (1986) 'The Festival of "Agathe": Comments on the Life of Constantinopolitan Women', in *Byzantium: Tribute to Andreas N. Stratos*, vol. 1, ed. N.A. Stratos, Athens: N.A. Stratos, 111–22.

Laiou, A.E. (1989) 'Ἡ ἱστορία ἑνὸς γάμου· ὁ βίος τῆς ἁγίας Θωμαΐδος τῆς Λεσβίας, in *Ἡ καθημερινὴ ζωὴ στὸ Βυζάντιο*, ed. C. Maltezou, Athens: Κέντρο βυζαντινῶν ἐρευνῶν, 237–52.

Laiou, A.E. (1992a) *Gender, Society and Economic Life in Byzantium*, Aldershot: Variorum.

Laiou, A.E. (1992b) 'Imperial Marriages and their Critics in the Eleventh Century: The Case of Skylitzes', *DOP* 46: 165–76.

Laiou, A.E. (1992c) *Mariage, amour et parenté à Byzance aux XIe–XIIIe siècles*, Paris: de Boccard.

310

Laiou, A.E. (1993) 'Sex, Consent, and Coercion in Byzantium', in *Consent and Coercion to Sex and Marriage in Ancient and Medieval Societies*, ed. A.E. Laiou, Washington DC: Dumbarton Oaks, 109–226.

Lampros, S. (1930) Λεύκωμα βυζαντινῶν αὐτοκρατόρων, Athens: Eleutheroudakis.

Laurent, V. (1930) 'Une princesse byzantine au cloître: Irene-Eulogie Choumnos Paléologue, fondatrice du couvent de femmes τοῦ Φιλανθρώπου Σωτῆρος', *EO* 29: 29–60.

Lefort, L. *et al.* (1985) *Actes d'Iviron*, 1: *Des origines au milieu du XIe siècle*, Paris: Lethielleux.

Leib, B. (1950a) 'Jean Doukas, césar et moine: Son jeu politique à Byzance de 1067 à 1081', *AB* 68: 163–79.

Leib, B. (1950b) 'Nicéphore III Botaneiatès (1078–1081) et Marie d'Alanie', *Actes du VIe Congrès international d'études byzantines (1948)*, vol. 1, Paris, 129–40.

Leib, B. (1956) 'Un basileus ignoré: Constantin Doucas (v. 1074–94)', *BS* 17: 341–59.

Leib, B. (1958) 'Les silences de Anne Comnène', *BS* 19: 1–10.

Lemerle, P. (1977) *Cinq études sur le XIe siècle byzantin*, Paris: Le Monde Byzantin.

Lemerle, P. (1979) *The Agrarian History of Byzantium from the Origins to the Twelfth Century*, Galway: Galway University Press.

Lilie, R.-J. (1996) *Byzanz unter Eirene und Konstantin VI. (780–802) (mit einem Kapitel über Leon IV. (775–780) von Ilse Rochow)*, Frankfurt am Main: Peter Lang.

Limberis, V. (1994) *The Virgin Mary and the Creation of Christian Constantinople*, London: Routledge and Kegan Paul.

Loernertz, R.-J. (1973) 'Aux origines du despotat d'Épire et la principauté d'Achaïe', *Byzantion* 43: 360–94.

MacCormack, S. (1981) *Art and Ceremony in Late Antiquity*, Berkeley: University of California Press.

McCormick, M. (1986) *Eternal Victory: Triumphal Rulership in Late Antiquity, Byzantium, and the Early Medieval West*, Cambridge: Cambridge University Press.

McCormick, M. (1995) 'Byzantium and the West, 700–900', in *The New Cambridge Medieval History*, vol. 2: *c. 700–c. 900*, ed. R. McKitterick, Cambridge: Cambridge University Press, 349–80.

McCormick, M. (1997) 'Emperors', in *The Byzantines*, ed. G. Cavallo, Chicago and London: University of Chicago Press, 230–54.

Macrides, R. (1987) 'The Byzantine Godfather', *BMGS* 11: 139–62.

Macrides, R. (1990) 'Kinship by Arrangement: The Case of Adoption', *DOP* 44: 109–18.

Macrides, R. (1992a) 'Dowry and Inheritance in the Late Period: Some Cases from the Patriarchal Register', in *Eherecht und Familiengut in Antike und Mittelalter*, ed. D. Simon, Munich: Oldenbourg, 89–98.

Macrides, R. (1992b) 'Dynastic Marriages and Political Kinship', in *Byzantine Diplomacy*, ed. J. Shepard and S. Franklin, Aldershot: Variorum, 263–80.

Macrides, R. and P. Magdalino, eds (1992) 'The Fourth Kingdom and the Rhetoric of Hellenism', in *The Perception of the Past in Twelfth-century Europe*, ed. P. Magdalino, London: Hambledon Press, 117–56.

Magdalino, P. (1984a) 'The Byzantine Aristocratic *oikos*', in *The Byzantine Aristocracy IX to XIII Centuries*, ed. M. Angold, Oxford: British Archaeological Reports, 92–111.

Magdalino, P. (1984b) 'The Not-so-secret Functions of the Mystikos', *REB* 42: 229–40.

Magdalino, P. (1988) 'The Bath of Leo the Wise and the "Macedonian Renaissance" Revisited: Topography, Iconography, Ceremonial, Ideology', *DOP* 42: 97–118.

Magdalino, P. (1991) 'Enlightment and Repression in Twelfth-century Byzantium: The Evidence of the Canonists', in *Tὸ Βυζάντιο κατὰ τὸν 12o αἰώνα*, ed. N. Oikonomides, Athens: Ἑταιρεία βυζαντινῶν καὶ μεταβυζαντινῶν μελετῶν, 357–74.

Magdalino, P., ed. (1992) *The Perception of the Past in Twelfth-century Europe*, London: Hambledon Press.

Magdalino, P. (1993) *The Empire of Manuel I Komnenos 1143–1180*, Cambridge: Cambridge University Press.

Magdalino, P., ed. (1994) *New Constantines: The Rhythm of Imperial Renewal in Byzantium, 4th–13th Centuries*, Aldershot: Variorum.

Magdalino, P. (1996) 'Innovations in Government', in *Alexios I Komnenos*, vol. 1: *Papers*, ed. M. Mullett and D. Smythe, Belfast: Belfast Byzantine Enterprises, 146–66.

Magdalino, P. and R. Nelson (1982) 'The Emperor in Byzantine Art of the 12th Century', *BF* 8: 123–83.

Maguire, H., ed. (1997) *Byzantine Court Culture from 829 to 1204*, Washington DC: Dumbarton Oaks.

Majeska, G. (1977) 'The Body of St. Theophano the Empress and the Convent of St. Constantine', *BS* 38: 14–21.

Makk, F. (1989) *The Arpads and the Comneni*, Budapest: Akademiai Kiado.

Mallet, C.E. (1887) 'The Empress Theodora', *EHR* 2: 1–20.

Maltezou, C., ed. (1989) *Ἡ καθημερινὴ ζωὴ στὸ Βυζάντιο*, Athens: Κέντρο βυζαντινῶν ἐρευνῶν.

Mango, C. (1959) *The Brazen House: A Study of the Vestibule of the Imperial Palace of Constantinople*, Copenhagen: Munksgaard.

Mango, C. (1962) *Materials for the Study of the Mosaics of St. Sophia at Istanbul*, Washington DC: Dumbarton Oaks.

Mango, C. (1963) 'A Forged Inscription of the Year 781', *ZRVI* 8(1): 201–7.

Mango, C. (1966) Review of F. Halkin, *Euphémie de Chalcédoine: Légendes byzantines*, *JTS* 17: 485–8.

Mango, C. (1967) 'When was Michael III Born?' *DOP* 21: 253–8.

Mango, C. (1972a) *Art of the Byzantine Empire, 312–1453: Sources and Documents*, Toronto: University of Toronto Press.

Mango, C. (1972b) 'The Church of Saints Sergius and Bacchus at Constantinople and the Alleged Tradition of Octagonal Palatine Churches', *JÖB* 21: 189–93.

Mango, C. (1973) 'Eudocia Ingerina, the Normans and the Macedonian Dynasty', *ZRVI* 14/15: 17–27.

Mango, C. (1975) 'The Church of Sts. Sergius and Bacchus Once Again', *BZ* 68: 385–92.

Mango, C. (1977) 'The Liquidation of Iconoclasm and the Patriarch Photios', in *Iconoclasm*, ed. A. Bryer and J. Herrin, Birmingham: University of Birmingham, 133–40.

Mango, C. (1978) 'Who Wrote the Chronicle of Theophanes?' *ZRVI* 18: 9–17.

Mango, C. (1980) *Byzantium: The Empire of New Rome*, London: Weidenfeld and Nicolson.

Mango, C. (1981) 'Daily Life in Byzantium', *JÖB* 31.1: 337–53.

Mango, C. (1982) 'St. Anthusa of Mantineon and the Family of Constantine V', *AB* 100: 401–9.

Mango, C. (1985) 'Deux études sur Byzance et la Perse sassanide', *TM* 9: 91–117.

Mango, C. and O. Pritsak, eds (1984) *Okeanos: Essays Presented to Ihor Shevchenko on his 60th Birthday*, Cambridge, Mass.: Ukrainian Research Institute, Harvard University.

Mango, C. and R. Scott (1997) (with G. Greatrex) *The Chronicle of Theophanes Confessor: Byzantine and Near Eastern History AD 284–813*, Oxford: Clarendon Press.

Mango, C. and I. Shevchenko (1961) 'Remains of the Church of St. Polyeuktos at Constantinople', *DOP* 15: 243–7.

Marinesco, C. (1924) 'Du nouveau sur Constance de Hohenstaufen, impératrice de Nicée', *Byzantion* 1: 451–68.

Martin-Hisard, B. (1991) 'La *vie de Jean et Euthyme* et le statut du monastère des Ibères sur l'Athos', *REB* 49: 67–142.

Martindale, J.R. *et al.* (1970–92) *The Prosopography of the Later Roman Empire*, 3 vols, Cambridge: Cambridge University Press.

Maslev, S. (1966) 'Die staatsrechtliche Stellung der byzantinischen Kaiserinnen', *BS* 27: 308–43.

Miller, T.S. (1985) *The Birth of the Hospital in the Byzantine Empire*, Baltimore: Johns Hopkins University Press.

Milner, C. (1994) 'The Image of the Rightful Ruler: Anicia Juliana's Constantine Mosaic in the Church of Hagios Polyeuktos', in *New Constantines: The Rhythm of Imperial Renewal in Byzantium, 4th–13th Centuries*, ed. P. Magdalino, Aldershot: Variorum, 73–81.

Missiou, D. (1982) 'Über die institutionelle Rolle der byzantinischen Kaiserin', *JÖB* 32.2: 489–98.

Moorhead, J. (1981) 'The Response of the Monophysites to the Arab Invasions', *Byzantion* 51: 579–91.

Moorhead, J. (1985) 'Iconoclasm, the Cross and the Imperial Image', *Byzantion* 55: 165–79.

Moorhead, J. (1994) *Justinian*, London and New York: Longman.

Morgan, G. (1954) 'A Byzantine Satirical Song?' *BZ* 47: 292–7.

Morris, R. (1976) 'The Powerful and the Poor in Tenth-century Byzantium: Law and Reality', *PP* 73: 3–27.

Morris, R. (1985) 'Monasteries and their Patrons in the Tenth and Eleventh Centuries', *BF* 10: 185–231.

Morris, R. (1988) 'The Two Faces of Nikephoros Phokas', *BMGS* 12: 83–115.

Morris, R., ed. (1990) *Church and People in Byzantium*, Birmingham: University of Birmingham.

Morris, R. (1994) 'Succession and Usurpation: Politics and Rhetoric in the Late Tenth Century', in *New Constantines: The Rhythm of Imperial Renewal in Byzantium, 4th–13th Centuries*, ed. P. Magdalino, Aldershot: Variorum, 199–214.

Morris, R. (1995) *Monks and Laymen in Byzantium 843–1118*, Cambridge: Cambridge University Press.

Mullett, M. (1984a) 'Aristocracy and Patronage in the Literary Circles of Comnenian Constantinople', in *The Byzantine Aristocracy IX to XIII Centuries*, ed. M. Angold, Oxford: British Archaeological Reports, 173–201.

Mullett, M. (1984b) 'The "Disgrace" of the Ex-Basilissa Maria', *BS* 45: 202–11.

Mullett, M. (1994) 'Alexios I Komnenos and Imperial Revival', in *New Constantines*, ed. P. Magdalino, Aldershot: Variorum, 259–67.

Mullett, M. and A. Kirby, eds (1994) *The Theotokos Evergetis and Eleventh-century Monasticism*, Belfast: Belfast Byzantine Enterprises.

Mullett, M. and D. Smythe, eds (1996) *Alexios I Komnenos*, vol. 1: *Papers*, Belfast: Belfast Byzantine Enterprises.

Nicol, D.M. (1964) 'Mixed Marriages in Byzantium in the Thirteenth Century', in *Studies in Church History*, vol. 1, ed. C.W. Dugmore and C. Duggan, London and Edinburgh (= *Byzantium: Its Ecclesiastical History and Relations with the Western World*, London: Variorum, 1972, IV).

Nicol, D.M. (1968) *The Byzantine Family of Kantakouzenos (Cantacuzenus) ca. 1100–1460: A Genealogical and Prosopographical Study*, Washington DC: Dumbarton Oaks.

Nicol, D.M. (1979) 'Symbiosis and Integration: Some Greco-Latin Families in Byzantium in the 11th and 13th Centuries', *BF* 7: 113–35.

Nicol, D.M. (1988) *Byzantium and Venice: A Study in Diplomatic and Cultural Relations*, Cambridge: Cambridge University Press.

Nicol, D.M. (1993) *The Last Centuries of Byzantium*, 2nd edn, Cambridge: Cambridge University Press.

Nicol, D.M. (1994) *The Byzantine Lady: Ten Portraits 1250–1500*, Cambridge: Cambridge University Press.

Nicol, D.M. and S. Bendall (1977) 'Anna of Savoy in Thessalonica: The Numismatic Evidence', *Revue numismatique*, series 6, 19: 87–102.

Nikolaou, K. (1994) 'Οἱ γυναῖκες στὸ βίο καὶ τά ἔργα τοῦ Θεοφίλου', *Symmeikta* 9: 137–51.

Nodia, I.M. (1978) 'Gruzinskie materialy o vizantijskoj imperatrice Marfe-Marii', *Vizantinovedcheskie etjudy*, Tblisi: 146–55.

Ohnsorge, W. (1958) 'Zur Frage der Tochter Kaiser Leons VI.', *BZ* 51: 78–81.

Oikonomides, N. (1963a) 'La dernière volonté de Leon VI au sujet de la tétragamie', *BZ* 56: 46–52.

Oikonomides, N. (1963b) 'Le serment de l'impératrice Eudocie (1067): Un épisode de l'histoire dynastique de Byzance', *REB* 21: 101–28.

Oikonomides, N. (1972) 'Quelques boutiques de Constantinople au Xe s.: Prix, loyers, imposition (*Cod. Patmiacus* 171)', *DOP* 26: 345–56.

Oikonomides, N. (1976a) 'Leo VI and the Narthex Mosaic of Saint Sophia', *DOP* 30: 153–72.

Oikonomides, N. (1976b) 'Leo VI's Legislation of 907 Forbidding Fourth Marriages: An Interpolation in the *Procheiros Nomos* (IV, 25–27)', *DOP* 30: 174–93.

Oikonomides, N. (1976c) 'L'évolution de l'organisation administrative de l'empire byzantin au XIe siècle (1025–1118)', *TM* 6: 125–52.

Oikonomides, N. (1978) 'The Mosaic Panel of Constantine IX and Zoe in St Sophia', *REB* 36: 219–32.

Oikonomides, N. (1980/81) 'St. George of Mangana, Maria Skleraina, and the "Malyj Sion" of Novgorod', *DOP* 34/35: 239–46.

Oikonomides, N. (1991a) 'Le kommerkion d'Abydos, Thessalonique et le commerce bulgare au IXe siècle', *Hommes et richesses dans l'empire byzantin*, vol. 2: *VIIIe–XVe siècle*, ed. V. Kravari, J. Lefort and C. Morrisson, Paris: Lethielleux, 241–8.

Oikonomides, N., ed. (1991b) Τὸ Βυζάντιο κατὰ τὸν 12ο αἰώνα, Athens: Ἐταιρεία βυζαντινῶν καὶ μεταβυζαντινῶν μελετῶν.

Oikonomides, N. (1994) 'La couronne dite de Constantin Monomaque', *TM* 12: 241–62.

Olster, D.M. (1993) *The Politics of Usurpation in the Seventh Century: Rhetoric and Revolution in Byzantium*, Amsterdam: Hakkert.

Ostrogorsky, G. (1968) *History of the Byzantine State*, tr. J.M. Hussey, 2nd edn, Oxford: Blackwell.

Oxford Dictionary of Byzantium (1991) ed. A. Kazhdan, 3 vols, New York: Oxford University Press.

Parry, K. (1989) 'Theodore Studites and the Patriarch Nicephoros on Image-making as a Christian Imperative', *Byzantion* 59: 164–83.

Patlagean, E. (1981) *Structure sociale, famille, chrétieneté à Byzance*, London: Variorum.

Polemis, D. (1965) 'Notes on Eleventh Century Chronology (1059–1081)', *BZ* 58: 60–76.

Polemis, D.I. (1968) *The Doukai: A Contribution to Byzantine Prosopography*, London: Athlone Press.

Poppé, A. (1971) 'La dernière expédition russe contre Constantinople', *BS* 32(2): 233–68.

Poppé, A.J. (1976) 'The Political Background to the Baptism of Rus': Byzantine–Russian Relations between 986–89', *DOP* 30: 194–244.

Previté Orton, C.W. (1914) 'Charles, Count of Vienne', *EHR* 29: 703–6.

Prosopographisches Lexikon der Palaiologenzeit, ed. E. Trapp *et al.*, Vienna: Verlag der Österreichischen Akademie der Wissenschaften, 1976–96.

Rambaud, A. (1877) 'Michel Psellos', *Revue historique* 3: 241–82.

Rapp, C. (1996) 'Figures of Female Sanctity: Byzantine Edifying Manuscripts and the Audience', *DOP* 50: 313–44.

Rapp, S.H. (1997) *Imagining History at the Crossroads: Persia, Byzantium and the Architects of the Written Georgian Past*, unpublished PhD thesis, University of Michigan.

Ringrose, K.M. (1994) 'Living in the Shadows: Eunuchs and Gender in Byzantium', in *Third Sex, Third Gender: Beyond Sexual Dimorphism in Culture and History*, ed. G. Herdt, New York: Zone Books, 85–109, 507–18.

Ringrose, K.M. (1996) 'Eunuchs as Cultural Mediators', *BF* 23: 75–93.

Rösch, G. (1979) 'Der Aufstand der Herakleioi Gegen Phokas (608–10) im Spiegel numismatischer Quellen', *JÖB* 28: 51–62.

Roueché, C. (1993) *Performers and Partisans at Aphrodisias in the Roman and Late Roman Period, JRS* Monographs VI, London: Society for the Promotion of Roman Studies.

Rubin, B. (1960) *Das Zeitalter Iustinians*, vol. 1, Berlin: de Gruyter.

Runciman, S. (1929) *The Emperor Romanus Lecapenus and his Reign*, Cambridge: Cambridge University Press.

Runciman, S. (1949) 'The End of Anna Dalassena', *AIPHOS* 9: 517–24.

Runciman, S. (1972) 'Some Notes on the Role of the Empress', *Eastern Churches Review* 4: 119–24.

Runciman, S. (1977) *The Byzantine Theocracy*, Cambridge: Cambridge University Press.

Runciman, S. (1978) 'The Empress Irene the Athenian', in *Medieval Women: Essays Presented to Professor Rosalind M.T. Hill*, ed. D. Baker, Oxford: Blackwell, 101–18.

Runciman, S. (1984) 'Women in Byzantine Aristocratic Society', in *The Byzantine*

Aristocracy IX to XIII Centuries, ed. M. Angold, Oxford: British Archaeological Reports, 10–22.

Rydén, L. (1985) 'The Bride-shows at the Byzantine Court: History or Fiction?', *Eranos* 83: 175–91.

Sarudi-Mendelovici, H. (1990) 'A Contribution to the Study of the Byzantine Notarial Formulas: The *Infirmitatis Sexus* of Women and the *Sc. Velleianum*', *BZ* 83: 72–90.

Savvidis, A.G.C. (1995) 'Romanus Boilas: Court Jester and Throne Counterclaimant in the mid-Eleventh Century', *BS* 56(1): 159–64.

Sayre, P.G. (1986) 'The Mistress of the Robes: Who was She?' *BS/EB* 13: 229–39.

Schlumberger, G. (1923) *Un empereur byzantin au dixième siècle, Nicéphore Phocas*, Paris: Boccard.

Schlumberger, G. (1932) *L'épopée byzantine à la fin du dixième siècle*, Paris: Hachette.

Schreiner, P. (1984) 'Das Herrscherbild in der byzantinischen Literatur des 9. bis 11. Jahrhunderts', *Saeculum* 35: 132–51.

Schreiner, P. (1991) 'Réflexions sur la famille impériale à Byzance (VIIIe–Xe siècles)', *Byzantion* 61: 181–93.

Scott, R. (1985) 'Malalas, The Secret History, and Justinian's Propaganda', *DOP* 39: 99–109.

Seibt, W. (1976) *Die Skleroi: Eine prosopographisch-sigillographische Studie*, Vienna: Verlag der Österreichischen Akademie der Wissenschaften.

Shepard, J. (1988) 'Aspects of Byzantine Attitudes and Policy Towards the West in the Tenth and Eleventh Centuries', *BF* 13: 67–118.

Shepard, J. (1995a) 'A Marriage too Far? Maria Lekapena and Peter of Bulgaria', in *The Empress Theophano: Byzantium and the West at the Turn of the First Millennium*, ed. A. Davids, Cambridge: Cambridge University Press, 121–49.

Shepard, J. (1995b) 'Slavs and Bulgars', in *The New Cambridge Medieval History*, vol. 2: *c. 700–c. 900*, ed. R. McKitterick, Cambridge: Cambridge University Press, 228–48.

Shevchenko, I. (1969/70) 'Poems on the Deaths of Leo VI and Constantine VIII in the Madrid Manuscript of Scylitzes', *DOP* 23–4: 184–228.

Shevchenko, I. (1977) 'Hagiography of the Iconoclast Period', in *Iconoclasm*, ed. A. Bryer and J. Herrin, Birmingham: University of Birmingham, 113–31.

Sola, G.N. (1916) 'Giambografi sconosciuti del sec. XI', *Roma e l'Oriente* 11: 149–53.

Spadaro, M.D. (1975) 'Note su Sclerena', *Siculorum Gymnasium* 28: 351–72.

Spain, S. (1977) 'The Translation of Relics Ivory, Trier', *DOP* 31: 279–304.

Spatharakis, J. (1976) *The Portrait in Byzantine Illuminated Manuscripts*, Leiden: Brill.

Speck, P. (1978) *Kaiser Konstantin VI*, 2 vols, Munich: Fink.

Speck, P. (1991) 'Juliana Anicia, Konstantin der Grosse und die Polyeuktoskirche in Konstantinopel', *Poikila Byzantina* 11, Bonn: Habelt, 133–47.

Stiernon, L. (1965) 'Notes de titulature et de prosopographie byzantines: sébaste et gambros', *REB* 23: 222–43.

Stratos, A.N. (1968–75) *Byzantium in the Seventh Century*, 6 vols, Amsterdam: Hakkert.

Stratos, A.N. (1976) 'Ὁ Πατριάρχης Πύρρος', *Βυζαντινά* 8: 11–19.

Striker, C.L. (1986) 'The *Coliseo de Spiriti* in Constantinople, in *Studien zur Spätantiken und Byzantinischen Kunst*, ed. O. Feld and U. Peschlow, vol. 1, Bonn: Habelt, 7–11.

Talbot, A.-M. (1984) 'Blue-stocking Nuns: Intellectual Life in the Convents of Late Byzantium', in *Okeanos: Essays Presented to Ihor Shevhenko on his 60th Birthday*, ed. C.

Mango and O. Pritsak, Cambridge, Mass.: Ukrainian Research Institute, Harvard University, 604–18.

Talbot, A.-M. (1985a) 'A Comparison of the Monastic Experience of Byzantine Men and Women', *GOTR* 30: 1–20.

Talbot, A.-M. (1985b) 'Late Byzantine Nuns: By Choice or Necessity?' *BF* 9: 59–102.

Talbot, A.-M. (1990) 'The Byzantine Family and the Monastery', *DOP* 44: 119–29.

Talbot, A.-M. (1992) 'Empress Theodora Palaiologina, Wife of Michael VIII', *DOP* 46: 295–303.

Talbot, A.-M. (ed.) (1996) *Holy Women of Byzantium: Ten Saints' Lives in English Translation*, Washington DC: Dumbarton Oaks.

Talbot, A.-M. (1997) 'Women', in *The Byzantines*, ed. G. Cavallo, Chicago and London: University of Chicago Press, 117–43.

Teteriatnikov, N. (1996) 'Hagia Sophia: The Two Portraits of the Emperors with Moneybags as a Functional Setting', *Arte Medievale* 10: 47–66.

Thomas, J.P. (1987) *Private Religious Foundations in the Byzantine Empire*, Washington DC: Dumbarton Oaks.

Thomas, R.D. (1991) 'Anna Comnena's Account of the First Crusade: History and Politics in the Reigns of the Emperors Alexius I and Manuel I Comnenus', *BMGS* 15: 269–312.

Tinnefeld, F.H. (1971) *Kategorien der Kaiserkritik in der byzantinischen Historiographie von Prokop bis Niketas Choniates*, Munich: Fink.

Tinnefeld, F. (1989) 'Michael I. Kerullarios, Patriarch von Konstantinopel (1043–1058)', *JÖB* 39: 95–127

Topping, E.C. (1982/3) 'Women Hymnographers in Byzantium', *Diptycha* 3: 98–111.

Tougher, S. (1996) 'The Bad Relations between Alexander and Leo', *BMGS* 20: 209–12.

Toynbee, A. (1973) *Constantine Porphyrogenitus and his World*, London: Oxford University Press.

Treadgold, W.T. (1975) 'The Problem of the Marriage of the Emperor Theophilus', *GRBS* 16: 325–41.

Treadgold, W.T. (1979) 'The Bride-shows of the Byzantine Emperors', *Byzantion* 49: 395–413.

Treadgold, W.T. (1982a) *The Byzantine State Finances in the Eighth and Ninth Centuries*, New York: Columbia University Press.

Treadgold, W.T. (1982b) 'The Unpublished Saint's Life of the Empress Irene', *BF* 7: 237–51.

Treadgold, W. (1988) *The Byzantine Revival 780–842*, Stanford: Stanford University Press.

Treadgold, W.T. (1997) *A History of the Byzantine State and Society*, Stanford: Stanford University Press.

Tritle, L.A. (1977) 'Tatzates' Flight and the Byzantine–Arab Peace Treaty of 782', *Byzantion* 47: 279–300.

Tsirpanlis, C.N. (1974) 'John Lydus on the Imperial Administration', *Byzantion* 44: 479–501.

Turdeanu, E. (1985) 'Nouvelles considérations sur le "Dit de l'empereur Nicéphore II Phocas et de son épouse Théophano"', *RSBS* 5: 169–95.

Turtledove, H. (1983) 'Justin II's Observance of Justinian's Persian Treaty of 562', *BZ* 76: 292–301.

Vannier, J.-F. (1975) *Familles byzantines: les Argyroi (IXe–XIIe siècles)*, Paris: Sorbonne.

Varzos, K. (1984) Ἡ γενεαλογία τῶν Κομνηνῶν, 2 vols, Thessalonika; Κέντρον βυζαντινῶν ἐρευνῶν.

Vasiliev, A.A. (1935) *Byzance et les Arabes*, vol. 1: *La dynastie d'Amorium (820–67)*, Brussels: Institut de Philologie et d'Histoire Orientales.

Vasiliev, A.A. (1950) *Justin the First: An Introduction to the Epoch of Justinian*, Cambridge, Mass.: Harvard University Press.

Vasiliev, A.A. (1968) *Byzance et les Arabes*, vol. 2.1: *La dynastie macédonienne (867–959)*, Brussels: Corpus Bruxellense Historiae Byzantinae.

Vikan, G. (1990) 'Art and Marriage in Early Byzantium', *DOP* 44: 145–63.

Vogt, A. (1934) 'La jeunesse de Léon le Sage', *RH* 174: 389–428.

Ward, B. (1987) *Harlots of the Desert: A Study of Repentance in Early Monastic Sources*, London and Oxford: Mowbray.

Weyl, A.M. Carr (1985) 'Women and Monasticism in Byzantium: Introduction from an Art Historian', *BF* 9: 1–15.

Whittemore, Th. (1942) *The Mosaics of Hagia Sophia at Istanbul: Third Preliminary Report. Work Done in 1935–1938: The Imperial Portraits of the South Gallery*, Oxford: Oxford University Press.

Whittemore, Th. (1946–8) 'A Portrait of the Empress Zoe and of Constantine IX', *Byzantion* 18: 223–7.

Whittow, M. (1996) *The Making of Orthodox Byzantium, 600–1025*, London: Macmillan.

Wirth, P. (1956) 'Wann wurde Kaiser Alexios II geboren?', *BZ* 49: 65–7.

Wolf, G., ed. (1991a) *Kaiserin Theophanu: Prinzessin aus der Fremde – des Westreichs grosse Kaiserin*, Cologne: Böhlau.

Wolf, G. (1991b) 'Zoe oder Theodora: die Braut Kaiser Ottos III.? (1001/1002)', in *Kaiserin Theophanu: Prinzessin aus der Fremde – des Westreichs grosse Kaiserin*, ed. G. Wolf, Cologne: Böhlau, 212–22.

Wortley, J. (1982) 'Iconoclasm and Leipsanoclasm: Leo III, Constantine V and the Relics', *BF* 8: 253–79.

Wroth, W. (1908) *Catalogue of the Imperial Byzantine Coins in the British Museum*, vol. 1, London: British Museum.

Yannopoulos, P. (1991) 'Le couronnement de l'empereur à Byzance: rituel et fond institutionnel', *Byzantion* 61: 71–92.

Zacos, G. and A. Veglery (1972) *Byzantine Lead Seals*, 2 vols, Basel: J.J. Augustin.

Zuckerman, C. (1995) 'La petite Augusta et le Turc: Epiphania-Eudocie sur les monnaies d'Héraclius', *Revue Numismatique* 150: 113–26.

INDEX

For emperors, empresses and patriarchs, see under Christian names. Illustrations are indicated by italic numbers.